PROJECT MANAGEMENT HANDBOOK

Project Management Handbook

Edited by
Dennis Lock

A Gower Handbook

© Gower Technical Press Limited 1987

All rights reserved. No part of this publication may be reproduced, stored in a retrieval system, or transmitted in any form or by any means, electronic, mechanical, photocopying, recording, or otherwise without the prior permission of Gower Technical Press Limited.

Published by
Gower Technical Press Limited,
Gower House,
Croft Road,
Aldershot,
Hants GU11 3HR,
England

British Library Cataloguing in Publication Data
Project management handbook.
  1. Industrial project management
  I. Lock, Dennis
  658.4'04   HD69.P75

ISBN 0-291-39741-7

Typeset by Action Typesetting, Gloucester
Printed in Great Britain by
The University Press, Cambridge

Contents

List of illustrations   xi

Notes on contributors   xv

Preface   xxi

PART I   PROJECT MANAGEMENT AND ITS ORGANISATION

1   The nature and purpose of project management   3
Dennis Lock
Characteristics of projects — Objectives — The project manager — Techniques of project management

2   Project organisation   15
Edmund J. Young
Defining 'organisation' — Role of the project manager — Matrix versus the pure project organisation — Project organisation with more complex arrangements

3   Establishing a project organisation   40
O. P. Kharbanda and E.A. Stallworthy
The three parties to a project — The role of the consultant — The contractor — Appointing a contractor — Communications the key — The owner's organisation — The contractor's organisation — The principle of accountability — Management by exception — Site administration — Appendix

Contents

PART II CONTRACT ADMINISTRATION

4 Contract law   69
   P. D. V. Marsh
   Contract formation — Contract terms — Vitiating factors — Contract law, jurisdiction and enforcement — Privity of contract and negligence

5 Contracts and payment structures   93
   P. D. V. Marsh
   Lump sum — Schedule of rates or bill of approximate quantities — Cost reimbursement — Management contracting — Terms of payment

6 Contract administration   119
   P. D. V. Marsh
   Variations in price and time — Disputes and arbitration

7 Insurance   131
   R. L. Carter
   Risk management and insurance — Contractual responsibilities — The benefits of insurance — Types of insurable risk — Limits to cover provided — Insurance for projects — Civil engineering and other construction projects — Manufacturing projects — Other projects — Delays in completing projects

8 Project definition   151
   Dennis Lock
   The project specification — Modifications, variations and other changes — Defining the project 'as-built'

PART III ACCOUNTING AND FINANCE

9 Financing the project   169
   Michael P. Bull and Keith H. Savage
   Some project financing situations — The role of the financial adviser — Funding methods — Limited recourse finance

10 Cost estimating — 188
David Ross

The nature of cost estimates — Estimating quality — Cost data collection — Interface with planning and cost control — Work breakdown structure — Estimating methods — Money of the day provisions — Contingencies — Cash flow — Estimating with and without a computer

11 Cost control — 214
David Ross

Overall control of project costs — Contract strategy in relation to project control — The control budget — Definition of cost control terms — Predicting trends and overspends — Collecting project costs — Cash flow — Cost reporting — Computer aided techniques — Historical costs

12 Controlling cash and credit — 238
John Butterworth

The impact of interest charges on the cost of money — Forecasting receipts — Forecasting payments — Forecasting net cash flow — Speeding up the cash flow — Collection of accounts when due

PART IV MANAGING PROJECT MATERIALS

13 Project purchasing — 265
Peter Baily

Some special characteristics of project purchasing — The project purchasing manager — Subcontracting — The purchasing cycle — Purchased materials and equipment

14 Inspection and expediting — 278
Bob Chilton

Organisation — Progressing and expediting — Inspection — Goods inwards inspection

15 Stock control and stores management 293
Dennis Lock
Project stock control — Management of factory stores for projects — Site stores management — The site materials controller

16 Packing and shipping 320
Graham J. McCleery
Feasibility — Planning — Freight forwarding — Communications — Contingency — Insurance of goods and insurance claims

PART V PLANNING AND SCHEDULING

17 Planning with charts 345
A. G. Simms
Bar charts — The line of balance chart

18 Critical path methods 357
A. G. Simms
Phases of project network planning and control — Activities and events — Relationships between activities — The arrow diagram — Project timing — Project control — Project network analysis as an aid to project management — Precedence notation — Using networks in project management

19 Resource scheduling 392
David A. Barrett
Network logic methods for indicating resource constraints — Scheduling goals: time limits and resource limits — Multi-project scheduling

20 Computer programs for network analysis — 1 405
David A. Barrett
Computer hardware — General factors concerning software — Software price factors — Choice between activity-on-arrow and precedence networks — Resource and calendar features — Error diagnosis

21 Computer programs for network analysis — 2   435
David A. Barrett
Complex relationships for activity starts and finishes — Probabilistic networks and risk analysis — Progress reporting — Computer aided network construction — Cost features — Database applications — Input, output reports and the user interface

PART VI MANAGING PROGRESS AND PERFORMANCE

22 Managing progress   463
Dennis Lock
The framework of progress management — Communicating the work programme — Monitoring and controlling progress — Modifications, changes and variations — Progress meetings — Progress reporting

23 Project quality assurance   489
L. E. Stebbing
The concept and philosophy of quality assurance — Objective evidence of quality — Organisation for quality assurance — Quality assurance procedures and systems — Developing the project quality plan — Design — Design controls — Control of procurement and vendors

24 Motivating the participants   529
F. L. Harrison
Organisational difficulties — The authority problem in project management — The engineer as a manager — Interpersonal behaviour in the project setting — Groups in the project setting — Team development — Intergroup conflict in the project setting

25 Integrated systems for planning and control   561
Ray Palmer
The project management process — The requirements for integration — Integrating the requirements of project staff — Integrating the computer hardware

Contents

26 An integrated project management system in action   **584**

Ray Palmer

The project information structure — How the system operates in practice — Design management — Materials management — Planning and scheduling — Allocating work and measuring progress — Cost management — Cost forecasting

Index   **611**

Illustrations

Figures

		Page
1.1	Example of organisation for a manufacturing project	11
1.2	Stages of project management	12
2.1	Project manager roles	18
2.2	Project co-ordinator in a design engineering organisation	22
2.3	Pure project team organisation	23
2.4	Matrix organisation	26
2.5	Joint venture organisation	33
2.6	Project manager relationships	34
3.1	Project development	41
3.2	The basic relationship	43
3.3	The role of the consultant	44
3.4	The project team	46
3.5	Logic diagram	47
3.6	Organisation chart for the design group	53
3.7	Typical construction site organisation	58
5.1	Contractor's expenditure in relation to payments received	111
5.2	Revenue and expenditure curves for overseas contract	111
6.1	Balancing cost factors of a contract variation	121
8.1	Project definition checklist	152
8.2	Network diagram used as project design checklist	157
8.3	Stages of project definition	164
9.1	OECD export credit rates	177
10.1	Work breakdown structure for a manufacturing project	197
10.2	Work breakdown structure for a large civil engineering or construction project	198
10.3	Example of a project cash outflow forecast	208
10.4	Estimating form for capital equipment	210
10.5	Estimating form for engineering manhours	211
11.1	Relationship between type of contract and control emphasis	218

Illustrations

11.2	Project variation summary form	228
11.3	Cash flow graph	232
11.4	Cost tabulation used for reporting purposes	233
12.1	A typical cash flow forecast format	246
13.1	Subcontracting procedure for a large contract	272
13.2	Example of a bid analysis form	273
14.1	Materials inspection and expediting in the project organisation	280
14.2	Inspection and expediting report summary	288
15.1	Summary of ABC stock control principles	296
15.2	Common stock parts	298
15.3	Materials organisation	300
15.4	Stores location	302
15.5	Stores documentation	307
15.6	Site materials status report	316
17.1	A project plan in bar chart form	346
17.2	Bar chart used for project control	348
17.3	Bar chart with resource scheduling	350
17.4	A line of balance chart for the construction of five houses	352
17.5	A line of balance chart for building 80 houses	355
18.1	An activity with its start and end event	360
18.2	Two independent activities	360
18.3	Simple sequence of two activities	361
18.4	Dependent activities — 1	361
18.5	Dependent activities — 2	362
18.6	Dependent activities — 3	363
18.7	Use of a dummy activity as a logical link	364
18.8	Dummy activity used to ensure unique activity numbering	365
18.9	The event symbol	370
18.10	Convention for earliest event times	371
18.11	Convention for latest permissible event times	371
18.12	A simple critical path diagram	373
18.13	Depicting critical activities	373
18.14	The concept of float	376
18.15	Time scaled network diagram	378
18.16	An activity on node network	383
18.17	Precedence logic notation	384
19.1	Simple example of resource conflict	393
19.2	Simple example of resource scheduling	398
19.3	Resource usage pattern typical of residual scheduling	404
20.1	Network representation of computing stages required to calculate two subnetworks	412
20.2	Scheduling of order and delivery activities	426
20.3	Start and end dangles	429

20.4	Logical loops in a network diagram	430
20.5	Multiple loops	431
20.6	Error detection report – loop analysis	432
20.7	Duplicate activities	433
21.1	Parallel activities – precedence system	436
21.2	Interpretation of precedence network duration	438
21.3	A paradox in precedence logic	439
21.4	Ladder networks and transit times	440
21.5	Computer generated network diagram – precedence system	447
21.6	Computer generated network diagram – activity on arrow method	448
22.1	A work-to list produced from a computer based resource schedule	464
22.2	More examples of work-to lists	468
22.3	A simple subcontract engineering order	473
23.1	Ideal relationship of quality assurance in project organisation	493
23.2	Project quality assurance department organisation	494
23.3	Typical quality assurance standards	496
23.4	Quality programme and quality plan	498
23.5	The quality assurance 'umbrella'	501
23.6	Matrix summarising the most important design controls	507
23.7	A document distribution matrix chart	512
23.8	A change control form	514
23.9	A change form for external issue to contractor	516
23.10	Form suitable for summarising the estimated costs of a change	517
25.1	Dataset principles	567
25.2	Selective drawings report	570
25.3	Integration of information	572
25.4	Combined report from integrated information	573
25.5	A user's view	575
25.6	Typical expediter's report	576
25.7	A cost forecast in graphical form	577
25.8	A graphical project summary report	578
25.9	Vertical integration	580
25.10	Typical configuration of computer hardware for a company using the ARTEMIS system for project management	582
26.1	A typical project information structure	585
26.2	Integrated system report for use by an expediter	591
26.3	A milestone report	593
26.4	A comparison bar chart	595
26.5	A detailed activity report	596

Illustrations

26.6	The hierarchy of project control levels	598
26.7	Updating job cards	599
26.8	Updating the project network from job cards	600
26.9	A project work breakdown structure (WBS)	602
26.10	Linking the project network to the cost dataset	604
26.11	A time/cost curve	605
26.12	Analysis of economic completion date	607

Notes on Contributors

Peter Baily (*Project purchasing*) has many years' experience as practitioner, researcher, consultant and lecturer in purchasing and supply management. After war service, he worked in machine tool and textile manufacturing industries as materials controller, chief buyer and assistant to group secretary before joining what is now the Polytechnic of Wales, where he started the Postgraduate Procurement Course of which he is still course leader. Mr Baily has written many articles and several books, including *Successful Stock Control* (Gower, 1971) and *Purchasing Systems and Records* (Gower, 1983) and, as co-author with D. H. Farmer, *Materials Management Handbook* (Gower, 1984).

David A. Barrett (*Resource scheduling, Computer programs for network analysis*). After working for IBM in the UK and abroad, he became joint managing director of K & H Business Consultants Ltd, where he was involved with the development of many project management packages. Since 1982, as managing director of K & H Project Systems Ltd, he has been responsible for the development of the Cresta project management system.

Michael P. Bull (*Financing the project*) is a senior manager in the international banking division of National Westminster Bank. His responsibilities have been particularly towards those projects, chiefly in the developing world, which have required the support of the export credit agencies of the industrialised world, bi-lateral aid or of multilateral aid available from international development agencies such as the World Bank. He is a frequent visitor to the countries of the developing world. Before joining National Westminster Bank in 1965, Mr Bull practised as a civil engineer.

Notes on Contributors

John Butterworth (*Controlling cash and credit*) has been successively credit controller, credit manager and executive director of International Factors Ltd. As director, his main responsibility was credit risk management. In 1986, Mr Butterworth joined the Royal Bank of Scotland plc to set up a new invoice factoring subsidiary. He is author of *Debt Collection Letters in Ten Languages* and co-author, with T. G. Hutson, of *Management of Trade Credit*, both published by Gower.

Robert L. Carter (*Insurance*) is Norwich Union Professor of Insurance Studies in the Department of Industrial Economics, Accountancy and Insurance at Nottingham University. Before his academic career, Dr Carter was with the Norwich Union and was assistant insurance manager with Dunlop Company plc. He is the author of *Economics and Insurance* (2nd ed. 1979, P.H. Press) *Reinsurance* (2nd ed. 1983, Kluwer) and *Theft in the Market* (Institute of Economic Affairs, 1976), joint author of *Barriers to Trade in Insurance* (Trade Policy Research Centre, 1979) and *Success in Insurance* (Murray, 1984), and editor of *Handbook of Insurance* and *Handbook of Risk Management* (Kluwer). He has contributed to many other books and journals and prepared tuition courses for the Chartered Insurance Institute. He is a Fellow of the Chartered Insurance Institute.

Bob Chilton (*Inspection and expediting*) is head of the management services group of Merz and McLellan, consulting engineers, whom he joined nearly 40 years ago. As co-ordinating engineer, he has been responsible for projects in India and Brazil as well as for BP, Alkan and British Steel, among others, in the UK. Mr Chilton is a Chartered Engineer and a Member of the Institution of Mechanical Engineers

F. L. Harrison (*Motivating the participants*) is Director of Operations in the largest public sector direct-labour organisation in Western Europe. He has been concerned with project management for thirty years, having worked for the National Coal Board, Cementation Ltd, ICI and Imperial Oil of Canada. His experience also includes ten years at a business school, teaching and acting as a consultant to a variety of manufacturing and public-sector organisations. Mr Harrison is the author of numerous papers on management, planning

Notes on Contributors

and control and of *Advanced Project Management*, published by Gower.

O. P. Kharbanda (*Establishing a project organisation*). After three decades in teaching and industry in the USA, the UK and India, Dr Kharbanda now runs his own consultancy advising clients in many parts of the world and across a wide range of industries. He is a Fellow of the Institution of Chemical Engineers, a Visiting Professor, and regular leader of seminars on corporate planning, cost estimating, project management and communication skills. Dr Kharbanda has published or contributed to eight books and more than 150 papers in scientific and technical journals.

Graham J. McCleery (*Packing and shipping*) has worked for 40 years in the transport and freight industries, including several years with shipowners Furness Withy Ltd and with J. Leete & Son, shipping, forwarding and airfreight agents, whose managing director he became in 1972. He is now development manager for Europe, Jardine Cargo International. Mr McCleery was made a Freeman of the City of London in 1963.

Peter Marsh (*Contract law, Contracts and payment structures, Contract administration*) qualified as a solicitor in 1951 and has an honours degree in management sciences. He was chief contracts officer of the National Coal Board which he left to become central contracts manager for AEI and then GEC. He later joined STC as manager, contract administration and later became projects manager for their Submarine Cable Division. Mr Marsh joined his present company, George Wimpey, in 1979 becoming commercial director for their subsidiary British Smelter Construction, and is currently director of business development for George Wimpey International and a director of Wimpey Major Projects. He is author of *Contracting for Engineering and Construction Projects* and *Handbook of Contract Negotiation*, both published by Gower.

Ray Palmer (*Integrated systems for planning and control, An integrated project management system in action*) has been involved with project management since the early 1970s. In addition to writing

xvii

Notes on Contributors

and implementing his own computer programs, he has been a user of a number of proprietary packages. His experience includes project management consultancy, training, and the design and installation of integrated project control systems in a variety of industries, including construction, aerospace, shipbuilding, off-shore and power generation. He has worked on projects in the UK, Europe, the Middle and Far East and the USA. Mr Palmer joined Metier in 1979 and, after working as a consultant and then in account management, became the UK marketing manager in 1982. He is now the business manager of the KERNEL project management system where he has overall responsibility for support, marketing, sales and research and development. His main interest remains the cost-effective application of computers to project management.

David Ross (*Cost estimating, Cost control*) is at present seconded to the Project Systems Division of BP International, responsible for the development of microcomputer based project management systems. Previously he spent five years with Westland Aircraft and Massey-Ferguson respectively, followed by fifteen years with Seltrust Engineering Limited, a subsidiary of BP Minerals International. His experience included a five year apprenticeship followed by project engineering involving new product introductions in the manufacturing industry. Subsequent work has been concerned with mining operations, principally in Africa. This included a three-year period in Zambia where he was responsible for the planning and financial control aspects of both underground and surface plant facilities associated with the copper mining industry. More recently, his assignments have broadened to include the creation and development of project management systems including the preparation of project policies and procedures manuals for BP Minerals International.

Keith H. Savage (*Financing the project*) is a senior manager in the International Banking Division of National Westminster Bank. He has overall responsibility for the bank's project financing activities and has been involved in structuring financial packages for the development of natural resources, downstream activities and infrastructure projects. Mr Savage has travelled extensively on behalf of the bank and has lectured on the techniques of project finance in several countries, including the People's Republic of China. He is an Associate of the Institute of Bankers.

A. G. Simms (*Planning with charts, Critical path methods*) first worked in the telecommunications industry on the early development of electronic telephone exchanges. He then lectured on statistics and operational research at Woolwich and Leicester Polytechnics, and at the Cranfield Institute of Technology; also as visiting lecturer at the Administrative Staff College, Henley, and the Royal Institute of Public Administration. He was a founder member of the Networks Study of the Operational Research Society, and Chairman of the British Standards Institution's Committee responsible for the Glossary of Symbols and Terms in Project Network Analysis. Since 1966 he has been Principal Scientific Officer at the Building Research Establishment.

Ernest A. Stallworthy (*Establishing a project organisation*) has for many years been a management consultant with his own company, Dolphin Project Management Services. He was previously a manager responsible for the cost control of large-scale projects in the petrochemical industry. He is a Fellow of the Association of Cost Engineers and a member of the American Association of Cost Engineers. Mr Stallworthy is co-author (with O. P. Kharbanda and L. F. Williams) of *Project Cost Control in Action* and (with Dr Kharbanda) of *How to Learn from Project Disasters, Total Project Management, International Construction* and *Management Disasters and How to Prevent Them* — all published by Gower.

Lionel Stebbing (*Project quality assurance*) has been technical director with Bywater Technology Limited since 1983. The company, which was formed in 1982, provides a range of professional quality and management related services to industry, and the author's responsibilities include consultancy services, and the development of training courses and seminars. Prior to joining Bywater, he was manager of quality assurance with Brown and Root (UK) Ltd, administering the technical management of quality assurance services relating to offshore drilling and production platforms, onshore installations and petrochemical plant. Mr Stebbing has more than 25 years' industrial experience, most of it being related to quality aspects

Notes on Contributors

in major capital plant projects, power generation (conventional and nuclear), petrochemical, pipe lines, military, civil engineering and open cast mining. Recent experience has included the application of quality assurance/management systems to service industries and small companies. He is the author of the book *Quality Assurance: the Route to Efficiency and Competitiveness*, published by Ellis Horwood Limited.

Edmund J. Young (*Project organisation*) is senior lecturer in charge of engineering management studies, Elton Mayo School of Management, South Australian Institute of Technology. A graduate of three disciplines — civil engineering, industrial management and economics — he worked first as an investigation and design engineer for six years with the Australian Government, then six years with Concrete Industries (Monier), Australia, as a field and project engineer, project manager and executive engineer in several Australian states and in South-east Asia, before full-time academic teaching in industrial management. In 1976, he was visiting lecturer in engineering management at the University of Newcastle-upon-Tyne and visiting lecturer in production management at Bradford University. Author of over 80 papers on management and engineering management, he is chairman of the Engineering Management Branch, South Australian Division, Institution of Engineers, Australia, and a member of the Institution's National Committee on Engineering Management. He is a member of both the British and Australia Institutes of Management and a member of the American Society for Engineering Management besides being a contributor to and consulting editor for *Engineering Management International*.

Preface

Project management is both a specialist and a non-specialist skill. It is specialist because it uses a family of highly developed techniques for planning and control — techniques which have to be learned and mastered by any self-respecting project manager. And yet, because the project manager must work with managers from a wide range of functions from within and from outside his or her own organisation, he or she must have a very broad (non-specialist) appreciation of the working methods used by everyone with responsibility for technical, fulfilment and commercial project operations.

This handbook deals with both of these aspects. There are chapters which cover, in practical detail, the methods for organising, planning, scheduling, cost control, and progressing — the recognised tools of the project manager's trade. These chapters range from first principles to some of the most sophisticated and advanced computer-based systems available. Alone, these chapters would have constituted a useful and practical textbook. Fortunately, however, the editor of a handbook such as this is free to draw upon the knowledge and experience of experts from the whole field of project management and general management practice. This makes possible the inclusion of chapters which deal with the total field of project management and its directly related subjects in a way which would not be possible in a single author work.

I should therefore like to introduce this *Project Management Handbook* to readers as a work which, through the collective contributions of its many expert authors, will provide both trainee and practising project managers with a source of reference that is unique in its authoritative and comprehensive coverage of the subject. For this achievement, I acknowledge my gratitude to all the authors who made this venture possible. At the request of many of these authors, I willingly extend this acknowledgement to those

Preface

working behind the scenes, checking scripts, collecting and verifying facts and running programs on computers to produce illustrations.

Dennis Lock
St Albans

Part I
PROJECT MANAGEMENT AND ITS ORGANISATION

1
The Nature and Purpose of Project Management

Dennis Lock

Projects have been part of the human scene since civilisation started yet the practice of project management is, on the historical timescale, almost brand new. Only in the last couple of decades has the subject appeared to any extent in management literature. Current budgeting and planning methods are all relatively recent. Perhaps the reason for emphasis on project management is that it is concerned with the management of resources, including the most expensive resource of all — namely the human resource. It is no longer the case that a few thousand slaves can be deployed to build some architectural extravagance regardless of their welfare and safety. Everything now depends on getting things done on time and within cost budgets. Moreover, there is competition. If one contractor fails to meet his obligations or targets, no doubt twenty others will be ready to jump in to take his place when the next job comes up. Management has been described as 'getting results through people'. Amend that definition to 'achieving successful project completion with the resources available' and you have a succinct definition of project management, the resources being time, money, materials and equipment, and people.

CHARACTERISTICS OF PROJECTS

Any sales engineer working for a company which sells products from a catalogue, off its shelves, will know that his job is to dissuade his customers from asking for anything not listed in the catalogue and standard price list. If the sales engineer achieves a full order quota on the basis of accepting a number of 'specials', the production management will probably be quite upset at the resulting disruption to their batched manufacturing programme and the inevitable cost penalties. Project work is exactly opposite. Everything is special and 'one-off' or in very small quantities. Designs are new and usually unproven. Every industrial or commercial project is a risk venture. The job of the contractor is to identify the risks and, through his project management, contain them.

Not all projects are industrial or commercial. While most have to be carried out to a critical timescale, and have to achieve some predetermined level of performance technically or functionally, not all are carried out for profit. In this book, many techniques and management practices are described. The application of these will depend on the size and type of project, and upon the relative priorities which are assigned to the cost, time and performance objectives. Three broad categories of project can be identified, each with its own characteristics and demands upon project management methods.

Manufacturing projects

Included in the category of manufacturing projects are specially designed and built machines or equipment ordered to some unique customer specification. Typically these involve original design work, possibly prototype testing, and then manufacture, assembly and testing or commissioning in a factory with subsequent delivery and installation at the customer's premises. Apart from possible installation and commissioning work, most of the contractor's work is carried out completely under his own control on his own premises and with his own management in command. The job has probably been sold for a fixed price with a target profit in mind. There will be a promised delivery date, and there should be a set of unambiguous data which defines the required project.

Development projects for new products fit into this classification, since they are carried out with internal resources using the company's own management. Development projects differ in management emphasis because there is no profit objective, but they still require

The Nature and Purpose of Project Management

definition of timescale, expected performance and cost budget limits.

Manufacturing projects need the project management techniques of definition, cost estimates and budgetary control and timescale planning and control (although small manufacturing projects may not need the application of network analysis and the more sophisticated forms of resource scheduling which are described in later chapters). Communication problems are not likely to arise, and the project manager should be able to monitor progress easily and obtain access to line managers for the purpose of getting deficiencies corrected.

The situation becomes more complicated when more than one major contractor is engaged on the project in a joint venture organisation, in which case the project more readily fits into the next category.

Civil engineering, construction, petrochemical, mining and other projects requiring external organisation

Projects which aim to establish buildings or operating plant at some site remote from the contractor's offices, or which require the major participation of other contractors in joint ventureship, need more attention to the problems of organisation and communication. It will almost certainly be necessary to prepare and issue a formal set of project administrative procedures, and to set up a management team at the site.

Assuming that projects in this category are likely to be bigger and more expensive than simple manufacturing projects, financial management to provide and control the flow of funds will need expert professional attention, while the contracts between participating companies will be more difficult to draft and agree.

The more expensive, the longer the duration and the more complicated the organisation, the more the project will be likely to benefit from the sensible application of modern sophisticated planning, scheduling and cost control techniques (almost certainly using computers).

Management projects

The categories of project described so far are the obvious cases which spring to mind whenever the words 'project management' are uttered. But all companies, whatever the nature of their business, encounter project management problems at some time. A company engaged in flow or batch production will be vitally interested whenever a production facility is modernised or reorganised, and project management techniques will be needed to ensure efficient installation and start-up of the new plant. Even a commercial company with no manufacturing base at all must exercise efficient project management when it enlarges or moves its offices. Under these circumstances, where there is probably little project management experience resident within the company, the employment of an external project manager or managing contractor is the sensible practice.

Project management techniques find their application in many situations far removed from the obvious industrial project scene, helping to manage changes of premises, new installations, refurbishment or maintenance of existing plant and facilities, company relocations and so on. Although scientific research projects may be too innovative and experimental to allow the definition of objectives, without which project management is unable to operate properly, setting up the research facilities in the first place will probably take less time and stand less chance of exceeding budgets if the principles of project management are applied.

Another kind of project which needs formal management of budgets and timescale is the systems development and implementation work seen when a team of internal or external specialists are engaged to investigate administrative or accounting procedures, suggest and develop alternative (improved) methods, and then implement them. In fact, the name 'project manager' is sometimes applied to the head of a team responsible for designing a special computer system application for a commercial user.

Most managers working in industry or commerce need the expertise of a project manager at some time during their working lives.

OBJECTIVES

The objectives of project management can be condensed under three headings. A successful project is one which has been finished on time, within its cost budgets and to a technical or performance standard which satisfies the end user.

Timescale

Provided that quality standards and design are satisfactory, it is a fairly safe assumption that projects which finish on time are likely to meet their other objectives, whereas projects that finish late overrun their budgets and cause customer resentment and other problems. Controlling the timescale must be a top priority for any project manager. There is no shortage of management techniques available to help in this quest. While it is true that strikes, failures by other contractors and unavoidable design errors are all hurdles to be overcome, nevertheless careful attention to timescale planning and progress control are essential if a project is to stand any chance of success.

A project costs money during every day, working or non-working, weekday or weekend day, from day one of the programme right through until final payment has been received from the customer. These costs arise from the obvious 'direct' cost elements of bought-out materials and all the manhours expended in design and production activities. There are also the costs of management and administration to be borne. Accommodation is another big cost factor in many projects, with all kinds of problems for future work schedules and subsequent projects if the work is not finished and cleared away on time. Other costs include the notional cost of money used or tied up in the project. This can include the obvious interest charges from banks or other sources for large projects with special financing, but it also includes the cost of money invested in work in progress. And work in progress does not only include the obvious work carried on in the factory or on a construction site, but it also encompasses all the costs of engineering and drawing which are buried in designs and drawings in progress or awaiting production or construction use.

Delays on a major project can amount to additional costs of thousands of pounds per day. If work is not finished, the contractor is unable to issue invoices or claim progress payments. And there can be the final ignominy of cost penalties in contracts which contain clauses providing the customer with the sanction of penalty payments for each day or each week by which the contractor fails to meet his delivery obligation.

Every project manager must ensure that his project is efficiently and sensibly planned and scheduled from the start, and that critical tasks are identified. Control has then to be applied to keep the work on time, if necessary by putting additional effort into critical jobs which are at risk of running late. Such control has to embrace all areas of the project and all subcontractors and vendors of equipment. If the contractor makes it clear from the start that he expects all participants to meet their delivery and work schedule commitments, and then proceeds to monitor progress closely, he stands a better chance of success. It is no good waiting until a supplier fails to deliver goods at the appropriate time, or being surprised that a specialist design subcontractor asks for more time to complete drawings. Only by a constant process of checking achievement against a series of intermediate, planned criteria or events can timely completion be assured. And the project manager should have rooted in his mind, if not actually displayed in his office, the axiom 'TIME IS MONEY'.

Project costs

Cost control starts with careful definition of the scope or work to which the contractor is committed, followed by division of the total project into a number of manageable parts: known universally as the work breakdown process. Each part of the work becomes a 'work package' to be cost estimated, budgeted and (subsequently) cost controlled. The actual process of cost control is, unlike timescale control, not always a direct procedure. Whereas, if a job runs late, management can take steps to expedite the work, it is more difficult directly to control costs. The process of containing costs within budgets is more a matter of applying sound control principles before money is committed.

The control of labour costs, including professional manhours, is largely one of controlling the timescale. If progress is maintained on schedule with the planned workforce, then no serious cost problem should arise.

The control of material and equipment costs is exercised before orders are placed, through the procedure of obtaining competitive quotations and by comparing quotations for similar items in a rational and orderly fashion. Formal procedures for the approval of expenditure commitments are essential, so that a responsible manager or organisation examines each significant item before issuing the purchase order. If equipment orders committed exceed the amount budgeted, then no amount of work can undo the damage. It will simply be too late to recover the over-expenditure.

There are project managers who believe that because they have good cost coding and work breakdown systems, possibly backed up by computers, that the resulting detailed reports constitute good cost control. They are mistaken. Cost reporting is not cost control. The purpose of accurate and detailed cost reporting is to provide early warning of dangerous trends, giving sufficient time for corrective action. But corrective action can, as already stated, only consist of rigorous progress control and formal vetting and approval of purchase commitments before they are made.

Other important factors in cost control concern the intrinsic costs of the project design. These are mentioned in the next section.

Performance

If a project is delivered on time and within budget the contractor will be well pleased. The customer should also be pleased, but he won't be if the finished result is below his functional or aesthetic requirements. This is not a technical textbook, and cannot deal with the intricacies of conceptual and detailed engineering which must be the jealously guarded capability of every reputable and competent contractor within each industrial field. There are, however, sound engineering management principles which fall within the scope of project management generally, and without which all the project objectives will be put at risk.

The first and obvious step in attaining the required performance is to define, from the outset, exactly what that performance is to be. Engineering then proceeds along guidelines which correspond with the cost and timescale objectives. All three objectives are interlocked, and the conduct and progress of engineering has to be managed to make sure that the design standards and concepts keep on the chosen track. Variations and modifications are inevitable in a large contract: these must be subjected to definition, vetting, approval and control along with the mainstream activities.

Some companies pride themselves upon their technical excellence. Pride in a company's products can be a wonderful motivating force. Care has to be taken, however, not to produce a result which far exceeds the requirements. There is a useful motto in this respect for engineering managers: 'Don't let the *best* be the enemy of the *good*!' Firms have been known to lose potential orders because their fundamental engineering standards were too good, and too costly to achieve. Sometimes their methods were actually wasteful: why use stainless steel where mild steel would do, and why use 50mm plate thickness when all the competitors would use the (perfectly adequate) thickness of 25mm? These are areas where companies can benefit from the commonsense techniques of value engineering and value analysis. A sensible company will involve the project manager and managers from the engineering and fulfilment divisions in pre-design meetings which aim to eliminate unnecessarily wasteful procedures, and to arrive at designs which, whilst functional, are practicable to produce.

Quality assurance is a vital function in the achievement of performance and, rightly, has a chapter of its own later in this book. As with control over time and costs, quality assurance must extend over all concerned with project fulfilment, whether they are working in the contractor's own factory, producing goods or equipment for supply through vendors, or carrying out construction, installation or erection on site.

THE PROJECT MANAGER

The role of the project manager, and the organisation of project management is discussed at length in the following chapters. It is, however, useful to reflect here on the emergence of project management as a distinct management specialisation. Major projects seem to demand more complex organisations these days, and we tend to marvel at the greatness and stamina of engineering giants such as Telford and Brunel, who personally directed all aspects of their projects. There now exist project managers with no direct responsibility for engineering, whose role is co-ordination and administration. It is to these administrative, co-ordinating and control functions and techniques that this book is addressed.

At its simplest, the need for the separate role of a project manager is seen in an engineering company faced with producing special one-off products which are large in relation to its total production

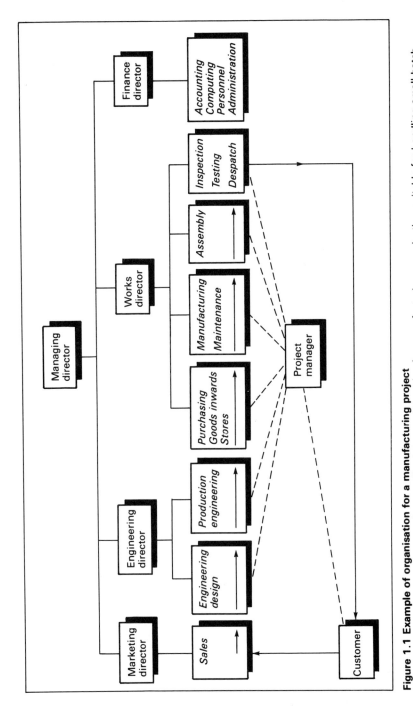

Figure 1.1 Example of organisation for a manufacturing project
Without the project manager, this diagram illustrates an example of a manufacturing organisation suitable for handling small batch production. When the output is, instead, large one-off special projects, the addition of a project manager is necessary to co-ordinate all activities and ensure that the project work flows smoothly within proper cost and time constraints

Project Management and its Organisation

Stage in project management	Method	See chapter
0 Feasibility	A preliminary stage, before project management involvement, in which appraisals are carried out to ensure that the project will be viable technically and economically, and that funds can be made available	
1 Definition of objectives		
— scope	Solution or feasibility engineering by potential contractors, often in consultation with the client	8
— costs	Evaluation of the proposed engineering solution as accurately as possible (given the limited amount of design information available) to arrive at provisional cost estimates. The project may have to be sold against such preliminary estimates	10
— timescale	An assessment of the project duration and its key dates, based mainly upon past experience of similar projects rather than on detailed planning. A simple bar chart may be produced or a network, but there is insufficient information or time available at this pre-contract stage to allow detailed planning	17
2 Arrange funding	The client, having decided that he wants to proceed with a contract, has to ensure that funds are arranged or are available from his own resources. Preliminary cash flow forecasts are necessary.	9
3 Agree the objectives	The successful contractor, by entering into a contract with the client, has accepted his commitments and agreed to the project objectives	4 5 6
4 Work breakdown	The project is divided into a set of manageable tasks, known as work packages. Each work package is a mini project, with its own objectives of scope, cost and timescale. Work packages are chosen so that they fit together into hierarchical (or family tree) fashion to constitute the entire project.	10 26
5 Work schedule	Barcharts or network diagrams are used to show all project activities in a logical sequence. Network notation is best suited to this process, but bar charts are acceptable for very small jobs.	17 18
	The duration of each activity is estimated, and the overall project timescale is calculated, together with the identification of all critical activities. The logic is re-examined if the timescale is too long.	19 20
	The resources needed for the project are calculated and scheduled, using a computer for all but the very smallest projects.	21

Figure 1.2 Stages of project management

The Nature and Purpose of Project Management

Stage in project management	Method	See chapter
6 Set the cost budgets	Re-estimate the project costs, in the detail afforded by the work breakdown and work schedule. Reconcile the new estimate with that used for the contract commitment, and take practical steps to limit the expenditure if this is initially estimated to exceed the total budget objective. Then set the work package budgets accordingly.	10 11
7 Work implementation	Set up the project organisation. Write and issue administrative procedures (unless standard). Issue an order authorising work to start. Issue detailed task lists and assign tasks to individuals. Set up purchasing arrangements. Identify and buy all long-lead purchased items.	3 22 13
8 Review the objectives	Reviewing the initial objectives is a continuous function of the project management team to ensure that any threat to them is acted upon promptly. Special attention must be paid to any proposals for project variations, to assess their likely effect on the overall scope, final costs and timescale.	8 11
9 Work follow-up	Expedite materials. Monitor, report and predict costs. Set up and carry out effective quality assurance procedures, to follow through until all work has been finished. Monitor work against key events or quantities, as appropriate. Ensure that personnel are well organised and motivated. Conduct progress meetings and report to the client and to the contractor's own management.	14 12 23 22 25 26
10 Close down	Assemble, summarise and archive a historical record of the project, showing final costs and scope of work, together with a technical description supported by as-built drawings. Include test certificates, calculations and copies of operating and maintenance manuals. This stage can be regarded as the final part of project definition, which started with the definition of objectives, continued as a constant review of these objectives, and (now) finishes with the objectives as they were actually achieved.	8

Figure 1.2 *(concluded)*

capacity, and which involve several departments. Whereas normal batch production is handled adequately by the existing production management, the larger project needs an independent co-ordinating eye to see the whole picture and keep everything controlled and co-ordinated. This concept is illustrated in Figure 1.1. The ordinary organisation of a factory contains no individual who can devote time, or has the authority to oversee all phases of the project. In industries such as construction, the need for project management is more apparent, and does not need further amplification.

TECHNIQUES OF PROJECT MANAGEMENT

This book contains much advice and explanation in the use of a number of management and commercial practices and techniques for project management. The armoury of such management tools is extensive and expanding. The choice of techniques, sometimes available on a selection of computers, is often a matter of personal preference. It is, however, necessary to be clear about the sequence in which the techniques should be used, and to know what they can and what they cannot achieve.

The sequence and choice of techniques

Faced with having to plan and control a large project, the inexperienced manager might well feel overfaced by the number of apparently conflicting and insoluble problems. Many decisions have to be made, and procedures established. The situation is, in some respects, analogous to the solution of a mathematical problem containing several unknown quantities. The way out of the dilemma is to use a logical method for eliminating the unknown quantities one at a time. The problem is then made manageable.

Please now refer to Figure 1.2. This shows the principle stages of project management, and provides a 'directory' to the chapters in this book which deal with the appropriate practices.

2
Project Organisation

Edmund J. Young

The Chinese philosopher Confucius once stated, 'The beginning of learning starts with the precise meaning of words'. Unfortunately, the fields of management in general and project management in particular are plagued by the problem of semantics. There are a number of different meanings of such terms as 'management', 'project management', 'project organisation', 'project teams', etc., and at present there is no general agreement or consensus of views on the precise definitions of these words.

DEFINING 'ORGANISATION'

While the term 'project' is more readily definable in terms of such attributes as a complete sequence of tasks that has a definite start and finish, an identifiable goal and entity, and an integrated system of complex but interdependent relationships, the term 'organisation' has several meanings. Consider the term 'global project organisation'. While the English author Harrison (1981) refers to it as 'the arrangement and relationships between client company, contractor and subcontractor organisations and their respective project managers who are all involved in undertaking a project in a particular environment', American authors Davis and Lawrence (1977) refer to it as meaning the arrangement and interrelationships of projects on a global or world-wide scale. So it is a matter of taking a point of view on what precisely one means by the various terms, and more importantly, on what is generally accepted in project practice.

'The term 'organisation' has four different, but related meanings, *viz*:

1. The systematic arrangement or division of work, activities or tasks between individuals and groups with the necessary allocation of duties and responsibilities among them to achieve common objectives.
2. A cohesive social group with formal relationships between members who combine together to achieve common goals, for example, a football club, a political party, a pressure group, etc.
3. The total aggregation of human and material resources that can be distinguished as a separate entity purposely combined together to achieve specific objectives, for example, a company, a government department, a construction project, etc.
4. The structure of authority and responsibility relationships in a cohesive social system that is a separate entity purposely set up to achieve specific objectives.

The relationships between these four definitions can be stated as follows: To achieve the objectives required in Organisation 2 or 3 entails Organisation 1 (involving arrangement or division of work) which in turn requires a structure of authority and responsibility that is Organisation 4.

Thus, organisations have specific objectives, a formal structure of authority with some persons in leadership roles and others in subordinate roles, division of work which entails specialisation by members in various activities or functions, a formal system of communications, and generally a set of formal procedures and customs that distinguish them from other social entities. Social scientists, from the German sociologist Max Weber early this century to today, called these features the attributes of 'bureaucracy' but it is difficult to see how organisations could continue to exist without possessing these attributes to some degree. The direct antithesis of 'organisation' is disorganisation, chaos and anarchy. In project organisation, accomplishment of the specific project in the most economical, efficient and effective manner within the constraints of time, budget and performance or quality standards is the prime objective.

ROLE OF THE PROJECT MANAGER

The problem of semantics relates also to defining the role of project manager. In practice, while all may be designated 'project managers', roles may vary considerably from one who is strictly a project monitor or expediter, through one who oversees or who exercises broad supervision over a project, to one who exercises total authority and accepts full responsibility for the execution of the project. The common element in defining the role of the project manager is that it relates to acceptance of managerial responsibility for certain aspects of the project. This managerial responsibility entails responsibility for planning, organising, co-ordinating, staffing, leading, major decision making, motivating personnel, monitoring and controlling operations on the project.

The varying roles can be seen in Figure 2.1 which depicts simply three organisations involved in the undertaking of a typical construction project. Organisation meanings 2 and 3 are implied here.

There is Organisation A — the principal, customer or client, who wants the project and is prepared to pay for it. If Organisation A does not have the resources and expertise to carry out such tasks as feasibility studies, planning, design, preparation of the necessary contract documents and general supervision of project execution, then it engages Organisation B to undertake these activities for a fee. Organisation B may be an architectural firm, engineering consultants, or a firm specialising in project management, depending on the nature and scope of the project. Organisation B is the second party involved and there is a contractual relation between Organisations A and B.

But to execute the project, a third party, Organisation C — the builder or contractor — with the necessary human and material resources, constructional experience and expertise, must be involved. Either by tendering or by negotiation a contractual relation is established between the principal or customer, Organisation A, and the contractor or seller, Organisation C. Organisation B then acts on behalf of Organisation A to supervise the project to be carried out by Organisation C. This is a typical situation where three parties are involved in a construction project. But if Organisation A was of such size and possessed all the resources to plan, design, supervise and

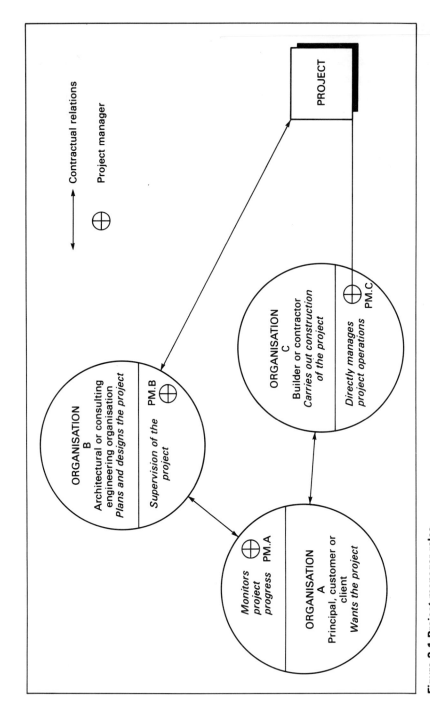

Figure 2.1 Project manager roles
Different roles of the project managers in three organisations involved in a construction project

Project Organisation

construct the project by itself (as in some socialist countries) then there would be no need for Organisations B and C. Likewise, if Organisation A had the resources and expertise to plan, design and supervise the project only, then Organisation B would not be needed. The arrangement of work to undertake the project is dependent upon the availability of resources, specialisation of functions between organisations and their roles, nature of the project and the environment.

The project depicted by the organisational arrangement in Figure 2.1 may be of such importance and complexity that all three organisations may each appoint their own project managers from within their own organisations. If we designate them by PM.A, PM.B and PM.C, with each relating to their respective organisations, then their roles will not be identical due to the division of work and responsibilities, and the particular roles and functions of their organisations.

PM.A's role would be more of a monitor, progress chaser, reporter and expediter. PM.A's duty would be to keep the top management of Organisation A informed on progress, expenditure, and likely delays on the project. He may approve progress payments by his organisation for work satisfactorily completed by Organisation C on the recommendation of the representative from Organisation B. Public relations for the project may be handled by PM.A. His top management has delegated the responsibility for the project to him to oversee. He is the key person to contact in his own organisation on all matters relating to the project.

PM.B's role would be more comprehensive insofar as it involves preparation of feasibility studies, advising the customer or client on best choice, planning, design, preparation of contract documents, analysis and recommendation of tenders, contract administration, checking quality and progress, and exercising general supervision over the project. In the investigation stage, PM.B may be involved with contacting and negotiation with local authorities.

PM.C's role is the one most directly involved with the actual execution of the project. This involves detailed planning, daily decision making, organising, co-ordinating, directing and supervising personnel, and controlling human and material resources in actually carrying out the project. Although not shown in Figure 2.1, he may be involved in the negotiation and supervision of subcontractors, and in dealing with suppliers and local authorities whose co-operation are necessary in implementing the project.

The role of the person designated as the 'project manager' would depend, therefore, on the arrangement of work and role of the organisation employing him in relation to the project. The focus of his duties and responsibilities is on the project.

The roles of the project manager can be viewed in terms of:

1 *Externally* — to others outside his own organisation, or to inter-organisational relationships, and
2 *Internally* — to members within his own organisation, or to intra-organisational relationships.

Externally, the project manager has to deal with the customer or client organisation, subcontractors, suppliers of materials and equipment, local authorities and other organisations which could affect the project. Of these the customer is the most important.

The project manager—customer relationship

One of the main reasons for the appointment of a project manager by his employer is the wish of top management to delegate the responsibility for monitoring, co-ordinating, supervising or managing the project from start to finish to one person — the project manager. In doing so, he becomes the key person whom the customer can contact on progress, complaints, taking corrective action, changes of plans or delays on the project. The project manager is in the key role for communications on the project. Both top management of his own organisation and the customer would consider him the main contact person on development or progress.

The project manager is also his organisation's representative for the project to the customer and others externally. He is his firm's chief spokesman and main negotiator on all matters relating to the project. For the project manager in a consulting engineering organisation (like PM.B in Figure 2.1) he has also the responsibility to advise the client or customer on best courses of action, costs of changes to plans, and to make recommendations on approval of progress payments to the contractor. Such services imply professional liability on the part of the consulting organisation which can be more than the straight principal–contractor contractual relationship.

Project Organisation

The project manager's relationships within his own organisation

Having recognised that there could be a number of different responsibilities that a project manager could assume, five major classes of responsibility can be identified, *viz*:

1. Project expediter, monitor or reporter.
2. Project planner.
3. Project co-ordinator.
4. Project supervisor or controller.
5. Project manager, administrator or director.

Wearne (1973) recognised nine degrees of relative project responsibility but the above simplified classification makes for easier identification in practice. Depending on the situation, it is possible for one person to assume one, several or all of these responsibilities. In Figure 2.1 PM.A assumed role 1, whereas PM.B carried out roles 2 and 4. PM.C assumed role 5 for his own organisation.

The role of the project co-ordinator (3) is more restricted in liaison and co-ordination with personnel outside his own department. Figure 2.2 shows an engineering design organisation in which the project co-ordinator in the civil section liaises with, and co-ordinates the efforts of, personnel in the other sections working on the same project. He is not allowed to exercise direct authority over these other personnel, but has instead to use more persuasion and other means of influencing them in carrying out their part of the project. At most, he can call co-ordination meetings to ensure that everyone involved reports progress and integrates effort.

The project co-ordinator has been delegated this task of co-ordination by senior management or by his superior (the chief civil engineer) on the basis that the major portion of the project is a civil engineering one, but requires inputs from the other engineering functions. Any conflict between personnel has to be taken up to the section engineers and ultimately to the chief design engineer for resolution. Within the civil section the project co-ordinator may be directly in charge of subordinates who, together, make up his own project team within the section. Then there exists line (direct) authority between the project co-ordinator and members of his own project team.

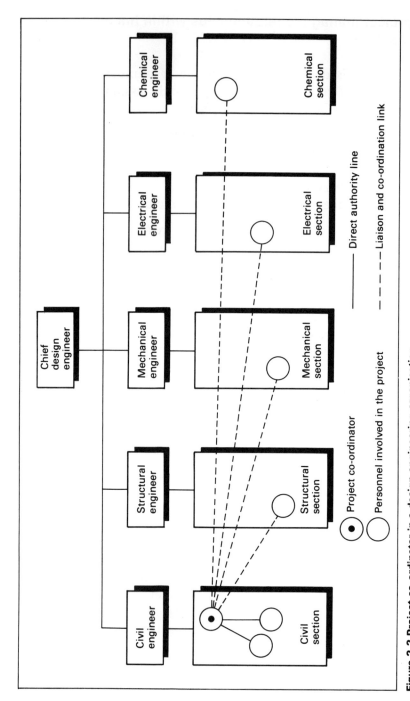

Figure 2.2 Project co-ordinator in a design engineering organisation
Example of a project co-ordinator based (in this case) in a civil engineering department with direct responsibility for the work in his own section and with liaison and co-ordination responsibilities with all the other sections

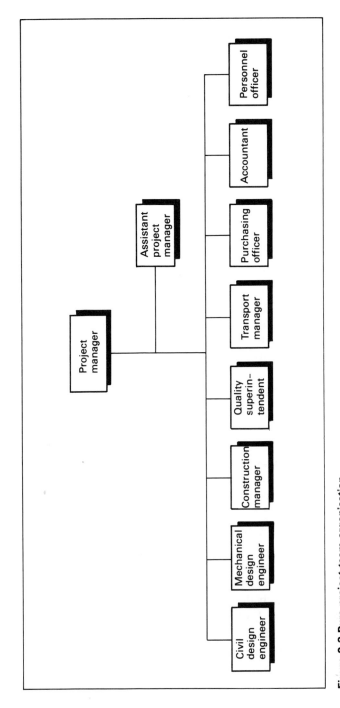

Figure 2.3 Pure project team organisation
Organisation in which the project manager is in total charge of the project

Figure 2.2 also shows the arrangement common to most organisations, which is functional organisation (organisation according to main functions or similar groups of activities). All civil engineering activities, all mechanical activities, and so on, are grouped together in their respective sections, with each headed by its appropriate specialist engineer. If, for example, the civil section had several major projects which were wholly or predominantly civil, it might be convenient to appoint project managers or officers with responsibility for each of these projects. This would become a form of project organisation within the functional department.

Pure project team organisation

The pure project team or projectised organisation is depicted in Figure 2.3 which shows the structure for an engineering construction project. Here the division of duties and responsibilities of personnel directly under the project manager and his assistant are according to main functions (which comprise civil and mechanical design, construction, transport, purchasing, etc.). The project manager exercises full authority and control.

Line and staff organisation

The prime tasks or functions of the enterprise are to design and construct the project. While the transport, purchasing, accounting and personnel activities are all a necessary part of the total set of operations, these sections are not directly involved with the prime tasks of design and construction. They are more in support or 'staff' roles. Their roles are to assist, aid, render counsel and advice, and to service the 'line' activities. The quality superintendent is in a more controlling role but is still considered as more a 'staff' function. While all the subordinates under the project manager are in line relationship to him, the organisation is also one of 'line and staff'. Thus, Figure 2.3 which depicts a pure project team organisation is really one that shows both line and staff relationships with some personnel performing line functions of design and construction, and other personnel rendering service, aid, counsel or support to those in the 'line'. A distinguishing feature of this pure project organisation is that the total efforts of all personnel involved are concentrated solely on the project. This is also the oldest form of project organisation. It was used by the ancient Egyptians, Chinese and Romans to build pyramids, walls, canals and roads.

Matrix organisation

In the early nineteen-sixties the concept of 'project management' was promoted by the US Defence Department and the aerospace industry as a new form of managerial organisation. The term 'matrix management' was conceived and applied to both client and contractor organisations in the United States. This raises the issue of whether there are different organisational relationships in different industries. We have considered the pure project organisation, which is common on large scale building and construction projects, and the line and staff organisation which is formed from a functional organisation. The pure project organisation is usually part of a broader line and staff-functional structure of the total enterprise. Where the project is of a small size and does not warrant accounting and personnel departments set up under the project manager (as shown by Figure 2.3) then it is usual to have 'staff' roles advising and assisting the project manager and his team from outside the project team structure.

A matrix form of organisation is depicted in Figure 2.4 which shows the functional organisations with engineering, production and other functional managers in charge of their respective departments with vertical lines of authority, and project managers A, B and C in charge of projects A, B and C respectively also exercising equal authority (shown by lateral or horizontal lines) with the functional managers.

This is a situation in which personnel in the functional departments could be responsible to two or more superiors. The diagram shows only the simple case, with a single person in each department allocated to one project (like the engineers X, Y and Z, allocated to projects A, B and C respectively). The situation would become more complicated if (for example) engineer Z were also to be assigned to work on project A. Or, suppose that project managers A, B and C all required the services of engineer Y. The result is a multiple command system which appears to violate the age-old principle of one man, one boss (unity of command).

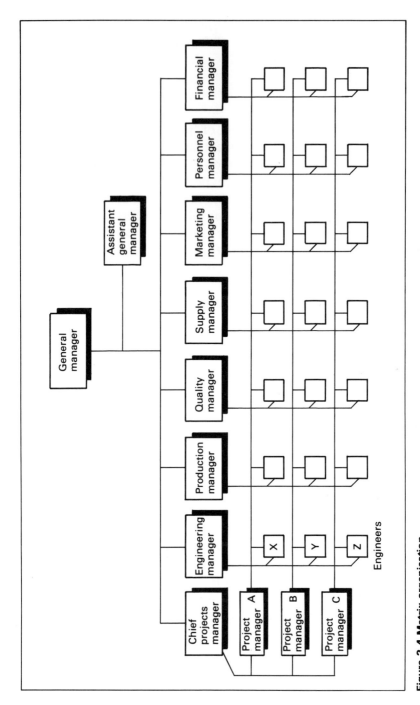

Figure 2.4 Matrix organisation
Project managers exercise equal (lateral) authority with functional managers

Figure 2.4 depicts the situation where a chief projects manager heads all the project managers A, B and C. This has the advantage that the span of control is reduced — the number of direct subordinates to the general manager is nine (assistant general manager, chief projects manager and seven functional managers). Without the chief projects manager, the three project managers would have to report directly to the general manager. The appointment of a chief projects manager enables more projects to be undertaken, with improved co-ordination between projects, and it allows consultation between the chief projects manager and the functional managers in order to settle any differences on project matters.

This matrix form of organisation was the 'spin off' from the US aerospace industry during the sixties and many organisations in various industries from manufacturing, consulting, construction, service to educational have adopted it with varying success (Kingdon, 1973; Davis and Lawrence, 1977; and Knight, 1977). Shannon (1972) maintained that the concept of dual or multiple authority relationships stemmed from the 'functional foremanship' theory of the American pioneer of scientific management, F. W. Taylor, with the basic difference that Taylor did not conceive it as applying to management of a project.

The matrix organisation may be one of two forms: shifting or fixed. In the shifting matrix (widely used in the American aerospace industry) personnel in functional departments were shifted between projects depending on the work load and project cycle. In the fixed matrix, personnel in functional departments are always assigned to the same project managers whatever the project. In the fixed matrix a project manager would be responsible for managing the projects in successive series; for example, projects P, Q and R would follow each other under the guidance and control of the same project manager. In the shifting matrix the personnel assigned to the project team are disbanded when the project is finished.

The concept of a project team can apply also within the matrix, where it relates to personnel in functional departments who work directly under the project manager in a team, group or task force. These personnel may either stay within their own departments or they can be grouped together and placed under the charge of the project manager in a place chosen for the duration of the project. But, in these cases, each person has two or more bosses — the project manager(s) and his usual functional manager.

In manufacturing industry, the concept of product manager is used to relate to the responsibility for conception, development, manufacturing, marketing and servicing of a particular product. Here, the matrix of Figure 2.4 still applies, but with the difference that the project managers are replaced by the product managers. In Figure 2.4 both line and staff personnel are used by the product managers to undertake project work. The matrix can also be developed in other dimensions, like services (Lloyd, 1979; Kerzner, 1979; and Cleland and King, 1983).

The basic organisation structures of line, line and functional, line and staff, or a combination of these can be identified irrespective of the industry being considered. The *project* organisation (whether in the form of pure project organisation or of project groupings within functional departments) focusses attention on the project. The *matrix* organisation combines functional structure with a project (or product) organisation overlay.

It should be noted that there are two other types of organisation which are not relevant for consideration here: these are committee organisation and military style general staff organisation.

MATRIX VERSUS THE PURE PROJECT ORGANISATION

Matrix advantages

Those who advocate the matrix claim a number of advantages for this type of organisation. It permits project managers to focus attention on all stages of the project from start to finish while operating in the traditional functional structure. It allows greater flexibility and so is more adaptable to changes in technology in that personnel can be readily transferred to different projects as in the shifting matrix. This facilitates balancing of workloads between the demands of all the projects being undertaken.

Better communications are maintained between all parties (especially with customers) as well as better utilisation of resources. Because the matrix can be considered as an overlay on the functional structure the benefit of functional specialisation in maintaining a high standard of technical excellence is another advantage. With the fixed matrix, functional personnel are likely to be more motivated because of continuity of projects whereas with the pure project organisation (and to some extent with the shifting matrix) motivation and morale can decline as each project approaches completion.

Matrix disadvantages

A prime disadvantage of the matrix is that it is a more complex form of organisation to operate. This is mainly due to its dual or multiple command structure with functional personnel being subjected to the authority of both their functional and project managers. It may lead to role ambiguity and conflict of interests. Cleland and King (1983) maintained that there can be a separation of responsibility in the sense that the project manager assumes responsibility for project planning, determination of project objectives, scheduling and budgeting while the functional manager assumes responsibility for the method of work and assignment of personnel. Such division and clarification of responsibilities can be assisted by the use of a Linear Responsibility Chart or Matrix developed originally by an American consultant, Serge Bern. Responsibility is divided into primary responsibility and support responsibility similar to line and staff responsibilities (Cleland and Kocaoglu, 1981). In practice it is difficult to separate the method of work from the time and cost aspects. Where highly talented or specialised functional personnel are involved, it is more likely for functional managers to give preference to these personnel for their own important jobs rather than allowing them to be used on project work. Thus conflict of interests can easily arise, and this involves conflict of loyalties.

Another disadvantage is the higher overhead costs involved in setting up project managers and the system of communications. Davis and Lawrence (1977) saw the problem of the delicate balance of power in the matrix form with tendencies to anarchy, power struggles, slowness of decision making, 'groupitis', and even collapse during business decline. They maintained that the three reasons for operation of the matrix form were due to: (a) outside pressure for dual focus; (b) pressures for high information-processing capacity; and (c) pressures for shared resources.

Operating the matrix

To use the matrix, personnel must be properly trained in understanding the concept, principles involved and the techniques of operation. Lines of authority and responsibility must be clearly defined, and any subdivision of responsibilities clearly allocated. This is where the Linear Responsibility Chart or Matrix can be an invaluable tool. The objectives and functions must be clearly stated for all components of the project, and the Work Breakdown Structure and Work Package concepts are useful aids in this regard. Clear guidelines on incentives, loyalties and promotional opportunities for functional personnel need to be stated. The system of communications between all personnel must be established early with provision for constant consultation as the project progresses.

The roles of each person must be clarified at the beginning with procedures established for resolution of role ambiguities or conflicts should they arise. The appointment of a Chief Projects Manager to co-ordinate the various projects, to avoid duplication of resources, and to help resolution of conflicts between the various project managers and the functional managers is a useful device to aid the operation of the matrix although it means higher costs. On the other hand, such an appointment would reduce the span of control of the general manager while adding another level to the organisation.

The project managers can also be viewed as a form of 'mini-general managers' and appointment to such roles is often considered good training for future promotion to general or top management roles.

Whilst many favour the matrix organisation in certain situations and some like Stickney and Johnson (1983) view it as an effective means of delegation, others like Sinclair (1984) are sceptical on whether such a form of organisation is really necessary in many situations.

Pure project advantages

The pure project or projectised organisation has the clear advantage of simplicity, with the project manager in complete control of the project and exercising total authority over all personnel involved. Functional specialisation is clearly demarcated and this permits a high level of technical competence. There is no confusion over line and staff roles and the chain of command is clear and direct.

Pure project disadvantages

On the other hand, the pure project form has some disadvantages. It may be more applicable to large-scale projects which can command the range of specialisations necessary. There may be unbalanced work loads due to variations in demand for resources in the project cycle and this makes for employment instability. The level of technical expertise may not be as high as in the functional organisation in the parent enterprise of which this project organisation is only a part. The morale and motivation of the project team members may decline as project approaches completion because the organisation is dismantled once the project is completed.

Matrix versus pure project

In weighing the use of the matrix versus the pure project team organisation, the advantages and disadvantages of each must be considered in light of the nature, scope and size of the project, the relative costs of each in terms of expected benefits, and the particular environment in which the project is to be undertaken. As an example of the environmental factor, a matrix organisation is more likely to be successfully implemented in a sophisticated aerospace company in a technologically advanced country than on a construction project in an underdeveloped country where pure project team organisation is the norm.

PROJECT ORGANISATION WITH MORE COMPLEX ARRANGEMENTS

The organisations of many projects involve more than just one contractor in undertaking the project. Subcontractors are employed to undertake specialised work which requires skills, expertise and resources not normally possessed by the main contractor but who, in turn, is still held accountable for their work by the principal or customer. Two or more contractors may combine together in a

Project Management and its Organisation

temporary partnership just to undertake a project forming a joint venture or consortium. Specialist consultants may be used by not only the principal but also the contractor to advise and render services on certain aspects of the project. Finally, the organisation of international projects requires consideration of special factors affecting organisational arrangements.

Joint venture organisations

Joint ventures are undertaken for large-scale complex projects where their accomplishment requires the use of skills and resources beyond that possessed by one contractor organisation. Two or more firms may form a temporary partnership whereby each firm sees advantages in utilising the skills and resources of the other in order to secure the contract and so mutually profit from the project. There may be forced partnership situations where governments in certain countries or organisations stipulate that a joint venture with certain firms known for some special expertise be included in the partnership. A common form of joint venture is where an overseas firm joins with a local firm in undertaking a project whereby both the expertise of the overseas organisation and the knowledge, experience and facilities of the local organisation are combined.

Like ordinary partnerships, there may be major and minor partners, or equal partners but the difference is that the joint venture partnership exists only to undertake the project. On completion of the project the joint venture partnership is dissolved. In forming joint ventures the most important document is the joint venture agreement which sets out the rights and obligations of each partner, sharing of profits or losses, provisions for default by any partner and especially should one partner drop out or go bankrupt during the course of the project. A common hazard of joint ventures is when one partner decides to withdraw from the project due to factors outside of the venture. Poor quality work and delays on the part of one partner could adversely affect the whole project, and responsibilities and obligations for such should be clearly defined in the agreement.

Figure 2.5 depicts a joint venture organisation structure for a project whereby a management committee comprising representatives from the various partners is made responsible for policy decisions on the project. The project manager is the chief executive officer and is

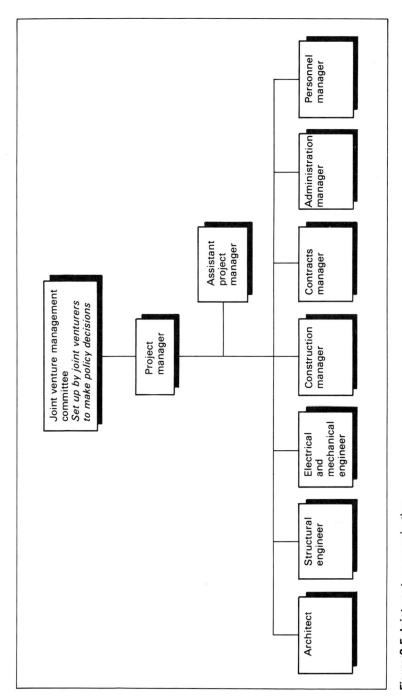

Figure 2.5 Joint venture organisation

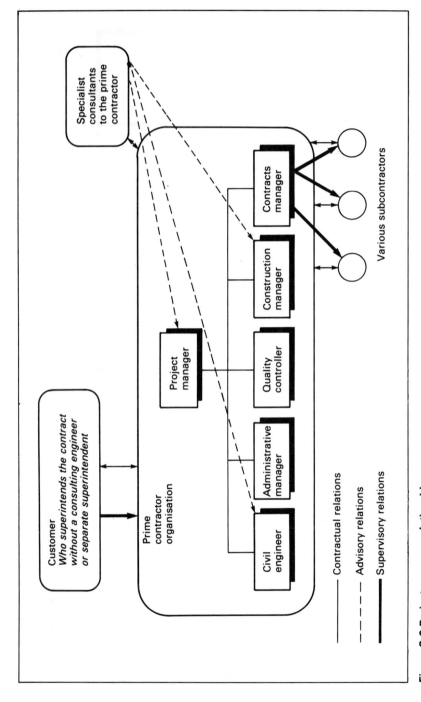

Figure 2.6 Project manager relationships
The project manager's relationships with customer, specialist consultants and subcontractors

totally responsible for the project. The organisation is of the pure project team form with subordinate personnel drawn from the personnel of the partner organisations but whose time and efforts are solely devoted to the project. The project manager may be chosen from the major partner or from whomever the joint partners deem most capable and experienced for the job.

Subcontractor organisation

Subcontractors are in contractual relation to the main or prime contractor with whom the principal or customer must deal. In the tender documents the principal may designate certain nominated subcontractors to be included in undertaking the project. The principal may approve or reject any subcontractor prior to start, but during the course of the project the main contractor has the responsibility for all work undertaken by the subcontractors.

Figure 2.6 depicts the situation whereby the project manager in the prime contractor organisation has delegated the task of co-ordination and supervision of the various subcontractors to a contracts manager on a major construction project. Unlike the joint venture the subcontractors are not partners on the project but are in a similar contractual relationship as between the prime contractor and themselves to that between the principal and the prime contractor. Thus they operate as separate entities rather than as a joint entity. Where the principal has a consulting engineer or superintendent acting on his behalf then dealings on any unsatisfactory work by the subcontractors must be through the prime contractor by the engineer or superintendent. Payments for work completed are made direct to the subcontractor by the prime contractor and not by the principal. The project manager of the prime contractor is responsible for all negotiations with the subcontractors, making agreements on their schedule of work and what part they contribute to the total project.

Organisation with specialist consultants

Specialist consultants may be employed at two levels; firstly, to the principal or customer, and secondly to the contractor. It is preferable for the principal to have a single prime consultant whether an architectural firm or an engineering consultant to be responsible for all consulting work, to design and supervise the project. Employing too many consultants would result in lack of unity of direction and co-ordination. The prime or major consultant can integrate and co-ordinate the work of the other consultants. This comes back to the situation depicted in Figure 2.1. Usually this is the level where most specialist consultants such as geologists, environmentalists, biologists, etc. (depending on the nature of the project) are used, especially in the planning and design stages of the project.

On some projects the contractor may require specialist advice and services on matters under his responsibility and not that of the consulting engineer. For a construction project, specialist consultants like work study, safety, ergonomics, and materials handling experts may be employed. In a manufacturing project, outside specialists like management consultants and consulting metallurgists may be employed to advise on the most economical production organisation and processes or usage of certain metals. Figure 2.6 shows the situation where the specialist consultants may be used to advise the project manager, civil engineer and construction manager of the prime contractor. This example also shows where the principal or customer plans, designs and superintends the contract implying that he has personnel under a project manager in his organisation who can carry out such functions.

Organisation of international projects

Organisation of international projects or 'off-shore' project organisation, like joint venturing, is increasing due to increasing project size and complexity, and to the drive for expansion and greater profitability. Most projects undertaken are of the pure project team organisational form but increasing use is made of the matrix especially with the third dimension of area or regional managers, where several projects may be undertaken in a geographical area or region.

Joint ventures are favoured with international projects whereby the overseas firm joins temporarily with the local firm to undertake the project. But in international projects the following special factors need to be considered:

    1 *Local incentive and assistance* — which refer to what induce-

ments the host country offers to undertake the project and what assistance the local government provides to assist the project. The search for greater profits, providing greater employment opportunities and assisting economic development, combined with provision of infrastructure facilities and tax-free inducements may all attract the organisation to undertake the project in another country.

2 *Language barriers and local customs* — in some countries the language barrier may pose some difficulties in that interpreters are needed, instructions have to be accurately relayed and local customs may restrict certain operations as well as impose contraints on project personnel on and off the job.

3 *Culture of the country of operations* — allied to (2) is the culture of the local people. It may be that traditions are such that quality, tempo and standards of operations acceptable to one country are not applicable to another. This makes for different styles of supervision and control. In many countries the Western notions of worker participation and participative democracy among personnel is entirely foreign to workers who are used to authoritarian styles of leadership and management.

4 *Logistics problems* — which relate to the transportation and storage of materials and equipment especially from overseas to the site of the project. The cost, protection and security may vary with the particular country.

5 *Personnel problems* — which relate to the availability of skilled personnel, industrial relation setting, training and safety procedures.

6 *Organisation of project work* — methods may vary with different countries and so the division of work may require a different organisation structure. In under-developed countries where labour costs are low and machines are expensive to operate and maintain, the organisation of work would be different to that for developed countries.

Generally a pure project team organisation structure is favoured for most project work but for high technology industries (like aerospace and electronic components manufacturing) operating internationally the combination of line and staff with matrix organisation is being increasingly used.

37

Organisation as a means to an end

Project organisation aims to achieve successful accomplishment of the project. Without proper and logical organisation there would be inefficiency, waste, and possibly chaos and delays on the project. Without systematic organisation there would be poor quality and performance, and cost over-runs. Without effective organisation, the efforts of personnel are duplicated and conflicts and frustration occur. The purpose of project organisation is clear — to achieve the project in the most efficient, economical and effective manner. As an American engineer, Russell Robb, a pioneer of organisation theory early this century observed, 'Organisation is but a means to an end; it provides a method'. The end is the successful completion of the project.

REFERENCES

Cleland, D. I. and King, W. R., *Systems Analysis and Project Management*, 3rd edition, New York: McGraw-Hill, 1983.

Cleland, D. I. and Kocaoglu, D. F., *Engineering Management*, New York: McGraw-Hill, 1981.

Davis, S. M. and Lawrence, P. R., *Matrix*, Reading, Mass: Addison-Wesley, 1977.

Dibner, D. R., *Joint Venture for Architects and Engineers*, New York: McGraw-Hill, 1972.

Harrison, F. L., *Advanced Project Management*, Aldershot: Gower, 1981.

Jerkovsky, W., 'The Roles of a Functional Manager in a Matrix Engineering Organisation,' *Proceedings of the 3rd Annual Meeting — American Society for Engineering Management*, Milwaukee, Wisconsin, October 17–19, 1982, pp. 5–14.

Kelly, K. L., 'Are Two Bosses Better Than One?', *Machine Design*, 1984, Vol. 15, No. 1, January 12, pp. 73–76.

Kerzner, H., *Project Management: A Systems Approach to Planning, Scheduling and Controlling*, New York: Van Nostrand Reinhold, 1979.

Kingdon, D. R., *Matrix Organisations*, London: Tavistock, 1973.

Knight, K. (ed.), *Matrix Management*, Aldershot: Gower, 1977.

Lloyd, B., *The Organisation of Engineering Work*, Melbourne: Macmillan, 1979.

Lock, D., *Project Management*, 3rd edition, Aldershot: Gower, 1984.

Purtell, M. L., 'Problems in Administering Overseas Projects', *Issues in Engineering*, 1982, Vol. 108, No. E12, April, pp. 140–144.

Shannon, R. E., 'Matrix Management Structures', *Industrial Engineering*, 1972, Vol. 4, No. 3, March, pp. 26–29.

Sinclair, J. M., 'Is the Matrix Really Necessary?', *Project Management Journal*, 1984, Vol. 15, No. 1, March, pp. 49–52.

Stickney, F. A. and Johnston, W. R., 'Delegation and a Sharing of Authority by the Project Manager', *Project Management Quarterly*, 1983, Vol. 14, No. 1, March, pp. 42–53.

Tatum, C. B., 'New Matrix Organisation for Construction Manager', *Issues in Engineering*, 1981, Vol. 107, No. E14, October, pp. 255–267.

Taylor, W. J. and Watling, T. F., *Successful Project Management*, Business Books, London, 1970.

Wearne, S. H., *Principles of Engineering Organisation*, Edward Arnold, London, 1973.

3
Establishing a Project Organisation

O. P. Kharbanda and E. A. Stallworthy

Of the three categories of project dealt with in this handbook, it is probable that civil engineering and construction projects, where a substantial part of the work is carried out on site, are the most complex in terms of project organisation. This chapter therefore deals with the project organisation appropriate to such complex projects, in order to present a comprehensive view of the possible requirements. Various aspects of the organisation outlined will however be relevant to the other two categories of project.

Before coming to consider project organisation in any detail it should be set into context. There will always be a *promoter* of the project, who could be the owner, 'employer', sponsor or user, but hereafter referred to as the 'owner'. Once the owner has decided to proceed with a project he always has first to establish feasibility and then ensure that the necessary funds are available. When a decision has been taken to proceed a project manager should be appointed. It is indeed implicit in the concept of project management that a project manager be appointed by the owner at a very early stage to 'manage' the project. This is illustrated in Figure 3.1. Once a project has been defined and is in preparation the project manager should become involved and it is he who will ensure that the project organisation appropriate to the project is set up. Part of his responsibility must be to consider the facilities available to him and assess what help he needs.

Establishing a Project Organisation

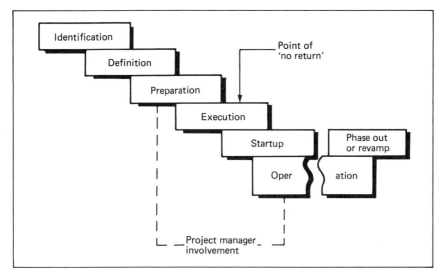

Figure 3.1 Project development
This diagram highlights the basic steps in project development. As time passes the commitment grows, and once the point of no return has been reached it costs more to cancel than to complete

As he begins his work the project manager has a variety of choices open to him. His choice will be determined to some extent by his own capability or (more often) by his own judgement of his capability — which might well be at fault. He can:

1. Do it all within his own company
2. Seek the services of a consultant
3. Seek the services of a contractor
4. Seek the services of both consultant and contractor.

THE THREE PARTIES TO A PROJECT

Since alternative 4 is the most complex, it is that which will be developed and reviewed. This means that at least three separate parties can be involved in a project. These are: (a) owner (b) consultant and (c) contractor. Their specific functions can well vary from case to case. No two projects are ever the same, even when they may appear to be. Each and every project is unique and so, therefore, are the roles of these three parties. Parties other than these three can be involved in the project, but they will not be directly involved in the project organisation. For instance, a process used in the project may be licensed, so the process licensor has an involvement, or finance may be secured from outside, so that a bank has an involvement, but these companies or organisations do not participate in the project directly. They do not become involved in the project organisation. It is true, however, that the project organisation has to take account of their existence.

In the concept of project management being developed here the three key participants have three distinct and separate roles to play, thus:

- The owner   oversees and pays
- The consultant advises
- The contractor does the job.

The potential relationship between these parties is illustrated in Figure 3.2. It is proposed to consider the project organisation which should be set up on the assumption that what is often called a 'managing contractor' is appointed (although the term 'contractor' will continue to be used). It then becomes his responsibility to set up a major part of the necessary project organisation. However, the owner will still have to set up an organisation of his own, which must be interrelated with the organisation set up by the contractor. Both should have a project manager. Were the owner to decide to 'go it alone' then his project manager would have to establish a project organisation such as is later outlined as part of his own project management facilities.

THE ROLE OF THE CONSULTANT

Of the three parties directly involved, the consultant occupies a separate and special position. He will advise the owner on the development of the project and its organisation. A consultant can be employed at various phases of project development and his degree of involvement will always depend on the needs of the owner. If the owner has previous experience, then his involvement may well be minimal or he may not be needed at all. But for the inexperienced owner he can be a most valuable asset.

Establishing a Project Organisation

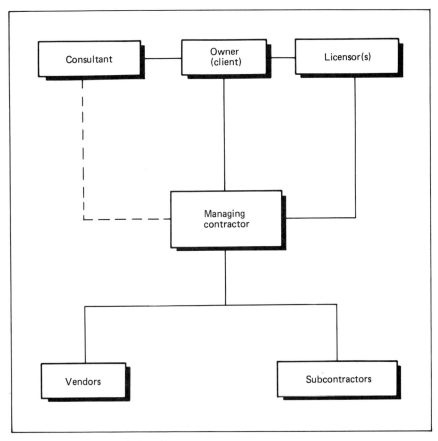

Figure 3.2 The basic relationship
Here we see the relationship between the various parties involved in a project as it develops

To set project organisation in the context of project development, Figure 3.3 illustrates all the phases through which a project will pass from identification onwards. It will be seen that the consultant can contribute to all the phases indicated with the exception of Phase 3. The degree of consultant involvement will depend upon the resources of the owner. It is recommended that a project organisation be set up when Phase 2 is entered, but it can only be in outline at that point, since decisions have still to be taken with respect to the involvement of outside parties.

Project Management and its Organisation

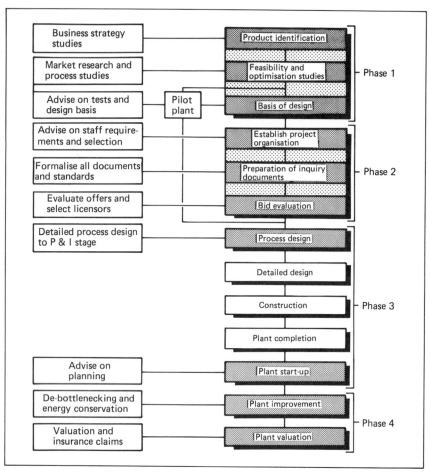

Figure 3.3 The role of the consultant
The steps in project development where the consultant can and should have a role are emphasised (Developed from data provided by Trichem Consultants Limited, London)

THE CONTRACTOR

When a contractor is used the project manager appointed by that contractor should be made responsible, within the contractor's organisation, for every aspect of the project. This is what one such contractor says of him:

> He is responsible for every aspect of the job from inception to completion. He is responsible for every service required

Establishing a Project Organisation

to carry out the work: planning, scheduling, costing, designing, engineering, purchasing, inspection, shipping, construction and commissioning. And he is responsible to you, our client. He is your direct contact. And you will know him personally. His position calls for wide experience, broad knowledge of every group within the organisation, the ability to control progress and make decisions.

However, the owner still has certain responsibilities which he cannot delegate to the contractor. These are effected through his own project manager. The organisational setup to achieve this is illustrated in Figure 3.4. From this diagram it can be seen that the owner and the contractor should be mutually supportive. This is indeed the way in which the relationship is seen by the contractor himself, since the layout shown in Figure 3.4 has been copied faithfully from a brochure illustrating the project team as proposed by one such contractor. The interrelationship shown in light rule is from the brochure. The heavy rule has been added to the chart as originally prepared and its purpose is explained below.

There is no doubt that this method of working both alongside and in parallel, just like a team of horses 'in harness' is highly successful and should therefore be completely acceptable to all the parties involved. How does it work? To quote once again from a brochure issued by a contractor:

> The project control team [refer to Figure 3.4] under the direction of the project manager sets the control guidelines for the project. On major projects a project control manager heads the project control team. Each supervisor within the engineering, procurement and construction areas is involved in the development of the project controls which affect his area of work. Thereafter, he is responsible for the execution of the project within the control plans and budget established for his area of work. The project manager, the project control manager and his project control team constantly monitor performance, making adjustments as may be required to plans as they may affect the interfaces between the speciality groups.

It is very clear that this contractor knows the road he has to follow.

Project Management and its Organisation

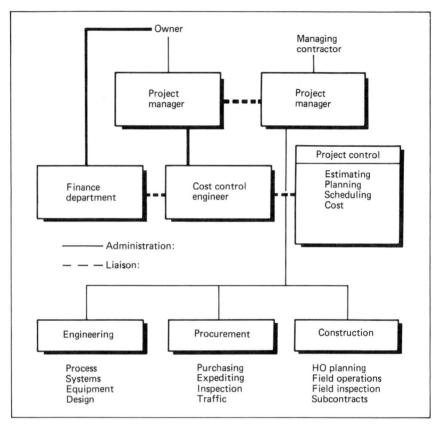

Figure 3.4 The project team
The chart shows (in light rule) a typical project team (with acknowledgements to the M.W. Kellogg Company, Houston). Added in heavy rule are the key functions that afford the owner control

But the owner also has a role to play and this is demonstrated in Figure 3.4. It is the 'heavy rule' addition to the original organigram produced by the contractor. Two key functions should be exercised by the owner, both functions that he should have or should establish within his own organisation. These are the functions performed by the finance department and the cost control engineer. They will have to work alongside the managing contractor's personnel day in, day out for the next three years — or however long it takes not only to bring the project to completion and commission it, but to pay the very last invoice. They will still be busy when the contractor's team has packed up, left the site and gone off on the next project.

Establishing a Project Organisation

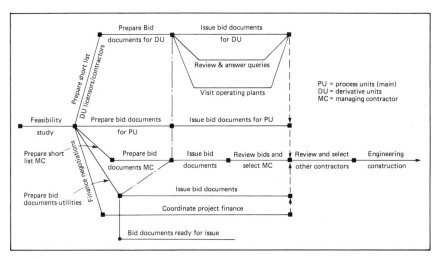

Figure 3.5 Logic diagram – bid document preparation and contractor selection
Outline of a typical plan for getting an approved project 'on the way'
(Data provided by Trichem Consultants Limited, London)

APPOINTING A CONTRACTOR

In the project organisation broadly outlined in Figure 3.4 a fundamental role is played by the contractor. Hence in order to establish a project organisation, once the decision has been taken to proceed, a contractor has to be appointed. It is here that a consultant (see Figure 3.2) may be called in to help. In order to appoint a contractor, bid documents will have to be prepared and issued. For the purposes of illustration it is assumed that the project has three main construction areas:

1. The process units, or manufacturing units.
2. Derivative production units.
3. Offsites, utilities and general facilities.

The particular approach adopted must depend upon the circumstances, but in Figure 3.5 a logic diagram is presented of the events that could lead to the appointment of a contractor. Great care is needed in the drafting of the bid documents, so that both the project specification and conditions of contract (subjects dealt with elsewhere in this handbook) are right in terms of scope. Another aspect of vital importance, which also affects both the project specification and the conditions of contract, is the financial arrangements, which are a specific element in the logic diagram, Figure 3.5. Once the bid documents have been prepared and are ready for issue, they have to be sent out to selected contractors under cover of an enquiry letter.

The primary enclosure with the enquiry letter will be the project specification. It is this document (which can be anything from a few pages to hundreds, even thousands of pages long) that defines the 'work' that the contractor will be required to do, in co-operation with the owner and other third parties. Whilst it is the project specification which is of prime and continuing interest to all those involved in the project, it has to be put into context. That is the function of the conditions of contract. They define the situation — the relationship of the various parties to the work to be done as described in the project specification, and also to one another in legalistic terms.

Choosing the contractor

When the various offers are received in response to the enquiry, a choice has to be made. The selection criteria include:

> Quality of personnel nominated to carry out the project, with special emphasis on the project manager.
> Cost incentive and liability arrangements proposed.
> Local currency content of the project cost and the total investment required for the project.
> Loan terms.
> Project organisation and relationship with local subcontractors.
> Workload of office where the design engineering will be carried out.
> Quality and contents of the technical proposal.
> Contractor's recent experience in the design and construction of similar projects.
> Appreciation and knowledge of local conditions at the job site.
> Ability to provide the owner with technical support services.
> Schedule for project completion.

The above criteria are not listed in order of importance. Whilst the price is significant (for example), it is only one of three financial considerations. The contractors selected to bid should have been chosen on the basis of their past performance, but what now matters is their *present* competence. This means that the specific personnel put out forward to form the project team are of crucial importance. Within the project team it is the project manager and his qualifications that need the most careful appraisal.

COMMUNICATIONS THE KEY

Once the contractor has been appointed, a working relationship has to be established between the owner and the contractor, and then between the contractor and the construction site, the subcontractors and others involved in the project. This is the responsibility of the contractor, but he should work closely with the owner in order to define the requirements of the project and its boundaries. This involves process decisions, fixing design standards, material supply, financing, transport and shipping, site conditions, subcontract services, and the parameters of performance and reliability.

In order to ensure that all possible activities involved in the project have been dealt with and the duties of the several parties properly defined, it is usual for the contractor, in co-operation with the owner, to set down and then issue what is called a project co-ordination procedure. This document will give all the information relevant to the administration and management of the project including the organisation, planning and control procedures to be used in order to complete the project successfully. A checklist is used to assist in the development of such a procedure and this is presented at the end of this chapter. This checklist has been relegated to an appendix not because it is relatively unimportant, but because it should not be condensed. All items are of importance and they should be reviewed one by one, the necessary information being written, reviewed and agreed with the interested parties.

A fundamental element in the operation of the procedures once implemented is the ability to communicate. These days a wide range of facilities are available, including the postal system, telephone and telex facilities, data transmission via computer and telephone and the like. These should be reviewed and the appropriate facilities provided, keeping in mind the site location and its possible problems. A courier service is often the most efficient means of transferring the substantial volumes of paperwork that have to be moved between the various offices and the site, especially when the latter is in a remote location not well served with modern communication facilities.

THE OWNER'S ORGANISATION

Figure 3.4 outlines not only the key elements in the contractor's organisation, but also those called for within the organisation of the owner. The owner should provide a project manager, with engineers to support him, a cost control engineer, with support staff and financial facilities. These latter should already be in existence, but specific arrangements are called for to co-ordinate the activities of the finance department in relation to the project.

The finance department is going to be responsible for authorising payment against the budget provided for the project. This role is centred in the accountant, who has two different functions. One is the regulating function of audit, that requires him to ensure the correctness of the accounts processed and paid. The other function, that of management accountant, requires him to monitor the financial progress of the project. Whilst in this he has many areas of common interest with the cost control engineer, their objectives will be different.

The cost coding system

The financial control exercised by both the accountant and the cost control engineer is achieved by means of what are called 'controllable items'. These are the separate cost items into which a total project budget is broken down for the purposes of cost control and financial administration. This calls for the use of what is called a 'code of accounts' or a 'cost code'. In establishing the project organisation, a cost coding system must be utilised for cost analysis. Normally, such a code should be set up for the specific project, although it may correspond to some degree with an established system employed in the finance department. Or the contractor may provide such a cost code. Whatever its source, it is an essential and integral part of the project organisation. The application and use of the code of accounts, or cost coding system, is dealt with in detail in Part III.

Project control

The purpose of the project organisation established by the owner is to give him real and effective *control* of the project. To achieve this, the owner must:

1 Give the project manager *total* responsibility for the entire project: design, engineering, procurement and construction. He should produce a monthly project cost control report.
2 Provide a cost engineering function to operate at the job site, responsible to the owner's project manager and headed by a senior project cost engineer.
3 Ensure that the finance department works in close liaison with the cost engineering function, whilst maintaining their own normal expenditure records and a cumulative commitment record.

The primary duty of the cost engineering function will be to establish the exact position of the total project in its 'controllable segments', from month to month, comparing actual progress with target progress. The finance department will check that the information provided in the project cost control report is in line with accounting records. They should also, in line with their standard procedures, check that all invoices for materials and services are duly authorised and that all materials are properly controlled and accounted for.

The audit function

The audit function does not appear on the outline project organisation but it is an essential element and makes a material contribution to project management. The owner should have or should employ accountants to act as an internal audit group. This group should examine both the financial and related operations of both the owner and contractor. The internal audit group would, at the very beginning and thereafter at intervals, examine the accounting policies of both parties with their related systems and procedures. It is their task to diagnose weaknesses in the project organisation as set up and then make recommendations for any necessary improvements to the system, specifically to protect the money being employed. This is for the benefit of those working on the project as well as for those whose money is being used. It protects those working on the project from accusations of fraud or the misuse of funds, or of giving undue advantage to companies or to persons. A formal report should be prepared by the accountants each time a review is undertaken, setting out the audit findings and the recommended corrective action. This should be followed by the discipline of receiving formal written assurance from the parties concerned within a stated period (say three months) that the recommended corrective actions have in fact been implemented. Weaknesses not remedied to the auditor's satisfaction should be reported to the project manager for the owner, for his further action.

The scope of such internal audits should not be limited to financial or accounting matters. With technical help from a consultant, auditors can and should review a wide range of routine activities carried out by the contractor and his subcontractors, particularly in relation to work assessment in the field. In the UK this latter work is carried out by quantity surveyors. For instance, contract letting procedures should involve competitive tendering, secret bidding and a proper comparison of offers. These are typical instances where an audit of the arrangements being made within the project organisation can be of real help. A proper internal audit system will always make a serious contribution to project management, bringing increased and more effective discipline to the contracting process.

THE CONTRACTOR'S ORGANISATION

The contractor brought in to handle a project on the behalf of the owner will have an established company organisation. Within that the contractor will provide a project organisation designed to provide the services required for the specific project. There are several ways in which a contractor can be organised, but the two most common are called the matrix and the team organisations, as have been discussed in Chapter 2.

The organisational matrix

Within any organisation there are bound to be certain conflicts of interest and this fact should be recognised, because it cannot be resolved. When a new project is introduced into the contractor's organisation, it immediately begins to compete with the other projects already in hand for services. This conflict becomes manifest as soon as a project team is formed to handle a project. Such a team will be drawn from a number of different disciplines within the

Establishing a Project Organisation

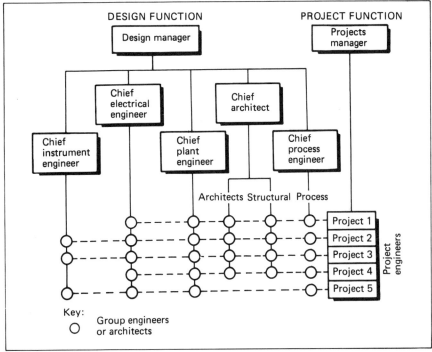

Figure 3.6 Organisation chart for the design group
This chart demonstrates the manner in which the design department should be grouped under section leaders in order to integrate with the project management function. Whilst the design department is necessarily internally streamed and managed in accordance with the several disciplines involved, the external integration is on a project basis

organisation, as illustrated in Figure 3.6. There will be a variety of design disciplines, each of which requires separate co-ordination and supervision for proper management and the administration of the particular design function. However, there is also a need for the close integration of the specific project requirements with the several design disiplines. This is achieved through the projects manager, who has a team of project managers (or engineers) who are responsible for individual projects. This concept is presented in Figure 3.6, each project engineer (five are shown) being responsible for a project. The requirements of the projects will differ in terms of the services they need, and such variation is indicated in the chart. Ideally, the resources of the design function should match the requirements of the project groups, with a slight reserve of capacity, but that never happens in practice. This leads to competition for services, which competition — and hence conflict — should be resolved by consultation between the various department heads.

THE PRINCIPLE OF ACCOUNTABILITY

If these organisational concepts are to be expressed in management terms, then the project manager (whether one considers the project manager working for the owner or the project manager working for the contractor) is accountable to his senior management for the project. An obligation is thereby placed, in the first instance, on the project manager to carry the project to a successful conclusion. But the usual problem is that whilst the project manager is held accountable, he is often not given the authority to discharge his obligation to management properly. Once made accountable he should have both the right and also the duty to make those decisions and to take those actions which he judges necessary within the scope of his responsibility without needing to seek prior approval from his superiors.

All too often there is a certain reluctance in this respect, from two sides. Senior management is reluctant to leave major decisions to the project group whilst, within the contracting organisation, the managers responsible for specialist functions such as design think that theirs should be the last word. The project manager may recommend, but *not* direct and instruct.

It is indeed true that limits of authority have to be established and must be established in relation to certain decisions. These decisions will involve factors and circumstances outside the scope and direct knowledge of the project manager, so that a measure of direction and control *must* in such circumstances be retained by senior management. A common instance in this context is in relation to money. Limits may well be placed on the project manager with respect to expenditure, despite the fact that blanket financial approval has been given to the project as a whole. Orders over a certain value, for instance, may well be referred to senior management for final approval before placing.

Care should be taken to see that these limits on the authority of the project manager do not inhibit him from discharging his

Establishing a Project Organisation

responsibilities. It is here that the owner, rather than the contractor, may err. The owner is more likely to be setting up a project organisation specifically for the project in hand and perhaps, even, for the first time. Contractors, inevitably, will have walked the road before and found by experience the constraints and restraints appropriate to the circumstances. The owner, however, especially if he lacks experience, may be over-restrictive. The best approach is to draw up all the guide lines, as part of the project organisation. Each person in a position of authority should be given a mandate. This should take the form of a written description, brief but explicit and positive, describing the basic objectives of the position, together with some detail of the activities considered implicit in the mandate. Not only should such documents be prepared, but the owner should seek to see the 'mandate' of the project manager, and perhaps other key personnel, appointed by the contractor to run the project.

MANAGEMENT BY EXCEPTION

The project organisation to be set up consists of two separate entities, one within the owner organisation and the other within the contractor organisation. The responsibilities of the personnel employed should be built around the principle of 'management by exception'. This is a long-established management principle, which implies that policies are established and plans are laid. In the context of a project the plans should be outlined in the project specification, together with the related project estimate and planning schedules. From then on, all that should be discussed are the deviations from those agreed policies and plans. If management by exception is to be successful there are four basic requirements which will have to be fulfilled. They are:

1 There must be a detailed, timed plan.
2 There must be the ability to delegate.
3 There must be confidence and trust placed in subordinates.
4 There must be a proper system of *management information*.

There are a number of separate areas for delegation in the project organisation that has been outlined above. First, the owner has delegated to the contractor the obligation to complete the project in accordance with the agreed plan. This plan will cover at least two key aspects of the project: cost and time.

For such delegation to be possible there must therefore be a project programme and a project estimate, which will become an integral part of the management information system. The term management information is intended to cover the various reports relating to both the physical and financial status of the project, which will provide the information needed at the successive levels of management on both sides to enable them to make the appropriate decisions. In all these reports there must be continuous comparison between the initial agreed programme and estimate and the current expectations. This reporting system is therefore an essential element within the project organisation. Its details are dealt with in later parts of this handbook.

Management needs to know the *deviations* from the plan once it has been agreed, for management by exception to be effective. It is the deviations, and only the deviations, that will call for managerial direction and action. It is therefore such deviations that form the substance of the various reports and the level that they reach within the management organisation will depend upon their significance and magnitude in relation to the project as a whole.

Good administration will result in only the essential information being provided. This means that data has to be edited, reviewed and condensed before reports are prepared. Of course, all such reports should be accurate, complete and up-to-date. Above all, reports at one level should not include data which is more properly the concern of subordinates at a lower level. Whilst the senior executives are entitled to ask for and receive specific information on any subject, excessive demands of this nature tend to undermine the concept of delegation. Then the basic principle around which the project organisation should have been built, that of management by exception, would have been destroyed.

Project liaison

It has already been stated that the basic need within a project organisation is the ability to communicate and the co-ordination procedure is designed to facilitate such communication. Both the owner and the contractor will be setting up project organisations which match at the top, as illustrated in Figure 3.4. This enables the two opposite parties to liaise on equal terms at each level. The administration established in accordance with the co-ordination procedure should ensure that the appropriate records are maintained, that all data is readily accessible and that those involved in the project are always informed of that which concerns them.

SITE ADMINISTRATION

A good, experienced, strong and comprehensive site organisation with sound administrative techniques is the best insurance possible against the multitude of problems that will arise once work begins on site. The contractor should not be allowed to skimp his efforts in this direction, which he may well be tempted to do if he is being remunerated via a fixed fee. A typical site organisation is presented as Figure 3.7 and of the many facets of site organisation and administration highlighted by this organigram, the following are probably the most significant:

1 Site planning.
2 Site cost control.
3 Control of subcontracts.
4 Quality control.
5 Industrial relations.

Site planning

The process of site planning involves manpower resource scheduling, progress reporting and the assessment of the particular site requirements. The most practical and economic construction method has to be selected, and due regard must be given to specific factors such as temporary work areas and site access. Safe working conditions have to be established, first aid facilities have to be provided and it is necessary to make provision for certain comforts (a place to eat, rest rooms, changing rooms, etc.). On a remote site housing may also be required. Transport is needed, not only to and from the site, but also all over the site, both horizontally and vertically. Communication facilities are essential and, apart from telex, it may be necessary to provide portable radios. There should also be a site postal system.

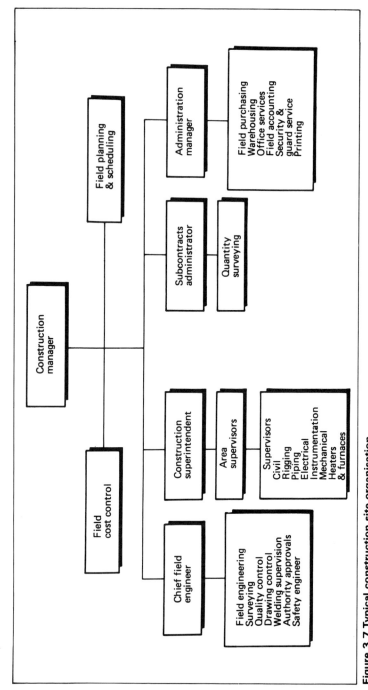

Figure 3.7 Typical construction site organisation
The number of personnel covered by this organigram will vary according to the size and complexity of the project

Co-operation is required from the shipping department to ensure the timely delivery of heavy and difficult loads. What are termed 'heavy lifts' require the provision on site of very expensive, specialised lifting equipment and personnel. It is therefore usual to establish a 'heavy lift' programme in order to bring all such work together and minimise the length of time such costly equipment is on site. This may involve traffic problems not only on or near the site but also hundreds of miles away. It may be necessary to make arrangements for movement of loads under police escort, routes will have to be carefully planned, obstacles on the route removed and later replaced.

Site cost control

All site costs, including the delivery of materials to site, should be closely monitored by the site cost engineer. It will be his task to prepare statements on the commitments and forecasts in relation to construction costs, including all the subcontracts, for inclusion in the overall project progress reports.

Site subcontracts

Whilst it is possible for the contractor to carry out some of the work on site by 'direct labour', that is, by people in his own direct employment, there will always be a considerable volume of work that is subcontracted to specialist contractors. The preferred approach for completely effective project cost control is for *all* work on site to be carried out by a series of subcontractors. With respect to the administration of such contracts, which are usually for a combination of materials and services, such administration is usually separate from the purchasing organisation handling materials. This is because the type of contract and the methods of assessing the value of work done for payment are very different.

The site contracts will normally be let one by one over a substantial period of time (probably over a period of at least two years with a project of any substance). As the contracts are let, their work content becomes gradually more predictable, because detailed design is progressing, and this allows for a change in the form of contract. Early contracts may well be let using a form of contract that employs a schedule of rates or some other form of cost reimbursement, whilst it should be possible to let the later contracts on a fixed price basis. The contract organisation should therefore establish procedures which allow this.

Quality control

All the work on site should be quality controlled. This is most important and the appropriate personnel should be incorporated in the site organisation with the relevant systems. Of the various aspects of quality control probably the most important is the quality control of site welding. There has to be detailed preparation for this, with the drawing up of welding procedures, the testing and certification of welders, the non-destructive testing of this work as it is done in accordance with the relevant specifications. All this requires not only the most meticulous supervision but proper administration of the related documentation, so that if necessary it can be later demonstrated that all is in order.

Industrial relations

Last, but not least, there is the matter of industrial relations, often hiding behind the cryptic letters IR. It is a subject kept well in the background but of supreme importance in relation to the successful execution of work on site. It is an area of possible confrontation, with two opposing parties each seeking their own ends. It is regrettable that such is the case, but it is a situation that seems to exist in most parts of the world these days. The problems will be different, dependent upon which country the project is being built in, but they will always be there. In the developed countries it is usual to tread warily, keeping in close touch with the unions at both local and national level. In the developing countries the problem may be very different: that for instance of training a completely ignorant, locally recruited workforce, or of satisfying the demands of expatriate personnel. Provision will have to be made within the site organisation for the appropriate facilities according to location, but above all it has to be recognised that the person or persons appointed to look after industrial relations *must* have relevant experience and be competent negotiators.

REFERENCES

The figures used for illustration in this chapter have been taken from one of the following two works:

Kharbanda, O. P., Stallworthy, E. A. and Williams, L. F., *Project Cost Control in Action*, Aldershot: Gower, 1980.

Stallworthy, E. A. and Kharbanda, O. P., *Total Project Management*, Aldershot: Gower, 1983.

APPENDIX: CONTENTS CHECKLIST FOR A PROJECT CO-ORDINATION PROCEDURE DOCUMENT

A typical co-ordination procedure checklist would cover the following items:

1 Introduction

1:1	Objective of document
1:2	Scope of work
1:3	Terms used

2 General policy

2:1	Relationship between parties
2:2	Facilities and information from owner

3 Co-ordination with owner

3:1	Project description
3:2	Project references and addresses
3:3	Correspondence to and from owner
3:4	Minutes of meeting with owner
3:5	Contractor's progress reports
3:6	Project programme
3:7	Approvals by owner
3:8	Change notice procedure
3:9	Code of accounts (cost code)
3:10	Project numbering system

3:11 Documentation issued to owner
3:12 Project information to be provided by owner

4 Co-ordination within contractor's organisation

4:1 Project team and their responsibilities
4:2 Contractor's key personnel
4:3 Co-ordination with owner and other parties
4:4 Recording and distribution of documents
4:5 Project memoranda and instructions
4:6 Minutes of internal meetings
4:7 Progress reports for owner and contractor

5 Introduction to project

5:1 Brief description of project
5:2 Basic contractual arrangements
5:3 Scope of contractor's services
5:4 Scope of contractor's supply
5:5 Scope of owner's supply and services

6 Engineering

6:1 General
6:2 Process requirements and design
6:3 Project and package units
6:4 Piping
6:5 Process plant and equipment
6:6 Mechanical and rotating machinery
6:7 Instruments
6:8 Electrical
6:9 Civil works, structural steel and buildings

7 Procurement

7:1 Procurement — scope of supply
7:2 Purchasing
    7:2:1 Conditions of order
    7:2:2 Preferred vendor's list

Establishing a Project Organisation

	7:2:3 Bid evaluations
	7:2:4 Document distribution
	7:2:5 Vendor's engineers
	7:2:6 Site address for delivery
7:3	Expediting
	7:3:1 Contractor's responsibilities
	7:3:2 Owner's responsibilities
7:4	Inspection
	7:4:1 Contractor's responsibilities
	7:4:2 Owner's responsibilities
7:5	Packing and protection
7:6	Shipping and delivery arrangements
7:7	Invoice procedure
7:8	Nominated subcontracts
7:9	Preferred suppliers
7:10	Discount arrangements

8 Project cost control

8:1	The cost control engineer
8:2	Variations
8:3	Extra work orders
8:4	Claims
8:5	Reimbursable or rate contracts
8:6	Lump sum contracts

9 Drawings

9:1	Agreed grid
9:2	Contractor's drawings
9:3	Manufacturer's drawings
9:4	Drawing approval by owner
9:5	Filing systems

10 Documentation

10:1	Contractor's documentation
10:2	Vendor documentation
10:3	Requisitions and orders

10:4 Internal distribution
10:5 Transmittal of documentation to site
10:6 Transmittal of documentation to owner
10:7 Operating manual
10:8 Engineering dossier
10:9 Destruction of documents and drawings
10:10 Microfilm or other records

11 Financial and accounting

11:1 Financial arrangements
11:2 Schedule of payments
11:3 Payment for extra services
11.4 Presentation of accounts
11:5 Insurance
11:6 Invoicing

12 Import procedures

12:1 General
12:2 Relevant regulations
12:3 Documentation

13 Site arrangements

13:1 Registration of site
13:2 Site address
13:3 Owner's responsibilities at site
13:4 Contractor's responsibilities at site
13:5 Site organisation
    13:5:1 Access
    13:5:2 Storage
    13:5:3 Warehousing
13:6 General site facilities
    13:6:1 Office accommodation
    13:6:2 Medical, fire, canteen and toilets
    13:6:3 Supplies from owner's stores
    13:6:4 Electrical power, steam, water, etc.
    13:6:5 Effluent disposal

13:7 Site regulations
      13:7:1 Site security
      13:7:2 'No smoking' areas
      13:7:3 Safety
13:8 Takeover by owner
      13:8:1 Procedures
      13:8:2 Takeover certificates

14 Commissioning

14:1 Contractor's responsibilities
14:2 Owner's responsibilities
14:3 Start-up procedures
14:4 Vendor services
14:5 Performance tests
14:6 Guarantees and penalties

15 Spares

15:1 Initial spares
15:2 Capital spares
15:3 Running spares

Part II
CONTRACT ADMINISTRATION

4
Contract Law

P. D. V. Marsh

The purpose of this chapter is to provide a brief outline and layman's guide to English contract law as it applies between commercial organisations. It is in no way intended to replace the need for legal consultation in cases of difficulty or dispute but rather to suggest ways in which such cases can be avoided. If however such problems do occur then it is essential that professional legal advice should be sought at the earliest opportunity and before action has been taken which can be prejudicial to the company's rights.

CONTRACT FORMATION

There are four essential elements for a binding contract to be formed between two companies. These are:

1. The intention to be legally bound.
2. Consideration.
3. Offer.
4. Acceptance.

The intention to be legally bound

Although this requirement exists it is of little practical importance as the courts have consistently held that between commercial organisations such a requirement can be assumed. Only if the parties have expressly stated in their agreement that it is not intended to be legally binding will the requirement take effect; then courts will hold that such an agreement is not binding. The agreement becomes a mere 'gentleman's agreement', not enforceable at law.

Consideration

Consideration is a highly technical doctrine which is peculiar to English law. It requires, in general, that an act or promise of one party must have been given in exchange for the act or promise of the other in order for a binding contract to exist. Normally no problem with the doctrine will arise since a commercial contract will be one under which the seller or contractor undertakes to provide goods or services in return for payment by the purchaser. But the doctrine may play a part in three instances which are of practical significance and deserve mention:

Standing offers

A purchasing organisation (such as a local authority) may consider that it will require a list of items over say a 12-month period without being certain of its specific needs. It will therefore invite tenders from suppliers indicating its likely requirements and notify those who have been successful that their tenders have been accepted for particular items. From time to time the authority will then call-off from those firms concerned the items they want and pay for these at the tendered prices. The question then arises as to whether or not the 'acceptance' of the firm's tender creates a contract since at that stage there would appear to have been no consideration provided by the authority.

The answer as so often is that it all depends on the wording used in the documents concerned, in particular as to whether or not the authority has actually promised to do anything. If for example the authority had stated in their enquiry that they would buy their requirements only from the firms whose tenders they accepted then this might be considered by the Courts as sufficient consideration to support the promise made by the supplier to supply at the prices specified in his tender. The importance of the distinction is that if no contract exists then, while the supplier must fulfill any orders which the authority places on him so long as his offer remains open, he is free to withdraw that offer at any time and clearly would do if for example there was an unexpected increase in his costs. If however a contract does exist then he must meet any orders which the authority may place on him during the period for which the contract remains in force.

Options

A case analogous to standing offers is that of an option. An example is provided by the tenderer who declares 'I will maintain the validity of my offer for a period of 60 days'. It has long been an established principle of English law that an undertaking to keep an offer open for acceptance is not legally binding, owing to the absence of any consideration. This can be particularly troublesome to a main contractor who has submitted his bid on the basis of prices provided by subcontractors only to find, when he is awarded the contract, that the subcontractors have withdrawn their offers.

In order to protect himself against that situation the main contractor would have had to create some consideration, however small, in order to establish a contract between himself and the subcontractor that the bid will remain open for acceptance for the specified period. It has been suggested that such consideration could be the supply of the contract documentation to the tenderer at his request. This would, of course, need to be stated in form of the invitation to tender.

Settlement of claims

It is important in an agreement for the settlement of a claim to recognise that there must be consideration for an undertaking by one party to waive rights which he has against the other. Since consideration need not be adequate, and can have a merely nominal value, it would appear that the withdrawal of a counter-claim which was unlikely to succeed would be treated by the courts as consideration but it needs to be expressed as such in the settlement documentation. In general the courts have shown considerable keenness and indeed ingenuity in finding consideration when it comes to upholding the existence of a contract and this appears to be an accelerating trend.

Offer

It is necessary to distinguish between an 'offer' and an 'invitation to treat'. An offer in law is both an indication of the terms upon which a party is willing to contract and an expression of willingness to do so if an acceptance is given of those terms. An 'invitation to treat' (of which the classic example is the display of goods in a shop window) is an indication of the terms upon which the seller is willing to do business, but not that he would accept any offer which was made. The commercial significance of this distinction is that an order made on the basis of a price list is not a binding contract until the order has been accepted by the seller, unless there are some special terms contained within the price list which would clearly indicate to the contrary.

As stated in the previous section an offer can be withdrawn at any time unless there is a separate contract under which it is to be kept open. However withdrawal of the offer (revocation, as it is termed) is only effective when it has been communicated to the person to whom the offer was made. Accordingly if the offer is accepted prior to the receipt of the notice of revocation then a valid contract exists and the purported revocation is of no effect.

Acceptance

An acceptance of an offer only becomes effective when it has been communicated to the person having made the offer. If the offer prescribes the form or manner in which the acceptance is to be made then the acceptance must be made in that manner, or in a way which is at least as beneficial to the party making the offer.

Since the last century the rule has been that the contract is complete when the acceptance is posted (properly stamped and addressed) even if the letter is never in fact received, although it is of course open to the person making the offer to state that he will not be bound until he actually receives the acceptance.

In instances where acceptance is by telex the general rule is different and acceptance is when the telex message is received. It would appear that receipt here means at the telex machine of the party making the offer, even if it has not been read, although it is not clear that this would necessarily apply if the telex was received out of business hours (because, for example, of time differences between the UK and overseas).

The principle difficulty with acceptance is that in order for a binding contract to be formed the acceptance must be in the same terms as the offer. In very many instances this is not the case. What purports therefore to be an acceptance is in fact a counter-offer which it is open to the other party to accept or reject. The issues which then arise are, first, whether or not a contract exists at all and, secondly, if a contract does exist, then on what terms? This problem is often referred to as 'the battle of the forms' since it most commonly arises between buyer and seller, each of whom is seeking to ensure that the contract is placed on his own standard terms and conditions.

In arriving at a solution to this problem the first essential point to be understood is that in English law:

> an offer falls to be interpreted not subjectively by reference to what has actually passed through the mind of the offeror, but objectively by reference to the interpretation which a reasonable man in the shoes of the offeree would place on the offer. It is an equally well established principle that ordinarily an offer, when unequivocally accepted according to its precise terms, will give rise to a legally binding agreement as soon as acceptance is communicated to the offeror in the manner contemplated by the offer, and cannot thereafter be revoked without the consent of the other party

per the Court of Appeal in the case of Centro-Provincial Estates *v* Merchants Investors Assurance Company 1983.

The practical result of this is that evidence of the party's subjective intentions in the matter is irrelevant. The test to be applied is the objective one of a reasonable observer. The second point is that nothing less than unequivocal acceptance will do. A response which raises questions (or, even more significantly, seeks to amend the terms of the offer in some way) even if it purports to be an acceptance will be considered as a counter-offer, which puts an end to the original offer and itself counts as an offer which it is up to the original offeror to accept or reject.

In ordinary purchasing practice the sequence of events could be:

Contract Administration

1 The buyer issues an enquiry.
2 The seller sends a quotation with his conditions of sale.
3 The buyer issues an order with his conditions of purchase.

At that stage no contract exists assuming (as is almost certainly the case) that the seller's and buyer's conditions do not coincide. It is therefore what happens next which is vital. There are many possibilities of which three will be considered:

1 Nothing is done to resolve the conflict in terms, but in due course the goods are delivered and accepted by the buyer. By delivering the goods the seller would be considered to have accepted the buyer's terms, unless there were documents accompanying the delivery which amounted to a counter-offer. The important point is that up until that time it is most probable that there is no contract between the parties at all although both may believe that there is.
2 The supplier returns the buyer's acknowledgment slip which is sent with the order and which refers to the order being accepted on the buyer's conditions. In that event there is a contract on the buyer's conditions.
3 The supplier returns the buyer's acknowledgement slip as requested but under cover of a letter which refers back to his original quotation. If the covering letter does not specifically refer to the seller's conditions of contract then the answer would very probably be, as happened in the leading case of Butler Machine Tool Co. Ltd *v* Ex-Cell-O Corporation 1979, that the court would consider the reference to the quotation as limited only to the price and identity of the goods and therefore of no contractual effect. The result would be again a contract on the buyer's conditions. If however the covering letter does refer specifically to the seller's conditions of sale then the position would be that this would constitute in law a counter-offer which the buyer could either accept or reject. If as is quite likely in practice there is no further reference to the terms of the contract, then there would be no contract between the parties until such time as the buyer had acted in some manner which constituted acceptance (for example by issuing a delivery schedule).

The general rule would seem to be, then, that the battle of forms is usually won by the party who fired the last shot. 'He is the man who puts forward the latest terms and conditions: and, if these are not objected to by the other party, then he may be taken to have agreed to them' per Lord Denning in the Butler case.

Letters of intent

Like many other expressions in common commercial use, letters of intent have no distinct legal meaning. In order, therefore, to determine what the parties meant when issuing and acting upon a letter of intent it is necessary to examine what happened. As was said in a recent judgement 'everything depends on the circumstances of the particular case'. It is difficult, therefore, to lay down any general rules but the following are offered as guidance:

1 Generally, a letter of intent does not give rise to any legal obligation on the part of the person issuing it nor on the part of the recipient. It is simply an expression of intentions.
2 If, however, it is clear from the facts of the case that the purchaser in issuing the letter of intent did mean to be bound and for the other party to act on the letter of intent as if it were an order, then the mere use of the expression 'letter of intent' will not avoid that conclusion. In a recent case after having telephoned an order and given an order number the purchaser sent the supplier a letter which amongst other things stated '(the suppliers) should accept in the meantime this correspondence as our letter of intent to purchase the items previously specified herein'. It was held that a binding contract existed.
3 Although the letter of intent may not amount to a binding promise to award the contract for the works concerned it may amount to a contract for the preliminary work to which the letter refers. Frequently the letter of intent will ask the supplier to proceed in the meantime with tooling, certain design work or the purchase of long lead items and these instructions will amount to a promise to pay for such work.
4 If the facts of the case are such that the letter of intent is just a stage in the negotiating process, but nevertheless acts as an encouragement to the supplier to proceed with the contract work while negotiations continue, and he does so proceed with

the full knowledge and indeed participation of the purchaser (for example, in inspection) then, if no contract is ever concluded because the parties never reach agreement on terms, the supplier will be entitled to be paid on a *quantum meruit* basis for the value of the work performed. The problem for the buyer in those circumstances is that if no contract is ever concluded then he has none of the contractual rights which he would otherwise possess, so if the supplier is late in making delivery he cannot claim damages for delay.

CONTRACT TERMS

The contract price

If a lump sum quotation is submitted and accepted for the carrying out of certain work or for the supply of specified goods, then it is the contractor's/supplier's obligation to complete his contract and without additional payment, even if the carrying out of the work becomes more difficult or entails work beyond that which the contractor/supplier originally contemplated — unless the contract specifically provides otherwise or there was misrepresentation on the part of the purchaser. In an old case involving a lump sum contract to build a house flooring was omitted from the specification and it was held that the contractor must put it in without additional payment as it was clearly indispensably necessary in order to complete the house.

Because the word 'estimate' is used it does not mean that the contractor is not bound by the figure which he submits. It depends on the facts and generally in the building trade 'estimates' are in practice treated as quotations which if accepted become lump sum contracts.

The price is not always agreed at the time when the order is placed. If it is left to be agreed between the parties at a later date and they fail to agree then the contract may be invalid for lack of certainty. However, if the goods have been delivered to and accepted by the purchaser then the court will almost certainly hold that the buyer must pay a reasonable price for them.

In times of inflation many contracts are placed on the basis that the contract price will be varied in accordance with a price variation clause or formula. In general such escalation clauses have been construed strictly by the courts in deciding on whether or not a particular increase in costs was included within their provisions. Thus where an escalation clause allowed a contractor to recover the additional costs arising from 'binding national awards' and a national award was made which included an element for a voluntary bonus scheme, the House of Lords held that this was not part of a binding national award and the increased cost to the contractor of complying with that part of the award could not be passed on to the employer. However it is equally clear that if a contract provides for escalation to be calculated in accordance with a price variation formula, then the contractor is entitled to be paid in accordance with the terms of that formula irrespective of the amount of his actual increase in costs.

Passing of property

The general rules as to the passing of property are laid down in the Sale of Goods Act 1979 and may be summarised as follows.

s.16. Property in unascertained goods only passes when they have been ascertained. Unascertained goods are those which are generic (for example, 100 tonnes of coffee beans), not yet built, or forming part of larger bulk. In general goods will become ascertained when they have been irrevocably attached to the contract, so that those goods and no others become the subject of the contract.

s.16 provides that if goods are specific or ascertained then the property in them passes to the buyer when the parties to the contract intend it to be passed. There are then in s.18 set out a number of rules which apply if the parties have been unwise or careless enough not to specify their intentions in the contract for sale. Of these the first and most important is that, if the goods are specific and in a deliverable state, then the property passes when the contract is made and it is immaterial if the time of payment or delivery or both are postponed.

The fact that the property in the goods has passed to the buyer but he has not yet paid for them, leaves the seller in a vulnerable situation in the event of the buyer ultimately defaulting and becoming bankrupt or going into liquidation. For this reason reservation of title, or as they are often today referred to as Romalpa clauses (after the name of the leading case on the subject) have become popular.

The legal effect of any clause will depend on the specific way in which it is drafted and the decided cases on the subject have to date left the law in a state of some uncertainty. However, the following is a guide to the current position:

1 The seller may be able to recover the goods from the buyer where they are still in his possession.
2 The seller may be able to recover possession of the goods from a person to whom they have been sold by the buyer.
3 If the goods have been used in the manufacture of other products and mixed with other goods then the seller would appear to have no right to recover possession or to receive any of the proceeds of sale.

Passing of risk

One reason for the importance of the clause relating to the passing of property is that, unless a contract for the sale of goods provides otherwise, the risk in the goods passes at the same time as the property does. Whoever is the owner of the goods takes the risk of their being lost or damaged (possibly in transit). If therefore the seller introduces a reservation of title clause which is effective, so that property does not pass until he is paid, he would be wise also to introduce a clause providing that the risk in the goods passes to the buyer at some earlier point such as when the goods are despatched.

Buyers also need to consider the question of the risk in goods when they wish for property to pass to them whilst the goods are still in the course of manufacture because they have made part payment. They should provide expressly that the risk remains with the seller until at least despatch, and that the seller insures accordingly.

Delivery

In one of the more old fashioned clauses the Sale of Goods Act s.29(2) provides that the place of delivery for specific goods is the seller's place of business. It is of course open to the parties to make other provisions and if the seller is required to make delivery to the buyer's premises then he discharges his obligations if he delivers the goods there without negligence to a person apparently having authority to receive them.

It is also provided in the Act that delivery to a carrier is presumed to be delivery to the buyer but this will only be so if the seller has made a reasonable contract of carriage on the buyer's behalf. In the case of Thomas Young and Sons Ltd against Hobson and Partners (1949) electric engines were sent by rail unsecured at owner's risk. The engines were damaged in transit. The buyer was held to be justified in refusing to accept delivery, as he would have had no remedy against the carrier, and the seller should have sent the engines at carrier's risk (which would have meant that they would have been inspected and required to have been secured).

Time for completion

In a contract for building or civil engineering works, and probably also a contract for the supply and installation/erection of electrical or mechanical plant, time is not of the essence unless the contract provides otherwise. In a commercial contract for the sale of goods however, time will generally be of the essence unless the contract provides to the contrary. The significance of time being of the essence is that if the supplier is late, even by a single day in completing delivery, then the buyer is entitled to cancel the contract and reject the goods. He will also be entitled to claim for damages. If time is not of the essence, failure to complete on time is still a breach of contract for which the purchaser is entitled to claim damages.

It is normal in construction and similar forms of contract to provide that the contractor is entitled to an extension of time if he is delayed either by the act/default of the employer or some other mitigating circumstance. There are two possible approaches to the drafting of an extension of time clause. The first is to provide that the contractor is entitled to an extension of time if he is delayed by 'industrial disputes or any cause beyond his reasonable control'. The second is to list out in some detail the circumstances which would entitle him to an extension — see for example Clause 30 of the FIDIC Conditions of Contract for Electrical and Mechanical Works (including erection on Site) Second Edition 1980.

There seems little advantage in adopting the second approach, particularly as inevitably (as in Clause 30 referred to above) the draftsman always finishes up with a sweeping-up provision like 'any cause beyond the reasonable control of the contractor'. One point, however, which does not often seem to be covered specifically, although it is in the FIDIC Clause referred to above, is the right of the main contractor to an extension of time if he is delayed by a subcontractor. The clause allows the main contractor the right to an extension if the delay on the part of the subcontractor is due to a circumstance which would have entitled the main contractor to an extension. This seems to be an equitable way of dealing with the difficulty.

One wording to be avoided is the use of the term 'force majeure'. The expression has no precise legal definition in English law. It was once said by a learned judge 'The precise meaning of this term, if it has one, has eluded lawyers for years'. It is defined in certain foreign codes of law, where the tendency is for it to be restricted to what we would more usually refer to as 'acts of God' and it is certainly more limited in scope than the normal extension of time clause to be found in standard conditions prevailing in the UK or in those recognised internationally such as FIDIC. But the real problem which its use creates is that of uncertainty which is always something to be avoided.

Damages

The object of an award in damages is to place the injured party in the same position financially as he would have been had the contract been properly performed, provided that the losses are not too remote.

Essentially the rule on remoteness is that the loss or damage which is recoverable is that which the parties could reasonably have contemplated at the time when the contract was made would be incurred from the breach in question. They could reasonably have contemplated a loss either because it would normally follow and arise naturally given that event, or because it should have been anticipated having regard to what was known to the parties at the time when the contract was made. Thus if a piece of equipment is delivered late, which it is obvious the buyer intends to put into immediate use, then the supplier will be liable for the losses which the buyer incurs as a result of such delayed delivery, provided that such losses are such as the supplier could reasonably have expected when he entered into the contract would follow from the delay. They would not therefore include exceptionally high profits which the buyer anticipated the machine would earn him unless when he issued his enquiry the buyer had brought that fact to the seller's attention.

Because of the difficulties and uncertainties surrounding the issue of what level of damages a purchaser will be entitled to if works are completed late the contract will often contain a clause specifying the damages which can be recovered. In commercial practice such a clause is often referred to as a penalty clause but legally there is a sharp distinction to be made between penalties and liquidated damages.

Liquidated damages are a genuine pre-estimate of the sum which the buyer considers he would lose in the event of the works being delayed, or, if he considers that would be excessive, some lesser amount. In practice such a clause nearly always contains a limit of liability although there is no legal need for this. It operates therefore both as a liquidated damages clause and also as an exclusion clause and to that extent is subject to the terms of the Unfair Contract Terms Act. Usually the clause is expressed either as a sum or as a percentage of the contract price payable per week up to a specified limit. The interesting question arises therefore as to the purchaser's rights once the period for liquidated damages has come to an end if the delay is still continuing. It seems unreasonable that he should be left in a position where he is without further remedy but it is by no means clear what his remedy would be. For a review of the possible solutions see K. F. A. Johnston's book *Electrical and Mechanical Engineering Contracts*, Gower, 1971, pp. 13–16.

It is to be noted that it does not matter whether the actual loss suffered by the buyer is greater or less than the amount of the liquidated damages or even it would appear whether in the event he suffered any loss at all. He is entitled to recover the liquidated damages provided that these were a genuine pre-estimate of the loss which he anticipated he would suffer from the delay.

The distinction between liquidated damages and penalties in English law (in other systems it is unknown) is that a penalty is a sum, greater than any loss which the buyer could anticipate suffering from the delay, included in the contract in an effort to compel the contractor to complete on time. If the sum is classified by the courts as a penalty then the clause is void and the penalty is irrecoverable by legal action. However this does not alter the fact that the contractor is late and in breach of contract, so he will still be liable for damages calculated under the normal rules. It makes no difference what the clause is called in the contract — the only question to be answered is whether or not it was a genuine pre-estimate.

Quality and performance

The issues of quality and performance are central to the carrying out of commercial contracts. The obligations of the seller and the rights of the buyer, as set out in the Sale of Goods Act, cover three broad areas:

1 *Description and sample.* Under the Sale of Goods Act goods must correspond to description and the bulk must correspond to sample. From our point of view the most important consequence of these provisions is that the goods must correspond to the specification. In the older cases which have come before the courts there have been a number of examples where the goods have not exactly corresponded with the specification and the courts have held that the purchaser was accordingly entitled to reject them. As an example, a case in 1921 (Moore and Co. v Landauer) allowed the buyer to reject tins of fruit because they came packed in 24 tins to the box instead of 30. Whether that case would be followed today is uncertain (unless the deviation made a significant difference to the buyer) because the buyer's motive in seeking to reject has often been to avoid what, by the time of delivery, has become an unprofitable bargain. This aspect was commented upon by the House of Lords in Reardon Smith v Hansen Tangen in 1976.

2 *Merchantable quality.* Where a seller sells goods in the course of business a condition is implied that the goods shall be of merchantable quality, that is to say that the goods are such that a purchaser would buy them as goods of that description. It does not mean that the goods are free of all defects. The question of the ability to use the goods or their resale for some purpose, and also the price at which they were purchased are both relevant factors. If the goods can be used or re-sold for some purpose then it is probable they will be regarded as being of merchantable quality. If the price is appropriate to a

particular level of use but not of another then again the goods are likely to be held of merchantable quality as happened in the House of Lords case Brown *v* Craikes 1970 when material suitable for industrial, but not dress, use was sold at an industrial material price.

There are two exceptions in the Act to the requirement as to merchantable quality. The first of these relates to defects specifically drawn to the buyer's attention. The second exception arises if the buyer examines the goods prior to contract and there are defects which that examination ought to reveal. If, therefore, the buyer is offered the opportunity of inspecting goods and does so, he must be careful to ensure that his examination is thorough enough. If it is only cursory (for example, looking at barrels from the outside only instead of examining them more closely) he will lose his rights under this clause.

3 *Fitness for purpose.* Under s.14 of the Act, if the buyer, expressly or by implication, makes known to the seller the purpose for which he requires the goods, then there is an implied condition of fitness for purpose, unless circumstances show that the buyer did not rely on, or it would be unreasonable for him to rely on, the skill and judgement of the seller. In some situations the purpose for which the goods are required will be obvious. In others however there may be difficulties either because the buyer has a particular purpose in mind for an item which is of general application or because the goods in question have more than one use and again the buyer has only one which he has selected. If the buyer is in one particular line of business (for example, mink farming) then clearly if he purchases feedstuffs the seller will be taken to know that he requires them for feeding mink and they should be suitable for that purpose (Ashington Piggeries *v* Hill 1972). But if there were (from the buyer's line of business) several possible uses, then it would be up to the buyer to indicate the one for which he was purchasing the goods.

Payment

Unless the parties otherwise agree, time is not of the essence as regards the time for payment. Delays in payment by the buyer do not, therefore, automatically give the right to the seller to terminate the contract. This point is of particular importance where the contract provides for stage payments. If the purchaser defaults on a single stage payment then whether or not the supplier or contractor has a right to terminate will depend on the size of the breach in relation to the contract as a whole and the likelihood of the breach being repeated. Because of the general uncertainty of the supplier's rights in this type of situation, it is important from the supplier's viewpoint that he should include express provisions in the contract covering his rights should the purchaser default on payment.

Interest on delayed payments can only be claimed by the supplier if the right was expressly included in the contract conditions. There is no general implied right to recover interest for delay in payment. It is important to note that inclusion of right to recover interest must be within the documentation forming part of the contract. Reference to it only on the invoice will not be effective unless the invoice is a part of the contract. It will only be so if the invoice constitutes the seller's acceptance of the buyer's order. In all other circumstances the invoice is a demand for payment under the terms of an existing contract and the rule is clear that once a contract has been made the terms can only be varied by mutual agreement and not by the unilateral act of one of the parties.

The contract should set out expressly the event or events on the happening of which the supplier or contractor is entitled to receive payment. It is one point on which the basic rules implied by law differ as between contracts for the sale of goods and contracts for services. Under a contract for the sale of goods s.28 of the Sale of Goods Act provides that, unless otherwise agreed, delivery of the goods and payment of the price are concurrent conditions. With a contract for services the general rule is that services are to be performed first and payment is only due when the whole of the services have been completed. So where there was a contract for the installation of a central heating system the contractor was only entitled to be paid when the work had been completed; that is to say, when the system had been made to work effectively.

Guarantees and exclusion clauses

For commercial reasons it has long been the practice of suppliers and contractors to limit their liabilities in damages for the supply of defective goods or for the carrying out of defective work. This practice even extends to excluding such liabilities altogether, offering the purchaser in return some limited undertaking to make good defects which arise within a specified period. At one time, under the general principle of freedom of contract, English law allowed the parties to make a contract on more or less any terms they chose, ignoring the reality of life that such freedom could be totally illusory if there was a significant difference in the bargaining power of the parties. In order to provide some rough kind of justice, particularly in cases where one of the parties was a domestic purchaser, the courts did on occasions strain the construction of exclusion clauses beyond any normal interpretation of the words, so as to be able to find that the clause did not cover the issue in question. They also invented the doctrine of fundamental breach which was to the effect that there were fundamental obligations under a contract which it was impossible to exclude, such as that in selling a car it had to be capable of self-propulsion. All that has now been swept away by a combination of decisions of the House of Lords and the passing of the Unfair Contract Terms Act.

First, the House of Lords in the Photo Production against Securicor Ltd case ruled that exclusion clauses in commercial contracts between businessmen were to be interpreted in accordance with the natural meaning of the words used and no strained constructions were to be applied. The doctrine of fundamental breach was firmly rejected. It was for the parties to decide how the risks involved were to be apportioned between them and if the meaning of the clause was clear the courts would not interfere. If there were any doubt as to the meaning then the court would approach the problem of construction of the clause by looking at who was in the strongest position (usually by way of insurance) to accept the risk involved.

Secondly, the Unfair Contract Terms Act has outlawed certain exclusion provisions and made others subject to the test of 'reasonableness'. Dealing only with commercial contracts the most significant provisions of the Act are:

1 Liability for death or personal injury due to negligence cannot be excluded or restricted by any contract term. In the case of other loss or damage due to negligence liability can only be

Contract Administration

restricted or excluded if the contract term satisfied the test of reasonableness.

2 The seller's implied undertakings under the Sale of Goods Act in respect of conformity of the goods with description or sample, or as to their quality or fitness for purpose, can only be excluded or restricted by a contract term if it satisfies the test of reasonableness.

There are five guidelines in the Act to be taken into account in deciding on whether or not a term is reasonable and the onus is on the party seeking to rely on the exclusion provision to show that the clause is reasonable having regard only to what was known (or ought reasonably to have been known) to the parties at the time when the contract was made. The guidelines are:

1 The strength of the bargaining positions of the parties relative to each other.
2 Whether the purchaser received an inducement to agree to the term or could have entered into a similar contract with someone else without such a term.
3 Whether the purchaser knew, or ought reasonably to have known, the existence of the term.
4 Whether it was reasonable at the time of contract to expect that it would be practicable to comply with the term.
5 Whether the goods were manufactured, processed or adapted to the special order of the customer.

It is still too early in the life of the Act to do more than indicate the factors which seem primarily to have influenced the courts in arriving at their decisions. Indeed the courts have said almost each time that they have decided the case on its particular facts and stressed that it does not mean that a similar but not identical case would be decided the same way. This is inevitable given that the court is trying to arrive at a balance. With that caveat the factors which seem most to have influenced the courts are:

1 Whether or not the parties have sought to renegotiate on the terms of the clause or have had the opportunity to do so. Failure to negotiate when the opportunity was there has been a factor in leading to the clause being held reasonable.
2 The possibility of the risk being insured against. If the seller

could have insured himself, and without materially affecting the price, this is a pointer to the clause being unreasonable.
3 The level of loss suffered by the purchaser and the degree of negligence of the supplier. The higher the loss and the greater the degree of negligence the more likely the court would appear to find the clause unreasonable.
4 A clause totally excluding liability is more likely to be found unreasonable than one which only partially excludes liability.

Finally, if the clause restricts liability to a specified sum then two additional guidelines become relevant:

1 The resources available to the supplier to meet the liability.
2 How far it was open to the supplier to cover himself by insurance.

On the first point it is not yet clear whose resources are to be taken into account when the supplier is part of a larger group. Is it just those of the subsidiary, or does it extend to those of the group?

VITIATING FACTORS

Mistake

The law has traditionally divided mistake into three categories:

1 *Common mistake*. If the parties both make the same mistake, as to say the suitability of the goods for a certain purpose, then they are still bound by the contract they have made. Only in the rare type of case in which the goods have later been found to have been destroyed, or even never to have existed, will the court declare the contract to be void.
2 *Mutual mistake*. In common parlance, the parties are simply at cross purposes. The courts then apply the objective test of the reasonable man, and ask if he would say that the parties had reached a binding agreement.
3 *Unilateral mistake*. This is where only one party has made a mistake, the other being well aware of the error since he himself is not mistaken. Usually these ones are cases of sharp practice, if not downright fraud. If the subject matter of the mistake is a

crucial part of the bargain then the courts have ruled that the contract is void.

Misrepresentation

A representation is a statement of fact made by one party to the contract to the other before the contract is made, which induces the person to whom it is made to enter into the contract, but is not itself a term of the contract. A misrepresentation is a representation which turns out not to be true. In general silence is not a misrepresentation except in cases requiring utmost good faith, such as insurance.

The law on misrepresentation has been developed both by the courts and by Parliament. In the briefest of outline there are four alternatives to be considered:

1. *Fraudulent misrepresentation.* This is where the misrepresentation is made knowingly or without caring whether it is true or false. The remedy is both damages and recision.
2. *Negligent misrepresentation.* A statement which is made carelessly during the course of negotiations by one side and is relied on by the other can be the subject of an action for damages. If the seller held himself out as an expert giving advice on some crucial aspect of the sale, and if that advice were given negligently and acted upon by the purchaser, then this would be the type of situation in which the purchaser could claim damages.
3. *Misrepresentation Act 1967, 2.2(1).* This gives a statutory right to claim for damages for misrepresentation which is negligent. The curious part of this provision is that it reverses the normal burden of proof once the falsity has been established, so that the person making the representation must then prove that he was not negligent.
4. *Innocent misrepresentation.* This is where the person making the representation honestly and reasonably believes it to be true. The remedy is that the other party can rescind the contract and claim an indemnity against those losses which he suffered necessarily from entering into the contract but not damages. However under the Misrepresentation Act s.2(2) the court now has the discretionary power to award that the contract shall be

continued and damages awarded to the party to whom the representation was made to compensate them for being obliged to continue with the contract.

Frustration

English law has always placed a very restricted interpretation on the doctrine of frustration. For it to apply there must have been an unforeseen event occurring after the contract, beyond the control of both parties, which makes further performance of the contract impossible. If the contract can still be performed, although only in a more expensive way, then it is not frustrated.

CONTRACT LAW, JURISDICTION AND ENFORCEMENT

The proper law of the contract

Where a contract is to be entered into with a company overseas it is important that the contract should specify by which law its conclusion and performance is to be governed. In the absence of such a provision it may be a difficult task for the court to decide upon what is termed the proper law of the contract. This has been described as 'the system of law by reference to which the contract was made or that with which the transaction has its closest and most real connection'. Unfortunately, if this is not stated in the contract much time and money may need to be expended to discover what it is. In general the strongest presumption which the courts apply in the absence of any statement in the contract, is the law of the country in which the contract is to be performed. Even that can create difficulties where the contract is to be performed in more than one country, say design and manufacture in England and installation and commissioning in Saudi Arabia. The court might even decide that although in general the contract is governed by English law, that part to be performed overseas must be regulated by the law of the overseas state. A reference to arbitration according to the rules of the International Chamber of Commerce (Paris) as is common in many contracts does not solve the problem since it only brings in the rules of the Chamber governing the conduct of the proceedings.

Jurisdiction

Again, it is highly desirable that the contract should state which court or arbitration tribunal is to have jurisdiction and it is to be noted that this question is quite separate from that of the proper law of the contract. Thus a case can be held in England with the court applying a foreign law. Since, however, this requires proof of that law through expert witnesses, the costs and time involved are considerable and the position is one to be avoided if possible.

Enforcement

This is perhaps the biggest problem for the English company where the other party to the contract is situated abroad with all his assets outside the jurisdiction of the English courts. An award by an English arbitration tribunal may be capable of being directly enforced if the other country is a signatory to the Convention on the Recognition and Enforcement of Foreign Arbitral Awards — the so-called New York Convention, or the Geneva Convention of 1927. With countries not signatory to these conventions enforcement may be difficult and in some instances impossible, particularly if the foreign territory is strongly nationalistic or under an autocratic government and the dispute involves a state organisation or government department.

PRIVITY OF CONTRACT AND NEGLIGENCE

Privity of contract

The general rule of English law is that a contract can confer rights and duties only on the parties to the contract. This means *inter alia* that there is no contractual right for an employer to take action directly against a subcontractor for defective work. Equally, a subcontractor is not protected by any clause of the main contract limiting the main contractor's obligations for damage to property or financial losses incurred by the purchaser arising out of any breach of contract, or any limitation of liability contained within the defects liability clause. An attempt was made in clause 30 (viii) of the Model Form A Conditions of the Institutes of Electrical and Mechanical Engineers to deal with this point by providing that 'the contractor (for the purposes of this sub-clause) contracts on his own behalf and on behalf of and as trustee for his subcontractors' servants and agents'. In the case of Southern Water Authority v Duvivier, reported in the June 1985 issue of the Building Law Monthly Monitor Press, it was held that the word 'trustee' in this clause did not entitle the sub-contractor to the benefit of the exemption provision since the notion of a trust was wholly inappropriate in such circumstances. However, the clause did indirectly provide the sub-contractor with protection. The Judge decided that the 'contract setting', in particular the inclusion of clause 30, so defined the area of risk which the employer had agreed with the main contractor to accept that it provided a justification for negativing the normal duty of care which the sub-contractor owed to the employer.

Negligence

The law of negligence is a rapidly changing scene, in particular as to the rights which a user has against a subcontractor for defective work or goods. At one time it was thought that there could only be such an action if the work or products were dangerous so that they created 'present or imminent danger to the health or safety of the occupiers' (as it was stated in a 1978 Canadian case). However the House of Lords in their 1982 decision in Junior Books v The Veitchi Co. Ltd decided that in certain circumstances an employer could recover against a subcontractor for pure economic loss although in subsequent cases in the Court of Appeal, particularly Muirhead v Industrial Tank Specialities, November 1985, it has been held that Junior Books was very much a case decided on its own particular facts. At present it appears that, in order to determine if the sub-contractor is liable, the test to be applied first is 'Was there a sufficient degree of proximity between the user and the subcontractor?' In the case of nominated subcontractors who are specialists in their particular field, as Veitchi were, that degree of proximity may well exist. With other subcontractors and suppliers it will depend on the degree of their involvement in the project. Did they know the identity of the user and the use to which their product or services was to be put?

Did the user rely on the skill and care of the subcontractor or supplier? If the answer to these questions is 'yes' then again the proximity test may be satisfied. The second part of the test is 'Whether there are any considerations which ought to negate, or to reduce or limit the scope of the duty (of care) of the class of person to whom it is owed or the damage to which a breach of it may give rise'. The difficulty with the second part of the test is just what are the considerations which would lead to the negation or reduction of the duty of care? At present the answer is unclear. One possible line of argument could be that if the user as the purchaser of the goods or services had contracted with the manufacturer or main contractor on terms which excluded the right to recover the damages in question, and if such exclusion was one which would be held as fair and reasonable were the purchaser to bring an action in contract against the manufacturer or main contractor, then the purchaser has benefited from a contract price which was related to such exclusion. Consequently it would be unreasonable for him now to recover in negligence what he had bargained not to be able to recover for in contract. Such a consideration seems to have been in the mind of Lord Roskill when giving judgment in the Junior Books case and indeed it formed the basis of the decision in the Southern Water Board case referred to above; but more decisions are needed in the higher courts to create any real degree of certainty.

Where it is a matter of rendering professional services, such as those of an engineer, architect, doctor or lawyer, then the normal rule is that the professional man's duty is to take reasonable care and to show such skill as may be expected of an ordinary competent person exercising that particular art. He does not therefore warrant the end result. However, there can be cases in which such a guarantee will be implied from the terms of the contract. One such could be where consulting engineers are employed by a package-deal contractor to design a building suitable for a particular purpose. It has also been clearly established now that if the design is novel and the consequences of failure would be dangerous then 'the graver the foreseeable consequences of failure to take care the greater the need for special circumspection'. So it is no defence to say that 'one is venturing into the unknown'. The answer is that in that event one has to think through the problems involved and if the conclusion is that they are too difficult to have any reasonable certainty of solution then it may be necessary not to proceed at all. The above comments are based on the judgments of the House of Lords in the Emley Moor case IBA against BICC.

5
Contracts and Payment Structures

P. D. V. Marsh

There are broadly three ways in which the contract price may be expressed or calculated:

1 Lump sum.
2 Schedule of rates or remeasurement.
3 Cost reimbursement.

These different ways are not necessarily mutually exclusive. Thus the above-ground element of a building contract may be on a lump sum basis whilst the foundations are subject to remeasurement; the supply portion of a plant contract may be a lump sum, whilst the installation of the plant is on cost reimbursement; a contract for a complex chemical plant may be on cost reimbursement but with the overheads and profit margin compounded as a lump sum.

The choice of which way to ask the contractor to price the work will depend very largely on the amount of information regarding the job, and the conditions under which it will be carried out, which the buyer can provide to the contractor in the time available for tendering.

LUMP SUM

From the purchaser's point of view the ideal is a firm lump sum. It establishes the amount of his commitment in advance, it provides the

Contract Administration

maximum incentive to the contractor to complete the work on time, and it reduces to a minimum the amount of administrative work involved after the contract has been let. But these benefits will be obtained only if it has been possible for the contractor to tender realistically. Any marked divergence between the contract price and the actual cost of doing the work may not only lose the purchaser the benefits he expected but, worse, may endanger or destroy the effectiveness of the contract as a means of achieving management's overall objectives.

In addition to the general information needed by a tenderer, in order to bid on a lump sum basis answers to the following questions must also be found, either from the prospective purchaser or from the contractor's own organisation:

1. Material quantities and specifications. These may be in the form of drawings from which the estimator can himself take off quantities.
2. Tolerances permitted and any special finishes required.
3. Labour hours and trades both for shop production and on site. This means that decisions on methods of production/construction affecting labour quantities and skills must have been made.
4. Description and quantities of bought-out items. This requires decisions to have been taken on, for example, sizes, capacities, and horsepowers.
5. Types of production or constructional plant which will be utilised both in the shops and on site, and the times or periods involved.
6. Where design is significant, and is not included as an overhead, the amount of design work involved.
7. The site organisation which will be needed and for what period.
8. Overtime to be worked in shops and on site.
9. Time when the work is to be carried out.
10. Factors which will affect labour productivity on site — climatic conditions, religious holidays, nationality of labour to be employed.
11. Geographical and climatic factors as they affect civil, building or mechanical and electrical site work. These would include

Contracts and Payment Structures

rainfall, presence of corrosive salts liable to attack steelwork, humidity, dust, availability of fresh water, general local facilities, supply of clean aggregates.
12 Local material availability: cement in proper condition and in the right quantities to meet programme, port off-loading and transport facilities including any heavy load restrictions on roads or bridges.
13 General local amenities and workshop facilities.

This is a formidable list. It confirms the need for the purchaser to be able to give complete and accurate information before a firm lump sum price can be tendered. It also indicates the time and cost in which the contractor is involved in lump sum tendering. What must be remembered is that every time a tenderer guesses, he may guess wrong, and every wrong guess costs someone money. Moreover that someone, if the tenderer is to stay in business, can in the long run only be the employer whether on that particular contract or another.

Just as the contractor's problem on lump sum tendering is to assess the risks involved, so the employer's problem is the time which it will take him to give the information necessary to reduce those risks to reasonable proportions. Some element of risk there will always be; that is in the very nature of contracting itself.

The problem of information against time arises particularly on contracts for building and civil engineering work where the employer is normally, though not necessarily, responsible for design, and two of the main factors affecting design are both largely outside the designer's control. These are, first, the nature of the subsoil and, second, the detailed requirements of the specialist contractors and subcontractors for plant and services. Increasingly, these latter form a major part of most building or civil engineering projects. If the start of construction were to be delayed until exhaustive bore-hole research had been carried out and detailed designs for the plant and services prepared, the element of uncertainty could of course be minimised. Managements, however, are not normally prepared to accept delays of this sort so that it becomes necessary to find some way in which the risks inherent in these unknowns can properly be shared between contractor and employer and a start made on the project.

SCHEDULE OF RATES OR BILL OF APPROXIMATE QUANTITIES

This leads to the schedule of rates or bills of approximate quantity method of pricing under which a schedule or bill is prepared, covering each of the items which it is anticipated may be met during the course of construction, for example excavation, concreting, brickwork, etc. These items are then priced by the contractor and he is paid at those rates for the amount of work actually carried out, irrespective of the quantity shown against the item in the schedule or bill. The problem has however always existed of where the change in the quantity from the estimated to the actual is such that it affects the contractor's method of working, perhaps a change to hand from machine work. It is now expressly provided in the 5th edition of the ICE conditions clause 56(2) that the contractor is entitled to an adjustment of the rate if there is a change in quantities which makes the rate 'unreasonable or inapplicable', and there is no minimum percentage change required.

In pricing a contract in this way a contractor has to estimate the quantity and cost of the labour, materials, and plant which will be required to execute the given quantity of work. Since the major elements are labour and plant, the assessment of productivity is a vital part of the estimating process. This in turn is closely related to the physical conditions under which the work will be carried out — for example, the time of year — and to the possibility of carrying out the work in a planned way with a reasonable degree of continuity — for example, drawings arriving on site well in advance of the commencement of construction of the work to which they relate. The importance of these points will be referred to again when discussing variations and claims.

As regards specialist subcontractors' work, these items are made the subject of prime cost or provisional sums. An amount is included by the employer in the bill which represents his best estimate of the cost of the item. When the sub-contract is placed (after the main contract has been let) that sum is deleted and replaced by the amount of the sub-contract. When tendering himself, the main contractor is only required to tender the margin he wants for handling the subcontractor, usually expressed as a percentage plus any sum he wants for attendance on the subcontractor, like providing scaffolding, storage, etc.

COST REIMBURSEMENT

With many industrial projects today, speed in getting work carried out is regarded as more vital than lowest initial capital cost. Moreover, apparent cost advantages at tendering stage may be lost by the time final settlement is reached on the payment of claims. On the other hand, simple cost reimbursement provides no incentive to the contractor to minimise costs, nor any penalty should he fail. Indeed the reverse is true. Most contractors in fact dislike straight cost plus because of the inefficiencies which it may breed within their own company. Costs can so easily be charged to cost-plus jobs if no other home can be found for them!

Various types of incentive, target cost or co-operative forms of contract have been devised, therefore, as a means of combining the flexibility and speed associated with cost reimbursement with a strong measure of cost discipline and an incentive to efficiency and economy. All these forms of contract have certain features in common:

1. The principle of design and construction in parallel as opposed to in series.
2. The early establishment of a target estimate either as a definite sum or on civil or building work as rates in an approximate bill of quantities, against which the work can be remeasured.
3. The recording of the actual costs incurred and their comparison with the final target cost. This is the original target cost adjusted to take account of authorised variations.
4. The sharing between employer and contractor of the difference between 2 and 3.
5. The payment of a management fee in addition to cost which may either be part of the comparison or paid quite separately as a lump sum or a percentage of the target estimate.

How the final contract price is arrived at under the conventional, and the target or incentive form of contract, can best be illustrated by the diagram overleaf.

Contract Administration

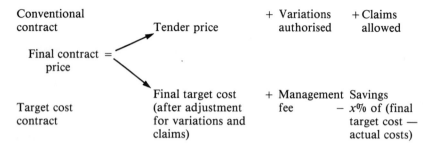

Two points need particular attention at the negotiating stage. First, the over-run, if any, above a defined ceiling should be borne wholly by the contractor. This ceiling may be the target itself or more likely the target plus a certain margin, the extent of which will reflect the unknowns inherent in the contract. Second, in the assessment of the target cost it is essential that the target should be built up from the component elements of labour, materials, plant, etc., which the contractor can be expected to use on the job, and has regard to the construction or manufacturing methods which it is anticipated that the contractor will adopt. It is not just a question of selecting 'average' competitive rates, but of seeing that they are tailored to the job in question and reflect its particular circumstances. The target must, however, contain a contingency margin which is sufficient to ensure that, provided the contractor uses proper efficiency, the target remains at all times credible to beat. The aim should be to set a target which ought to be beaten by a low margin, say 10 per cent.

If time is particularly vital, it is possible to build in an additional incentive by varying the share of the savings accruing to the contractor according to the extent to which the contract is completed early or late. This may be done as under:

Period in weeks by which contract is finished before or after target completion date	Contractor's % share of savings
−6	90
−4	75
−2	60
0	50
+2	35
+4	20
+6	nil

With this type of scheme, while the contractor is given an incentive to complete early, he is at the same time encouraged to achieve that result by greater efficiency and productivity, rather than by excessive overtime.

The target method is not, however, suitable in all cases where time is vital. Sometimes, because information is lacking, it may not be possible to establish the target, and it may be necessary to place the contract initially on a cost reimbursement basis with the intention of firming up the price into a lump sum at a later date. Also, to administer a target cost contract effectively imposes a substantial burden on the employer and may require the services of outside quantity surveyors, thus pushing up the total cost by the amount of their fees. This applies with certain contracts for complex chemical plants. In this type of case the contract price may have to be broken down and dealt with as set out below.

Design

This is usually paid for on a man-time basis, the unit of time — hour, day, week, month, or even year — being selected to suit the individual contract. To the actual wages or salary of the draughtsman or engineer the contractor will add his design overhead. The following points need watching when considering these rates:

1 In respect of which classes of staff are they payable? This may be only actual engineers or draughtsmen or may extend through bills of material clerks to clerks, typists, and the like. Obviously this alters substantially the allowance for overheads; the smaller the chargeable base the higher the overhead.
2 Are the overheads included in the rates the whole of the company's overheads, or only those related to design? Practice differs on this according to whether the firm's normal selling unit is design time or not. If it is, then normally all overheads (other than possibly those relating purely to construction or procurement) will be charged against design.
3 The above two points have a tremendous effect on the overhead as a percentage. The swing can be as much as from 75 to 300 per cent.
4 Do the rates include:

Contract Administration

    (a) Overtime?
    (b) Travelling and subsistence?
    (c) Telex, cables, and telephone calls?
    (d) Printing and reproduction costs?
    Or are these chargeable at net cost?
5 Do the same rates apply to sub-contract design?
6 The rates may be expressed as so many pence or pounds per time unit, in which event they are usually based on an average of the salaries of the designers expected to be employed or as the actual wages plus percentage.

Obviously from the employer's point of view the more elements which can be properly made the subject of lump sums the better; particularly if the job is going out to competition. It is extremely difficult to compare either percentages or hourly rates; percentages because these have no validity by themselves but only when related to a base, and it cannot be assumed that the base will be the same for all firms; hourly rates because these have no validity unless one is in a position to assess the real value to be placed on the work which will be turned out in an hour, and quite simply one is not.

Thus firm A may offer design at £15 an hour, firm B at £19 an hour. But by themselves these figures mean nothing. Firm A may take 50 000 man-hours and produce a design which costs £2 500 000 to build. Firm B may take only 35 000 man-hours and their scheme result in a final price of £2 300 000. The same sort of reasoning applies to labour rates for construction or erection work.

Procurement

This is usually paid for as a percentage of the value of materials purchased after deduction of trade but not cash discounts. It includes purchasing, expediting, and inspection. Again one needs to check that travel and subsistence, which may be high, are included.

Materials

Net price after deduction of trade but not cash discounts. The total value of discounts can be very substantial, particularly on items such as motors, valves, pipework, and so on, and should not be regarded as the estimator's contingency.

Site supervision, UK contracts

This may be negotiated as a lump sum, or a weekly rate. It will include:

1 Salaries, allowances, and charges, National Health Insurance — for example, for site supervisory staff.
2 Site huttage.
3 General services — for example, telephone, lighting.
4 General site transport.
5 Consumables.
6 Canteen.

Erection labour, UK contracts

Charges for erection labour on a per hour basis will normally include:

1 Wages and allowances — for example, subsistence and radius allowance, condition money, etc.
2 Bonus.
3 National Health Insurance, holiday with pay, redundancy fund payment, etc.
4 Common law insurance.
5 Hand tools.

Care needs to be taken in dealing with the non-productive element of overtime. This will affect only a small proportion of the overhead charges related to wages.

Site supervision overseas

On overseas contracts the indirect charges for supervisory staff may easily amount to 150–200 per cent of the man's payroll costs. Such charges may include:

1 Provision of accommodation, its maintenance and services costs, such as charges for electricity and water which are often substantially higher than in the UK.
2 A car and its running/maintenance costs. Although, depending on the territory, petrol may be cheaper than in the UK, maintenance and depreciation may be very high due to unfavourable climatic conditions and the poor state of the roads.

3 Food allowance.
4 Air fares to and from the UK.

Practice on housing and food varies both from company to company and according to the size of the supervisory team.

On projects involving only a small team some firms pay a fixed allowance per day leaving it to the man to find his own accommodation and food. This is often preferred by the supervisory staff since it leaves them free to choose their own standard of living and sometimes to form local 'liaisons'. It does however weaken the company's control and may lead to staff living and behaving in a manner which lowers the firm's reputation.

With larger contracts it would be normal for the company either to set up a camp containing shopping, laundering and recreational facilities in addition to the accommodation or select itself the accommodation for its staff according to their grades. In remote areas or where there is no suitable expatriate type accommodation, there is no alternative and the company must totally establish its own facilities, often including drinking water, sewerage, catering facilities, cottage hospital, etc.

A further complication is caused on long-term contracts by the need to offer at least senior staff married contracts. There are then the problems of children's education, either paying fees for a local English/American school if there is one or if not providing a school with a teacher for juniors and paying at least part of boarding school fees for older children. Whilst batchelors can be accommodated in flats or barrack-type blocks on site, families need houses. If suitable ones do not exist locally then pre-fabricated ones, air-conditioned and complete with all services, must be provided. Shopping and medical and recreational facilities will need to be expanded to cater for the needs of wives and children or additional allowances paid to allow use to be made by families of local facilities which are normally expensive. Air fares to the UK for mid-term leave and for children at boarding school for at least one holiday per year with parents need to be included.

Finally if the overseas territory imposes income tax there may be the vexed question of taxation to be considered, and the following issues will arise:

1 Is there a double taxation convention between the overseas territory and the UK? If so what are its terms?

2. On what basis will the individual be charged tax in the overseas territory — on his living allowance only or his total earnings as assessed by the local tax authorities?
3. Does an exit visa from the territory depend on the issue of a tax clearance certificate?

Although firms often take the line that while giving general answers an individual's tax affairs are his own business they inevitably get drawn into the problem since the individual who goes to work overseas is only interested in the net remuneration package. American companies since the introduction of legislation taxing a person in the USA on his combined American and overseas earnings including benefits have found this out to their cost and at the time of writing are busy replacing American engineers with those of other nationalities, primarily from the UK, at substantially reduced all-up expense.

To the extent that a contractor is able to utilise locally recruited administrative and professional staff then the costs of supervision will necessarily be reduced by the allowances for housing, accommodation, air fares, etc., although in territories in which such staff of an appropriate calibre are available base salaries are not likely to differ widely from those in the UK. Depending however on the nationality of such staff, problems may arise in terms of differences in social and religious habits and customs and these will be accentuated if both the ex-patriate and local staff are required, because of the site's isolation, to live as well as work together.

Overseas erection and construction labour

On overseas contracts construction and erection labour will be either local or recruited from third national countries: for example, in the Gulf States and Saudi Arabia labour including skilled tradesmen will come from either India, Pakistan or the Philippines. Different considerations, all of which affect pricing, apply to the employment of local as opposed to third national labour and may briefly be summarised as follows:

Third national labour

1. Recruited through a labour contractor in the country of origin on a one- or two-year contract.

2 Trade testing normally carried out in country of origin.
3 Payment includes recruitment fee and return air fare.
4 Wages are generally subject to control of the government of origin.
5 Accommodation and food must be provided.
6 Work permits and visas are usually restricted to employment by the contractor and the man must return to his country of origin on termination of his contract.

In practice at the time of writing the employment of third nationals on the above basis has had the effect of largely protecting the contractor against escalation or labour disturbances but has also meant that he lacks flexibility in being able to hire and fire. Labour costs become in effect semi-fixed instead of a variable which could have a major impact if the work programme becomes subject to changes or delays outside the contractor's control. Productivity becomes largely a function of the number of men on the site relative to the available quantity of work.

Local labour. In general it is not recommended that contractors working overseas should directly employ local construction/erection labour for the following reasons:

1 Local labour laws which can be tough in their theoretical provisions will be strictly enforced against an expatriate contractor and complying with them to the letter in terms of working hours, redundancy payments, bonuses, etc. will be expensive. Local contractors however have a way of getting round these provisions or at least minimising their cost impact.
2 Local working and amenity practices will be unfamiliar to the expatriate contractor and even when he does become aware of them they will be difficult for him to apply, which again will cost the contractor money.
3 Trade testing and qualifications may not exist.
4 The problem of language.
5 Local contractors will already have an established network of relationships with government and union officials, client's inspectors, etc. and also with sources of reliable labour which an expatriate firm on its own will never achieve.

Contracts and Payment Structures

The only circumstances under which an expatriate firm can successfully employ any quantity of local labour is if it has formed a joint venture with an established local contractor and matters related to the employment of local labour and dealing with local officialdom are made the responsibility of the local partner who is obliged therefore to take an active interest in the partnership.

Constructional plant

There will normally be a schedule of weekly hire rates. The following points need covering:

1. Do the rates include any element of profit?
2. Are they tied to a number of hours?
3. Do they include for driver?
4. Do they include fuel, lubricants, spares, maintenance? There is a danger of paying twice.
5. Do they include charges for transport to and from site? These are often heavy.
6. Where the plant belongs to the contractor what allowance has been made for depreciation and what residual value has been assumed?

On overseas projects unless exemption is granted by the government then the problem may arise regarding import duties. First, even though the plant is only being imported temporarily, duty may be payable on certain types of plant or on particular makes in order to protect local industry or exclusive dealer arrangements. Even if this is not the case duty or a bond in lieu may require to be deposited which is in theory returnable on that item of plant being re-exported but is forfeit if the plant is sold in country. Unfortunately in practice temporary importation procedures tend to be so drawn-out that in desperation to get moving the contractor will pay the import duty and hope to recover it. The actual practice of temporary importation in the territory in question needs to be carefully examined both by the contractor and by the employer's negotiator.

Management overheads and profit

Preferably a lump sum which can be made the subject of competitive tender. Sometimes, depending on the information available, it may be possible to include in this lump sum the design element and even perhaps the site supervision, leaving only the direct materials, sub-contract, and labour costs to be either reimbursable or negotiated during the contract period.

MANAGEMENT CONTRACTING

Management contracting covers a number of possible contractual arrangements between client and contractor. These are discussed in a useful guide to the whole subject, *Management Contracting*, published by the Construction Industry Research and Information Association (Report number 100). There is also a standard form of project management contract, prepared by FIDIC. The principal issues peculiar to management contracting which affect pricing are given below.

Management contractor — agent or principal?

The question is whether the management contractor, when entering into contracts with others for supplying equipment or services, is doing so as an agent for and on behalf of the client or as a principal. To put the matter another way, who takes the risk of the supplier's default, and who is ultimately liable to the supplier for payment — the client or the management contractor?

Responsibility for results

The issue here is whether the management contractor is basically providing professional services and is liable only for his own negligence, or is acting as a contractor responsible for the achievement of an end result. Although it would be difficult to imagine a case in which the management contractor was acting as principal and not responsible, as regards the equipment to be supplied and the work to be performed in the same way as a contractor would normally be, the issue could still arise regarding the design which the management contractor was carrying out himself. If he is acting as an agent for the client, then it is necessary to be quite clear as to the responsibilities for

Back-to-back agreements

The extent to which it is practical for the management contractor to enter into back-to-back agreements with the subcontractors and suppliers will depend in part on the nature of the works and in part on the willingness of the client to pay an acceptable level of profit. The more integrated the plant, the more difficult it will be to break into major packages and only if it can be packaged in that way can the management contractor reasonably expect to obtain back-to-back cover. As an example, an electrical supply system could be purchased as separate units (switchgear, transformers, cables, motors, etc.) and be co-ordinated by the management contractor. Alternatively it could be purchased as a total system from one subcontractor. If there is one system subcontractor, then he can be expected to accept broadly the same terms for payment and warranty liability as the management contractor, whose risk is then mainly limited to the interface risk between the electrical subcontract package and the other subcontract packages (mechanical, building and civil works, etc.).

If, however, the management contractor has to place purchase orders for individual items himself, then there is bound to be a gap between his contract conditions with the client and those which he can place on the supplier (for example, the supplier is only likely to accept a 12 months warranty period ex works or FOB whereas the management contractor's own liability to the client for warranty may not start until the acceptance of the total project, which could be many months or even years later.

Obviously this will not be a problem for the management contractor if he is acting as agent and buying for and on behalf of the client, since it is assumed that his only liabilities for warranties will be co-extensive with those he obtains from the suppliers. But it does become a major issue if he is buying as principal and is giving his own overall warranty. Naturally it has to be someone's problem and in the agent case it is that of the client. He can finish up with as many different warranty periods as there are suppliers, and most of these warranties will have expired before the project is commissioned. But the difference in the management contractor's risk is, or it should be, reflected in his fees.

The route for payments

Do payments to the subcontractors and suppliers pass through the management contractor's books, or do they go direct from the client? If they go through the management contractor he will be able to increase his profits by taking advantage of the period of time for which he can hold payments received from the client before passing them on to the supplier or subcontractor. As an example, if it is assumed that the period of retention is 30 days, and if payments average £2 000 000 a month over a year, then with short term interest rates at 12 per cent the management contractor can add £240 000 interest to his earnings. At the same time, unless he has his subcontractors and suppliers on 'pay when paid' terms, he does have the ultimate contractual liability to them for payment.

If the payments do not pass through the management contractor's books, and he only certifies the amounts which are due to subcontractors and suppliers, then this removes from him both the opportunity to increase his profits and his potential liability for any default in payment by the client.

TERMS OF PAYMENT

Policy considerations

Terms of payment are a matter on which the commercial/technical and financial sides of the employer's business may find themselves pulling in opposite directions. The employer may attain the best commercial and technical result if he offers to the tenderers terms of payment which, while providing the employer with reasonable contractual safeguards, impose the minimum strain on the contractor's financial resources. By so doing the employer will:

1 Avoid having to restrict the tender list to large firms possessing the resources to finance the contract, whose overheads and prices will be higher than those of smaller companies. (This assumes of course that such smaller companies are otherwise technically and commercially competent to carry out the work.)
2 Ensure that the tenderers do not have to inflate their tender prices by financing charges. In many instances the rate of

interest which the contractor has to pay when borrowing will be higher than that paid by the employer.
3 Give encouragement to, and be able to take advantage of, firms possessing technical initiative who would otherwise be held back from expanding by lack of liquid cash.
4 Minimise the risk of being saddled with a contractor who has insufficient cash with which to carry out the contract and of having, therefore, either to support the contractor financially or terminate the contract.

On the other hand, to offer such terms means that the employer has to finance the work in progress and tie up his own capital in advance of obtaining any return on his investment. Particularly with a project such as a new factory or power plant, it would impose the least strain on the employer's financial resources if he could avoid having to pay anything at all until the project is earning money, and make the payments wholly out of revenue. With very major contracts of this type overseas, particularly in the under-developed countries, buying on credit in this way is not a matter of choice but of necessity. The authorities or companies concerned are not in a position to do anything else. As usual, however, the price which a customer pays for credit is high. Even with preferentially low interest rates for exports the cost to the purchaser of the financing charges on a long-term credit contract may easily amount to a third of the 'cash' selling price.

The factors related to cash flow and contract risk/profitability on both home and international contracts were analysed by Roland B. Neo in *International Construction Contracting*, Gower, 1976. However, only construction contracts under which payment is related broadly to the value of work carried out were considered and on overseas contracts the effect of having to provide bonds cashable by the purchaser on demand was not taken into account, a factor which seriously diminishes the author's conclusions on risk assessment.

On civil engineering and building contracts carried out in the UK either under the ICE or JCT forms or some major customer's adaptation of these, the contractor is paid monthly for the value of work done and materials delivered to site for incorporation into the permanent works in the preceding month, less a percentage for retention money: the relationship of the contractor's expenditure related to payments received is broadly illustrated in Figure 5.1. The

Contract Administration

shape of the expenditure curve will be affected by the labour/material ratio and the proportion of the work to be undertaken by nominated subcontractors. The higher the ratio of labour to material the steeper the expenditure curve as the less the contractor will be able to benefit from delaying payment to suppliers. Equally the higher the proportion of nominated suppliers and sub-contractors who can demand payment be made to them of the amount certified by the engineer/architect within x days of certification, again the less room the main contractor has to delay payment.

Roland Neo mentions but does not take account of two other actions which a main contractor can take to improve cash flow; over-measurement in the early months of the contract and front-end loading by artificially increasing the value of the rates for the work to be carried out early. These practices are common both in the UK and more especially overseas and unless carried to excess the engineer or quantity surveyor will often turn a blind eye to them as being a matter of custom and practice. Indeed during a time of high or sharply rising inflation, if the contract is subject to Contract Price Adjustment they can work to the contractor's disadvantage by diminishing the amount of escalation recovered relative to that incurred.

The other factor which may materially affect cash flow is the extent of variation orders issued by the architect/engineer which are not covered by rates and prices contained within bills of quantity and the time taken to get such rates and prices agreed. Although payment for such variations will normally be made on interim certificates on a provisional basis the amount certified will inevitably be conservative.

But the major factors in determining the cost to the contractor of financing the contract are:

1. Time between execution of work and the receipt of payment as the contract proceeds.
2. Time taken to settle the final account and release the final portion of the retention money.

The example in Figure 5.1 is based on the following assumptions:

1. 50 per cent of the contractor's expenditure relates to staff, labour and plant which must be paid for in the month in which it is incurred.
2. 20 per cent is represented by the contractor's own sub-contractor's on 90-day credit.

Contracts and Payment Structures

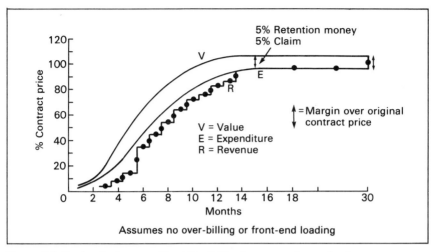

Figure 5.1 Contractor's expenditure in relation to payments received

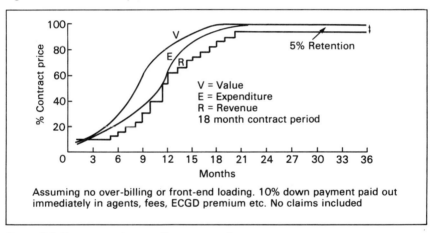

Figure 5.2 Revenue and expenditure curves for overseas contract

3   30 per cent is represented by nominated suppliers/subcontractors on a 30-day credit.
4   Certificates are issued by the engineer within 14 days of the end of the month in which the work is carried out and payment is made by the employer 30 days later.
5   Retention is 10 per cent, 5 per cent to be released on the issue of the certificate of practical completion and 5 per cent at the end of the 12 months' defects liability period. In practice the final account is not settled until 6 months after the end of the

contract and includes settlement of claims equal to 5 per cent of the contractor's costs.
6 The contract work is substantially carried out according to programme.

It will be seen that the contract is funded by the contractor to the extent of 16.58 per cent of the contract sum for one year which at 15 per cent p.a. interest represents an interest charge of 2.58 per cent against profit. Had completion of the contract been seriously delayed then the position would have been significantly worse since the contractor's preliminaries would have continued at broadly the same rate regardless of progress and the same would to an extent apply to plant costs.

On overseas construction contracts for which the contractor can expect to receive a down payment of say 10 per cent of the contract price then it might be expected that the amount of 'capital lock-up', to use Neo's term, would be less; indeed that is his suggestion. Whether however this is the case in practice will depend on the following factors:

1 The amount of the contractor's initial expense for such items as ECGD premiums, bonding charges and agents' fees which are payable on contract signature. These may easily amount to 10 per cent of the contract price.
2 Mobilisation costs in the overseas territory, e.g. setting up the site establishment, importation of plant, and whether these are paid as a separate item from the down payment, are deemed to be covered by the down payment or amortised over the billed rates and recovered pro rata to progress. Only if they are paid as a separate item is the contractor's cash flow likely to be other than negative particularly on any contract such as road construction which is plant-intensive.
3 Delays in certification and payment either deliberate or the result of bureaucratic inefficiency. This applies especially to payments for escalation or variations. Certification delays may be mitigated if the contract is being supervised by international consultants but those for payment can usually only be reduced by personal attention being given to each person in the chain of required signatures to ensure that your piece of paper is moved ahead of others.

4 Delays in the release of retention monies usually due to the unwillingness of overseas clients to take the responsibility of releasing their hold over the contractor.

Although not directly affecting the cash flow situation of the individual contract the contractor's financial position as a whole will be materially influenced by any on-demand bonds which he is required to put up under the terms of the overseas contract. The value of these will be regarded by his bank as liabilities when deciding on the extent of the facilities they are prepared to make available to him. A contract of say £20 million on which the amount of bonding averaged 15 per cent could therefore reduce the contractor's overdraft limit by £3 million.

Typical revenue and expenditure curves for a medium-sized civil engineering contract overseas are given in Figure 5.2. It will be seen that the interest charges against profit amount to 35 per cent, again assuming an interest rate of 15 per cent. The periods for certification and payment have however been increased to 30 and 60 days respectively.

For plant and equipment contracts it has been traditional within the UK for payments only to be made against the value of materials delivered to site so that the burden of the financing costs during manufacture has fallen entirely on the contractor. Continental practice has however for a long time been to make payments in stages during manufacture and this practice appears to be spreading within the UK.

In the author's view objection can reasonably be taken to the principle of expecting the contractor wholly to finance the work either up to delivery or to the commencement of site erection. First it imposes on many companies a substantial and continuing strain on their cash flow position. This is particularly so when the company is seeking to expand or to take contracts of longer duration. Second, it is against the national interest in that it puts such firms at a disadvantage when competing against continental companies who would normally expect in their domestic market to be paid as much as 30 per cent of the contract price with order. Clearly such companies do not have to include within their overheads for the financing of work in progress; their money is turned over faster, capital employed is reduced, and they can invest more, for example, in development and

Contract Administration

new machinery. These are formidable advantages.

So far as retentions are concerned, the purchaser is obviously sensible to withhold an appropriate percentage of the purchase price until he is satisfied that the plant is working properly and has met its guarantees. Provided that the retention moneys are considered in this way and not as a form of finance for the purchaser then the contractor can have no reasonable objection to them.

To sum up, provided the employer can possibly afford to do so he is likely to get the best bargain if he, rather than the contractor, largely finances the contract. By so doing he will also be acting in the national interest and indirectly therefore in his own, by assisting British companies to compete abroad on level terms.

Contractual safeguards

In order to safeguard the interests of both parties the contract should:

1. Define precisely the events against which payment becomes due.
2. Relate those events to the achievement of some particular objective.
3. State the amount due at each stage or provide a mechanism by which such amount can be determined.
4. Establish a time limit within which payment must be made.
5. Provide the contractor with an effective remedy should the employer default in payment.
6. Provide the employer with means by which he can obtain or recover the value of payments made before completion should the contractor default and be unable to complete.

Definition of events (1 and 2)

Where the contract includes for the issue by the nominated engineer of certificates, then provided the criteria for these have been properly established no problem should arise unless for any reason, other than the contractor's default, the issue of a certificate is delayed. To cover this possibility two provisions are required:

1. The certificate must be issued within a stated time of an application which the contractor was entitled to make.
2. If issue of the certificate is delayed because the event itself is

delayed, that is guarantee tests cannot be held because employer's other work is not ready, then after a suitable time interval the contractor must become entitled to the payment. The same applies in relation to delayed delivery because of non-readiness of the employer to receive the goods.

If, however, entitlement to payment is to be determined solely by reference to an event, for example delivery of the goods f.o.b., together with relevant shipping documents, then it is important if misunderstandings are to be avoided to ensure that the event is clearly described and that it is kept simple.

It is desirable to avoid multiple requirements wherever possible, since it will often be found in practice that one of them takes much longer to comply with than the others.

From the employer's point of view it is inadvisable for payment to be related solely to time, for example six months after placing the order, unless this is qualified by a requirement as to the progress which must also have been achieved. This can be done very simply by providing that the engineer must be satisfied that progress is to programme, or, if not, then he can reduce the amount to be paid.

Alternatively, if the work is being controlled through network analysis, values can be allocated to certain key activities, and the contract can provide that payment of these sums will be made as those activities are completed. Properly planned, the linking together of payment and programme in this way can be most effective.

A problem which can arise on the sums due on commercial operation or take over is that often the contractor has carried out all but a small amount of the work involved but, because there is still some work outstanding, the engineer is unwilling to issue his certificate, so that retention money to the value of very many times the outstanding work continues to be withheld. Provided what has still to be done does not significantly affect the operation of the works, there is no reason why the engineer should not issue the certificate with an appropriate endorsement and release the retention money, apart from whatever he considers appropriate to retain in order to ensure satisfactory completion of the outstanding work. This is specifically provided for in Model Form *A* conditions (clause 34(ii)).

Determination of amount due (3)

Only rarely will the contract state a definite sum to be paid at the various stages of completion; usually it will refer only to percentages, for example:

10 per cent with order.
80 per cent on delivery.
 5 per cent on take over.
 5 per cent on final acceptance.

As with any percentage, it is important that no ambiguity should arise as to the base to which it relates. On supply and erection contracts there are broadly two possibilities:

1. All percentages relate to the contract price as a whole.
2. The percentages due on delivery are calculated on the contract value of the materials delivered (excluding therefore the erection and commissioning element of the price), and those elements are paid for separately as the work is carried out. In that event the 80 per cent payment might be expressed in the contract as 80 per cent of the value of materials delivered to and work executed on site (see, for example, condition 31(ii) of the Model Form *A* conditions).

The contract should also clearly establish the method of payment for variations and price escalation.

Variations

It is suggested that variations should be paid without any down payment and that the down payment is recovered therefore only against the original value of the contract. Retention money however would normally be deducted from the value of the variations executed.

Escalation

If the contract is subject to Contract Price Adjustment then it is essential to establish the data necessary for the calculation of the amount of escalation due on the variation unless for simplicity the

Contracts and Payment Structures

price for the variation can be settled on a fixed price basis. Payment for escalation, it is proposed, should be made with each monthly certificate at 100 per cent of the value properly claimed. There seems no justification for involving escalation payments with either the recovery of any down payment or percentage deductions for retention.

Care however needs to be taken in the contract drafting particularly in respect of the use of the term 'contract price'. If the contract price is defined as 'the sum named in the contract subject to such additions thereto or deductions therefrom as may be made under any provisions of the contract' and the term contract price is then used in the payments clause without qualification it could be argued that both down payment and retention provisions apply to variations and escalation alike. It is preferable to set out separately the payment terms for both these items so that no ambiguity can arise. In fact the ICE and JCT conditions retention is withheld from payments made for escalation and the argument for doing this in relation to the ICE conditions is that the contractual entitlement to any payment for escalation is derived from the payments clause 60(2) and the amounts certified by the engineer under this clause are subject to retention.

Time limit for payment (4 and 5)

No one likes paying bills before they are obliged to do so. The accountants for big companies have been quick to see the money which can be saved by not paying their creditors until the last day for payment (unless a discount for cash has been offered). The short-term investment of daily cash balances can make a useful contribution to company profits. The administrative procedures of large organisations, both public and private, can of themselves impose substantial delays in the money actually being paid. Main contractors, to protect their own position, have developed the habit of only paying subcontractors on 'as and when' terms, that is when they themselves have been paid by the employer.

All this emphasises the need for the contract conditions to lay down a clear time limit within which payment should be made, which is practical in the circumstances of the contract. It is better to lay down a rather longer time initially, which stands a reasonable chance of being kept, than to include the standard 28-day clause knowing that it is unlikely to be honoured and to be faced with the inevitable bickering which follows.

Should payment not be made within the prescribed time, the contractor's normal remedy (which in practice is seldom applied) is to claim interest, or, in an extreme case, to stop work.

Recovery of payments made (6)

Where payments are made in advance of delivery to site the two rights which an employer will usually seek to have included are:
1. A bond to be lodged for not less than the amount of the down payment. The making of the payment and the lodging of the bond should take place at the same time, and the contractor should check that the time limits for doing both are the same. Cases have been known in which the time for lodging the bond ran from acceptance of the contractor's tender, while the time for making the down payment ran from the signature of the formal contract.
2. That where progress payments are made during manufacture:
   (a) Plant to the value of the payment made is identified, becomes the property of the purchaser and is marked as such.
   (b) Such plant remains, however, at the sole risk of the contractor and is insured by him accordingly.

Retention money

Reference has already been made to the principle that retention moneys should be considered by the employer as a contractual safeguard, not as a cheap form of finance. The fixing of the level of retention money should take this into account so that no higher amount is retained than is reasonably necessary. Where the works are completed and taken over in sections these retention moneys should be released on a sectional basis.

The higher cost to the contractor of retention moneys on many plant contracts lies in the 5 or 10 per cent retained during the defects liability period.

It is to the contractor's advantage, therefore, to press strongly for the release of the final retention after take over against, if necessary, a bank guarantee. Nor is it considered that the employer's contractual interests would be harmed by such action.

6
Contract Administration

P. D. V. Marsh

This chapter deals briefly with two aspects of contract administration, namely contract variations and the arbitration of disputes.

VARIATIONS IN PRICE AND TIME

Variations may not unfairly be described as the cancer of contracting. In quantity their cumulative effect can operate to destroy the best of contracts: the habit of ordering them is in itself a disease. What causes this disease? The causes are many but the principal ones may be summarised as follows:

1 Inadequate allowance for thinking time. It is distressing but true that many managements are still not convinced that progress is being made unless holes are being dug on site or plant manufactured.
2 Inadequate specifications. One finds a great reluctance amongst people to be completely specific as to what they require, as to the services which the employer will himself provide or the actual conditions under which the work will be carried out.
3 Insufficient attention paid as to whether what the tenderer is offering is in fact precisely what the purchaser wants to buy. The tendency to say 'That's a matter of detail we can sort out later.'

Contract Administration

    4 Lack of discipline. In the matter of variations it is often far easier to say 'Yes, while we are about it we might as well have that done' than to say firmly 'No, it's not necessary.'
    5 Improvements to avoid obsolescence. With the rapid rate of technical change taking place today any major plant is likely to be out of date in some respects long before it is completed. There is always the temptation to try to avoid this by incorporating improvements in the design.
    6 Genuinely unforeseeable circumstances. It would be idle to pretend that no variation is ever justified. There will be times when conditions do arise when it is essential to vary the works — for instance, the existence of unsuspected drains or cables which have to be diverted.

What is often not fully appreciated is the effect which even quite a simple change of specification can have on a contractor. This may involve him in:

1. Design work which because of the change is now abortive.
2. Additional design work including studying the consequential effect of the variation on a number of drawings.
3. Cancellation of, or modification to, orders already placed on his own works or on outside suppliers.
4. The placing of new orders.
5. Delay and/or rephasing of the manufacturing programme to accommodate the variation.
6. Delay in delivery of material to site due to action under 3 above.
7. Rephasing of site works or concentration of work into a shorter period with consequent additional overtime costs and loss of productivity.
8. Extending the period to the contract.

It follows from the above list that unless the variation is ordered very early in the contract indeed, the assessment of the effect of the variation either in terms of cost or time is not easy. Consider first the question of the assessment of the change in the contract price for a plant due, say, to the deletion from the specification of one item and the substitution of another.

    The listing in Table 6.1 represents the direct financial balance between the item originally included and that now ordered as a

Contract Administration

Additions	Deductions
1 Works or bought-out cost of the new item.	Works or bought-out cost of the item to be replaced.
2 Percentage for overheads and profit related to works or bought-out costs.	Percentage for overheads and profit related to works or bought-out costs.
3 Man-hour costs for installation of new item.	Man-hour costs for installation of the item to be replaced.
4 Percentage overheads and profit related to installation costs.	Percentage overheads and profit related to the installation costs.
5 Charges for additional design work including overheads and profit necessary to incorporate new item.	Charges for any detailed design work which will no longer be required including related overheads and profit.
6 Design, labour, and material costs and related overheads and profit on any consequential modifications or alterations to the remainder of the plant, including study of drawings to determine whether any such are necessary.	
7 Cancellation charges payable to outside supplier or costs of any work actually carried out in contractor's works.	

Figure 6.1 Balancing cost factors of a contract variation
Ignoring possible effects on timescale, the listings compare factors which are taken into account when considering the costs of a variation which requires that one or more items of equipment are to be deleted from the specification and replaced by other items

variation. It takes no account of the factor of time. Taken in isolation this is correct, unless the single variation itself is so major that it does have an immediate effect on the overall programme. It also takes no account of the double administrative cost effect on the contractor of having to go through the same operation twice. The contractor's staff, whose services are recovered for under the estimate as a percentage of prime cost, will have been involved to some extent on the item already in estimating and procurement, but under this listing the contractor would recover for such services only once for the new item. Again, if it is only one item, few contractors would seriously quarrel with this, accepting it as one of the hazards of contracting. The trouble starts when it is not one variation but a series of variations, when the programme is affected, and when the time spent by the contractor's head office staff starts to become totally disproportionate to the value of the contract. Under these circumstances the employer must expect that the contractor will seek to recover additionally for:

1. Abortive time spent by head office staff not otherwise directly charged to the contract.
2. Prolongation of the contract period on site — for example, hire of huts, supervisors' salaries.
3. Loss of productivity and overtime working due to changes in the programme.

It is easy enough to set down the basis on which single variations should be priced in the manner which has been done above. It is often, however, another matter actually to negotiate the alteration in price. The purchaser will be thinking the contractor is trying to take him for a ride, but may additionally be genuinely unappreciative of what trouble and cost his simple instruction has caused. He will also be acutely aware that he cannot get competitive quotations. The contractor may be anxious to recover some of the ground he lost in post-tender negotiations. Neither side is likely to be in the mood for concessions, but the purchaser will probably be in the weaker bargaining position.

Partially for this reason attempts are sometimes made to establish in advance the main tender rates on which variations can be calculated. It is possible to do this for civil engineering or building work or for structural steel or pipework, although the value of doing so seems questionable. This is because in putting forward his rates the contractor must make certain assumptions regarding the quantity and complexity of work which will be involved, the plant required, and so on, and as to whether it will be convenient to do the work in parallel with or as an extension of existing work of the same nature; or whether it will be something quiet separate for which perhaps plant and a gang of men must be specially brought to site. For this reason, and also because it is difficult to take rates for the purpose only of pricing variations into account in deciding on the award of the contract, the tenderers have every incentive to assume the worst conditions and price accordingly.

In general therefore it would seem preferable from the purchaser's point of view, despite the difficulties involved, to negotiate when the occasion arises and on the facts of the particular variation without being tied in advance. The contractor may, however, press, for quite a different reason, for at least the overhead percentages and margins to be fixed and stated in the contract.

It is often assumed that contractors welcome variations in that they can use them to recoup any losses they may have made on the main contract or at least improve their overall rate of recovery on the job. While, as explained above, the contractor may be placed in a favourable negotiating position when it come to settling a price for the variation, it has also been pointed out that the cumulative effect of a number of variations on his main contract programme can be extremely serious and result in disruptions of work, loss of productivity and so on. These losses, while real, may often be difficult for him to quantify or to claim from the employer. In any event he is likely to be involved in protracted claims negotiations which are both time- and cost-consuming in themselves and may well be detrimental to his chances of obtaining further business from the employer concerned.

For this reason some contractors seek to put forward as part of their tender, rates or percentage charges for different classes of work which may be involved in handling variations — for example, design — which are deliberately so high as to be penal. In this way the contractor seeks to utilise the contract as a means of disciplining the employer's engineers.

While obviously such an arrangement can be open to abuse, there does seem considerable merit in any system of pricing which will bring home to those responsible for administering contracts the real cost involved in having frequent changes of mind. Accordingly a system of differential pricing for work as a variation as compared with the same work under the main contract seems justified. If as a result variations become a luxury which can be afforded but rarely, then so much the better. It might also help to avoid the other practice, of including an allowance within the original tender for the 'messing about' which, from past and often bitter experience, the contractor knows that he is likely with certain clients to receive.

A vital factor in the successful control of variations is the timing of price negotiations. Only too often because of the pressure for physical progress with the work and the complexities in assessing the price change, instructions are given to the contractor to make the change, with the alteration in price to be negotiated later.

Ideally the sequence of events should be:

Contract Administration

1 Purchaser decides that a particular variation would be desirable.
2 Contractor is instructed to assess the effect of the proposed variation in terms of:
 (a) Price.
 (b) Time.
 (c) Performance.
3 Contractor submits his proposals under the above three headings.
4 Purchaser decides whether he can afford the variation taking all factors into account.
5 If purchaser decides to proceed with the variation, then he negotiates amendments to price, time for completion and specification.
6 Purchaser issues formal variation order in writing, using a standard serially numbered form.
7 Contractor proceeds with the work.

This seems a long series of steps; the temptation is there to go straight ahead and tell the contractor to start work. Indeed there will be genuine emergencies when it is necessary to do just that and tidy up the paper work afterwards. But in doing so not only is any possible negotiating advantage lost, but also any curb on the enthusiasm of the purchaser's staff to make variations is removed and financial control of the contract is made impossible. Except in the case of a real emergency it should be made difficult to make variations.

However, while it may be possible at the time to assess the direct effect of the individual variation on the contract price and time for completion, it is much more difficult to assess the indirect or consequential effect. This with one variation may be small, but as the number of variation orders grows so do the consequential effects increase, often at a much faster rate.

While therefore, ideally, one should treat each variation order separately and assess finally its effect on the contract price and time before it is issued, there are occasions when it is just not practicable to do this. In order to retain as much control as possible in these circumstances it may be necessary to divide the negotiation of variations into two stages:

1 The assessment of the direct effect of the variation.

2 The assessment of the consequential effect of the variation on the contract price and the overall time of completion.

Stage 1 should be completed for each variation order before it is issued. Stage 2 cannot be completed until the design has been finally frozen. At that point the cumulative effect of the variation orders can be reassessed and any necessary adjustments to the contract price and programme made. Obviously the earlier the design-freeze date, and so the final contract value and programme, can be established the better for both parties. What is vital, however, to do at the time is to record and agree with the contractor the facts on which the stage 2 negotiations will be based. There is no excuse for there not being accurate records of, for example, the time plant was on site and the periods during which it could not fully be utilised.

Not all variations relate to the physical content of the works. The employer may wish either to speed up completion or to slow it down, or possibly to put the contract into suspense. Any such actions are bound to have a serious effect on the contract price.

The simplest case is probably trying to speed up completion. Time may be bought by:

1 Working additional overtime or at weekends.
2 Putting on an additional shift.
3 Offering suppliers or subcontractors a bonus to deliver or finish earlier.

By such methods small improvements can be obtained fairly easily. But above quite a low level the law of diminishing returns starts to operate and it becomes more and more expensive to purchase smaller and smaller improvements. Once a certain level has been passed the productivity value starts to drop rapidly, and on double shifting the productive effort may be 25 per cent or more below normal. Moreover, the longer one tries to continue with excessive overtime or double shifting, the lower the return one obtains for the increased expenditure.

As regards pricing, provided the make-up of the labour charges already included within the contract is known, this presents no real difficulty. For site work the make-up will normally comprise:

1 Basic wage which may in these days bear no relation at all to the

Contract Administration

so-called basic wage agreed nationally between the union and the employer's federation concerned.
2 Bonus often related to productivity.
3 Condition money which may cover such things as working in dirty conditions, wearing rubber boots, etc.
4 Subsistence allowance for men lodging away from home or radius allowance for those living within a certain distance from the site.
5 Travelling time.
6 Allowance for overtime. It is virtually impossible today to obtain site labour without a guarantee of a certain number of hours' overtime a week.
7 National Health Insurance, holidays with pay and common law insurance, all of which bear a direct relationship to wages costs.

To these the contractor will add his charges for supervision, small tools and consumables and other erection on-costs including normally a margin to cover his head-office erection department.

One important point to ensure, when negotiating an addition to cover for extra overtime, is that where such an addition is to be charged on a percentage basis, such percentage is charged only on those costs which are directly proportional to wages, or alternatively that the percentage is adjusted to take account of the non-variable items. Item 4 in the above list, for example, is a flat weekly charge which will not alter.

Slowing down a job is rather more difficult, in that it will involve the contractor being engaged for a longer time on the contract and will therefore tie up his resources for a longer period, so reducing his potential earning capacity over that period. For this reason the contractor may reasonably claim under the following headings:

1 Charges for plant, huts, etc., retained on site for an extended time.
2 Salaries and overheads of supervisory staff so retained.
3 Some additional charge for wages costs due to less productive work.
4 Additional costs for any work which is now to be carried out under different and more arduous conditions, for example excavation to be carried out in the winter instead of the summer.
5 If the contract is on a fixed price basis an addition to cover:

Contract Administration

  (a) any increase likely to be met in the extended period;
  (b) the proportionately more serious effect which increases occurring earlier in the contract period will have, over the allowance made for these when the estimate was prepared. For example, 40 per cent of the contract work may now be carried out after the date when a wages award will take effect, instead of the 25 per cent on which the estimate was based.
6 Additional interest charges due to retention moneys being outstanding for a longer period.

Where the contract is put into suspense, consideration will need to be given by the buyer to following points:

1 Should the contractor's site organisation plant, huts, etc., be removed from the site? Obviously, if all or any part of it remains, the contractor is going to want to be paid for it. On the other hand the costs of taking it away and then re-establishing it may also be heavy. The buyer must weigh up the advantages of each course, taking into account the likely period for the suspension.
2 Work partially completed on site must be properly protected; loose items not yet incorporated or built into the works must be identified, labelled or marked, and properly stored. If the contractor's organisation is being removed from the site then the responsibility for such storage and safe custody will vest in the purchaser.
3 Items in course of manufacture or not yet despatched must be similarly treated. In this case, however, they should remain at the risk of the contractor; this needs making clear explicitly; also the buyer will want to make sure that the contractor has insured the items against all insurable risks.
4 The contractor will seek to ensure that he is not prejudiced by the suspension as regards the time when payments under the contract should be made. Thus if the contract provides for retention money to be released on completion, and completion is delayed as a result of the works being suspended, he will want to be paid the retention moneys relating to work already executed not later than the date by which they would originally have been released. This is reasonable, and certain standard

conditions of contract do make provision for this. It is also reasonable to make payments on account of work partially completed in the contractor's shops but not yet delivered or ready for delivery, provided that it has been identified as the purchaser's property. The buyer will want to make sure that such parts are correctly marked and so on, and that they are covered by all-risks insurance.

5   From the buyer's point of view it also seems reasonable that he should not as a result of the suspension lose the rights he may have in respect of any defects which may occur in the works after they have been finally completed. In other words, payment of retention moneys in respect of the partially completed job must be without prejudice to the defects liability period, which should only start to run after the actual completion of the job. Where, of course, equipment which suffers natural deterioration no matter what care is taken is stored for any period, this must be subject to the contractor's right to inspect and make good the results of any such deterioration at the buyer's expense.

Variations on overseas contracts

Variations, unless they are of a minor nature which can be accommodated within existing resources and the contract programme, are even more troublesome when the contract is being executed several thousand miles from the contractor's home base.

First there is the problem that the design or planning for the variation may have to be referred back to the UK or personnel sent out from the UK specially to site for that purpose which all takes time and costs money.

Second, the contractor's site organisation and facilities will have been geared to the contract as it is known and will lack the flexibility for adjustment which is possible within the UK. A major variation will therefore have that much greater impact on the economic utilisation of existing resources — plant and labour may have to be retained even if there is no immediate use for them — and additional resources of a different character which may be required will take time to have available.

Third, as has been indicated earlier the high cost of retaining supervisory staff on site is that much higher because of the expenses of housing, feeding, etc., so that the labour costs associated with the variation will be substantially increased.

DISPUTES AND ARBITRATION

Technical disputes and law

It is still widely believed that in arbitration the arbitrator is free from the need to follow legal principles and to apply what is sometimes referred to as 'palm-tree' justice, that is to say to decide the case on what he considers to be its merits. In reality this is not so and the arbitrator is bound to comply with the established principles of law, otherwise his award may be subsequently challenged in the courts. One of the advantages of arbitration is where the matter in dispute between the parties is entirely technical and no matter of law is involved, since it is then possible for the arbitrator to be chosen by the parties because of his particular expertise in the area. If the dispute is a matter of law, then it is far preferable to allow for the issues to be adjudicated in the courts at the beginning, since that is where almost certainly they will finish up in the end, after the additional time and costs of arbitration have been incurred. Of course in practice many issues involve both questions of law and technical expertise. For example a question as to whether the testing of the works has been properly carried out may involve both the correct interpretation of the contract as well as the manner in which the tests were conducted.

Arbitration or settlement

The advantages of settling a dispute rather than allowing it to go to arbitration are substantial. Indeed, the very threat of taking proceedings is often sufficient to force a settlement. While proceedings in arbitration are private, which may be a definite advantage for the parties, there is no guarantee that in the end they will be speedier or cost less than taking the issue to court. One thing is certain: the arbitration proceedings will tie up one's own staff to a significant extent in the preparation of evidence, so that they cannot be used for any more productive purpose.

Contract Administration

Then there is the problem of 'discovery of the documents' (as lawyers refer to it) which involves the collections of all files and papers relevant to the case and their disclosure to the other party. Estimating papers, inter-office memoranda, general correspondence, even private diaries will all have to be disclosed if they are relevant. Generally, only documents passing between a party and his lawyer will be privileged. On a major contract the documents to be disclosed could run into many hundreds of pages. The party concerned will, of course, need to scrutinise them himself before 'making discovery' to see what they are going to reveal.

Arbitration is not, then, a process to be embarked upon lightly in the belief that it is a quick and simple way of resolving a dispute.

7
Insurance

R. L. Carter

Associated with all of the types of project dealt with in this book are many risks which may result in substantial losses and liabilities being incurred. Only some of those risks can be handled by insurance. Insurers (i.e. insurance companies and Lloyd's) are reluctant to provide insurance if:

1. The loss-producing events are virtually certain to occur and/or are not fortuitous so far as the insured is concerned.
2. The insurer does not have access to a large number of similar risks.
3. Past loss experience does not provide a reliable guide to the future.
4. There is a possibility that the insured may benefit from the insured event occurring.

So, for example, insurance is not normally available for business risks of a speculative nature which, therefore, must be handled in other ways. For example, foreign exchange futures contracts can be used to hedge against the potential impact of foreign exchange rate fluctuations on the costs and revenues of overseas projects.

The fact that a risk can be insured does not mean, however, that it should be insured. Insurance is only one of the ways in which risks can be handled.

RISK MANAGEMENT AND INSURANCE

If risks are to be managed efficiently, first they must be identified. Only then can the potential loss frequencies and severities be evaluated, which will provide the information on which to base risk handling decisions. Failure to identify a risk may leave the firm exposed to severe, hidden threats to its financial stability. The basic approaches to the management of risks are through physical loss control and financial loss control.

Physical loss control

Physical loss control involves taking measures to reduce the probability of loss-producing events occurring and/or the potential size of losses. Loss control is a specialised field of management, but two points merit mention here. First, most countries have extensive legislation covering such matters as the safety of employees, consumers and members of the public, product safety, pollution or other damage to the environment, etc. Failure to comply with statutory regulations may be a criminal offence, and in any event would strengthen the case of an employee or third party for compensation for any injuries sustained as the result thereof. Secondly, measures to improve safety are often the most cost effective way of handling a risk, particularly when the occurrence of a loss may cause prolonged interruption of work on a project.

Financial loss control

Financial loss control involves taking measures to finance the losses that do occur, so that the cost of losses which could cause severe financial strain are spread over a longer period, thereby smoothing out the profit performance of the firm. The measures may be either *ex ante*, *ex post* or concurrent with the time of the loss. They may also either involve the firm absorbing the loss itself, or transferring the risk to another party.

Risk transfer

Insurance is the most common form of risk transfer. It is simply a contractual arrangement whereby an insurer, in return for the payment of a pre-determined premium, undertakes to meet the cost of any loss which the policyholder may incur due to some specified uncertain event occurring during the period of the insurance. It is a form of *ex ante* risk financing in that usually the premium, or a major part of it, is payable at the inception of the insurance.

The transfer of risks also frequently forms part of the contractual arrangements for major projects. Particularly hazardous jobs may be subcontracted to specialists. Also, responsibilities for injury or damage arising out of the performance of the works may be allocated between the contracting parties through the inclusion in the contract of 'hold harmless' and similar clauses.

Risk retention

Risks not transferred will be retained within the organisation. Losses which are too small to have any significant impact on cash flows and liquidity may be absorbed as part of the current operating costs, but if larger losses are to be retained their costs will need to be spread over a longer time. Provision may be made in advance by setting aside readily realisable assets to create an internal contingency fund to finance future losses: this is often called 'self-insurance', though there is no transfer of risk outside the firm. (Many large industrial, commercial and construction groups have taken 'self-insurance' a stage farther by forming their own 'captive' insurance companies to insure part of their risks.) The alternative method of financing large losses is to try to arrange guaranteed lines of credit to be made available if required, so that the cost of any loss is spread over the future.

Insurance versus risk retention

The choice as to the methods employed for the financing of risks is constrained by statute and contract conditions. Most countries have compulsory insurance legislation which requires persons and corporate bodies that undertake certain activities to effect insurance with an authorised insurer. In Britain, for example, owners of vehicles used on a public highway must effect third party insurance, and employers must insure against their liability for injury to employees.

Some countries have far more extensive compulsory insurance regulations. An obligation to insure certain risks is also a common feature of leases, debenture deeds, construction and other contracts.

Even if there were complete freedom of choice in the handling of risks, the choice between risk transfer and retention would still depend upon various factors, including the firm's corporate objectives, its management style and attitudes to risk, its financial situation, and tax considerations. Consequently it is impossible to say precisely what risks should or should not be insured. However, as a general rule insurance should be effected only for those risks with a low frequency of occurrence and a potential high severity of loss which could cause financial strain. To insure high frequency/low severity risks is to indulge in a 'pound-swapping' exercise in which each year premiums charged will exceed losses recovered because the insurer needs to cover his costs of handling a large number of small claims. Most insurable risks are of a type where losses may vary from low value/high frequencey to high value/low frequency. Then instead of fully insuring, it is usually more economic to insure subject to a deductible amount so that the policyholder pays the first £x of every loss, so excluding small losses from the insurance.

CONTRACTUAL RESPONSIBILITIES

When decisions are being taken regarding insurance, the interests of various people and organisations need to be taken into account, notably:

1. The parties to the contracts associated with the project.
2. The employees of all of those contracting parties.
3. Members of the public.
4. The owners of surrounding land, buildings and plant, including coastal, river, and other water authorities, and so forth.

There may be a large number of organisations and contracts associated with a single project. For example, a harbours board may arrange for consulting engineers to design a new dock, and for the construction to be undertaken by a main contractor, who may place part of the work with subcontractors: then each contractor may place contracts for the purchase of materials, plant, etc. with several

Insurance

suppliers. The legal rights, responsibilities and liabilities of each of the contracting parties for any injury, damage, impairment of the environment or other infringement of property rights, arising out of the performance of the project, including their liabilities to injured employees or members of the public, would be determined according to the terms of their respective contracts and the laws of tort.

As noted above, the contracts may include conditions:

1 Imposing on one of the parties a liability for losses arising out of the performance of the contract, including possibly losses for which he otherwise would have no responsibility.
2 Requiring one party to indemnify the other for any liability the latter may incur towards third parties for bodily injury, damage to property or other losses they may sustain due to the performance of the contract.
3 Requiring one party to insure against such losses for the protection of both.

Such provisions form part of all the standard forms of contract used for construction and engineering projects (e.g. in Britain, the RIBA, JCT, ICE, FAS, ACA, EB/BEAMA, I MECH E/IEE and, for government contracts, the GC/Works/1 (Edition 2) Conditions of Contract). Therefore, one of the first steps for anyone engaged in project management should be to examine the terms of any contracts into which his organisation enters, paying particular attention to the options that may be exercised under, or amendments that may be made to, the standard forms of contract. It is necessary to check:

1 What are the organisation's responsibilities for any losses which may flow from the occurrence of loss producing events arising from the carrying out of the project.
2 Whether any other party is required to effect insurance, and if so whether the insurance arranged is satisfactory in regard to the scope of cover, sums insured, period of insurance, and the financial standing of the insurer(s).

It is normal for insurance policies to contain a condition relieving the insurer of any liability which the policyholder has accepted under the terms of any contract, for which he otherwise would not be responsible. Therefore, when any insurance is being arranged it is essential that the insurer is informed of any liabilities which the policyholder may have accepted, or any rights which he may have waived, under the terms of any contract. Insurers are well aware of the terms of standard industry contracts, and are prepared to provide cover accordingly: when necessary, the insurance can be arranged in the joint names of the parties.

THE BENEFITS OF INSURANCE

A well designed insurance programme provides a number of benefits to all who may be involved in the carrying out of a project.

It will provide a guarantee that if some loss-producing event does occur, funds will be available to meet the resulting losses. Thus a contractor has the assurance that he is protected against any contractual liability he may incur for material loss, damage or injury under the terms of his contract, even if the loss was caused by a sub-contractor, provided the latter had either effected the required insurances or had been included in the contractor's own insurance arrangements. Equally an employer knows that if, say, his property is destroyed, or if he becomes liable to compensate some third party injured during the course of the work, he will not be dependent upon the contractor being in a financial position to indemnify him or to rebuild the damaged property. Also, if during the course of any particular contract a major loss should occur, the cost to a contractor or an employer will not fall wholly on either that contract, or on the profits for the year in which it occurs.

TYPES OF INSURABLE RISK

The risks for which insurance is available fall into six main classes.

1 *Property insurances*, covering loss of or damage to buildings, furniture, plant, machinery, stocks and other property, caused by fire, explosion, riot, storm, flood, theft and other perils.
2 *Transportation insurances*, covering loss of or damage to land vehicles, mobile plant, railway rolling stock, aircraft, ships, other vessels and goods in transit, and liabilities arising from the use of vehicles, aircraft and ships.

3 *Liability insurances*, covering legal liabilities to compensate third parties for bodily injury, damage to property, financial losses, or infringement of property rights, due to accidents occurring in the course of business, including products liability, professional negligence, pollution and employer's liability for injury to employees (or workmen's compensation in some countries).
4 *Pecuniary insurances*, covering credit, embezzlement by employees, suretyship, legal expenses, and miscellaneous financial losses, including losses arising from business interruption.
5 *Personal accident, sickness and medical expenses insurances*
6 *Life annuity and pensions insurances*

Often several classes of insurance are packaged together in one insurance contract; for example travel policies usually cover loss of baggage, personal accident; medical expenses; personal liability; losses due to enforced cancellation of the journey, etc. Insurances may be arranged to cover losses caused by specified perils, or be on an 'all risks' basis covering loss from any cause, other than losses specifically excluded from the insurance.

Although a checklist of the types of insurance available is useful when considering insurance needs, the danger is that by concentrating on the types of risks listed some unusual risk(s) may be overlooked.

LIMITS TO COVER PROVIDED

The amount of insurance provided by most policies normally is limited in amount.

Apart from life and personal accident policies which undertake to pay a stated, guaranteed sum if the insured event occurs, all other classes of insurance are subject to the principle of indemnity, which basically limits the amount recoverable from the insurer to the financial loss incurred by the policyholder at the time of loss. So a liability policy will indemnify the policyholder for damages which he is legally liable to pay to a third party, plus any costs awarded and costs incurred in defending the action with the insurer's consent. Provision frequently is made under property insurances for the principle of indemnity to be amended, so that the insurer accepts liability for the full cost of repairing, replacing or rebuilding damaged property (without making any deduction for wear, tear and depreciation), plus costs of: removing debris; professional fees incurred in the rebuilding or replacement; and additional building costs incurred in complying with planning authority regulations.

Normally the insurer also limits his liability in respect of any one loss or a series of losses in any one period of insurance. In the case of property insurances the insurer's maximum liability for any one loss is limited to the sum(s) insured on the item(s) involved, and in the event of a claim, the sum insured is reduced by the amount paid unless an additional premium is paid to reinstate the full sum insured. Liability policies are made subject to limits of indemnity: the nature of those limits depend on the type of risk insured but may include a limit on the amount payable in respect of all claims arising out of a single loss-producing event plus an aggregate limit on losses occurring in any one year. Business interruption insurances are made subject to both a sum insured and a limit to the period of interruption for which a claim will be paid.

If the amount of cover available in the event of a loss is not to prove inadequate, it is essential that the basis of the cover is fully understood and the limits negotiated are adequate not just at inception but to cover the eventual cost of settling a loss at some future date. Therefore, when fixing sums insured or limits of indemnity, allowance must be made for future inflation. Most property insurances are subject to the so-called condition of average which reduces the amount payable by the insurer if the sum insured is less than the full value of the property at the time of loss. The whole area of the basis of cover, sums insured and limits of indemnity is one on which expert advice is necessary.

INSURANCE FOR PROJECTS

The insurance needs of the various parties involved in any project vary according to both the nature of the project and, as explained above, the terms of the various contracts involved. In every case each party will need such basic insurances as third party insurance for motor vehicles and mobile plant used on a public highway; employers' liability insurance; property insurances for its own

Insurance

property, etc. Also in every case architects, consulting engineers, surveyors and anyone else engaged in design or supervision work will need to ensure that their professional liability insurance is adequate to cover any liability that may arise in connection with the contract in question. Attention will now be focused upon the specific forms of insurance associated with different types of project.

CIVIL ENGINEERING AND OTHER CONSTRUCTION PROJECTS

Specially designed Contractors' All Risks (CAR) insurances are available to cover the contractual responsibilities of contractors and their employers both during the period of construction and any specified maintenance period thereafter, for:

1. Any loss of or damage to the contract works; that is, the permanent works in course of erection, temporary works that may be removed as the work progresses, materials, temporary buildings and their contents, plant, equipment, tools and other property brought on to the site.
2. Where relevant, loss of or damage to the employer's existing property on or adjacent to the construction site caused by accidents arising during the course of the works.
3. Liability for injury to, or damage to the property of third parties and employees, or damage to the environment, etc., arising either from accidents occurring during the course of the works or the maintenance period, or from defective design or construction.

Thus, the insurance covers both property and liability risks.

Dècennale liability

Architects, consulting engineers and contractors working on construction contracts in France, former French colonies, Belgium, Holland, Luxembourg, Switzerland, Egypt, Iraq and other Middle Eastern countries, also need an additional dècennale liability insurance. In those countries designers and builders have a statutory liability extending for a period of ten years after the completion of the

Contract Administration

contract for any damage to the building or injury to third parties arising from any defect in the construction of the building or the ground on which it stands. In Britain the purchasers of newly constructed private houses have for many years had similar protection under the NHBC scheme, and dècennale liability insurance is now available to architects and contractors on a selective basis.

Clause 19(2)(a) of the RIBA and clause 21.2.1 of the JCT forms of contract also provide that the employer may require the contractor to insure in their joint names in respect of —

> any expense, liability, loss, claim, or proceedings which the employer may incur ... by reason of damage to any property ... caused by collapse, subsidence, vibration, weakening or removal of support or lowering of ground water arising out of or in the course of or by reason of the carrying out of the works.

Excluded from such an insurance is any liability for damage:

1. To the contract works.
2. Caused by the negligence, omission or default by the contractor or subcontractors.
3. Attributable to errors or omissions in design.
4. Which can reasonably by foreseen to be inevitable given the nature of the work.
5. Arising from nuclear or war risks.
6. Which is at the risk of the employer under the terms of the contract.

The requirement to insure is invoked where a provisional sum is inserted in the bills of quantities, which must also specify the amount of the indemnity required. Similar clauses appear in other forms of construction contract, including civil engineering contracts.

Arranging the insurance

In every case the insurer(s) must be supplied with all of the material facts (i.e. those facts which could influence the underwriter's decisions) regarding the contract, including the relevant plans and technical data. Insurers retain their own consulting engineers and they normally wish both to carry out a site survey and receive periodical reports as the work progresses. Although it is not the function of insurers to interfere in the way a job is to be performed, they may wish to recommend additional safety measures.

In the case of large projects it is usually advantageous to employ an insurance broker who specialises in CAR insurances. The broker will assemble the information required, arrange for the insurance survey, and after having negotiated terms with the leading underwriter, will then place the insurance with a number of insurers, each of whom will be separately liable for the share it writes.

CAR policies are issued to contractors on an annual basis whereby all contracts undertaken that are below an agreed monetary limit are automatically insured (though care must be taken to ensure that if a contract is subject to any special features details must be supplied to the insurer(s) and their agreement obtained). The alternative is to arrange a separate CAR policy for individual contracts. For very large contracts involving a consortium of contractors, with each contractor having a number of subcontractors, it is usually more satisfactory for the employer to arrange an 'umbrella' policy covering all the parties involved. When only one main contractor is involved, although the employer may still effect an insurance on the contract works, it is usually preferable that the contractor should be responsible for doing so: he can ensure that it fits in with his normal insurance arrangements and that it covers his contractual responsibilities and liabilities.

Property damage

The 'all risks' insurance

This cover may be defined as follows:

> The insurers will indemnify the insured in respect of loss of or damage to any of the property described in the Schedule arising from any cause whatsoever (except as hereinafter provided) occurring during the period of insurance.

The property insured

This will typically be defined as:

1 The works and temporary works erected or executed in performance of the contract and materials for use in connection therewith.
2 Construction plant, tools, equipment, temporary buildings, and any other property;

all belonging to the insured or for which they are responsible and not otherwise insured by or on behalf of the insured, while on or adjacent to the contract or in transit thereto and therefrom anywhere in (the territorial limits). The cover is extended to include:

1 Architects', surveyors' and consulting engineers' fees necessarily incurred in the reinstatement of damaged property and
2 Debris removal and propping-up costs consequent upon an insured loss. No cover is provided for the cost of fees incurred in preparing a claim.

Exclusions

It is not possible to list here in detail the normal exclusions to the property insured and the losses covered, but the main exclusions are:

1 Waterborne or airborne vessels and craft.
2 Motor vehicles other than construction plant.
3 Cash, bank notes, cheques, stamps, deeds, bills of exchange, etc.
4 Property of the employer existing at the commencement of the contract.
5 Damage to the permanent works after they have been taken over by the employer, except as provided for in the policy.
6 Defective material or workmanship, but damage to other property resulting therefrom is covered.
7 Damage to plant caused by breakdown, its self-explosion or derangement, but consequential damage to other parts of the plant or other property is covered.
8 Loss or damage caused by nuclear risks, sonic boom, war, civil war, requisition and nationalisation, and in Eire and Northern Ireland, by riot and malicious damage.
9 Delay or non-completion penalties, and other consequential losses.

Excesses

It is normal for insurers to require the insured to pay at least the first £250 of each and every claim, and some large contractors accept substantially larger excesses.

Period of insurance

This should be the same as the period of construction and maintenance, with provision for it to be extended if the contract is not completed on time.

The sum insured

This should be based on the estimated contract price, plus any professional fees, debris removal and the value of temporary works and buildings, plant, equipment, etc. which are to be insured.

Liability insurance

Insurance against the liability of employers, contractors and subcontractors for injury to third parties or damage to their property may be included as part of a CAR policy or it may be effected separately. A typical policy wording would set out the cover as follows:

> The insurer will indemnify the insured during the period of insurance in respect of all sums which the insured shall become legally liable to pay for:
> 1   Accidental bodily injury to any person
> 2   Accidental damage to property
> arising out of the performance of the contract described in the Schedule.

The insurance extends to include (i) costs and expenses awarded against the insured; and (ii) costs and expenses incurred with the consent of the insurers in resisting a claim. A limit of indemnity is applied to the aggregate cost of all claims arising from one occurrence but normally the cover is unlimited over the period of insurance. When product liability is included the cover may be subject to a limit over the period of insurance. It is vital that any limit is sufficiently high to cover all possible claims, bearing in mind the nature of the contract, the site and its surroundings, and the size of awards for personal injury.

Exclusions

The normal main exclusions are:

1. Liability to persons under a contract of service with the insured for injuries or disease arising out of and in the course of their employment.
2. Liability arising from the ownership or use of road vehicles other than construction plant.
3. Liability arising from the ownership or use of locomotives, waterborne vessels, aircraft and steam pressure vessels.
4. Damage to property, land or buildings occasioned by subsidence, collapse, vibration, the removal or weakening of support.
5. Loss of or damage to property belonging to or under the control of the insured.
6. Liability arising out of any contract or agreement, unless the insured would have been liable notwithstanding such contract or agreement.

In view of the nature of construction projects and contract conditions, usually certain of the above exclusions will need to be deleted; e.g. contractual liabilities, damage caused by subsidence, etc., property in the insured's custody or control.

Territorial limits

Care must be taken to ensure that the territorial limits stated in the policy are sufficiently wide to embrace the insured's area of activity. If work is conducted abroad, the policy should cover not only actions brought against the insured in a UK court but also in the courts of the country where the injury or damage occurs, and preferably worldwide.

The insured

The definition of the insured must be sufficiently wide to protect all of the parties needing to be indemnified under the policy according to the contract terms. So an insurance effected by a contractor may need to be extended to indemnify the employer and possibly subcontractors too. The trade or business of each of the insured must be stated in the policy.

JCT Contract clause 21.2.1 insurance

When clause 21.2.1 of the JCT form of contract, or similar clauses in other contracts, are invoked the insurance will need to be specially arranged, either as an extension to the contractor's public liability insurance or as a separate policy. Even if a premium and other terms cannot be agreed with insurers before the contract commences, temporary insurance should be obtained from the start of the works.

The objective of the clause is to protect the employer:

1 Against any liability he may incur for damage to adjoining property.
2 For damage to his own property not forming part of the contract works, including consequential losses (damage to the contract works would be covered under the CAR policy);

which he cannot recover under the indemnity clause of the contract because the damage is not due to any negligence on the part of the contractor or his subcontractors.

The insurance has to be arranged in the joint names of the contractor and employer, though the indemnity applies solely to the employer. As the employer will be indemnified either under the contractor's public liability policy (if the damage is due to the contractor's negligence) or under the clause 21.2.1 insurance, it is highly desirable that both insurances should be placed with the same insurer(s) to avoid any problems in the event of a dispute as to the cause of the damage.

The cover provided follows the wording of the relevant contract clause, but because it is not limited to accidental damage, the insurance will be subject to the specific exclusion of damage which can reasonably be foreseen to be inevitable. It will not cover damage due to errors or omissions in the designing of the works which would be the responsibility of the designer and fall under his professional indemnity insurance.

Sole responsibility for deciding upon the limit of indemnity under the insurance falls upon the employer.

Policy conditions

There are three conditions common to all policies which it is vital that the insured should observe:

1 Any change in the material facts existing at the date of the policy must be notified immediately to the insurers in writing;
2 all reasonable measures must be taken to prevent accidents and, if an accident does occur, to minimise the loss; and
3 immediate notification must be given to the insurers upon receiving notice of any claim or accident, and all of the provisions regarding claims must be observed, such as passing on writs, summons, etc., supplying information, providing assistance, giving insurers access to the site, and so forth.

Failure to comply with any of the above conditions may result in the insured being unable to recover under the policy for losses incurred. Therefore, the insurance arrangements must be administered efficiently and steps taken to ensure that there is good communication between the site management and the individual responsible for insurance administration. The employer will need to ensure that the required insurances are kept in force and that the conditions are observed.

MANUFACTURING PROJECTS

The insurances needed in connection with the erection and commissioning of a new plant are much the same as for construction projects. The standard forms of contract for the supply and installation of plant and machinery (e.g. the EB/BEAMA and the I MECH E/IEE forms of contract) contain similar clauses to those in construction contracts in respect of (a) the liabilities of contractors and subcontractors for loss or damage to the contract works and for third party injury and damage; and (b) their obligations to insure. Therefore, engineering insurers offer 'all risks' contract works insurances similar in scope to CAR insurances.

The remarks regarding the arranging of construction insurances equally apply to engineering projects. Usually contractors maintain annual 'all risks' and liability policies to cover all contracts undertaken up to a predetermined limit, but for large projects special arrangements may be made by either the contractor(s) or the purchaser.

Transit risks

Engineering projects often involve moving valuable plant and machinery from the manufacturer's premises to the site by road, rail and possibly by sea or air. Therefore, besides the site insurances, cover is also required for transit risks. During transit sensitive plant and machinery may suffer latent damage which may not become apparent until its erection and testing has reached an advanced stage, when it may be difficult to prove that the damage occurred during transit, particularly if the shipper or carrier has been given a clean receipt. Therefore, both the transit and erection insurances ideally should be placed with the same insurer(s), possibly under the same policy.

Engineering all risks insurance

Even if under the terms of the contract the contractor is only responsible for loss or damage to the contract works by specified perils, normally 'all risks' insurance is arranged. It needs to provide for:

1. Loss or damage from the time of unloading on site, during the period of erection and testing, until a taking-over certificate is issued.
2. During the contract maintenance period.

Besides covering the contract works, temporary buildings, construction plant, equipment, etc. can be included in the insurance. The policy exclusions (including excesses) and other conditions are similar to those applicable to CAR policies, but two points are worth noting:

1. The wording of the exclusion of mechanical and electrical breakdown of plant (but not damage resulting therefrom) occurring either during commissioning or during the maintenance period and caused by defective workmanship, materials or design, needs to be studied carefully. In its strictest form it

Contract Administration

could mean that not only are the insurers not responsible for repairing or replacing the defective part itself, but also that they accept no liability for the costs of gaining access to the defective part and reassembling after the rectification of the fault and repair of the damage. Such access costs could be the most expensive part of the work involved. In the case of export contracts there is the possibility too that part of the plant may need to be returned to the manufacturer's works for repair, so that substantial shipping costs may be incurred. It may be possible to reach agreement with the insurers for at least the costs of gaining access for rectification of the fault and repairing the resulting damage to be shared.

2   The insurance provided for the maintenance period needs to be tailored to meet the contractor's liabilities under the terms of the contract. In its narrowest form the insurance will only cover damage to the plant whilst the contractor is on the site to carry out his obligations under the contract. Usually such 'visits risk' insurance is insufficient to cover the contractor's contractual responsibilities and liabilities, and a wider form of insurance is necessary.

The same considerations apply to the fixing of sums insured, and territorial limits for the 'all risks' insurance as for CAR insurances. Likewise purchasers, consulting engineers, contractors and sub-contractors need to make the same sort of arrangements for the insurance of their liabilities to third parties for bodily injury or damage to property which may arise out of the performance of the contract as in the case of construction contracts.

Other aspects of manufacturing projects

When instead of commissioning consultants and contractors to design, supply and erect new plant a firm undertakes the work itself, it will need to make special insurance arrangements. 'All risks' insurance can be purchased to cover both installation of new plant, and major resiting operations of existing plant, during both installation and test running of the plant. In every case, arrangements need to be made to extend existing property insurances to cover new buildings and plant from the time that they are taken over from contractors, and other insurers may need to be informed of the new developments so that business interruption, engineering, employers', public and products liability, etc. policies are extended to cover the new products/operations.

Finally, engineering insurers offer comprehensive inspection and testing services covering the design, erection and commissioning of new plant.

OTHER PROJECTS

It is impossible to deal with all of the other types of project included in this book. It must suffice to say that:

1. Care must be taken to identify all of the risks associated with the project.
2. The firm's insurance arrangements must be reviewed to ensure that they adequately cover any responsibilities and liabilities it has accepted under any contract, not forgetting that existing policies will probably contain an exclusion of any liability accepted under contract unless the insurer's agreement is obtained.
3. Special insurances are available to cover certain types of project.

An example of such a special form of insurance is that available for exhibitors covering both material damage and public liability risks. It might also be desirable to extend the firm's business interruption policy to include cover for loss of profits on anticipated orders if due to the operation of an insured peril the exhibition either cannot take place or is brought to an abrupt end.

DELAYS IN COMPLETING PROJECTS

If the completion of a project is delayed it will delay the date when the new investment will begin to generate revenue to cover fixed costs and eventually provide a profit. It is possible to obtain advance profits insurance to cover such a contingency. However, the market for such cover is limited and it is advisable to discuss the matter with insurers at an early stage.

FURTHER READING

Association of Insurance and Risk Managers in Industry and Commerce, *Company Insurance Handbook*, 2nd edition, Aldershot: Gower, 1984.

R. L. Carter (editor), *Handbook of Insurance*, Brentford: Kluwer, 1973 (updated).

R. L. Carter and G. N. Crockford, *Handbook of Risk Management*, Brentford: Kluwer, 1974 (updated).

S. R. Diacon and R. L. Carter, *Success in Insurance*, London: Murray, 1984.

F. N. Eaglestone, *Insurance for the Construction Industry*, George Godwin, 1980.

8
Project Definition

Dennis Lock

If project management can be summarised as managing resources so as to achieve the three objectives of performance, timely completion and containment of costs within budgets, then project definition is the process of ensuring that these objectives are clearly set out before any work starts. Too often, projects are finished months, even years later than their promised dates, costing millions of pounds more than the original estimates, and with the technical content quite different from that envisaged at the outset. Project fulfilment will always be a risk undertaking, but careful definition will at least remove those risks which are preventable through careful planning and forethought.

THE PROJECT SPECIFICATION

The project specification is (or should be) the document which contains all the elements, technical and commercial, of the project definition. Starting from the first client enquiry to the contractor, and following through all the various technical and sales discussions between the parties involved in the establishment of a contract, a large volume of data is amassed for any project of significant size. This information must be recorded faithfully, its interpretation has to be clear and uniformly appreciated by both client and contractor and, most important of all, this information has to be communicated through the project manager to all participants to ensure that the

Contract Administration

Project site

Availability of utilities (power, water, sewerage, etc.)
Local taxes
Import restrictions
Political restraints on purchasing sources
Statutory or mandatory local regulations relating to labour and environmental controls
Site accessibility by road, rail, air, sea
Site conditions — seismicity tectonics
Climatic conditions (temperature, humidity, precipitation, wind direction and force, sunshine, dust, barometric pressure)
Site plans and survey
Soil investigation and foundation requirements
Local manufacturing facilities
Sources of materials, manpower and construction equipment
Transportation, insurance, etc.
Access restrictions (e.g. low bridges)

Contractual and commercial

How firm are proposals?
Client's priorities (time/money/quality)
Termination points and responsibility
Client's cost expectations/budget available
Client's programme requirements
General contract matters
Scope of work envisaged:
— Full detailed design or basic design only?
— Procurement responsibility — ourselves, client or other?
— Construction responsibility — ourselves, client or managing contractor?
How accurate are existing estimates (ball park, comparative?)
Check below-the-line estimate items with the checklist in the estimating manual
How is project to be financed?
Any restraints on purchasing owing to financing requirements?

Initial design and technical definition

Flowsheets
Layouts
Urgent specifications for long-delivery purchases
Identify other critical jobs
Are further investigations necessary?
Is further information required from the client?
Process parameters
Design parameters
Design standards, drawing sheets, etc.
Engineering standards
Design parameters
Is information from previous similar projects available for retrieval and use?

Figure 8.1 Project definition checklist
This example was developed by a mining engineering company for use in the early stages of a project or potential project

Project Definition

Organisation

Names, addresses, telephone and telex numbers of participants and
    nominated project representatives for correspondence
Communication methods available (telephone, telex, mail, couriers, facsimile,
    etc.)
Work breakdown
Sectional responsibilities for project management, specialist functions,
    procurement, construction
Manpower resources
Organisation chart

Programme

Timescale targets
Are targets realistic?
Have long-delivery items been considered in target dates?
Transport time expected to site
Initial bar chart or network

Control techniques and procedures

Methods and management tools involved
Site capability for handling techniques (e.g. Is computer available?)
Procedures for updating the programme and updating frequency
Methods for expediting and programme control
Methods for cost control
Transportation procedures to be used
Arrangements for project meetings
Arrangements for site visits
Design approvals
Drawing approvals
Purchasing approvals
— enquiry specifications
— bid evaluations and choice of vendors
— authority for placing orders and for committing costs
Purchasing procedures
— arrangements for paying vendors' invoices
— inspection arrangements
Numbering systems to be used on this project — as specified by the client,
    or our usual standards?
Distribution of documents, who gets what and how many copies?
Define all procedures by issuing project standing instructions

Figure 8.1 *(concluded)*

project is carried out in the manner intended by the client and the original sales team.

During the sales negotiations for any major project, and in the formulation of the sales proposal document, it is customary for the contractor to invest a considerable amount of initial engineering design. Often working with the client, the contractor's sales engineers come to understand the client's technical requirements, suggest or recommend one or more particular solutions, and then develop a solution into a fully cost estimated, defined and timed proposal. This process is sometimes termed solution engineering, and it will certainly involve leadership from one or more senior technical people. Whenever possible, it is excellent practice for the contractor to ensure continuity of purpose and understanding by arranging that if the proposal becomes a contract, then the person principally responsible for heading the solution engineering team should transfer to the 'production' side of the organisation and become the project manager.

Some typical contents of a project specification are now described: actual formats of such documents will obviously vary according to company styles and project requirements but all must include functional, financial and timescale sections if the project is to be defined properly.

Functional definition

The most obvious elements of functional definition are the quantitative data expressing performance. These might be the output rate and production tolerances of a machine, together with its capacities, power requirements, foundations, dimensions, control methods, types of fixtures and jigs, and so on. Alternatively, the project might be a construction venture, in which case the functional aspects are expressed in terms of dimensions, layout, architectural style, standards of accommodation, lighting, heating, environmental control, and many other factors. All functional details are expressed by means of schematic or outline drawings, data sheets, and other engineering documents. All this is very obvious, and should not come as a surprise to any reader who has ever worked in an engineering company. Unfortunately, companies quite often get the initial definition wrong, either by error or by omission. One of the worst

Project Definition

phrases with which a contractor can confront his client is 'unforeseen difficulties' when trying to make excuses for failure. Often, the difficulties should have been avoided by giving more thought to the original specification.

The environment into which the project is going to be delivered or constructed is a vital factor to be examined. For a civil or construction project (for example) is the territory subject to earthquakes, subsidence, excessive humidity, high or low temperature extremes, hurricanes, torrential rain, dust, blown sand, destructive pests or other natural hazards? Are there good road, rail, sea and air communications? What materials handling equipment already exists at the site and what must be provided additionally? What are the power supply standards? In addition to the natural conditions, man-made regulations are also important. Governments impose all kinds of statutory conditions concerning health and safety and working regulations, and there are also likely to be local technical standards which differ from those used in the home country of the contractor.

Each project has its own set of rules, and every contractor has his own particular bank of experience from which to cope with these problems. Sensible contractors develop standard checklists which can be used to try and ensure that no important item is forgotten. Figure 8.1 is an example, taken from the mining industry, of a checklist used by engineers during the early stages of a new project. Obviously the application of this example is specific to one industry, but each contractor should be able to establish a checklist which has particular use for his own field of activity.

Establishing the project ground rules can be a time-consuming business. They include some items which have to be sorted out between the client and the contractor after the contract has been signed, but before serious work can really get started. Such things as drawing numbering standards, the types of drawing sheets to be used (the clients', the contractors', or entirely new sheets for a joint venture?) and some technical principles have to be defined. One machine tool specialist developed a standard network diagram to serve the purpose of checklist and control document for carrying out these preliminaries. While these preliminary investigations cost money in terms of engineering manhours, they are more significant in relation to the elapsed time taken up in getting answers to the questions posed. Against all the usually accepted commercial rules, it

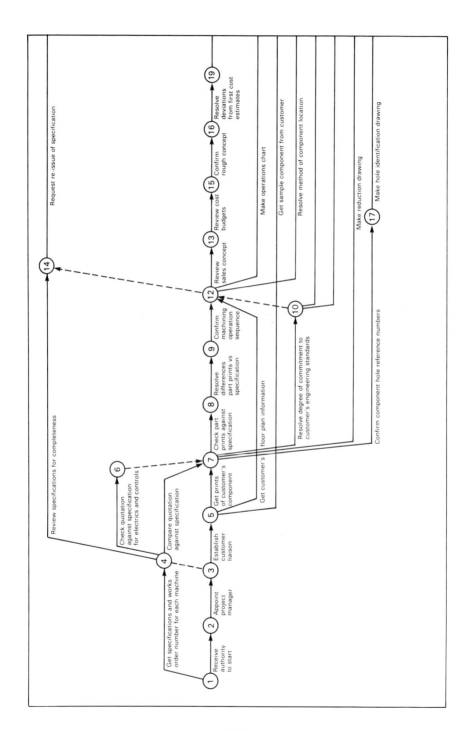

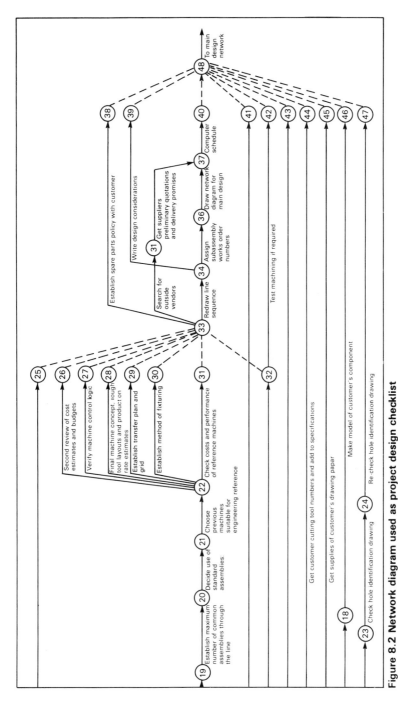

Figure 8.2 Network diagram used as project design checklist

This simple network diagram includes activities likely to prove necessary before a particular specialist contractor can start the main work of design on heavy machine tool projects. In practice the network is edited to remove activities which do not apply to a particular case. Since most of the activities consume time rather than any considerable amount of design manpower, the company sometimes allows these activities to be carried out before a contract is signed with the customer. Although a small cost risk is thereby accepted, the reward is to gain several weeks on the overall programme

157

Contract Administration

may be worth a contractor's while to commit limited resources to these preliminary tasks before an order is received. The risk is relatively small compared to the size of the eventual project, since the work level is right at the front, low end of the familiar 'S' curve or resource build-up, and the reward can be a gain of several weeks or months on the overall timescale. Figure 8.2 shows the standard preliminary network which was indeed put into action before receipt of an order on occasion by a major American machine tool company.

Financial and commercial definition

The financial and commercial aspects of the specification are based upon the cost estimates, expanded into prices, terms of payment, and all other contractual conditions. These factors are described in Chapters 5 and 10.

Timescale and delivery promises

It might be thought (and some textbooks might say) that projects are given delivery date promises on the basis of sophisticated planning using critical path networks and other detailed considerations. Real life can be quite different from this ideal. When the contract is signed there is usually no information upon which to base detailed planning of any sort. The dates promised are far more likely to be based on the contractor's expert judgement. If a company has built a number of hospitals, for example, of different sizes and on sites of varying degrees of difficulty, it should be able to gauge a new sales opportunity by comparison with one or more of its earlier projects, where the overall timescales are recorded in their records. What happens in practice is that projects are sold with the technical and cost/price details calculated with some care, and with the timescale promises made on a 'broad brush' basis. This does not mean that the delivery promises are not valid, and it implies no sense of impropriety or dishonesty. The company is simply using its experience to make a reasoned judgement. The purpose of all the detailed project management and planning and scheduling which must follow is to ensure that the reasonable promises made at the outset are fulfilled in practice.

The detailed network diagrams and other schedules produced later may quite possibly indicate that the initial promises are too optimistic. In such cases the network logic has to be re-examined to change working methods and sequences to make sure that the dates are met. The sequence of timescale definition is, for practical purposes, seen as:

1. Delivery promises made on the basis of reasoned judgement, possibly assisted by the drawing of very simple bar charts.
2. The preparation of detailed schedules, made with the objective of achieving the dates already promised by the sales and higher management team.
3. The revision of detailed schedules, in the event that they predict a project duration which is unacceptable, but certainly not carrying out such revision simply by making impossible reductions in the estimates for activity durations — timescale shortening can only be planned by rearranging the logical working sequence in a practical way.
4. The subsequent updating of schedules as work proceeds in order that they remain valid and workable as actual results and progress are substituted.

Project schedules typically provide some events which stand out from the others as 'milestones' or 'key events' as denoting completion of important phases of the project. Some of these milestones will be related to the various promises made in the original proposals, and as such the original project specification defines the timing of the more important project phases and sets the total framework for the critical path planning.

Publishing the first issue of the project specification

Ideally, when the authorisation is received for a project to proceed there should be a logical and orderly handover from the contractor's sales organisation to the departments responsible for carrying out the work. If the project manager has been involved in the sales engineering activities or, better still, has transferred from the function of leading the sales or solution engineering process, then so much the better. The important objective at this stage is to ensure that all the objectives are set out in the specification so that there is minimum risk of their misinterpretation.

Contract Administration

The specification itself is not something which has been written in a few days at the end of the selling operation. It is, rather, a compilation of documents which have accumulated over a period of discussions and negotiations with the client. As such, it probably has undergone several changes. Central to the specification is a descriptive text, supported by a contents list in which all the relevant documents are catalogued. Ambiguity is removed by giving the specification itself, and each of its constituent documents some form of unique reference number. Further, since the documents have undergone development and change, it is vital that each document number is qualified by the appropriate revision or issue number.

Thus, at the time of project start-up, the original sales specification upon which the sales enquiry was based has become a valid project specification. Since the accurate definition of work to be done depends so much upon having the correct drawing and document numbers and revisions, it is relevant to discuss briefly some aspects of the document numbering systems used.

Numbering systems within the specification

It is assumed that the contractor will use a general document numbering system which is dictated either by his normal practice, or (alternatively) by the demands of the client. The subject of numbering systems is discussed elsewhere in this book, especially with relevance to cost coding and work breakdown packages, but care should be taken to keep the systems as simple as possible, avoiding the need for numbers containing great numbers of digits. Such numbers irritate and confuse those who have to work with them, and they are often designed by systems or computer engineers in the (mistaken) belief that they will afford great benefits of detailed cost analysis and effective control.

Starting with the project number itself, this can form the prefix to all drawing and cost code reference numbers in a well regulated system. One good idea is to start with the last two digits of the year, and then allocate a serial number. Thus, the tenth project started by a contractor in the year 1987 might be numbered 87010. If the project splits nicely into two or more major parts, rather than complicating the numbers by adding subcodes a block of numbers can be used in a series: for example the supply of five special machines, all different, but all comprising one project, could be covered by allocating number 87010 for the main project, with 87011, 87012, 87013, 87014 and 87015 as the subproject numbers for the separate machines. Main assembly codes and, within them, subassembly codes can then be suffixed.

If the main specification is given the number 87010SPEC (for example) the revision number at the time of start-up must also be given in any works order or project procedure authorisation. If (again for example) the specification is issued at revision 4, then its contents list is also at revision 4. Thus the specification issue number should automatically define the issue or revision number of all constituent documents, since all these document serial and revision numbers are listed in the contents list.

It is good practice to highlight the items which have changed in any document at each revision. This will be a familiar practice to engineers working with drawings, where the details of changes are listed in tables on the borders of the drawings, while the relevant revision numbers are used to annotate the actual drawing changes by placing them in triangles adjacent to the altered dimensions or views. This practice can be extended to the specification itself, with the revision numbers entered in the margins alongside the paragraphs which differ from earlier issues. One company uses the simple device of ruling a vertical line in the margin against items which have changed at the first revision, two parallel vertical lines for those affected at the second revision, three parallel lines for the third revision, and so on. The project manager, and anyone else interested, can see where the text changes have taken place and get an accurate picture of how the technical and commercial specification has been developed with the customer.

MODIFICATIONS, VARIATIONS AND OTHER CHANGES

Production of the project specification at start-up is only one stage in project definition. As work is done, so client-generated changes, production difficulties, alternative methods chosen for expediency and essential engineering changes for reasons of safety or performance assurance can all lead to divergence from the details contained in the first active issue of the project specification.

Contract Administration

At any stage in a project, each participant who is working to documented instructions must be clear that he or she has the correct issue of the document. This may or may not be the latest issue (for example, it is possible for more than one batch of components to be in production at the same time which must be built to different issues of the same drawing because some are for prototype use while others are being made for project stocks for use on later assemblies). And so, the concept of the master record index or build schedule has developed. This document, which is an amplification of the original contents list in the project specification, lists all production documents needed by number, description and revision number. Where more than one main assembly or batch of equipment is being produced, and where these are built to different designs owing to changes, then there must be a build schedule or master record index for each situation.

The control of engineering changes and project variations is usually formalised, with a change committee appointed to consider and approve or reject all proposed changes according to their technical merit, inconvenience or risk value towards achieving the project on time, and their effect on overall costs. Changes that are approved must result in new or updated and revised drawings, with new or revised issue numbers. Other changes to documents occur retrospectively, following deviations which are allowed during production or construction activities: it is then said that the drawings are updated to 'as built' condition.

Management and supervision of drawings and engineering documents has to be carried out strictly to ensure that drawings are, in fact, modified when they should be and, also, that the revision numbers are correctly updated and recorded in all the appropriate places. At one time it was possible to enforce this rule by insisting that every original drawing was placed in central files as soon as it was checked and finished. Only prints could then be issued, unless the drawing were needed for modification or redrawing, in which case the drawings clerk or registrar could keep an eye on the modification process to make certain that a revised issue number did appear. Better still, when the modification was the result of a change committee approval, the committee itself could follow progress to ensure that the drawing revisions were carried out according to the approved system.

Project Definition

The control situation became somewhat complicated when 35mm microfilm aperture cards were introduced as the source of prints, with the original drawings kept locked in files. The microfilms, possibly existing in duplicate or triplicate, might be used as masters for obtaining new prints after the original drawings had been modified and re-filmed. This danger was overcome by insisting that only one set of centrally filed aperture cards were used to print drawings for production or construction. When any original drawing was removed for modification, the master microfilm aperture card was taken out also, and used as a loan card in a separate file from which printing was prohibited. Only when the modified drawing was returned, with its new aperture card microfilm, could printing resume, and the old microfilm card would be destroyed or archived according to requirements.

With the advent of computer aided engineering, the situation has become perilous indeed. At one time an original drawing was easily recognised as such, and copies were easily identifiable as prints (even when they were printed on translucent paper or polyester film). Now it is a simple matter to call off prints from the computer plotter, each of which can be on clear film or tracing paper, and each of which becomes an apparent original. Great care is needed to ensure that revision numbers are in fact added as changes are made, and that the original is clearly identifiable as such. In one example, for instance, a drawing was generated of a floor plan for an engineering and drawing office. The same outline was used in the computer to produce 'overlays' which showed in turn the electrical, air conditioning, flooring and furniture arrangements. Because the drawing number appeared on the original plan as part of the outline data, all these drawings bore the same number. Very bad drawing management and extremely confusing for the contractors employed on site.

DEFINING THE PROJECT 'AS-BUILT'

In Figure 8.3 a sequence of stages is depicted which shows that a project cannot be fully defined until it has been finished. Changes to engineering drawings may be necessary right up to the very last stages of commissioning. Vendors' drawings, operating manuals, test certificates and results, spares lists and the specifications against

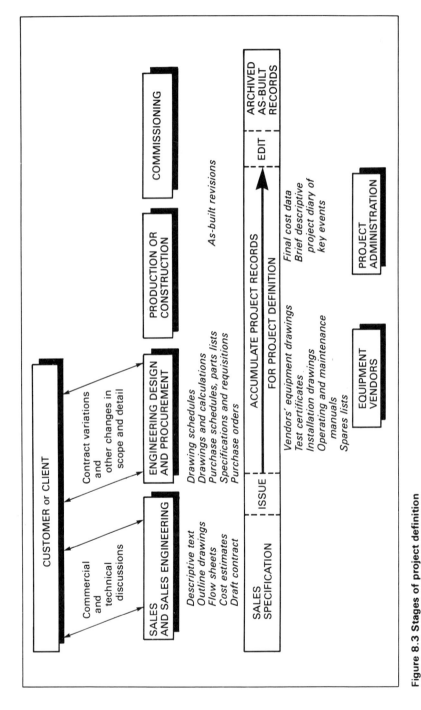

Figure 8.3 Stages of project definition
The sales specification is only the first stage in defining the project. The process of definition is not complete until as-built records are safely archived for future retrieval

Project Definition

which the equipment was purchased all form part of the project records. This information has to be assembled and kept in order that the contractor is able to fulfil later commitments to the client if rectification work is needed, or if the client needs operating advice or later extensions to the project. The contractor is obliged to make sure that he knows and retains in archives all information needed to define the project as-built.

When the project started, final costs were available only in the form of estimates. When the project has been finished, the actual costs should be known. These, if recorded, are valuable data towards the comparative cost estimating of similar projects to be undertaken in the future.

Some companies arrange that a concise 'project diary' is filed with the archives, describing briefly the scope and course of the project, together with any key events and particular problems, difficulties or successes. Coupled with the filing of contractual documents, calculations and other engineering data, such a diary can be invaluable should disputes arise between client and contractor concerning plant operation or safety, or any other contractual matter. When it is borne in mind that the active life of some built projects is sufficiently long for problems to arise several years after initial completion, the need for careful historical definition is very important. Project managers come and go. If a serious defect arises which gives rise to a claim for damages, the contractor organisation will be in a stronger position to mount a fair defence if his records are properly archived in a readily readable and retrievable form.

Part III
ACCOUNTING AND FINANCE

9
Financing the Project*

Michael P. Bull and Keith H. Savage

Project finance has developed over a number of years and the term has acquired several different, and sometimes rather specialised, meanings. For the purpose of this chapter the term 'project finance' will be used in its broadest sense, meaning the arrangement of adequate funds to finance the development and construction of a specific major project.

The particular way in which finance is arranged will depend upon the type of development and will vary from project to project. For example, the scheme needed for an infrastructure project in a developed industrialised country will differ from that required in a lesser developed country and both of these will be different from the type of financing arrangements appropriate to the development of a natural resource such as a mine or an oilfield.

In some projects the sponsors will undertake full responsibility for arranging the financial package, leaving the contractor to produce the technical response to the tender invitation. In others the sponsor will require the contractor to produce a technical proposal supported by a full financial proposal. Whichever approach is adopted, there is a wide variety of financial options available. These might include, for example, capital issues, commercial borrowing, export credits, bi-lateral and multi-lateral aid.

This chapter describes some of the options available and the ways in which a bank can provide professional advice and arrange the necessary financing. Intended as a guide to the types of funding and

*Copyright National Westminster Bank plc.

financial services which are available from banks and other lending institutions, the chapter starts from the point where a project's viability has been established (at least to the borrower's satisfaction) and the decision has been made that the project should be financed from external sources.

SOME PROJECT FINANCING SITUATIONS

Projects in developed countries

There is a long history of arranging finance for projects in the developed countries. Project sponsors are usually well experienced in the traditional methods such as utilising funds raised by taxation, the subscription of equity by private investors, the issue of capital bonds and the arrangement of loans against an acceptable security. However, the enormous increase in development costs in recent years has placed many projects, even in developed nations, outside the scope of the traditional methods and project sponsors and contractors increasingly are required to design alternative financing schemes.

Financial assistance is available, for example, from many governments as part of their internal programmes of industrial and social development, and these can provide a useful source of project funds. Again, many projects, which at one time might have been considered the responsibility of the public sector, are now beyond the resources of that sector and are being considered for privatisation. Whilst this is an important concept it must not be assumed that privatisation will relieve the public sector of all its financial responsibilities towards a project. Many of the projects which might be suggested for privatisation are provided for the public good and as such it is inevitable that they will have continuing environmental, social and infrastructural implications which will remain the concern of governments and for which governments will retain at least partial financial responsibility.

To summarise, therefore, whilst it remains important to understand the conventional methods of financing projects in the developed countries, it is also necessary to examine some of the alternatives that are now available.

Projects in developing countries

Most major projects in developing countries are in the public sector. If finance is required for these projects, the sponsor will usually be the government and the project will also probably be part of a larger scheme contained within, say, a national economic or development plan.

Few projects of this kind can be assessed in conventional balance sheet terms and it will be impossible for lenders, other than the World Bank and similar development agencies, to determine whether a project is viable within the context of the national plan as a whole. The lending institution will often have to content itself with an examination of the social and political situation within the borrowing country and the ability of the economy to generate sufficient foreign earnings to repay the loan. It will also consider the extent of its existing exposure to the borrowing country. If it is satisfied with all these factors it may be prepared to lend against the guarantee of the government of the borrower.

This is not to suggest, however, that project financing in the developing nations fits neatly within specific categories. Some projects may be part self-financing and part government sponsored, whilst others may involve the participation of major corporations, possibly in partnership with a government entity. Furthermore, the project itself may qualify for funds from a wide variety of sources including commercial banks, export credit agencies, development agencies, bi-lateral aid, or indeed any combination of these. Such considerations make it necessary to examine all the available methods of funding so that the sponsor can obtain the best mix of financing facilities; both sponsors and contractors may wish to call upon an experienced international bank to assess the alternatives and recommend the best solution.

Projects for the development of natural resources

Many projects for the development of natural resources are undertaken by major corporations whose financial position is often sufficient to enable them to undertake the projects, backed by the strength of their own balance sheets. However, the cost of some projects is now so large that these same corporations are becoming increasingly unwilling to make disproportionate financial commitments towards one particular project and are seeking other means of arranging the necessary finance.

In order to meet this requirement, the technique of 'limited recourse financing' has been developed so that the financial commitment and the risks associated with a project can be shared between the project sponsor and the lending institution, the lender's recourse for repayment being limited primarily to revenues from the project itself. Projects in the energy, mining and other natural resource industries are particularly suitable for such treatment. Limited recourse financing is discussed in more detail later in this chapter.

THE ROLE OF THE FINANCIAL ADVISER

Project sponsors do not always have the resources to identify and evaluate the variety of financing options that are available. Independent financial advisers may therefore play an important part by identifying those alternatives, in helping to prepare a financial plan and in co-ordinating the implementation of the eventual financing package. Project sponsors will turn to the international banks in seeking this advice and the adviser's task will include the consideration of both non-financial and financial factors.

Non-financial factors

Non-financial factors relate to the interrelationship between the project originator (who will probably also be the paymaster) the executing authority and the project manager. It will be most important to recognise the respective roles of these three entities and to make sure that the arrangements between them are such that there is no delay in the execution of the project because of misunderstanding or poor communications. For example:

The statutory framework

The need to ensure that the project will not be disrupted because of statutory requirement, financial constraints or foreign exchange problems.

The status of the project sponsor

As a borrower, the sponsor's past experience of borrowing, ability to administer debt, legal position, his legal position vis-à-vis state and federal authorities and his method of funding.

The contractual methods

Whether the project will be conducted on a turnkey basis or under the management of the sponsor, the position and responsibility of the main contractor and that of the subcontractor.

Financial factors

On the financial side the adviser's task will be to recommend the way in which the project can be financed in a manner which will be of maximum benefit in terms of total financing cost, economy and ease of execution. The following are some of the factors that the adviser will consider:

Advice on the project's financial structure

The adviser will provide advice on the level of borrowing which the project can support with different equity structures, a recommendation on the optimum mix between different types and sources of funding and advice on the structure of an appropriate security package for offshore loans, export credits and any local currency facilities.

Negotiation with potential lenders

The adviser will assist with the selection of, and approaches to, potential lenders in the international Eurocurrency market, with negotiations of credit terms with export credit agencies, and with the obtaining of possible aid allocations from governments and from such agencies as the World Bank and the Asian Development Bank.

Accounting and Finance

Evaluation of financing proposals submitted in support of contractors' bids

It will be necessary for the project to obtain the best and most flexible terms available from concessionary and commercial sources in terms of interest rates, maturities, repayment schedules and currency options. A bank will apply computer based techniques involving discounted cash flow (or present value) analysis to the various financing proposals, so as to present an evaluation of the alternatives.

Choice of currency

There are superficial attractions to borrowing money in a currency which carries a low interest rate (for example, the yen, Deutsche mark or Swiss franc) but the lower interest costs might be offset by movements in the exchange rate over the borrowing term. This, when it comes to repaying the loans, could mean that the overall cost of borrowing in a low interest currency does not result in cheaper borrowing than in a higher interest currency.

The services of an adviser may be especially relevant to the selection and negotiation of export credits and to negotiations on bi-lateral and multi-lateral aid (see later sections in this chapter). Experience has shown that (notwithstanding the guidelines) a degree of flexibility is exercised by various export credit agencies, and it is often the practice to use bi-lateral aid funds to supplement export credits in order to produce a blended export credit package.

FUNDING METHODS

There are a number of alternative ways in which project finance packages can be assembled and some of the sources of funds which are available and some of the techniques that are used in deploying those funds are described below.

Eurocurrency market

Substantial funds can be raised in the Eurocurrency market either through borrowing from a number of individual banks, or through a syndicated loan from a group of banks. Such loans are available in many of the major currencies (although Eurodollar loans predominate) and are usually arranged at a margin of interest above a floating indicator rate, such as LIBOR (London Interbank offered Rate).

The terms of a Eurocurrency loan can be designed to give a great deal of flexibility. For example, it is possible to incorporate a multi-currency option which gives the borrower the right to switch part or all of the loan in any fully convertible currency (e.g. US dollars, pound sterling or Deutsche marks). Currency and interest rate 'swaps' may be combined with a Eurocurrency loan to provide additional benefits. For example, if a loan has been put in place on a US dollar floating rate basis, it may be possible at a later date to convert the loan into fixed rate debt in another hard currency (say, yen or Swiss francs) through a technique involving interest rate and currency swaps which, when combined with long dated currency exchange risk protection, can achieve savings in interest costs and a hedge against currency exposure. Borrowers of fixed interest export credits are well placed to offer their loans to this market.

If the size of the Eurocurrency loan is such that it will be necessary to syndicate it amongst a number of banks, the choice of a bank to lead the syndication (the lead manager) will be an important matter. It will be the lead manager (in liaison, if appropriate, with the financial adviser) who will be responsible for preparing an Information Memorandum and inviting other banks to participate in the loan. It will also be the lead manager's responsibility subsequently to negotiate a loan agreement acceptable to all parties. It is therefore essential that the bank appointed as lead manager should enjoy the confidence of the banking community.

Export credits

Most industrialised nations have government-supported export credit agencies which provide short and medium term export credit insurance and guarantee schemes which, subject to certain conditions, are readily available to exporters. In addition, subsidised finance on medium and long term credit is generally available to support the export of capital goods and services.

The terms upon which the majority of the industrialised nations

Accounting and Finance

make export credits available are arranged in accordance with agreements made under the auspices of the Organisation for Economic Co-operation and Development (OECD).

These agreements are intended to prevent harmful competition and are known as the 'consensus terms'. Twenty-four nations accept the consensus terms, including the members of the European Economic Community, Japan, USA, Canada, Switzerland and the Scandinavian countries. A few countries which are not members of the OECD (Brazil, for example) have their own credit schemes which operate outside the agreed terms.

Interest rates under the consensus terms are offered at standardised fixed rates and are revised every six months. These rates are dependent upon the economic rating of the country of the borrower and upon the currency of the loan. (The rates which were current at July 1985 are shown in Figure 9.1). Although at a first glance the consensus rates may not appear particularly attractive when viewed in isolation against market rates, there are inherent advantages in opting for this type of financing which are not always available in the more conventional forms of borrowing:

1. Interest fixed at a rate that is probably lower than the prevailing commercial rate.
2. A maturity period that is longer than that normally associated with commercial fixed interest lending.
3. A grace period on repayment covering the construction or supply phase.
4. Progress payments covering the construction phase.

Export credits are normally available for up to 85 per cent of the value of the export portion of the contract. The actual funding is frequently routed through commercial banks and, where there is a shortfall between the export credit element and the contract value, the banks are often willing to lend the shortfall or 'front-end' element, in the form of a commercial Eurocurrency loan.

Export credits are made available as either buyer credits or supplier credits. In the case of supplier credits, the exporter sells on deferred payment terms whilst borrowing from a commercial bank to finance the agreed payment period. The export credit or insurance agency will normally insure the exporter against political risks together with some of the commercial risks relating to the buyer and will provide a

Financing the Project

> Importing countries are divided into three categories, with credits divided between medium- and long-term maturities. The consensus rates set in July 1985 and which apply where normal commercial rate of interest is higher than the consensus rates (i.e. US dollars, sterling etc.) are:
>
> | Maturity | Category 1 (relatively rich) % | Category II (intermediate) % | Category III (relatively poor) % |
> |---|---|---|---|
> | 2 – 5 years | 12.00 | 10.7 | 9.85 |
> | over 5 years | 12.15 | 11.20 | 9.85 |
>
> **Low interest rate currencies (LIRCs)**
> Where a currency's commercial market rates are below the maximum consensus rate of 12.00 per cent, credits denominated in that currency may be given support at an agreed reference rate plus a margin of 0.2 per cent. Although not all of them qualify at present as LIRCs, reference rates have been established for yen, Swiss francs, Deutsche marks, guilders, schillings, Finnmarks, the US dollar, Canadian dollar and sterling. The reference rates are adjusted at least monthly, based mainly on the movements in each country's government bond rates, plus a spread to represent the additional cost of commercial borrowing.

Figure 9.1 OECD Export credit rates as at July 1985

guarantee of repayment to the lending bank. In the case of buyer credits, the loan is made to the overseas buyer and the exporter receives direct payment from the lending bank on the instructions of the buyer. The bank which grants the loan is the beneficiary of the guarantee issued by the export credit or insurance agency.

It is usual for export credit agencies to match terms offered by other agencies in order to ensure that a potential exporter from the country in question is not placed at a competitive disadvantage. It is therefore important that the project sponsor should consider the strategy to be adopted in respect of export credits at the earliest possible stage.

The capital markets

The international bond markets in Europe, the United States and the Far East each offer to borrowers of undoubted strength the advantage of fixed and variable rate funding in a wide range of currencies and maturities. The markets are relatively free from regulation and offer enormous flexibility. Bonds are generally issued for up to 20 years, depending upon the currency, and in amounts per issue of up to US$100 million. International bonds are issued outside the country of residence of the issuer and, whilst the majority of issues have been in US dollars, Swiss francs, Deutsche marks or pounds sterling, more limited markets are available in Canadian dollars, French francs, Australian dollars and European currency units. Bonds offer the borrower enormous flexibility at a cost that can be below that of a conventional syndicated loan.

The advantages of these markets therefore include savings in financing costs, the availability of long-dated maturities and fixed interest rates, flexibility and the fact that the markets attract non-bank investors and thereby widen the funding sources available to the borrower.

Multi-lateral aid

Multi-lateral aid funds are those made available by subscribing countries to such development agencies as the World Bank and the Asian Development Bank. These funds are on-lent, normally on concessionary terms, in support of developmental projects in those countries which are members of the development agencies. The governments of these member countries will maintain contact with the development agencies and will decide a list of priorities for using aid funds. A project which the government considers suitable for development aid support will be submitted to the appropriate agency who will undertake an assessment of the viability and acceptability of the project. If support is agreed the agency will require the project sponsor to act as buyer and to invite tenders on an international competitive basis.

Bi-lateral aid

Bi-lateral aid is provided on a direct country to country basis. The governments of the developed countries operate their own individual bi-lateral aid programmes, the policies and objectives of which differ and which have been developed as a result of discussions between donor and recipient nations. Each donor country has established its own organisation; in West Germany for example, the Kreditanstalt für Wiederaufbau (KfW) and in Japan the Overseas Economic Co-operation Fund (OECF). The United Kingdom's aid programme is

Financing the Project

administered by the Overseas Development Administration (ODA).

The ODA is responsible for allocating funds between recipient countries and, in consultation with those countries, for selecting viable and worthwhile projects. United Kingdom industrial and commercial interests are taken into account and the acceptance of UK goods and services can sometimes be a condition of the provision of aid.

A small portion of United Kingdom bi-lateral aid funds is set aside each year for 'Aid and Trade Provision' (ATP). This is a fund which is available to support British firms tendering for projects in developing countries where Britain does not normally provide aid or where an allocation is already committed. Usually aid allocated under ATP is made available in association with export credits to enable UK exporters to match aid-assisted bids made by foreign competitors; this technique is sometimes known as 'credit-mixte'.

The United Kingdom's bi-lateral aid is also distributed indirectly through the Commonwealth Development Corporation (CDC). This is an investment institution supported by loans from the aid programme and by self-generated funds. The purpose of the CDC is to assist in the economic development of lesser developed countries and, whilst its support is not necessarily tied to British goods, CDC requires that United Kingdom suppliers should be allowed an equal chance of tendering alongside other international contractors.

Leasing, forfaiting and confirming

These are financing techniques which limit the contingent liability on either the buyer or the seller and in some circumstances could usefully be introduced as part of a financing package.

Leasing

Leasing is based upon the concept that profit is generated by the use of an asset and not by its ownership. Under a leasing agreement the goods remain the property of the leasing company (the lessor) to whom the user (the lessee) will pay a rental. The lessor will often be able to make use of local taxation allowances and grants, the benefits of these allowances being reflected in the rental calculation, and it is therefore usually advantageous for a leasing facility to be arranged in the country of the overseas client.

Forfaiting and confirming

Exporters who wish to offer medium term credit in support of their exports but wish to avoid the consequential recourse liability, might consider either forfaiting or confirming. Both methods involve the provision by a bank of fixed interest funding against the purchase of the supplier's bills of exchange. In the case of forfaiting, the financing will be at commercial rates of interest and will require the guarantee of an acceptable bank in the importing country. In the case of confirming, the finance will be at export credit rates and the guarantees will be provided by the export credit agency.

Bonds and guarantees

A bond or guarantee is a document issued on behalf of an exporter to a buyer by a third party, for example a bank, whereby the latter indemnifies the buyer against the failure of the supplier to comply with the obligations of a contract. There are many types of bonds and guarantees of which the following are the most common.

Tender bond

A bond provided by a bank to the buyer providing compensation, usually on demand, in the event that a supplier declines to enter into a contract in conformity with the bid that has been put forward.

Advance payment guarantee

A bond given to the overseas buyer in the amount of the advance payment and which will remain valid until progress on the contract equates to the amount of the advance payment.

Performance bond

A bond provided by a bank or an insurance company to the buyer providing compensation in the event that the contract is not completed or the goods supplied do not perform within the agreed specifications.

LIMITED RECOURSE FINANCE

A project sponsor may wish to limit his obligations to lenders and to restrict the lenders' interest and repayment rights solely to the assets and revenue of the project. This section describes a lending technique known as limited recourse project finance, which goes some way to satisfy this requirement.

The advantages and disadvantages of limited recourse finance

Some of the advantages of limited recourse finance are:
1 Certain projects demand a degree of financial commitment beyond the resources of the asset owner and limited recourse financing is one means of obtaining the level of finance required.
2 Project sponsors may wish to reduce the extent of their financial exposure, either because of the technical nature of the project or of its particular location, or because of the uncertainty of future price levels.
3 The repayment of the financing may be tailored to reflect the actual performance of the project.
4 Constraints on the debt/equity ratios of a sponsor may be overcome by the creation of a credit structure which will give favourable balance sheet treatment to obligations and the associated debt.
5 Any security pledged in support of the financing can be isolated from the borrower's other assets, thereby avoiding the impact of cross default clauses on other borrowings, should the project fail.

Some of the disadvantages of this type of financing are:
1 The interest cost may be higher than for a normal corporate or sovereign financing to reflect the additional risks the lender is asked to accept.
2 Other charges sought by the lender may be higher to reflect the greater complexity of the loan structure.
3 Project revenues may be locked-in to the project during the term of the financing.

Risk sharing

For purposes of explanation, the issues discussed in the following paragraphs relate particularly to petroleum projects. However the principles can be applied to other resource industries, to processing projects and to other types of project that have an identifiable future revenue stream. The risks involved fall into three broad categories:

Technical

The extent to which lenders will accept technical risk will depend upon the sponsor's own technical evaluation of the project and upon a review by an independent consultant.

Such a review would cover:

1 Geological and geophysical features and field delineation;
2 Calculation of proved and probable reserves and estimation of recovery factors;
3 The feasibility of the development programme;
4 The adequacy of the proposed production and transportation facilities and a consideration of any untried technological features.

Economic

Lenders will usually undertake:

1 An appraisal of the capital expenditure budget as proposed by the operator.
2 An assessment of anticipated operating costs.
3 A market study to assist in forecasting future prices.

Political

Political considerations can be divided into fiscal and non-fiscal, both of which may have a direct or indirect impact on cash flow:

1 Fiscal, including taxes, royalties, miscellaneous provisions and allowances, and exchange controls.
2 Non-fiscal, including regulations concerning field developments and production.

Normally, lenders will be able to obtain appropriate consents, undertakings and assurances from government that new or amended regulations will not be introduced which will affect their rights to obtain repayment of the debt.

Historical considerations

The willingness of international banks to assume risks in project financings has increased steadily in line with their familiarity with those risks and their ability to understand and assess them. For example, in the first major North Sea financing, banks were willing to assume (only) the reservoir risk — that is the risk of whether the oil was actually in place, regardless of technical or economic recoverability and that only after completion of the field facilities had taken place. In some more recent North Sea financings, banks have assumed all technical and economic risks on a proportion of the loan from the outset.

The terms of each financing will reflect not only the characteristics of the development itself but also the prevailing economic conditions and the future outlook for the industry as forecast by both lenders and borrowers. The bank invited to create a loan structure will be anxious to meet the defined objectives as expressed by the borrower, but it is vitally important, for successful syndication, to ensure that the structure devised for the project represents the banking market's attitude towards risk sharing.

Completion risk

Many projects, particularly offshore oil fields, have inherent production and development problems. For this reason lenders usually retain recourse to the sponsors until physical completion has taken place as defined by a completion test. Following a completion test, debt service may be a function solely of the revenues generated by the continued operation of the project. The terms of a completion test will always be tailored to meet the characteristics of each project, but in the case of an offshore oilfield, for example, will require evidence of:

1 Completion of the physical facilities in accordance with the development plan.

2 Cumulative production of a specified quantity of crude oil.
3 Average daily production of a specified quantity of crude oil from a given number of wells over a specified period; and (if appropriate)
4 the efficiency of operation of a water and/or gas injection programme.

A completion test for a coal mining project would be similar in nature but would place rather more emphasis on the successful progress of the associated infrastructure development, such as roads, railways and coal distribution facilities. The completion test will usually be undertaken by an independent consultant acting on behalf of the lenders.

Cover ratio

A loan may be designed in such a way that once a completion test has been satisfied, lenders will assume some, or all, of the technical and economic risks of a project. However, in most cases, the amount of the resultant non-recourse loan will be limited by reference to recoverable reserves and future revenues. Customarily the revenue will be expressed in net present value terms and will take account of operating expenses, royalties and taxes. The discount factor used in this calculation will usually be related to the market view on interest rates during the life of the loan. The ratio between this revenue and the amount of the loan is the cover ratio. This ratio will have to be satisfied, for example:

1 At the time of drawdown of the non-recourse loan.
2 At the time of conversion of any part of the loan from recourse to non-recourse.
3 Following any repayment of principal.

The actual cover ratio to be maintained will be negotiated between lender and borrower and will reflect the perceived economic and technical viability of the development. In typical petroleum development financings cover ratios of outstanding loan to future revenues have ranged from 1:1.5 to 1:2.0 over the loan life.

The calculation of the cover ratio will usually be performed either by an independent consultant for the lenders, or by the borrower, but with the lenders having the right to call for an independent audit in the event of disagreement, and to impose their own assumptions in such areas as future market price for the product. Depending on the circumstances, the revenue that will be calculated is that accruing over either the full life of the reserves, or the loan life. In calculating future revenues it will be necessary to estimate:

1. Likely production levels of the remaining proven reserves.
2. Future prices.
3. Government royalties.
4. Operating expenses.
5. Taxation.
6. Any other project costs.

In the case of coal or gas projects (which unlike oil do not have large open markets) the lenders, when evaluating the revenue stream, would wish to be assured that firm sales contracts, probably with a fixed floor price, had been signed with first class purchasers.

Repayment profile

Banks will view the proposed repayment profile as extremely important in assessing the acceptability of project risks. The repayment arrangements on project financings are normally set to balance two requirements:

— the borrower's desire to achieve a reasonably long maturity with perhaps a fairly even repayment schedule and to retain a portion of the revenue; and
— the lenders' wish to avoid undue extension of the loan period, with a consequent increase in the risks being assumed, and to protect themselves against a deterioration in production or some disaster occurring during the life of the loan.

It is therefore likely, that lenders will require a combination of the following repayment provisions:

1. The dedication of a specified percentage of available revenues from the preceding period on each repayment date.
2. A minimum repayment schedule over the life of the loan, with a provision that if repayments at the specified dedication

percentage fail to maintain that schedule, the percentage may be increased up to 100 per cent while the shortfall exists.

3   A requirement that the dedication percentage should also be increased up to 100 per cent in the event that the cover ratios cease to be satisfied. (It is also possible to provide for a reduction in the dedication percentage if the ratios improve significantly — subject to an overall minimum repayment schedule.)

Whatever repayment arrangements are built into the loan agreement, lenders will require that a significant volume of proven reserves remain to be lifted after the expected final maturity of the loan.

Other considerations

Amount of project loan

The amount of a project loan will depend on the requirements of the sponsors and would typically be up to 70–80 per cent of development costs. In each case, the prime consideration will be the magnitude of the future revenue available for debt service.

Abandonment

Lenders have normally been willing to allow sponsors to cease production and abandon the project once production becomes uneconomic, for example once total costs of production in any period have not been covered by the proceeds of sale. In circumstances of abandonment the lenders will normally (of course) have the right to exercise their security.

Interest-rate premium

In order to compensate for the additional risks being assumed by lenders, they will usually seek a premium above the normal margin payable by the sponsors on a straightforward corporate or sovereign credit. The size of the premium will depend on the risks being assumed and the length of the loan.

FURTHER READING AND INFORMATION

Development Forum – Business Edition, twice monthly, from United Nations, CH 1211, Geneva 10, Switzerland (includes *Monthly Operational Summary of World Bank and Inter-American Bank*).

The Courier, bi-monthly from EEC Commission, Rue de la Loi 200, 1049 Brussels, Belgium. (Information about the European Development Fund.)

Britain's Aid Programme and *Overseas Development*. Six editions a year. Obtainable from Information Department, Overseas Development Administration, Eland House, Stag Place, London SW1E 5DH, United Kingdom.

Export Intelligence Service. An information service for UK exporters. Obtainable from British Overseas Trade Board, Lime Grove, Eastcote, Ruislip, Middlesex HA4 8SG, United Kingdom.

ECGD Services, Export Credits Guarantee Department, Aldermanbury House, Aldermanbury, London, EC2 2EL, United Kingdom.

10
Cost Estimating

David Ross

Accurate cost estimates form the bedrock upon which all aspects of project pricing, budgeting and cost control are built. This chapter explains the various categories of cost estimates that the project manager will encounter, outlines the principles for their compilation, and examines some of the procedures associated with computer based techniques. While the examples quoted are taken from projects in the mining and minerals industry, the practices described illustrate how the application of sensible work breakdowns, the use of a logical code of accounts and the employment of checklists all act as practical aids in achieving estimates without avoidable omissions and with the degree of accuracy relevant to their purpose.

THE NATURE OF COST ESTIMATES

Cost estimates prepared by the client or project purchaser (referred to from now on as the owner) are likely to be concerned with the life cycle costs of the project, in order that the overall economic viability can be assessed in advance as part of the project appraisal techniques used to ensure that his projected investment is likely to prove worthwhile.

The owner's cost estimates will be objective, embracing the pre-project, active project and post-project phases. The owner will need to estimate for:

1 Capital costs.
2 Operating and maintenance costs.
3 Plant and equipment replacement costs.
4 Working capital requirements.
5 End-of-life costs.

Capital cost estimates

A potential contractor preparing to tender for a project is likely to be concerned mainly with the initial capital cost estimates for the project rather than the subsequent operating costs. He will need the most accurate estimates possible, given the information available, in order that his senior management can be provided with the best possible figures in which to base their pricing (taking into account all the current market forces and competition).

Capital costs include the acquisition of fixed assets together with the associated costs of bringing the fixed assets to operational level.

Acquisition costs

include supply, packing and transport (including any import duties, port charges and the like) installation and commissioning charges associated with the permanent works.

Associated costs

include engineering design, project management, construction management, contractors' preliminary and general costs, strategic and initial spares, consultancy services, temporary installations which will not form part of the permanent works and charges for energy consumed (air, water, power, gas, etc.). Associated costs also include the following, where these are directly attributable to the capital project:

1 Interest on finance.
2 Fees on dedicated loans.
3 Legal fees.
4 Owner charges and overhead expenses.
5 Land acquisition or rental.
6 Insurances.

Operating cost estimates

Operating costs may include provision for maintenance costs, but will normally exclude the costs of replacing plant. Typically included are operating labour, materials, energy, plant and equipment maintenance costs, engineering services and other service costs which the owner must meet to manage and operate the plant that has resulted from the capital project.

Plant and equipment replacement costs

Replacement costs include all costs needed for the replacement of the fixed assets. These embrace costs for the replacement of worn out assets on a like for like basis together with any enhancements to the fixed assets. Replacement costs include for the supply, transportation installation and commissioning of replacement equipment together with any downtime costs associated with loss of production and/or profits.

Working capital costs

That part of a company's total capital which is tied up in stocks, work in progress and the provision of credit to customers is the working capital. It is equal to the total value of all stocks, customers' debts and cash less the amount owing to suppliers.

End of life costs

End of life costs are all costs associated with the de-commissioning of the fixed assets at the end of the project life less any monies received from the sale of the assets. These costs include: dismantling, disposal, land reclamation together with costs associated with health, safety or environmental considerations.

ESTIMATING QUALITY

A contractor preparing to tender for a project is likely to be concerned mostly with the initial capital cost estimates for the

Cost Estimating

project, rather than with the subsequent operating costs. He will need the most accurate estimates possible, given the information available, in order that his senior management have the best possible basis upon which to set their pricing (taking into account all the current forces of the market and competition).

There may be instances where the owner's and contractor's expectations are in opposition. The owner is concerned with preparing an objective and comprehensive cost estimate which will satisfy the company's financial criteria for investment, such as rate of return, payback and the sensitivity of the project to shifts in capital cost, operating cost, revenue from sales, etc. Alternatively, the contractor will be seeking to satisfy the owner's technical specification whilst simultaneously maximising contribution to profit and overhead at the owner's expense.

While recognising that an owner and a contractor need cost estimates for different reasons, similar principles apply to the compilation procedures in both cases. Where it is necessary to assume a viewpoint in this chapter, then the role of the owner has been used, since this encompasses a broader and more complete view of project costs over all phases.

Such is the complexity and duration of many projects that it will be necessary to repeat cost estimates at various stages in the project life as definition becomes more precise. Efforts will be made to keep financial exposure to a minimum in the early development of the project until scope definition improves to the extent that major decisions having a significant financial impact on the owner can be taken with greater knowledge and confidence. To satisfy this phased approach it is desirable to establish criteria against which cost estimates may be prepared and later independently classified in respect to accuracy. The estimating criteria needed for phased classifications will need to be established to suit the particular business. However, typical technical definition classifications are described below.

Ball park estimates

Viewed from the contractor's standpoint, as opposed to the owner, cost estimates prepared with a paucity of information are sometimes referred to as 'ball park estimates'.

Accounting and Finance

Ball park estimates can best be illustrated as the type of inspired guess which an experienced manager can make with no access to detail drawings, quotations for equipment, or any other data other than his own intuition and broad knowledge of the size of the task confronting him together with an idea of the costs experienced with projects of a similar size and scope in the past. The use of ball park estimates is obviously limited. They have an application in the pre-tender period, and will help the contractor to decide whether or not he has the resources available which would make him want to tender. The financial standing of the potential customer (i.e. his potential ability to meet payment) is one of the factors which the contractor will consider at the pre-tender stage, and knowledge of the ball park extent of total costs will prove useful.

Pre-development cost estimates

Engineering design may be only 5–10 per cent complete. Criteria which satisfy the needs of the cost estimate may include:

1. Pre-development study and report completed and scope developed.
2. First relevant programme prepared, which may be of bar chart form.
3. Main statutory requirements known.
4. Preliminary budget type quotations sought for significant or for unfamiliar equipment items or any unusual construction requirements.

After inclusion of a contingency, the upper accuracy limit could be as high as $+50$ per cent. A typical accuracy rating would be $-20 +40$ per cent. An estimate of this type would be suitable for the first application for funds to advance the project through the next phase.

Feasibility cost estimates

Engineering design may be in the order of 10–15 per cent complete. To prepare a cost estimate the following criteria may need to be satisfied:

1. Feasibility study completed in draft form.
2. Process flowsheet frozen.

3 Engineering plans developed; preliminary plant and building arrangements prepared; utilities requirements defined; layouts and general arrangements completed together with piping and instrument diagrams. All major equipment specified and budget quotations obtained.
4 Preliminary take-offs for bulk materials completed.
5 Significant site, environmental and geotechnical data evaluated.
6 Project and contract strategy established.
7 Preliminary critical path network programme agreed.
8 Capital contributions by or to public authorities, utility companies, etc., established.

After inclusion of a contingency the upper accuracy limit could be as high as $+30$ per cent. A typical accuracy rating would be $-10 +25$ per cent. An estimate of this type would be suitable for application to full project sanction or alternatively would allow:

1 Review of an existing project estimate to establish any significant trends, and to re-run economic evaluation.
2 Identification of long delivery items and facilities for procurement.
3 Approval of further funds for continued project activity.

Definitive cost estimates

Engineering design would be at least 30 per cent complete. To prepare a definitive cost estimate the following criteria would need to be satisfied:

1 Detailed engineering by the main contractor (or others) substantially complete such that procurement can be advanced to an extent where vendors' firm prices and deliveries are known.
2 Contracts critical to programme achievement are awarded and preliminary prices obtained on other contracts.
3 Detailed network programmes developed and agreed.

Where a lump sum bid covering a defined scope has been received, and after detailed evaluation has been judged acceptable, then this would qualify as a definitive cost estimate.

After inclusion of a contingency the upper accuracy boundary should not exceed +15 per cent. An example of an accuracy rating would be −7 +10 per cent.

An estimate of this type would be suitable for full scale review of the project estimate to establish any further significant trends, and to re-run economic evaluations. It also provides an opportunity for the owner to affirm commitment to the total project development.

COST DATA COLLECTION

Current cost data

The quality of cost data available to the estimator will depend upon the degree of project scope definition. However the estimator should have access to a 'cost data bank'. For international contracts involving local costs in unfamiliar territories or countries, it will be necessary to obtain local cost data on a more formalised basis. This may necessitate preparing preliminary bills of quantity and contract scope definitions for issue to local contractors in order to obtain pricing details. Other cost collection methods will include written quotations received from potential suppliers in response to enquiries, order of magnitude costs elicited over the telephone, and so forth.

Cost data bank

A comprehensive and up to date cost data bank, preferably located on a computer database, provides a powerful tool for building cost estimates.

The data bank should clearly separate capital, operating/maintenance, replacement, working capital and end-of-life cost entries. It is desirable that cost data is coded so that rapid access can be achieved. A code of accounts convention will assist in this respect. Cost information will need to include such details as:

1 A precise definition of the cost record.
2 The date ruling for price details.
3 The source of the information, supplier details.
4 Actual/estimated costs, purchase order number, etc.

At the conclusion of a project actual cost information should be

Cost Estimating

recovered and stored in the cost data bank for application to future projects.

When employing historic cost data it is essential that the composition of any bulk material cost rates is clearly defined. For example, a cost rate for imported steel may need to include all or some of the following elements:

1. Price ex works.
2. Packing and transportation to port.
3. Ocean freight costs.
4. Special rates for heavy lifts.
5. Import duties and sales tax.
6. Inland freight costs to site.
7. Handling and storage at site.

Similarly equipment prices of each item will require a precise definition of the contents of each item. When applied to a specific project, historic costs will need to be updated selectively to a ruling base date to ensure uniformity across all the estimates. This must be done before any calculation of escalation/inflation rates applicable to the life of the project.

INTERFACE WITH PLANNING AND COST CONTROL

Cost estimates are compiled with costs relating to a particular point in time or base date. In order to make provision for escalation apparent during the life of the project it will be necessary to spread the base date cost estimate over the programme. This task can be simplified to an extent if the project programme is developed around the code of accounts or work breakdown structure. Reference to a coding structure will also help to ensure that the network is comprehensive in respect to all the items in the cost estimate.

After the decision to proceed with the project, cost control measures will be needed to ensure that the project is completed within its authorised budget. For this reason, it is important to bear in mind the future needs of the cost control function when the estimates are compiled. As with the project planning task, the business of relating cost estimates to elements for cost control is simplified by the use of a logical and well ordered work breakdown into work packages, built around a comprehensive, formal code of accounts. If this is appreciated during the cost estimating process, then this will help to avoid any need for wholesale restructuring of either planning or cost control when the project goes live. Unnecessary work of this nature is wasteful of time, error prone, and not in the best interests of efficient project management.

WORK BREAKDOWN STRUCTURE

The project work breakdown structure breaks the total task down into a logical series of smaller tasks, each of which is chosen for size and scope to fit in with the management structure of the project so that it can be subjected to efficient planning and execution. The policy upon which this breakdown is conducted is sometimes called the project strategy. Work packages, in addition to being related to the control possible from the particular organisation, are also related to the cost control breakdown for the project, whether this is for cost estimating, cost control or for the authorisation of expenditure on particular tasks or purchases. It follows that the work packages must be related logically to the code of accounts applicable to the project.

At the simplest level, a work breakdown structure can be likened to the division of tasks represented by a manufacturing 'goes into' chart (see Figure 10.1). This chart shows how the work breakdown and cost coding structures are related. In the manufacturing environment such correlation can be extremely useful, especially if the manufacturing drawings can also be numbered to correspond with the coding. Firms using these techniques find them essential for standardisation of designs across different projects or works orders, and it is far easier to retrieve information from past projects for use on future work, whether this is design information or cost data. At the level of Figure 10.1, the situation is applicable to the manufacturer supplying equipment to the larger projects with which this chapter is principally concerned.

Work breakdown structures and codes of accounts for large international projects are a little more complex. Figure 10.2 illustrates the concept. Here, the work breakdown is concerned with relevance to authorisations for expenditure. Each authorisation for expenditure will be divided into one or more contracts, as defined in the contract

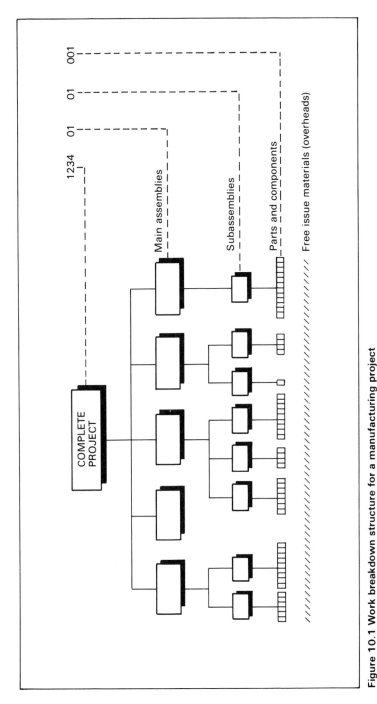

Figure 10.1 Work breakdown structure for a manufacturing project
This hierarchical or 'family tree' breakdown is typical of many manufacturing projects. Sometimes known as 'goes into charts', the version here is very simplified. The complete project might be, for example, a transfer machinery line, built against a works order numbered 1234. Each main assembly is a machine along the line (milling, drilling, etc.) numbered -01 upwards. Then there are the subassemblies (heads, fixtures, transfer sections) which have their own identifying numbers. And so on down to the individual parts and components. The numbering system can be used for cost accounting and estimating, and for the drawing numbering system

197

Accounting and Finance

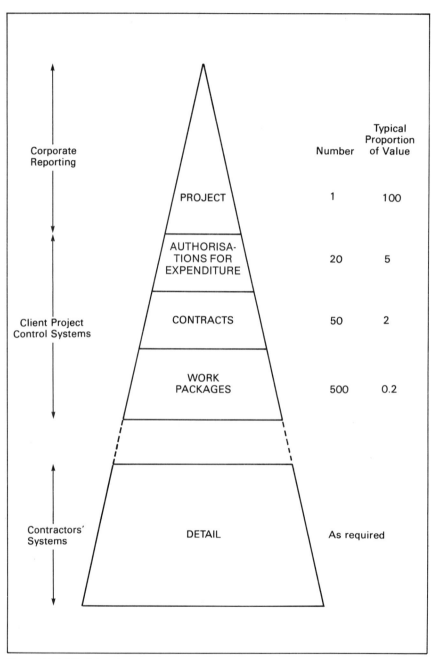

Figure 10.2 Work breakdown structure for a large civil engineering or construction project

Cost Estimating

strategy, allowing the project to be summarised into authorisation for expenditure format to allow control and reporting relevant to financial, partnership and commitment aspects as well as providing breakdown into the contract format commonly used for engineering management control. Each authorisation for expenditure is then split into its constituent work packages.

The work breakdown structure will provide the basis for project reporting. Subdivision of the cost estimate into the work breakdown structure will also assist in estimating the cost of later contracts and authorisations for expenditure which may be a requirement of the owner's approval or sanctioning process.

Code of accounts conventions

In order to compile a project cost estimate it is beneficial to subdivide the project into its constituent work packages. One approach to this problem is to devise a plan unique for the particular project which details how it is to be subdivided.

An alternative approach is to have available a standard code of accounts which provides a more formalised approach to subdividing the project. A typical coding convention is included later. The code of accounts will enable the later needs of cost control, planning, accounts and project reporting to be recognised at an early stage. Application of the coding structure therefore enables the project to be broken down into a number of 'work packages'.

A work package is a logical element chosen to suit the requirements of engineering, planning, contract administration and cost control (for example, individual foundations as part of a civil works contract). Each work package also carries a duration and cost estimate, the detailed content of which varies with the nature of the contract (lump sum, reimbursable, etc.) and the degree of budgetary control to be exercised during its execution.

Application of the coding convention ensures that all work packages are assigned a code number. The actual structure of the coding convention is tailored to suit the needs of the particular company. The development of a comprehensive code of accounts, updated regularly from experience gained on successive projects, enables the coding structure to act also as a checklist. By applying the same discipline to planning and cost control it also encourages a unity of approach to these related functions.

Contract strategy

The contract strategy can be a major influence on the cost estimate. It may be a requirement, for example, that the cost estimate recognises finance sources, high risk contracts, procurement policy and so forth. It will be useful therefore to note some aspects of contract strategy. The strategy would clearly depend upon the particular business but may not include the following subjects:

Management

How will the project be managed? Joint venture, owner as operator or vice versa?

Finance

How will the project be financed? Owner/joint venture sources, bank financed loans?

International policy

For projects of an international nature what will be the procurement policy — local or imported equipment or both?

Project team

Having split the work up into a number of suitable contract packages, does the owner's project team have the capacity to manage one or more main contractors or is it necessary to appoint a managing contractor as its agent?

Control

How closely does the owner's project team wish to exercise control over the work of such contractors?

Definition

How well defined is the scope of work? Poor early definition may result in inefficient working, delay and overspending.

Risk

In general the concept of fairness should operate. However, as with insurance, there is a premium to be paid for passing on risks to a contractor, who may even then not have sufficient substance to bear those risks. Consequently the project team may opt to retain the risk itself.

Compatibility

What other contracts, or other owner company project team investments, will be undertaken concurrently? Industrial relations problems may arise if parallel contracting operations, close enough to interact, are implemented using different forms of contract.

Some or all of these factors may influence the composition of the cost estimate, provisions for contingency, work breakdown structure and so forth.

ESTIMATING METHODS

Estimating instructions

Before embarking on a cost estimate for a particular project estimating instructions should be prepared. These will be issued to departments participating in the compilation of the cost estimate and should include:

1. The project title and case number.
2. Technical scope definition including engineering design, drawings, equipment lists and so forth.
3. Estimate base date.
4. Estimate currency.
5. Estimate exchange rates to be used.

Accounting and Finance

6. Principal unit cost rates (bulk materials) to be employed and their composition.
7. Escalation/inflation rates to be used.
8. Work breakdown structure and code of accounts conventions.
9. Contract strategy (if defined).
10. Project programme.

Formal issue of the estimating instructions, including any later revisions, will help to ensure the consistency of the cost estimate and hence its accuracy and scope.

In their widest context cost estimates may need to embrace total life cycle costs including:

1. Capital costs.
2. Operating and maintenance costs.
3. Replacement costs.
4. Working capital costs.
5. End of life (or de-commissioning) costs.

These estimates should be prepared to a base date with separate provisions for future escalation and currency fluctuations to create 'money of the day' values.

Factoring methods

In those instances where in-house actual cost information is available for a similar project, or alternatively where there is a paucity of scope information, then factoring techniques may be considered for cost estimates completed in the pre-development phase.

Factoring techniques utilise historical project cost information which is escalated to an estimate base date using factors that take account of:

1. Escalation/inflation rates apparent between the historic cost data and the new project base date.
2. Variations in scope between the historic cost and the new project.
3. Variations in location between the historic cost and the new project. Location factors may attempt to recognise technical, economic, environmental, social and political factors.

4 Variations in project/contract strategy and/or operating philosophy between the historic data and the new project.

After factoring the historic costs to a common base date separate allowances will be made for:

1 Items unique to the new project and not available in the historic data.
2 Inflation/escalation over the period from project base date to commissioning including any allowances that are to be made for estimated fluctuations in currency exchange rates.
3 Contingency provisions.

Detailed and factor methods

Alternatively, detailed methods may be used in respect of high cost specialist disciplines. Other less significant costs will then be estimated as a percentage factor of the high cost disciplines with separate allowances for escalation and contingency.

Detailed methods

To satisfy the requirements of feasibility or definitive estimates, detailed estimating methods should be used. This necessitates subdividing the estimate into work packages. Reference to a standard code of accounts may help in defining work packages.

The estimators will need to interpret process flow sheets, general arrangement drawings, detailed drawings (where available), bulk material take-offs and the like. Engineering designs created using computer aided techniques (CAD or CAE) will be suitable for rapid generation and revision of material take-offs. For the major, high cost items of equipment it is usually appropriate that written quotations should be obtained from the potential suppliers.

Computer based systems which can extend quantity and rate data into base source cost and project currency equivalents will permit rapid assembly of the cost estimate. In this context systems that can access a library of bulk material commodity rates are particularly beneficial insofar as rate data are consistent and less prone to error. Commodity rates of this type can be modified at a later date if this proves necessary and the estimate re-generated. Careful consideration will be given to the compilation of these bulk material unit rates.

Accounting and Finance

MONEY OF THE DAY PROVISIONS

After the cost estimates have been prepared according to a single 'base date' it will be necessary to assess the effects of future inflation over the life of the project. This establishes 'money of the day' values, relevant to the dates in the future when the money will actually be spent. In the cases of projects involving several foreign currencies (international projects) it may also be policy to allow for expected fluctuations of all the currencies, measured with respect to the project currency.

Escalation

Escalation rates have to be determined relevant to the inflation expected for each currency involved. It may also be necessary to adopt different escalation rates for different kinds of project work, especially for different disciplines (civil, mechanical, electrical, etc.).

It depends upon the accuracy needed whether or not to attach escalation as a single total value to an estimate, or to apportion it separately to each work package. When the project proceeds to the construction phase it will, in any case, be desirable to show the escalation attributable to each work package, subcontract or authorisation for expenditure document, for cost control purposes.

Escalation provisions should be related to the forecast value of work done (and, therefore, to the value of work remaining). Using the project schedule, escalation amounts are calculated from the project base date for each currency, and according to the value of work done. The results are conveniently grouped into periods (months, quarters, half-years etc.).

Ideally computer aided techniques will be used to identify escalation provisions for each work package. These can later be grouped into purchase orders, contracts and authorisation for expenditures. If computer aids are used it becomes possible to alter the escalation rate assumptions with respect to time. For example, escalation assumptions may state:

> Assume 5 per cent p.a. for UK manufactured components for the period January 1985 to December 1985, then use 7.5 per cent p.a. for the period January 1986 to August 1986 and so forth.

Currency exchange rates (for multi-currency estimates)

For international projects the cost estimate will incorporate a number of different currencies. It is usual to nominate a common currency in which costs can be summarised: this is known as the 'project currency'. All costs should be estimated in the currency of origin or anticipated payment, referred to as the 'source currency'.

By identifying the source currency applicable to each work package it will be possible to subdivide the cost estimate into its constituent currencies. It will then be possible to make provision for anticipated currency fluctuations. Whilst calculations of this type are relatively simple the volume of data can be formidable and computer aided techniques are therefore needed.

Ideally the estimator will forecast the movements in exchange rates over the project life. All fluctuations should be stated with reference to the starting project base date and, relevant to the project currency. For example, if the project currency happened to be US dollars, and a particular item or work package is to be paid for in pounds sterling, then the estimator might define the likely changes over the period from project base date in a simple table:

Table 10.1
Project XYZ Exchange rate forecast ($ per £)

April 1985 (base date)	– December 1985	1.25
January 1986	– August 1986	1.35
September 1986	– March 1987	2.00
April 1987	– August 1988	2.50

and so on ... (all figures here fictitious, for illustration only!)

Obviously such forecasts are subject to a great deal of intuition and luck. Once agreed forecasts have been tabulated, these can be used to adjust the values of work scheduled to be done (or equipment scheduled for purchase) according to the relevant payment periods. In other words, the project cash flow plan can be used for this purpose, and is itself modified as a result.

Using a computer, it is possible to calculate exchange rate fluctuation effects for each work package, similar to the approach adopted for escalation allowances. Manual techniques preclude this level of detail, and the estimator will be content with working out currency fluctuation effects on the basis of total expenditure amounts for each currency.

After using a computer to calculate currency and escalation allowances, each work package value will include the basic cost, the escalation allowance, and the anticipated effects of currency changes, all relevant to the point in time when the expenditure for that package is to be paid for — the money of the day value for the particular work package.

CONTINGENCIES

There are wide ranging and differing concepts about contingency. A traditional view is that contingency is an allowance made to cover unforeseen errors and omissions. Other concepts will attempt to quantify risks associated with the project and the accuracy of the estimates: for example stating that by the addition of a quantifiable 'allowance' to the cost estimates there is a 50 per cent chance that the estimated costs will prove sufficient to complete the project. By adding further allowances in the form of 'comfort money' the probability of completing the project within the revised, higher, cost estimate is further increased (to 80 per cent, for example). The amount of comfort money to be added is obviously a matter of judgement — in fact a management decision. In all cases where such additions are made, clear definition of the terminology is a prerequisite.

Returning to the traditional approach, contingency allowances can be defined as:

> Financial provisions intended to cover items of work which will have to be performed or elements of cost which will be incurred, and which are considered to be within the scope of the project covered by the estimate, but are not specifically defined or foreseen at the time the estimate is compiled.

The actual provisions that are included in the estimate require a blend of experience, historical data and knowledge of the current commercial conditions applied to a technical understanding of the project.

Cost Estimating

In order to avoid confusion in the later requirements of cost control after project go-ahead it is necessary to define three further components of contingency. These are:

1 Estimate contingency.
2 Budget contingency.
3 Forecast contingency.

Estimate contingency

These provisions specifically exclude any change in scope to the project that would later be the subject of a project variation. In so far as contingency provisions are intended for those items that are unforeseen, or not specifically defined, then the provisions may be retained as a single lump sum. However if the rationale of determining contingency provisions allows for calculations on either a discipline or commodity basis, then the contingency total will be apportioned in like manner. The estimate contingency sum included in the cost estimate prior to project approval is not related to its usage or allocation after sanction during the execution of the project.

Budget and forecast contingency

These terms are associated with cost control as opposed to estimating. Budget contingency is the sum, usually the same in value as estimate contingency, included in the control budget after project go-ahead. It is allocated by the project manager for whatever purpose is deemed appropriate. Forecast contingency is quite separate from budget contingency insofar as it is concerned with provisions against future costs not yet committed to the project.

CASH FLOW

Cash flow statements can be interpreted and presented in a variety of ways. The concepts are, however, simple. On the one hand are the cash outflows, which is the expenditure of money needed to fulfil all aspects of the project. The cash outflow statement has to be phased to agree with the timing of payments, so that the organisation providing the project funding can be given a forecast not only of how much has

COST ITEM	COST CODE	1986				1987				1988				TOTAL BUDGETS
		1	2	3	4	1	2	3	4	1	2	3	4	
ENGINEERING	A													
Design	A105	10	20	50	100	100	80	60	20	5				445
Support	A110			2	2	5	5	4	4	4	3	2		31
Commissioning	A200										2	2	1	6
Project management	A500	4	5	7	8	8	8	8	8	6	4	2		68
EQUIPMENT PURCHASES	B													
Main plant	B110				400		500	400	1100	400	200	10		3010
Furnaces	B150							200	250					450
Ventilation	B175						20		20		20			60
Electrical	B200					5	20	25	60	40	10	2		162
Piping and valves	B300				10	5	5	10	15	20	5			70
Steel	B400				80	100	100	100	30					410
Cranes	B500			50					100	100	50			300
Other	B900	2	1	4	1		5	25		2	4	2		48
CONSTRUCTION	C													
Plant hire	C100			1	2	10	10	8	6	4	2			43
Roads	C150			4	6	10	20	15	10	2				67
External lighting	C200				2	2	4	1	1	1				11
Main building Labour	C300				10	30	100	150	200	400	200	50	5	1145
Materials	C325			12	20	20	80	100	50	20	30	2	1	335
Stores building Labour	C400				5		15	15	15	20	10	2	2	94
Materials	C425				2	5	15	15	5	10	2	1		55
Racking	C450								5					10
Fork trucks	C460											120		120
	C470													
CONTINGENCY SUMS					20	10	5	20	50	20	10	5	1	142
ESCALATION PROVISION						16	50	58	97	106	56	20	1	404
QUARTERLY TOTALS		16	26	131	668	331	1042	1214	2042	1161	618	220	11	7486

XYZ PROJECTS LIMITED
Cash flow schedule for FERTILISER PLANT
Client BEANZ-TALK INC.
Project No. 1005-85
Issue date DEC. 1985
QUARTERLY PERIODS — ALL FIGURES ARE DOLLARS × 1000

Figure 10.3 Example of a project cash outflow forecast
This is an illustration of the format which a manually prepared capital cost outflow might take. Obviously the level of detail included in a real project would be greater, and would therefore be tedious to revise with every change in project scope. Computerised techniques can speed up the process

Cost Estimating

to be paid, but when. A cash outflow statement cannot be prepared without the benefit of detailed cost estimates and a project programme.

Cash inflow statements are more relevant to the operating phase of the project, when the plant has been constructed and is earning money for the owner. A full cash flow statement balances these inflows against outflows to arrive at net figures for each period considered, and the results can either be inflows (profit) or outflows (loss).

In calculating a project cash (out)flow statement, the project manager must ensure that all costs are taken into account, suitably augmented for escalation and currency fluctuations to arrive at 'money of the day' values. These are related to the forecast values of work done, as derived from the project programme. Material and equipment costs, for example, are timed to fall into the periods when their invoices are expected to fall due for payment. Likewise, equipment being purchased against contracts which allow progress payments will result in each progress payment estimate being scheduled in the appropriate cash flow period. The person making the cash flow table uses his judgement to allow for the normal delays which occur in commerce in the payment of invoices, so that an invoice for £100 000 payable for goods scheduled for delivery in March 1986 might be shown as a cash outflow of £100 000 in April 1986 where the contract terms are 30 days. These delays in payments, sometimes called the payments pipeline, can be of considerable durations on major international contracts.

The scope of the cash flow statement needs to be defined. Is it, for example, intended to cover capital costs only, or is it to be a full inflow/outflow statement including operating costs, revenue from sales, tax, and so on?

An example of a cash flow statement is given in Figure 10.3. This is limited to the capital cost outflow.

ESTIMATING WITH AND WITHOUT A COMPUTER

Estimating systems may be either manual or computer aided. Within the computer aided category systems can be made available on micro, mini or mainframe computer installations. Systems will benefit by utilising a coding structure such as a code of account convention and work breakdown structure.

ESTIMATE OF CAPITAL COST			Estimate No.
Company Project No. Plant Plant Section	All values are in • Curr = Currency in which value is to be paid Exchange Rates Estimate Base Date	Estimate Identifier Sheet of sheets Estimator (s) Approved by	Rev. 0 1 2 3 4 5

Description	Discipline / Detail	Detail Extension	Classification	Quantity	Unit	Supply				Freight			I.D.S.T			Sub-contract			Total cost
						Unit Rate	Cost Fob/For	• Curr	Gross/Ocean Tonnes	Rate	Cost	• Curr	Rate	Cost	• Curr	Rate	Cost	• Curr	
Sheet Totals																			

Figure 10.4 Estimating form for capital equipment
This is an example of a form suitable for listing and estimating major items of equipment to be purchased for a project

MANAGEMENT INFORMATION SYSTEM

ESTIMATE OF MANHOURS

DEPARTMENT DETAILS

WORK FUNCTION (See note 1)	DESCRIPTION	UNIT	HOURS EACH	No OFF	MANHOURS BY GRADE 11	21	22	31	41	51	52	61	TOTAL HOURS	% METHOD (See note 2)	LINE NO
	DRAUGHTING THIS SECTION TO BE COMPLETED BY ENGINEERING DEPARTMENTS ONLY (See note 3)														
1 1	Flowsheets Single line diagrams	Dwgs			–	–	–					–			1
1 2	Studies Schematic diagrams Panel layouts	Dwgs			–	–	–					–			2
1 3	General arrangement & layouts Piping arrangements Power layouts – Ints. plot plans	Dwgs			–	–	–					–			3
1 4	Details Isometrics – Hook ups Lighting & small power	Dwgs			–	–	–					–			4
1 5	Reinforcement schedules Supports – Ints. indexes Cable & termination schedules	Dwgs			–	–	–					–			5
1 6	Architectural	Dwgs			–	–	–					–			6
1 7	Other SEL drawings	Dwgs			–	–	–					–			7
					–	–	–	–	–	–	–	–			8
1 9	Other drawing office work (See note 4) including supervision				–	–						–		*	9
	ENGINEERING THIS SECTION TO BE COMPLETED BY ENGINEERING DEPARTMENTS ONLY (Depts. 41 – 46 Inc.)														
2 9	Engineering supervision & dept. supervision (See note 5)									–	–	–		*	10
	GENERAL THIS SECTION TO BE COMPLETED BY ALL NON-ENGINEERING DEPARTMENTS														
9 9 9	Totally unclassified & default for reconciliations only													*	11
	GRAND TOTAL BY GRADE														12
	GRADE TOTAL AS % OF GRAND TOTAL														

Notes

PROJECT			PROJECT No.
Senior Engineer	Chief Engineer Department manager		PLANT
			DEPARTMENT
Date			EST/CV REV SHT OF

Figure 10.5 Estimating form for engineering manhours
This form allows clerical collation of estimated manhours for the engineering and draughting of a project. The forms are assembled in batches, one for each discipline (civils, structural, mechanical, piping, electrical, process control, general office). The total engineering estimate is assembled on another of these forms, used as a summary sheet

Manual systems

Manual systems are enhanced by the use of standard forms together with an accompanying definitive procedure. An example form is illustrated in Figure 10.4. An obvious drawback with manual systems

Accounting and Finance

is that change is difficult to accommodate. Last minute adjustments to exchange rate assumptions, alterations in scope, re-compilation of bulk material cost rates and the like cannot be easily accommodated.

However, circumstances may be such that access to a computer system is not possible, or alternatively the estimate is not voluminous and may be completed more rapidly manually. Careful attention should be made to the design of forms supporting a manual system. Another example, relating to the estimation of design hours, is shown in Figure 10.5.

Computer based systems

The choice of a system will depend on the type of computer installation favoured by the company. Where a central company estimating department exists a mainframe computer may be ideal. Alternatively, a micro system will allow independent operation, minimising the risk of complete system breakdowns. Microcomputers also have the advantage of being suitable for use in remote sites, or as portable systems.

Where large cost estimates are being prepared and it is desirable to link the data with other systems, such as cost databanks, network schedule data, cost control activities and so on, then minicomputers or mainframe systems may be preferred.

The actual design features of an estimating system must obviously depend on the nature of the business. Aspects to be considered are:

1. Estimates derived by factoring historical costs held in a databank.
2. Estimates built up in detail for individual work packages.
3. Combinations of both of these.

Features to be included in the estimating system could also include:

4. Definition of the project base date.
5. Various foreign currencies and their conversion to the common currency used throughout the project, using the relevant exchange rates.
6. A library of cost rates for bulk materials.
7. A library of the code of accounts and work breakdown structure codes.

Cost Estimating

8 Extension of quantities, appropriate units and cost rates to obtain cost estimates.
9 Automatic allocation of basic cost estimates to the values appropriate at the times of the relevant work packages.
10 Automatic calculation to factor-in the level of escalation as required, and provisions for handling fluctuations in the exchange rates used for overseas currencies.
11 Generation of money-of-the-day cost estimate tables, either detailed or in summary form, or distributed for the project duration.
12 Selecting factoring of estimates.
13 Reworking estimates to different basedates and timescales.

11
Cost Control

David Ross

Effective control of project costs is an obvious requirement within the total project management function. It is important to the buyer, and to the contractor. The emphasis of cost risk between buyer and contractor must depend on the type of contract (e.g. fixed price, cost-plus, etc.) but, whatever the contract type, it is in the best interests of all concerned that costs are contained within pre-planned (i.e. budgeted) and authorised limits. Even with a fixed price arrangement the buyer is faced with risk when excessive costs arise, since the contractor (at best) may be inclined to cut corners and try to skimp, while (at worst) the contractor's financial viability could be brought into question as a result of the substantial losses that he must incur. This chapter examines some aspects of cost collection and control, including the viewpoints of the project buyer (i.e. the eventual owner) and the contractor.

OVERALL CONTROL OF PROJECT COSTS

Within the owner company it will be important to establish authority levels at which financial commitments can be made. The nature of these authority levels will depend on the size of the owner company and the nature of its organisation but they will typically be based upon some sort of hierarchical structure. Thus, there will be levels of authority set which can:

1. Sanction the use of funds.
2. Approve authorisations for expenditure (AFEs) for specific items or work packages.
3. Authorise contract conditions.
4. Specify individual levels of authority (usually according to rank or status).

Authority to sanction funds

As an example of a hierarchically-based structure of authorising levels, a large owner organisation might assign the following limits of authority on its management:

1. Chief executive of subsidiary company. Principally responsible for buying the project — up to £2 million.
2. Group managing director — up to £5 million.
3. Main board of subsidiary — up to £15 million.
4. Main group board — over £15 million.

Authorisations for expenditure

After the sanctioning of funds by the appropriate authority, it may be necessary to establish a formal system of authorisations for expenditure (known as AFEs for short). Obviously the total sum approved for expenditure through AFEs must never be allowed to exceed the amount of funds sanctioned. Thus, it is necessary to arrange that every significant contract or purchase order commitment is subject to AFE approval in advance of the actual commitment being made.

Contract committee authority

Assuming that a committee exists for the consideration and approval of contracts, this committee's involvement would only be invoked for purchase order commitments or for new third party contracts which exceeded some predetermined financial commitment level. Such a committee's duties might also include the approval (or rejection) of overall strategies for contracts. Contract committee approvals are primarily concerned with technical and commercial aspects, and could include:

1. Approval of project contract strategy.
2. Approval of lists of bidders.
3. Approval to award a contract or purchase order.

Individual authority levels

After each AFE has been approved, there will be individual levels of authority, at which various members of management are able (within the constraints of overall funds sanctioned, AFE levels, and the dictates of the contract committee) to commit expenditure. A large multinational company might, for example, subdivide individual authority levels on the basis of:

1. Approval of indents and purchase orders.
2. Authority to place orders and contracts with third parties.
3. Authority to approve payments to third parties.
4. Authority to approve expenses, travel requisitions and the like.

Within each of these categories various levels could apply, for example:

1. General manager — unlimited within authorised funding.
2. Divisional manager — up to £1 million.
3. Departmental manager — up to £500 000.
4. Project manager — up to £200 000.
5. Resident engineer — up to £20 000.

and so on down the line.

A small contracting company might take the view that their project manager has absolute authority to commit company funds. In any event, the recognition and definition of individual and collective levels of authority is an important criterion before funds are committed on a project. Although at first glance a formal authority level structure might appear to be cumbersome and time consuming, it is an essential feature of project cost control for the larger business because it ensures that every aspect of the project is considered before expenditure is committed and not after (when it would be too late to exercise any control). Summing up, such consideration within the sanctioning process would consider essentials such as project finances, risk factors, relevance to company (rather than project) strategy, and so forth. The procedures are also supportive to the project manager in those cases where his assessment of a particular situation is endorsed through a consensus process involving a group.

CONTRACT STRATEGY IN RELATION TO PROJECT CONTROL

After recognition of the overall requirements, another key aspect of project control is the development of the project contract strategy. The contract strategy seeks to define the number, scope and types of contracts that should be used. These considerations are important to the owner, and to the contractor responding to an invitation to bid. The arguments also apply to contracts for work to be done by other (third) parties. Some of the major factors to be taken into account are:

1. *Management* — does the owner have sufficient management resources or expertise to undertake the project, or will it be necessary to appoint a managing contractor?
2. *Control* — how closely does the owner wish to exercise control over the contractor?
3. *Definition* — how well is the scope of work defined?
4. *Risk* — how is risk to be apportioned between the owner and the contractor?
5. *Motivation* — how best can the contractor, and subcontractors be motivated by contract terms to work for the benefit of the project team?

These factors can be summarised and explained in outline by the comparative table in Figure 11.1. The owner will need to exert maximum control over the contractor for cost-plus contracts, and least control for fixed price or turnkey projects.

THE CONTROL BUDGET

It must be assumed that, for the basis of sound project control, a

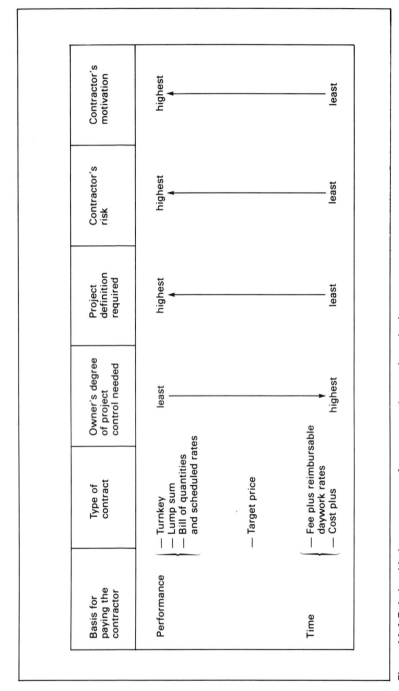

Figure 11.1 Relationship between type of contract and control emphasis
Choice of the type of contract greatly affects the way in which project control and risk will be apportioned between the contractor and the owner of the project

logical work breakdown structure and code of accounts exists, and that the project cost estimates are properly tabulated and assigned into the relevant parts of this structure. The number of work packages will obviously depend upon the size of the project and the accuracy to which it has been defined. As the project definition becomes refined, work packages can be grouped into contracts and contracts can be assigned to specific authorisations for expenditure (AFEs).

Work packages provide the basis for grouping costs which are budgeted, committed, actually spent and estimated (or actually recorded) at the final level of expenditure. Cost summaries can be made at the levels of individual contracts, and at the levels covered by each AFE. Where work packages are derived from a logical code of accounts, it should be possible also to prepare cost summaries according to the specialist disciplines working on the project, or by any other subdivision suggested by the accounts coding structure as required by the project management.

Money-of-the-day provisions

The control budget must be expressed in money-of-the-day terms. This means that it has to include provisions for escalation and, where different currencies are involved in international projects, allowances for fluctuations in exchange rates. Since like must always be compared with like, it will be necessary to include similar allowances when considering or reporting committed costs, cost estimates to complete work and estimated final costs.

When (inevitably) changes are made to the project scope, these will need to be properly evaluated and authorised through a formal change (or variation) order procedure, with the resulting changes in money-of-the-day costs added to the control budget after approval.

Contingency provisions

A contingency sum should be included in the control budget. This is intended to cover work or expenditure which would be considered to lie within the scope of the project covered by the estimate, but where such work or expenditure cannot be defined or even foreseen at the time the budget is compiled.

Contingency sums can be set aside in a separate part of the budget,

Accounting and Finance

to be allocated to relevant AFE areas by the project manager as the project proceeds and the actual contingencies arise. This allocation has to be carried out on a debit/balancing credit basis in order that the total amount of the control budget remains unchanged. The application ('drawdown') of contingency sums after final sanction would normally be at the discretion of the project manager for whatever purpose is deemed appropriate by him. All such drawdowns must be explained in the regular project reports.

DEFINITION OF COST CONTROL TERMS

Before proceeding to describe cost control methods, it will be appropriate to list and define some of the terms used. These are typically used in reports, and their clear understanding is essential to the correct interpretation of those reports.

Committed costs

Committed costs represent the total value of all work and expenses contained in contracts and purchase orders awarded to third parties. In the case of reimbursable or measured work contracts, committed costs are calculated in respect of the defined scope of work as at contract completion.

For control purposes, costs must be regarded as being committed after the approval of each purchase requisition (or indent) or contract. In the case of imported equipment or materials the committed value will need to include all costs associated with getting the goods to site. These associated costs include elements such as freight, import duties and taxes, insurance, etc.

Although costs incurred overseas will be committed in the relevant foreign currencies (the 'source currencies') they must be converted at current exchange rates to their equivalents in the common project currency. All calculations, together with any assumptions, should be recorded.

The purchase order or contract relating to committed costs should show the budget work package numbers against which the costs are to be allocated. Where more than one work package number applies to a single contract or purchase order, the value of the committed costs must be apportioned appropriately between those work packages.

Cost Control

Sunk costs

Sunk costs are the total costs, at a given time, that would be incurred should the project be cancelled. In addition to costs already experienced, these would have to include any cancellation charges arising from purchase orders and contracts. Proceeds from the resale of any surplus equipment or materials are deducted from sunk cost calculations. Insofar as sunk costs are always related to a given point in time, a degree of judgement is necessary to determine the value of work done, and the likely cancellation charges that would arise in the event of cancellation.

Project expenditure

Expenditure is the total cost of work done, of goods received, and of services used, whether or not these items have actually been paid for. Expenditure therefore includes accruals and provisions (see the separate definitions for these items below).

Expenditure has to be recorded in the source currency by invoice for each work package to show invoices paid and accruals. Separate allowances should be made for provisions. For the purposes of cost reporting, source currency amounts should be converted into the common project currency at the exchange rates ruling when payments are made. By definition the expenditure in source currency will never exceed the commitment value (unless incorrect payments have been made and not put right).

Accruals and provisions

Sums of money due to suppliers of goods or services at the end of a month (or other accounting period) where the invoices have not actually been paid, but where the amounts themselves are reasonably certain, are termed accruals when they are included in expenditure reports. Where the invoices have not been received, and the amounts due are less certain, the allowances made in expenditure reports are termed provisions.

Outstanding commitments

The outstanding commitments are the total costs committed minus

Accounting and Finance

expenditure (at any given time). The value of outstanding commitments will, therefore, tend to zero as work proceeds. A negative value for outstanding commitments will require scrutiny because it could indicate an accounting error or an erroneous payment.

Estimate to complete

The estimate to complete is the best estimate that can be made at any given time of remaining costs not already reported as expended or committed, taking into account the current project scope and performance trends to date.

At the start of a project, before any costs have been spent or committed, it is usual for the estimate to complete value to be equal to the control budget. As the project proceeds, the value of the estimate to complete will reflect all known financial changes to the project which have not already been included in the total committed costs. Such changes are likely to include:

1. Discrepancies between the estimated quantities and those currently being used.
2. Changes of project scope authorised in variation orders.
3. Changes of project scope which are apparent, but which have not yet been made the subject of variation orders.
4. Discrepancies between the estimated inflation or escalation amounts and those actually being experienced.
5. Future exchange rate fluctuations.

Forecast contingency provisions are not usually included in individual work package estimates, but are more likely to be listed separately as a lump sum provision.

Estimated final cost

The estimated final cost is the best estimate which can be made at any given time, taking account of the project scope and of trends to date, of the final cost of a work package, contract or AFE. Bearing in mind the previous definitions, the estimated final cost is seen to be equal to the committed costs to date plus the estimate to complete. This subject is expanded in the following section.

PREDICTING TRENDS AND OVERSPENDS

The most difficult and challenging aspect of cost control is in determining the estimated final cost of the project. To complete this task there is no substitute for a detailed knowledge of the project from both a technical and commercial aspect. The cost engineer will therefore need to communicate with discipline engineers not only in respect to work that is presently being undertaken, and the likely problem areas, but also in the scope of future work not yet committed. In particular there is a need to be aware of any scope changes that are either being contemplated or are in the approval process.

Contract conditions

The type of contract (lump sum, reimbursable, etc.) will influence the prediction of future cost trends.

Lump sum conditions

Under lump sum contract conditions the contractor supplies plant (or carries out certain works), the scope of which has been clearly defined in advance, for a stated price. In most cases the contract price can be regarded by the owner as the final estimated cost, after correcting for any scope changes and their associated variation orders.

Measured work

Where contract terms rely upon an element of measurement, such as a schedule of rates applied to quantity values, the cost engineer will need to quantify the scope of work yet to be completed. For large contracts this will mean collaborating with specialist discipline engineers and with quantity surveyors. The estimated final costs will therefore be:

> Expenditure to date + Future work to be done

In this instance expenditure includes invoices received to date plus provisions for work done but not yet invoiced. Future work will need to recognise the:

1. Quantity of future work (m^3, hours, tonnes, etc.).
2. Contract rate per unit (£/m^3, £/hour, etc.).

As with lump sum conditions all scope changes both real or apparent will need to be included in the assessment.

Reimbursable work

Under reimbursable conditions the supplier or contractor is reimbursed his costs for work completed. This may also include a fee, or alternatively the rate under which he is reimbursed may already include a profit element. As with to measured conditions the cost engineer will need to assess the hours content of work yet to be accomplished, including any scope changes apparent at the time, in order to estimate the cost at completion.

Like for like comparisons

It will be remembered that the control budget comprises:
1. Basic cost estimates for the original scope of project work.
2. Contingency allowances.
3. Cost estimates for approved project variation orders.

With all the above corrected for:
4. Provision for cost escalation with time.
5. Allowances for fluctuations in the exchange rates of relevant overseas currencies.

All of which together provide a control budget which is expressed in 'money-of-the-day' terms.

It follows that prediction of the estimated final cost must take account of all these factors, in order that the predicted costs are directly comparable with the control budget.

Since the escalation allowances for each work package or AFE depend so much on the timing of expenditure, the cost engineer will need to be familiar with the project schedules. He will, therefore, have to collaborate closely with the planning and scheduling engineers in order to be aware of the schedule details, and to understand the extent and effect of any programme changes on the phasing of costs.

The estimated final costs differ in content very slightly from those made for the control budget, since predictions have to take sensible account of changes which are expected, even though they might not have any approval or authorisation at the time of prediction. Thus, although the control budget only includes project variations which have received approval, the estimates of final costs should include the costs of all project variations, including those which (although apparent) have not yet received formal approval.

Relationship between the cost control and planning functions

Accurate cost predictions must depend in part upon the establishment of a close rapport between the cost engineer and the planning function. Obviously, in addition to their influence on escalation, any significant programme changes can have other effects on total costs (in the case of a bad delay, for example, leading to possible contract penalties).

When making assessments on expenditure the cost engineer will need access to information on invoices paid, and on the accrued value of all invoices received but not yet actually paid (accruals). When making allowance for provisions (work done but not yet invoiced by the contractor) the cost engineer may need to seek advice from the planning engineer. The planning engineer should be able to make or obtain estimates for the proportion of each contract or order which has been finished. These estimates of work completed (usually expressed as a percentage of the total contract or order hours or cost) must be a true assessment, and not merely an assumption based on the proportion of money, manhours or time spent (a job might be half-way through its time and cost estimates but only 30 per cent complete, for instance).

Changes in project scope

By their very innovative nature, all projects undergo change during their fulfilment. These changes can be technical, contractual, financial, programme, or some combination of these.

Technical changes

They are concerned with the design of the finished project. For example, in some projects they might be represented by changes to process flow sheets, including changes in the processing capacity or configuration of plant.

Contractual changes

are those which alter the defined contract strategy.

Financial changes

will include any alteration to project funding arrangements (especially loan funds) which can affect subsequent procurement policy.

Programme changes

are those which include major alterations to the planned construction sequence where these do not of themselves constitute technical changes, but which will delay or shorten the programme. There may also be increased or decreased project capital costs resulting from such programme changes.

For the purposes of predicting cost trends and controlling costs, changes in scope can be classified as either defined or apparent.

Defined scope changes

are those which can be quantified in the same manner as the original project. Thus they will include a scope of work, programme and cost estimate. Defined changes occur as project variations or as contract variations.

Project variations

are defined changes which alter the scope of the project with the authorisation of the owner or client. They can be formally recorded by the project manager and, when approved by the client, they will normally be included in the control budget total as authorised changes.

Cost Control

Contract variations

are defined changes in the scope of work agreed between the project manager and a contractor or a supplier of equipment. After approval, contract variations can be recorded and become formal contractual documents. In the cases of purchase orders, these kinds of variations will probably require the issue of purchase order amendments.

An example of a form used to summarise and record a project variation is shown in Figure 11.2.

Apparent scope changes

are those where, although a change is foreseen or inevitable, the implications have not been formally recorded or approved as a project variation. For example, a project might require the sinking of a mine shaft in ground which has been considered dry. If water is hit during the works, this situation will have to be recognised in the contract conditions existing between the project team (representing the owner) and the shaft sinker. However, it could be difficult, in such a case, to prepare a well defined project variation request. The rate of water ingress into the shaft could be speculative, and the total amount of water present might not be known. The cost engineer has to quantify the financial implications by the best means available to him, and make a provision in the future cost forecast for the apparent change of scope. Other changes falling within the category of apparent changes are those where additional work is completed, with the formal variation being agreed later.

Earned value concepts

An earned value system makes use of reported actual progress to apportion the budgeted manhours in order to arrive at an 'earned value' of the work completed. Thus when a job is finished its earned value is equal to its share of the control budget: when the job was (say) 30 per cent complete, its earned value would have been 30 per cent of the relevant portion of the control budget. These earned values are not derived from the actual manhours or time expended. They are an attempt at expressing the true value of work done, related to the control budget, in order that the remaining work and future costs can

Accounting and Finance

PROJECT VARIATION SUMMARY				
COST DATA				
Total increase/decrease in cost =				
PROGRAMME DATA				
LIST of RELEVANT DOCUMENTS and DRAWINGS				
DESCRIPTION of CHANGE (Use continuation sheet if necessary)				
APPROVALS				
Originator	Project Manager			
Date	Date	Date	Date	Date
PROJECT TITLE		AFE No:		
		PV No: ⌊_⌋P⌊V⌋_⌊_⌋		
		Rev No:		
VARIATION TITLE		Sheet of		
		Date:		

Figure 11.2 Project variation summary form
Example of a form used to summarise details and approval (or rejection) of a change in the defined project scope

be evaluated so that the project manager is able to advise the owner at any time during the life of the project on the likelihood of all work being completed within the constraints of the control budget.

By deriving ratios of the actual cost of work performed to the earned values (or budget cost of work performed) a measure of productivity is established. The productivity factor is applied to all budgeted work not completed or started in order to re-assess the estimates for that work, and to help in the calculation of the final project cost predictions.

Forecast contingency

In addition to all the other elements of final cost prediction and cost trend observations, it will be necessary to include an overall provision to cover future contingencies on the costs which are not yet committed.

COLLECTING PROJECT COSTS

Whilst the more difficult aspects of cost control are concerned with the prediction of future trends, it is obviously important that committed costs and expenditures are monitored and recorded.

Committed costs

To ensure that financial commitments are identified promptly, the cost controller will need to be party to, or have access to, the approval process before commitments become contractually binding. In particular the estimated committed cost will need to be known and compared with the relevant part of the control budget before approval. Any potential cost overrun implications are therefore highlighted at or before the time of approval, and not afterwards when it is too late to exercise control.

Expended costs

The final authority for the approval and payment of invoices often rests with accountants, but the time lag between the work being done and the resulting payments is usually too long for the purposes of cost control. The project manager and, more particularly, the cost engineer will therefore need to be party to the auditing of suppliers' and contractors' invoices as early as possible. Then the implications for expenditure (the value of work done) become known well in advance of the actual payments. In cases where payments are dependent upon the actual hours worked (e.g. daywork rates) it is sometimes possible to implement control through the use of timesheets. This would need to be stated in the proposed contract conditions before the award of a contract or purchase order. More recently microcomputers have been used to record the hours worked by contractors at the project site. Such records can then be used by the cost engineer to assist in calculating expenditure in advance of the invoices being received.

CASH FLOW

Cash flow can be defined as an estimate of the amount of cash flowing into the project (earnings — usually nil before the project becomes operational) and the cash outflows (expenditures) divided into convenient control periods (monthly, quarterly or yearly) throughout the life of the project. Each element of forecast income or expenditure is assigned to the period when money is expected actually to be received or spent. Thus a cash flow statement becomes a time related schedule of receipts and payments. Within each period, incomes and payments are taken together to arrive at a net overall inflow or outflow of cash for the period. It is obvious that an accurate cash flow forecast of this type is crucial to the organisation that has to provide funds for the project, since it gives advance notice of the amounts of funds needed and the timing.

There may be circumstances where project funds are to be supplied from a number of loan sources, possibly in more than one currency. The cost engineer will need to be aware of such arrangements in order to be able to advise the owner accordingly.

In most cases the cost engineer will be concerned with the capital costs of the project. Other cash flow studies relating to the project during its operational phase (operating, maintenance, working capital and so forth) would need to be considered separately from the

Cost Control

mainstream project control activities, although operating cash flow information is usually forecast and considered very carefully by the owner or his advisers before a project starts as part of the project appraisal studies. In other words, cash flow information is used to decide from the outset whether or not a project is likely to be financially viable.

Forecast cash flow calculations for the capital costs of a project will need to include:

1. The estimated value of work done over the project timescale, expressed in terms of the base cost.
2. Calculated provisions for escalation and any exchange rate changes, based on the estimated value of work done, in order that the value of work done is expressed in money-of-the-day terms over the project timescale.

The forecast cash flow is then calculated by:

1. Estimating when invoices are likely to be received in relation to the value of work done (in money-of-the-day values).
2. Estimating when invoices are likely to be paid. The cost engineer uses his experience of his company's speed (or otherwise) in paying incoming invoices to assess the likely overall delay between the completion of work and the actual payment date. The total delay is made up of the contractor's own delay in preparing his invoice and sending it, postal delays, and the delays within the paying company caused by internal approval procedures, inter-office messenger delays and the time spent in obtaining cheque signatures.

The forecast cash flow will need to take account of the estimated value of work done, expressed in money-of-the-day terms. In the absence of information to the contrary, it may sometimes be necessary to assume the receipt of invoices in accordance with the value of work done. The cost engineer will then make an allowance for payments which are 'in the pipeline'. In those cases where work has been committed but not yet paid for, recognition for the purposes of the cash flow schedule will be based on the terms of payment stated in the contract or purchase order. The value of actual cash outflows (invoices paid) would normally be recorded by the project accountant.

An example of a cash flow report is shown in Figure 11.3.

Accounting and Finance

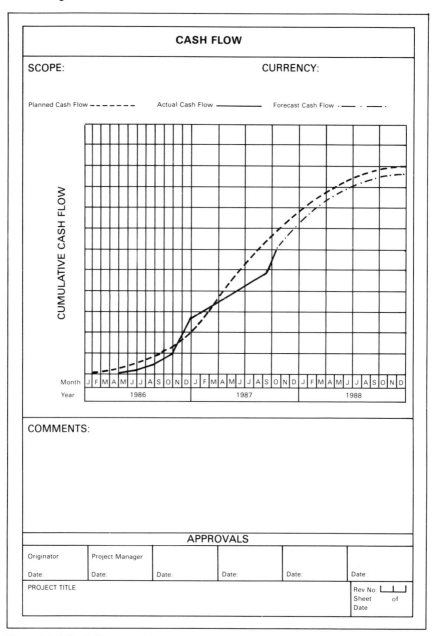

Figure 11.3 Cash flow graph
This is an example of a cash flow forecast in graphical form. It is usually necessary also to provide this information in tabular format, with the columns representing the months, quarters or other control periods spanning the project life, and with the amount of cash outflow or inflow expected entered for each period

CAPITAL SANCTION STATEMENT

FINANCIAL SANCTION			
Date	Memo No.	Amount £,000	Adjustments

PROJECT

Company
Currency
Date of report
Cut off date
Date printed

COST REPORT							EXPENDITURE			
1	2	3	4	5	6	7	8	9	10	11
AFE Budget No	Description	Approved control budget Estimate class	Authorised for expenditure	Commitment as at	Estimated final cost (EFC)	Over (under) budget	Current year: Estimate for year	Current year: Actual as at	Previous years	Cumulative to date
		Dated				6 3				9 · 10
	Sub Total									
	Contingency									
	Total									

Notes	Accruals & Provisions Included above

Figure 11.4 Cost tabulation used for reporting purposes
This form is an example of a report used to show the status of capital sanctions on a large project at a given report date

Accounting and Finance

COST REPORTING

The content and frequency of project cost reports will clearly depend upon the requirements of management, and the nature of the project or projects being undertaken. Where a considerable number of small projects are being undertaken, each of which is of relatively short duration, weekly reporting might be appropriate. Larger projects, including those extending across international boundaries or involving joint ventureships, would probably be reported monthly.

Cost reports typically include data summarised in tabular format, backed up by graphs which show trends against the passage of time.

Figure 11.4 illustrates a monthly report format which has been used for large international projects. Of particular importance is the relationship between the estimated final cost and the control budget.

In addition to the commitment and expenditure profiles there might be cases where sunk costs need to be plotted in a project's early stages. Cash flow statements could also be important, in which case it would be desirable to plot invoices received and the value of the invoices paid.

The cost engineer will need to compile and keep detailed cost records from which to support the summary cost reports. If computer based techniques are used the system should be capable of producing:

1 Budget, commitment and expenditure listings.
2 Analysis type reports which enable comparison of the budget, committed and expended cost records.
3 Movement reports. These identify movements in cost totals within a given reporting period.

COMPUTER AIDED TECHNIQUES

Under the rigorous financial constraints within which projects are now completed it is very desirable to use computer aided techniques for cost control functions. These allow information to be gathered and analysed rapidly, and can react quickly to dynamic situations.

Unlike planning systems it is not usually possible to purchase cost control systems 'off the shelf'. It is more usual to select a relational database which is then structured to suit the particular needs of the

Cost Control

company. When selecting a system there are a number of factors to be considered. These include the following:

1. Existing company policy on hardware selection and availability.
2. Existing databases (such as procurement, accounting, time-sheeting, etc.) that would need to be accessed.
3. Operating environment of the system (in-house, remote site, etc.).
4. The needs of the project (large international project(s) requiring numerous terminals or small scale local enhancements, etc.).
5. The needs of the user (cost engineer), a system that is simple to operate or, alternatively, technically excellent but difficult to use without computing skills.

Computing equipment already available within the company may well dictate the outcome. Where however it is necessary to operate in a remote environment, or projects are low cost, selection of a microcomputer based system may be preferable to mini or mainframe configurations.

A major advantage of computer based systems is their ability to sort, select and subtotal data rapidly, coupled with the convenience of being able to interrogate the system. For example, if the cost engineer needed to review escalation provisions for work not yet committed, then by entering these constraints into the computer a list of the cost records that would satisfy the chosen parameters could be obtained quickly.

Timesheet systems

One useful application of computers is in the analysis and presentation of data recorded on timesheets within the head office (or home office, depending on the preferred terminology). One company produces monthly reports which have twelve columns of data, with the following headings:

1. *Original budget manhours.* The hours approved by the project manager when the project is sanctioned (or awarded).
2. *Approved contract variations.* Includes hours that have been approved.
3. *Current budget hours.* By definition equals original budget hours plus approved project variations.

4 *Hours this month.* The total hours allocated via timesheets during the month.
5 *Hours to date.* The cumulative hours allocated to date via timesheets.
6 *Budget hours remaining.* By definition, equals current budget hours minus the actual hours to date.
7 *Forecast hours total.* This is the best estimate of the total hours needed for the project at completion.
8 *Per cent budget spent.* By definition, equals hours to date divided by current budget hours, multiplied by 100.
9 *Per cent forecast spent.* By definition, equals hours to date divided by forecast hours total, multiplied by 100.
10 *Per cent complete.* This represents the best estimate of project completion at the report date. Where appropriate this will include quantitative methods of measurement (e.g. the completion status of each drawing). To obtain an overall percent completion for the project, departmental totals are summated using forecast hours total as a weighting factor.
11 *Forecast over or under run.* By definition, equals forecast hours total minus current budget hours.
12 *Per cent overrun.* By definition equals forecast over/under run divided by current budget hours, multiplied by 100.

The hours report can be converted to costs by applying a cost rate per staff grade, together with the addition of project expenses not covered by timesheets.

HISTORICAL COSTS

At the end of the project, the actual cost details should be recorded carefully for future reference, possibly in a comprehensive cost databank. This task is simplified if a standard code of accounts is in use, since classification of costs will be uniform and access to the records for information retrieval will be easier and quicker. Historical cost records have obvious use as an aid to the estimating of future projects. It is important that such details as the scope of the project and relevant dates are clearly associated with the cost records for each project or contract. Since cost escalation can quickly render historical cost information less useful and more inaccurate with the passage of time, the records must include the manhours associated with the costs.

12

Controlling Cash and Credit

John Butterworth

Profit is measured in money. All forms of industrial or commercial performance are perforce measured in or reduced to money terms. Every successful industrial project has therefore to be measured in money as well as in the time taken to completion and its technical excellence. For project managers with a financial background this will be obvious. If a project manager's training and discipline is non-financial he has nevertheless to understand and control the financial elements of the project under his command if it is to be concluded successfully.

The amount of time taken to complete a project has a direct relationship with the money invested or otherwise tied up in the project. Quite apart from the completion of all work within estimated manhour durations, and estimated material costs, a project will generally cost more than another with the same work content if it takes longer to finish. This is simply due to the employment of resources such as space, plant and management for the longer time. These are resources which have to be paid for. Money is also a resource, and money costs money to employ for as long as it is tied up in the work in progress. Time is money.

If the project manager's employers have access to all reasonable funds, then efficient resource management, including the management of funds, will simply maximise project success and demonstrate that it has been professionally managed. If the contractor's funds are limited, then inefficient fund management could produce a crisis — even a disaster — owing to lack of finance

Controlling Cash and Credit

at crucial stages in the project. For example, supplies vital to project completion might be witheld by the vendors if there is doubt concerning the contractor's ability to meet their bills promptly through lack of cash. This chapter, therefore, deals with the management of funds from the planning aspects of cash receipts from customers, of scheduling and providing for cash outgoings, and in the collection of overdue amounts from customers.

THE IMPACT OF INTEREST CHARGES ON THE COST OF MONEY

Developing the foregoing arguments further, just as money saved means interest earned, so money spent means interest forgone. This is true regardless of whether the contractor is a net borrower or has money on deposit, because even to spend less of the money which would otherwise be on deposit would produce higher deposit account interest.

The interest element also means that money spent at the beginning of a long project will effectively cost more than money spent much later, towards the end of the project. Efficient use of money is an essential part of project management.

FORECASTING RECEIPTS

As with most other things in life, financial management becomes easier with practice, so that with successive projects planning the finances becomes more and more a matter of routine.

The fundamental point to note about cash flow management is fairly obvious but is nevertheless worth stating. The cash impact of a project is not necessarily the same as the physical implementation but is usually subject to leads and lags in time. Assuming the project involves the commissioning of a new production line it will be readily appreciated that sales of products from this production line, if sold on 30 days' credit terms, will produce cash only after 30 days following date of sale. In other words cash receipts lag behind physical sales. (Note that in the examples in this chapter all accounting is assumed to be on a calendar monthly basis, with holidays ignored, and with every month comprising 30 days unless otherwise stated — for simplicity). In a perfect world the new production line results might look as follows, given an arrangement which allows the customer 30 days' credit:

Table 12.1

	Month 1	Month 2	Month 3	Month 4
Invoiced sales	50	75	100	100
Cash receipts	Nil	50	75	100

However, it is an unfortunate fact that customers rarely pay on the due date. Suppose that the average amount of credit taken by customers is 45 days (quite normal in practice) the table of receipts, or *cash inflows*, is further distorted, as follows:

Table 12.2

	Month 1	Month 2	Month 3	Month 4
Invoiced sales	50	75	100	100
Cash receipts	Nil	25	62.5	87.5

If the customers are allowed to deduct a discount for prompt settlement the cash receipts will be reduced by the amount of discount granted. Assuming, for example, that customers all deduct 2½ per cent discount, the position for 45-day credit payments becomes:

Table 12.3

	Month 1	Month 2	Month 3	Month 4
Invoiced sales	50	75	100	100
Cash receipts	Nil	24.38	60.49	85.31

This table is not entirely realistic, as it assumes that all customers deduct 2½ per cent discount, whereas it has been assumed that some customers are paying late. The principle is, however, clear. The management will have to estimate the proportion of customers who will avail themselves of the discount offer, and then forecast the

Controlling Cash and Credit

effective level of discount averaged over all customers (possibly 1.8 or 1.9 per cent of turnover, or as the case may be).

Offering a cash discount to speed up customers' payments is not always cost effective. A 2½ per cent cash discount to speed up payments by 30 days is equivalent to a rate of interest of 30 per cent per annum. And some customers may deduct the discount and still pay late, giving rise to even more hassle.

A further consideration may be the length of time goods are held, on average, in stock. This would be highly relevant for a production or distribution unit forecast. Ignoring the discount shown in Table 12.3, but using the example in Table 12.2, consider the cash inflow time lag after output on the additional assumption that all goods are held in stock for an average of 30 days before they are sold. The result is as follows:

Table 12.4

	Month 1	Month 2	Month 3	Month 4
Production	50	75	100	100
Cash receipts	Nil	Nil	25	62.5

Further complications can be added. For example, 10 per cent of the turnover might be over the counter for cash. Or there could be (say) two products, one of which is held in stock for 30 days and the other for 60 days. If the cash flow is to be accurate the forecast sale volumes of each product must be established with some degree of accuracy, and also the proportion of each product (if any) which is sold for cash.

Remember also if turnover is subject to Value Added Tax that this is added to the value of the goods or services when these are invoiced. The VAT becomes a cash receipt when the invoices in question are paid but is subsequently accounted for separately to the VAT authorities.

The conventional way to show these aspects in a cash flow forecast is to list cash sales separately from credit sales and to provide a third line for other cash receipts (such as rent receivable, proceeds of sale of a capital asset, new capital paid into the project or the proceeds of loan received from head office or from a bank). Where the characteristics of the products differ, as with the two different

Accounting and Finance

stocking periods suggested above, or possibly due to longer terms of sale to a different market, it is recommended that separate subsidiary schedules are drawn up for each product or market, etc. The totals of these subsidiary schedules can then be combined into the monthly cash flow forecast, with the format similar to that of Table 12.5.

Table 12.5

Receipts:	Month 1	Month 2	Month 3	Month 4
Cash sales				
From credit customers				
Other receipts				
Total receipts				

FORECASTING PAYMENTS

Just as receipts are subject to leads and lags relative to the physical movement of goods etc., the same is true of payments. Obviously every project is different, but the following notes should be of help to the reader drawing up a cash flow forecast for the first time.

Cash purchases, like cash receipts, have immediate impact. If the project involves a new venture it may be necessary to pay cash for a higher proportion of purchases than if it is part of an established operation. Indeed on a new project it may be necessary to pay for certain requirements in advance. The project manager may be wise to take a conservative view of the proportion of purchases paid for on a cash basis. Obviously cash in this context would include immediate payment by cheque and not merely petty cash disbursements.

Where cash purchases are significant it may be necessary to split them into those subject to VAT and those not so subject remembering that the VAT is paid with the invoice.

Goods and services not purchased for immediate cash payment result in an element of credit received from the creditors. This period of credit gives rise to a time lag before these purchases impact on the cash flow, exactly in the same way as do sales made on credit terms — except that this time the time lag delays the cash outflow and thereby reduces the project's cash needs. As in the sales forecast, in so far as cash settlement discounts are available to the project then cash needs

Controlling Cash and Credit

are reduced still further. Beware of planning to take longer than usual credit from suppliers however. The suppliers do not always cooperate, and may retaliate by cutting off supplies. On a project with tight time constraints the project manager will need the maximum co-operation and goodwill from his suppliers.

Capital expenditure may or may not be significant, but in many projects substantial payments for major capital items will be required. The project manager must estimate this expenditure, possibly with the assistance of his technical management. He should be aware that for many capital items cash is required in advance of delivery. The sums of money required may be significant, even for head office.

Where capital expenditure is sizeable, a complete schedule of capital expenditure should be prepared and agreed with the relevant technical departments and with the organisation responsible for providing the funds (head office, the client, the bank, or other source of finance). It is also worth mentioning that any sizeable capital expenditure needs to be sanctioned before all the other work involved in the cash flow forecast is carried out, since a decision by the funding source (e.g. head office or client) to phase such expenditure over a different period must affect all aspects of the project and might mean rescheduling all activities and producing a complete new cash flow forecast.

Value added tax (VAT) must be calculated wherever it is involved in either purchases or sales. The UK procedure is to complete the VAT return quarterly, showing the amounts of VAT charged to customers or clients and the amounts paid out to suppliers of goods and services. The resulting balance becomes payable 30 days from the date of the return. Failure to complete returns on time will incur the wrath of the authorities.

Liability to VAT runs from the date it is invoiced — not from the date it is paid by customers. If customers or clients pay very slowly, it is possible that the contractor will become liable to pay VAT to the authorities before he has collected it from his customers. This is one important reason for maintaining good credit control.

VAT payable on goods imported into the UK becomes due when the goods are cleared through the customs. It can only be delayed if the importer provides a formal bank guarantee to the authorities.

Where the product or service provided by the contractor does not

Accounting and Finance

carry VAT, but where the goods and services bought for the project do, then the VAT becomes a net receivable item and a credit. In these circumstances VAT may be shown under the receipts section of the cash flow forecast.

Corporation tax is normally paid annually. Few projects will have to provide for this charge, but some kind of tax may be payable for overseas projects.

Labour costs comprise wages or salaries plus other elements such as employee tax and social security payments. Wages are usually (but not invariably) paid weekly. If the cash flow forecast is made on a monthly basis, then some months will have four pay days and others five. This will distort the cash flow, and payments must be scheduled accordingly. Salaries, on the other hand, are almost always paid at the end of each month, with no month to month variation. Income tax (pay as you earn) and National Insurance elements of wages and salaries become due 14 days from the end of the month in which the wages or salaries were paid. Other points to bear in mind when scheduling the costs of labour are:

1. Any bonus payments which may arise.
2. Holiday pay, which is often paid in advance.
3. The impact of periodic pay reviews which could increase pay rates, reflecting the rate of inflation.

Rent, rates and water may be payable monthly, quarterly or half-yearly. There may be a degree of payment in advance demanded for some of these items. Light, heat and power are normally payable quarterly in arrears, and their due dates may not fall at the end of a calendar month. These payments for public utility services have to be made promptly to avoid danger of the service being withdrawn.

Costs and timing of payments for transport and packing will vary enormously in their impact on the cash flow schedule. It is sometimes possible to establish an arithmetic relationship between these items and, say, the value of goods being despatched.

Among the many other payments to be considered are the charges levied by the bank or other financing authority providing funds for the project. If funding is from head office on an interest-free basis, only the current account commission of the administering bank will have to be provided.

FORECASTING NET CASH FLOW

The format of a typical cash flow schedule is shown in Figure 12.1. This brings together, spaced according to their appropriate timings, all the receipts (inflows) and payments (outflows) discussed in the two previous sections of this chapter to arrive at a net monthly inflow or outflow figure, and uses these results to predict the level of the current account bank balance each month.

If receipts are greater than payments the resulting credit to the bank balance will increase any credit balance or reduce the debit balance as the case may be.

If payments are greater than receipts the converse will be the case. Obviously the closing bank balance for Month 1 becomes the opening bank balance for Month 2.

Most managers make a point of preparing a separate schedule for each line in the cash flow forecast to show how each month's figure has been calculated. This is worth doing even if the forecast expenditure for an item is the same, regular, small amount every month (simply note on the relevant schedule sheet, for example, 'Repairs and renewals estimated at £50 per month'). These schedule sheets can be kept in a loose leaf folder behind the master schedule, where they are easily available for reference.

Reviewing cash flow forecasts

Cash flow preparation can be a daunting task at first, but it becomes increasingly straightforward with practice, provided the manager subjects himself to the vital discipline of examining the variances. This means writing in as month succeeds month the actual figure on each line against the forecast. Any fool can write down a forecast but it may be wildly inaccurate. It is only by comparing the actual with the forecast figures that the relationships become apparent.

To do anything successfully in business the manager needs to carry out three separate activities:

1. Plan.
2. Do.
3. Review.

This is the review phase. It may be late, extremely hot, and the boys

Accounting and Finance

CASH FLOW FORECAST FROM _____ 19   TO _____ 19

RECEIPTS	Jan	Feb	Mar	Apr	May	Jun	Jul	Aug	Sep	Etc →
Cash sales										
From credit customers										
Other receipts										
Total receipts (A)										
PAYMENTS										
Cash purchases										
Creditors for goods and services										
Wages and Salaries										
Rent, rates, water										
Light, heat, power										
Transport and packing										
Repairs and renewals										
Bank and finance charges										
Capital expenditure										
Value added tax (net)										
Corporation Tax										
Other payments										
Total payments (B)										
Net inflow (A − B)										
or										
Net outflow (B − A)										
± opening bank balance										
= closing bank balance										

Figure 12.1 A typical cash flow forecast format
The list of payments shown is not exhaustive. Other relevant items may include, for example, advertising, royalty payments, audit fees and other professional charges

Controlling Cash and Credit

may be having a party next door, but this review must be carried out if the manager is to exercise control of current and future projects. It is what he learns from the current review that will improve his control in the future.

Finally cash flow forecasts should be regularly revised if the project is to last much more than say three months or so. Variances are bound to arise. The review process will highlight them. If they are not to reverse themselves they need to be built into a revised forecast. Head office will prefer to be warned in good time if the original forecast was too optimistic rather than be faced with a mini cash crisis.

A second reason for regular revisions is that in any forecast the error factor must increase with time. It is quite reasonable to expect a high degree of accuracy for three months or so and then an increasing ± error factor for succeeding quarters as the variances build up and compound.

It is not usual to prepare detailed cash flow forecasts more than twelve months ahead but the business may require a 'rolling' forecast, that is, a forecast for the next 12 months to be reviewed after six months with a view to producing another twelve month forecast as at the date of the review.

SPEEDING UP THE CASH FLOW

The remainder of this chapter deals with collections. A better description might be 'safeguarding and speeding up the cash flow'. Once a project manager has worked out his cash flow forecast he has two basic tasks:

1   To implement the project in accordance with the timetable.
2   To ensure that the client or customer pays for it, and that the budgeted profit duly accrues to the project in cash.

Of course the major part of the project is the implementation. Successful achievement of this will produce the flow of product or services (or in some projects will eliminate the costs) which is the ultimate objective of the project in the first place. Successful implementation on time will help to ensure that the budgeted costs do not overrun. This aspect therefore is quite vital.

However, the project will not be successful — indeed it may break

Accounting and Finance

down completely — if implementation does not result in the anticipated cash receipts. If these are not achieved on time the project manager will be running up bills and paying out money with the risk of running out of cash funds. If head office or higher management are not aware of the bills being accumulated without funds with which to pay them, when the day of reckoning arrives the situation could be, at the least awkward, at the worst a crisis. Every possible step has to be taken to ensure that money due is paid promptly by the customer.

The contract

The first consideration of the project manager must be the contract with the customer or client. This contract may have been written by the contractor (in consultation with his legal advisers) or may be a contract imposed upon the contractor by the customer (in consultation with *his* legal advisers). On the other hand, the contract could be a standard, general purpose contract. The subject of contracts generally is dealt with in Chapters 4, 5 and 6.

The experienced project manager will have a good idea of the payment stipulations he requires and will, if at all possible, have tried to be present personally at any negotiations with the customer on this point. If it is (say) a construction project, and the manager is an engineer he should not simply concentrate on the engineering aspects and leave the payment clauses to someone else. These are vital to the successful completion on budget of the project. If the manager is responsible for the project, he is also responsible for getting paid as this is the real object of the whole operation.

But mention must be made of lawyers. Assuming the project manager is using his own lawyers, they will put in as tough a set of payment conditions as they can draw up. Make sure from actual experience that these are reasonably enforceable in the field or in the market concerned. Otherwise they become at best pointless and at worst a future stumbling block. The lawyer needs to have a clear understanding of the nature of the work and the sorts of problem likely to be encountered. The project manager may need to prepare a detailed briefing for his lawyer. This may seem unnecessary or tedious but time spent on these points will pay dividends when it comes to getting the money in later. Of course most projects follow, in broad terms, a previous job and the conditions of the last job can be used for

Controlling Cash and Credit

the new one, provided that the manager learns from any problems experienced previously.

It might be appropriate to include a provision for payment of interest by the customer in respect of any late payment. The lawyer will cheerfully draft a paragraph to this effect but only the project manager will know how best to implement this condition. For example it must be clearly seen what are the due dates of the payments. If this kind of detail cannot be established beyond reasonable doubt the best lawyer's contract will not be enforceable in the matter of interest on late payments. This is an example of how the project manager needs to work closely with his lawyers.

In many cases the manager will be faced with the customer's own set form contract. Here the boot is on the other foot and the customer's lawyers have been at work in strictly the customer's interest. In such a case read the contract carefully and check the provisions for payment and those covering arbitration over disputes. Make sure that they are workable and reasonably fair. Discuss with the customer if necessary how he implements these conditions in practice. If the contract says payment 30 days from an event find out if the customer's own accounts department is efficient. If dealing with, say, the customer's engineering department, they will probably be very happy to say (for example) 'Should you experience payment delays, which is unlikely, contact our Mr White who can sort them out very quickly'. Make a note of Mr White's name and his telephone number.

Consider any foreseeable snags arising out of the customer's contract. What are the critical conditions? In certain construction contracts certification of work done will be critical. Consider how to obtain this promptly when required. The customer's contract may (for example) say that payment will be made so many days from certification or measurement of work done by the customer's architect or surveyor or engineer, etc. Make sure that the person who is to certify the work will be available to do this when required. If considered appropriate, obtain written confirmation that this work will be done promptly. A letter along the following lines could be used:

> In consideration of our carrying out the work/building/ providing the services covered by your contract No.00101

dated ... April 198.. and for which payment will be made following certification of work done by your nominated architect/surveyor/engineer please confirm our discussion of yesterday (by signing and returning the enclosed copy of this letter) that your nominated architect/surveyor/ engineer will attend the site to carry out the necessary certification work within 7 days of being requested by us to do so.

Such a letter could prove very useful at a later date if payments are delayed through no fault of the project manager, who might be instructed by his superiors to claim interest for the late payment. Even if interest is not shown in the contract as payable on late payments, a letter such as that shown above will help to safeguard prompt payments.

If the project is large, the contract will probably have a clause setting out arrangements for settling disputes. This clause should be read carefully to ensure that it is workable and, it is to be hoped, in line with previous similar projects undertaken. If it is not considered workable, the project manager should endeavour to have it changed to a practicable arrangement which is agreed as fair by both parties. It always has to be remembered that the work has got to be performed correctly in the first place for payment to be due: this is fundamental.

In the writer's experience set form contracts drawn up by engineering orientated companies tend to be fairly straightforward. After all the company in question simply wants the work to be done to the required specification within the time scale agreed and at the stipulated price. Set form contracts drawn up by financial organisations tend to be a lot tougher in the conditions they contain.

Consider also in the light of the main contract what implications there may be for the project manager if he, in turn, is proposing to subcontract part of the work to a third party or parties. It is difficult to be specific here because of the wide range of work and conditions for carrying it out. But subcontractors have to be paid, sometimes extremely promptly, and this fact may need to be reflected in some way in the project manager's own contract with the end customer.

Terms of payment

Careful consideration must be given to the terms of payment in the contract. These affect not only the cash flow, but also the endemic risk of the work. As a general rule, the greater the risk in the project the greater the need for a mobilisation of 'up-front' payment by the customer. The manager's objective in this case should be to arrange matters so that the customer has a clear financial interest in the completion of the work because he has already paid in advance for a proportion of it.

Perhaps the most extreme need for up-front payments is in foreign markets where there is the possibility of political problems or even of a revolution. In Iraq in the 1950s and again in Iran in the 1970s, following their respective revolutions there was widespread abrogation of commercial contracts by the new rulers. A number of companies suffered severe losses or went bankrupt. It is, of course, easy to be wise after the event but the lesson is clear. Contracting companies which have been paid up-front, even if only in part, will:

1. Be able to save at least something from the situation.
2. Have a valuable bargaining counter if the contract has to be renegotiated.

In most normal commercial situations it is the second point which is most important. If the contractor has been paid partly in advance he is in a far better position to negotiate with the customer when something unforeseen occurs. He can actually threaten to lay off his men or slow down the completion rate. If he has no money in hand such threats will have far less effect. The customer may regard them with disdain, inviting the project manager to go ahead and carry out his threatened action if he dares — in which case the customer will simply replace the present contractor with another.

Every project manager, wherever he is operating, needs to take this point into his calculations. If he cannot reduce the risk by means of a down payment by the customer he needs something else as a bargaining counter. This might be the withholding of part of the technical know-how from the customer's operatives, for example.

Length of credit terms

Terms of credit also contribute to the risk. The longer the terms the greater the risk and vice versa. Quite apart from the question of cash flow, if the customer is to pay on 90 day terms rather than 30 day terms there are two effects:

1. Three times as much money is owed by the customer. If the customer is a credit risk, the project manager has three times as much money at risk. In the absence of any down payment, if the customer fails the resulting bad debt will be three times as great.
2. The manager will have far less warning of deteriorating payments. If, for example, the payment terms are 30 days and payment is not forthcoming, the project manager is put on notice that something is wrong and can take steps to remedy the situation before any more time is lost. If, however, the payment terms are the 90 days of our example the project manager cannot react until much later and this delay could turn out to be a serious matter.

It will be appreciated that the greater the credit risk is considered to be, the lower should be the maximum amount of credit to be granted to the customer and, accordingly the shorter the terms of settlement. If the work involves payment by the customer of £5000 per week and if we do not want to grant to the customer more than £10 000 credit outstanding at any moment of time then the terms have got to stipulate 7 day payment. This permits 1 week's work in progress prior to invoice plus 1 week's credit to the customer. If he does not pay on the due date the work force must down tools or the credit exposure will rise above £10 000. Of course things are never quite as simple as this but the principle is clear. Short terms mean less risk.

Retentions and guarantees

For many contracts it is usual for the customer to withold payment (typically 10 per cent) of the total amount invoiced. This 'retention' amount becomes payable after an agreed period, which might be six months or even a year. Payment of the retention amount might be related to an event, such as the commissioning of a machine or production process. If retentions are applicable to the project in question, there is little that the project manager can do about them except to:

Controlling Cash and Credit

1 Remember to include them in the cash flow schedule.
2 Recognise that they increase the credit risk (if the customer becomes insolvent before they are paid they become a bad debt).
3 Arrange for these retentions to be accounted for properly and ensure that they are followed up for payment as soon as they become due.

Another way in which risk may be reduced is by incorporating in the contract a guarantee by a third party such as a bank. Where there is a significant risk the project manager should always bear in mind the desirability of obtaining such a guarantee, particularly since he may have considerably more at risk than the amount invoiced and outstanding. There may be considerable work in progress awaiting certification. He may have liabilities to subcontractors. He may have run up other bills himself, not yet due, or entered into firm purchase contracts which he must fulfil regardless of whether he is paid by his customer. In these circumstances he may be wise to have the contract guaranteed by a substantial third party such as a bank or other financial insititution.

A limited amount of security can be obtained by specifying payment under a letter of credit. This is a document issued by a bank in which the bank undertakes either to pay cash or to accept a bill of exchange (which in turn can be discounted for cash) up to a specified maximum amount against receipt of specific documentation. This documentation is usually evidence of shipment of goods such as invoices and bills of lading but can include certificates of work done by a nominated authority.

The very fact that the customer has provided a letter of credit is evidence that he has the funds to pay for the project. The project manager has to be extremely careful, however, that the documentation which he lodges with the bank in order to obtain payment complies in every way with the terms of the letter of credit. Letters of credit carry expiry dates for completion of the work or shipment of goods and for the presentation of the claim documents. Late completions or late submissions will not be eligible for payment, which will have to be renegotiated with the customer.

Accounting and Finance

COLLECTION OF ACCOUNTS WHEN DUE

Having done as much preparatory work as possible in the way of examining the contract, ensuring that all paper work required is in order and obtaining the most secure or risk-free terms as possible (not to mention implementing the actual project) the time will come when the customer is due to pay. What steps should the project manager take to ensure that payment is received promptly?

Of the many different types of project, the following sections of this chapter will consider two categories for the purpose of collection of accounts. Firstly there are the major projects, of which the contractor will only be handling a few (even only one) at any particular time. At the other end of the scale are the smaller projects, so that the contractor could be handling a larger number, involving collections from a considerable number of customers.

High cost, major projects

Projects which, by their size and value, generate the collection of substantial sums obviously deserve treatment as special cases by the accounts department. Because the sums owing are large, the impact on the cash flow (for the contractor and for the project) is great and the effects of any late payments generally more serious than for one of a series of smaller projects. For example, if the annual rate of interest is running at 12 per cent, a debt of £50 000 would cost over £16 a day, or £115 a week, in finance costs. The impact of late payments on the viability of a large project is clear.

Under the terms of the contract governing the project it may be necessary to apply for payment in a specified way. This will be either set out in the contract or will be required in a form which is usual in the trade or industry concerned. In either case it is important to apply for payment by the method laid down, be it by invoice and statement or by application for stage payment etc. as the case may be. By following this laid down procedure strictly the project manager makes it easier for his customer to process the payment through *his* own administration. For example, quoting the customer's own order or job number on the invoice may be quite vital if prompt payment is to be obtained. If the project manager has delegated this follow-up or collection activity to a subordinate, it is most important that the

Controlling Cash and Credit

person in question fully understands the contract or trade requirements.

The first and obvious step to take if money is not forthcoming is to telephone the customer. When this call is made depends upon the circumstances. It might be prudent to telephone *before* the account is due and whilst still raising the paper work. Such a call could be used to ensure that the paper work was accurate, sufficiently comprehensive and was addressed to the right payment authority at the right address. Just one telephone call at the beginning might save great frustration and delay throughout the remainder of the project for, in the matter of collecting debts, there is absolutely no substitute for getting the paperwork right first time.

Alternatively the telephone call might be made *after* the paperwork has been dispatched, but before the account falls due. Here the purpose of the call will be to ensure that the customer has received the paperwork and to ascertain that there are no 'problems'.

The project manager may feel that these telephone calls are unnecessary. The author would question such a view, especially if significant sums of money (for example, over £20 000) are involved, preferring to telephone after the account falls due. In such a case the call should be made within 7 days of the due date.

Many customers are simply late payers, resulting from a mixture of laziness, weak administration and poor cash flow. Obviously a customer whose administration is weak is not likely to be efficient when it comes to getting his own money in. Some customers are slow payers because they are financially weak and, therefore, bad credit risks. The assessment of credit risk is a specialised subject. If necessary, the reader should consult a specialist textbook on this subject such as that by T. G. Hutson and J. Butterworth, *Management of Trade Credit*: Gower, 1984. But by far the most common reason for late payments is some technical administrative problem, which the project manager or one of his team can sort out quickly. So, the reasons for the early telephone call are:

1 To put pressure on the customer to pay.
2 To identify any problem and get it sorted out as quickly as possible.

If a couple of telephone calls do not clear the matter up it may be necessary for someone from the project team to visit the customer.

But who should be visited? It is now that the work recommended earlier in this chapter will bear fruit. The project will have its own contact personnel in the customer's organisation. If they cannot help or do not know why payment is being withheld it is time to visit the Mr White who the project manager in his early discussions discovered was the official in charge of the customer's purse strings.

If these telephone calls and visits do not produce the required results and if the problem is not due to failure in some way by the project manager or his team, then the manager must seek to escalate the confrontation to the most senior official he can identify in the customer's organisation. Here the right approach might be another telephone call or a carefully worded letter or another visit. It really depends on the manager's own personal style. Arriving at the customer's premises and politely refusing to leave until either a meeting takes place with the required official or better still a cheque is handed over is a procedure which does actually work. It is far preferable to the next step, which consists of either slowing down the work rate or complete withdrawal of labour from the project. The latter action in particular is tantamount to crossing the Rubicon. It can never be taken lightly. It may sour relations with members of the customer's own staff with whom good relations are important. It may even give rise to a counter claim by the customer for unfinished or late work. In other words it is a step which should only be used by a project manager when he is entirely certain that he has carried out *to the very letter* his side of the contract. If he is not sure on this point he should take advice from his superiors.

Finally the project manager can instruct his solicitors to write to the customers. Before doing so he should again be satisfied that he has completed the work he has contracted to carry out and has billed the customer for. The solicitor's letter should specify the amount owing and the contract under which it is due. If the customer does not respond to such a letter with either a cheque or a valid reason for non payment the solicitor has the following main options open to him (at English law):

1   To obtain a court's judgment against the customer.
2   To seek to enforce this judgment by having the court's officials seize the customer's assets with a view to selling them for the benefit of the creditor or, alternatively

3 To use the existence of the judgment to petition the court at a subsequent hearing to wind up the customer compulsorily if it is a limited company or to make the customer or its partners bankrupt if it is a sole trader or firm.

There are a number of other, more specialised, remedies available to an unpaid creditor but the ones set out above are the most commonly used.

It will be appreciated that legal action will differ in detail in other countries and the project manager's local solicitor will advise on local practice. Regardless of the market one point remains the same and that is that if the customer disputes his liability to pay, judgment is unlikely to be obtained and the dispute will have to be negotiated. Normally speaking negotiation is better carried out before in effect the project leader crosses his Rubicon and escalates the problem out of normal day to day commercial relations. With a few customers escalation may be inevitable. With the majority a face to face meeting will solve the problem. Nevertheless the importance of the early preparatory work suggested throughout this chapter will readily be appreciated since this, it is to be hoped, will prevent later crisis management.

Multiproject collections

Where a relatively large number of small value projects are being undertaken for a number of customers the collection process will need streamlining to some extent at least. Exactly how the contractor decides to do this will depend on the available resources. The following suggestions provide a guide which can be varied in the light of circumstances. For the sake of illustration, it is assumed that there are 100 customers to whom the value of goods or work provided ranges from £250 to £10 000 each month.

Obviously, bearing in mind the fact that money carries its own financing costs, more strenuous efforts must be exerted to recover overdue payments from the larger value contracts. A telephone call to collect a £10 000 debt will cost no more to make than a call to a customer owing only £250, but the payback for such a call is 40 times as great. It is suggested, therefore, that at least two collection programmes are drawn up, with one arrangement for debts exceeding

Accounting and Finance

(say) £1000 and another for smaller debts. These arrangements could be organised as follows:

1 *Collection programme for debts exceeding £1000*

Timing	Action
Every month	Send detailed statement of account
14 days after due date (if unpaid)	Telephone call
21 days after due date (if unpaid)	First letter
28 days after due date (if unpaid)	Final letter/second telephone call
35 to 40 days unpaid	Solicitor's letter

2 *Collection programme for debts under £1000*

Timing	Action
Every month	Send detailed statement of account
14 days after due date (if unpaid)	First letter
28 days after due date (if unpaid)	Second letter
44 days after due date (if unpaid)	Final letter
60 days after due date (if unpaid)	Solicitor's letter

It will be noted that the telephone is not used in this example for chasing smaller debts. Although there is no reason why it should not be used it is more expensive in clerical time than letters, which can be standard texts produced by machine.

Examples of debt collection letters

Here are a few examples of standard collection letters which are suitable in many cases.

1 A first reminder letter designed to accompany statement of account.

Controlling Cash and Credit

Dear Sirs,
We enclose your statement of account giving details of an overdue balance of £   .
Would you kindly look into this and let us have your cheque in settlement or state your reason for witholding payment.
Yours faithfully,

2   A first reminder letter designed for use without a statement of account.

Dear Sirs,
We have already sent you details of your account, on which there is now an overdue balance of £   .
Would you kindly look into this and let us have your cheque in settlement or state your reason for witholding payment.
Yours faithfully,

3   Second letter, for use without a statement of account.

Dear Sirs,
Despite one reminder we are still carrying forward an overdue balance of £   .
May we therefore have your immediate payment.
Yours faithfully,

If a statement of account is to be enclosed with this letter, the words 'as can be seen from the enclosed statement' can obviously be added after the overdue amount.

4   Letter to a customer who has paid only part of his account.

Dear Sirs,
We thank you for your payment of £   in reduction of this account.
There remains, however, a balance of £   which is extremely overdue and we must insist on receiving this sum/a further substantial payment* within the next seven days.
Yours faithfully,

*whichever is appropriate.

5 Example of a final demand, prior to a solicitor's letter.
   This may be sent by recorded delivery, for greater impact.

FINAL APPLICATION

Dear Sirs,

Account £

We note with regret that our previous applications for settlement of your now long overdue account appear to have been ignored.

It is with reluctance that we must inform you that unless we receive your remittance or your explanation for not making settlement within seven days of the date of this letter we shall be left with no alternative but to take whatever steps we consider necessary to secure collection.

Please help us to avoid this unpleasant step.

Yours faithfully,

Collection letters generally should be polite, firm and as short as possible. They are unlikely to be filed, let alone framed by the recipient. The final demand is a little different, being intentionally slightly high-flown in style and rather longer. It implies that the sender is about to take further action (i.e. to cross the Rubicon, as suggested earlier) without being specific. The project manager, in sending this final demand, can keep his options open — but he must do something when the seven days are up. If he does nothing then his credibility disappears, and any subsequent threat made by the project manager or his team will have less effect.

CONCLUSION

Various ways in which accounts receivable can be collected when they fall due have been discussed. As stressed continuously throughout this chapter, the three main points to be remembered remain:

1 Careful preparation will always be worthwhile and pay dividends.
2 Efficient work execution and accurate records are vital in order to establish the basis for a strong cash flow.

3 Prompt, polite but firm follow-up of overdues is most important in all circumstances.

Given these ingredients, the project manager will be less likely to suffer problems with his projects' finances.

Part IV
MANAGING PROJECT MATERIALS

13
Project Purchasing

Peter Baily

Purchasing for projects differs in some ways from other kinds of purchasing, but certainly also it has a great deal in common with purchasing generally for productive organisations.

Purchasing has been defined as 'the process by which organisations define their needs for goods and services, identify and compare the suppliers and supplies available to them, negotiate with sources of supply or in some other way arrive at agreed terms of trading, make contracts and place orders, and finally receive the goods and services and pay for them' (P. Baily, *Purchasing and Supply Management*, 4th edition, London: Chapman and Hall, 1978). It is in the details of this process that project purchasing differs from purchasing for batch production or continuous production, rather than in the aims and objectives.

Aims and objectives at their most basic are to arrange for the supply of goods and services of the required quality at the time required from satisfactory suppliers at an appropriate price; but to achieve these basic aims, purchasing departments may need to engage in a variety of activities aimed at subsidiary objectives, including purchase research, supplier development, and so on.

Project purchasing has two main sub-divisions: buying parts and materials, and placing subcontracts. Closely associated with these buying activities are the related activities of expediting (or progressing), which is intended to ensure delivery on time, and inspection and quality control, which is intended to ensure delivery to specification, together with stores management and stock control. These associated activities are the subject of later chapters in this part of the book.

SOME SPECIAL CHARACTERISTICS OF PROJECT PURCHASING

Differences between project purchasing and purchasing for other types of production are most noticeable in the case of very large projects. Very small projects do not differ so much in their purchasing requirements from jobbing production or (if they are undertaken on a regular and frequent basis) from batch production. Batch production, with most batch sizes in the six to six thousand region, accounts for about two-thirds of UK manufacturing output. As far as printer and binder are concerned, this *Project Management Handbook* is itself part of batch production, although for the editor and publisher it is more an example of project production.

Differences exist in the way specifications are arrived at (with a single client playing a dominant role); in the way suppliers are identified and compared (with the client often involved and sometimes insisting on the use of particular sources of supply) and in the often complicated details of cash flow and payments in and out.

Project production is essentially discontinuous, in comparison with batch production and continuous production. Even though the company concerned may expect to undertake a series of projects of similar type, nevertheless each project stands on its own and it is therefore very important to devise and negotiate terms and conditions of contract which are appropriate for the individual project and which so far as possible cover all eventualities.

Differences also exist in the way the purchasing people, and those on associated activities, are slotted into the organisation structure. For large projects, the project manager may have full-time staff, including a purchase manager, attached to him for several years. Much has been written about matrix organisations, which do not comply with classical organisation theories because senior people answer to at least two bosses. The project purchasing manager for instance would be responsible both to the project manager and to his own purchasing director in the permanent organisation structure. He would in principle have line responsibility to the senior project manager and functional responsibility to the purchasing director: one would be concerned with *what* is to be done, and *when*, while the other would be concerned with *how* it should be done. In practice things are not always quite so clearcut, which is why people in matrix organisation structures have to be able to cope successfully with fluid situations, political pressures, uncertainty and conflicts of interest.

A major responsibility of such a project purchasing chief for a very large project would be manpower planning, which would be done in consultation with his two immediate bosses, of course. Some purchasing staff would be seconded to the project for the whole of its duration, or at any rate the greater part of it. Others would be attached to the project for a shorter period. It might be necessary to cope with peak work loads by hiring outside personnel on short contracts. At the other extreme, some of the purchasing work could be dealt with no doubt by permanent staff who had not been attached to the project full-time, as part of their normal work.

THE PROJECT PURCHASING MANAGER

A sample job description for a project purchasing manager on a very large project taking years to complete follows.

The project purchasing manager:

1. Reports directly to the project manager and liaises with all other managers in the project team.
2. Provides a procurement service to the project manager. This includes subcontracting, ordering equipment and materials, expediting, inspection and shipping.
3. Represents the project manager in meetings with the client on all procurement matters.
4. Prepares procurement procedures for the project in agreement with the project manager, corporate procurement management and the client.
5. Ensures that the project procurement procedures are adhered to.
6. Directly supervises the chief subcontracts buyer, chief buyer,

Managing Project Materials

senior project expediter and the senior project purchasing inspector.

7 Reviews and agrees regularly with the project manager and with corporate procurement management the manpower needs of the project procurement department.

8 Maintains close liaison with corporate procurement management on all project procurement activities.

9 Supervises the preparation of:
Conditions of contract and subcontract
List of approved suppliers and subcontractors
Detailed inspection procedures
Shipping documentation
All other documentation required for project procurement.

10 Agrees the names of firms to be invited to tender, in conjunction with the client.

11 Attends at the opening of tenders when sealed tender procedures apply.

12 Monitors and reviews procurement progress on a continuous basis and prepares monthly status reports. Attends and reports to project progress meetings whenever the progress of purchases and subcontracts is being considered.

13 Signs bid summaries before their submission to the project manager and the client, after ensuring that the correct procedures have been followed.

14 Supervises the placement of all procurement commitments, whether these are by letter of intent, purchase order, contract, or any other form.

15 Ensures that copies of purchase orders, correspondence, and all relevant documents including drawings, specifications, test certificates, operating and maintenance manuals, are correctly distributed to the client, the project manager, or elsewhere as laid down in the project purchasing procedures.

16 Obtains from suppliers and subcontractors schedules of work compatible with the project programme.

17 Ensures that negotiations concerning orders and subcontracts are properly conducted, and takes personal responsibility if they are critical.

18 Ensures that invoice queries from the invoice checking section are promptly dealt with by procurement staff.

SUBCONTRACTING

Major projects are usually the subject of one main contract between the client (or customer, purchaser, or employer if these terms are preferred) and the main contractor. The main contractor will then place a number of subcontracts, which themselves constitute contracts between him and the subcontractors. The client is not legally a party to these subcontracts, but will usually take part in the process of awarding them, deciding on the subcontractors, approving the terms and conditions, etc. In effect the client is subcontracting part of his purchasing activity to the main contractor, and will naturally want to keep an eye on things (except in turnkey contracts) and perhaps also to stipulate that certain preferred firms should be used as subcontractors. This can be seen from the paragraphs numbered 3, 4, 10 and 15 in the project purchasing manager's job description example given above.

Computerised databases are being used increasingly to assist in finding the names of possible subcontractors and suppliers. One such database, launched in 1985, was aimed particularly at the offshore oil and gas industries. Suppliers paid £300 a year for being listed in the appropriate subsection of the fifty product groups covered. The information listed included each supplier's name and address, the five most recent contracts, and details of the parent company and any associates, etc.

Suppliers have a long way to go between bringing their name to the notice of a possible customer, and actually getting the business. Quality capability is important. Track record is very important. A few years ago when the whole British off-shore oil and gas industry was getting under way, the government set up the Offshore Supplies Office, mainly to ensure that available business was not pre-empted by overseas-based organisations which had built up track records in offshore work in South America, North America and in other parts of the world to the exclusion of home-based organisations which were trying to break into new market opportunities. A voluntary agreement between the Offshore Supplies Office (OSO) and the operators includes such clauses as:

1 All potential suppliers selected to bid are given an equal and adequate period in which to tender, such period to take into

account the need to meet demonstrably unavoidable critical construction or production schedules of the operator;
2 Any special conditions attached to the materials, the source of supply of components and materials, and the inspection of goods are stated in the specification or enquiry documents;
3 Stated delivery requirements are not more stringent than is necessary to meet the construction and/or production schedules of the operator;
4 Where the requirement includes the need to develop equipment or proposals in conjunction with the operator, all bidders are given equal information at the same time;
5 When the operator is unable to identify a reasonable number of suitably qualified UK suppliers for his invitation to tender, he will consult the OSO before issuing enquiries;
6 The enquiry documents require the potential bidders to estimate the value of the UK content of the goods and/or services to be supplied.

and:

7 When the operator has determined his decision for the award of contract, in the case of non-UK award, he will inform OSO prior to notifying selected suppliers and will give OSO a reasonable time, in the circumstances applying, for representation and clarification. This procedure will be followed in the case of sub-contracts referred by main or subcontractors to the operator for approval. Where the operator does not intend to call for prior approval of subcontracts the procedure for adherence to the Memorandum of Understanding and this Code of Practice will be agreed between the operator and OSO. Where this gives OSO access to the operator's contractors and subcontractors this procedure will not diminish the direct and normal contractual relationship between the operator and his suppliers. The principle shall be adopted that following disclosure of prior information to OSO on intended awards no subsequent representation to the operator by a potential supplier, other than at the express request of the operator, shall be entertained.
8 To satisfy the OSO that full and fair opportunity is being given to UK suppliers operators will, on request, make available to officers of the OSO such information as they may reasonably

require about:

(a) the programme of intended enquiries to industry necessary to implement the anticipated overall programme of exploration and/or development to the extent that this information has not already been made available to the Department of Energy. (The operators may supply this information in any format convenient to themselves provided it is sufficiently comprehensive to enable OSO to assess the potential opportunity for UK industry)

etc. ...

How long such agreements should last, and indeed whether or not there is still any justification for them, are matters outside the scope of this chapter.

THE PURCHASING CYCLE

Conventional notions of the purchasing cycle which apply in batch production, mass production or in merchandising are less appropriate to the realm of the complex project.

Large complex projects such as the construction of complete factories, fully equipped hospitals, offshore oil rigs, are carried out all over the world. Purchase departments are involved on both sides of the contract: on the client's side, in obtaining and helping to analyse tenders and in contract negotiation, and on the contractor's side, in obtaining information from subcontractors and suppliers which is needed in preparing the bid or tender. Once the contract is settled, a large number of orders and subcontracts need to be placed by the contractor's purchase department, usually with the approval of the client.

It is often desirable to use the expert knowledge and experience of contractors in converting the preliminary functional specification into the final build specification. Two-stage tendering is sometimes used for this purpose. There are several versions of this. The World Bank, in its booklet *Guidelines for procurement under World Bank loans*, suggests that the first stage could be to invite unpriced technical bids. Based on these, a technical specification would be prepared and used for the second stage, in which complete priced bids are invited.

It is admittedly difficult to reconcile the public accountability

Managing Project Materials

requirement that all tenderers have equality of information and are bidding for the same specification, with the common sense purchasing principle that exceptional expertise on the part of a supplier should be used in preparing the specification. To expect a contractor with unique design and construction ability to tell the client the best way to do a job, without payment, and then in the second stage to lose the contract to a low bidder with less design capability, seems unlikely to work out. Such firms sometimes insist on some version of the cost-plus contract or on negotiated contracts.

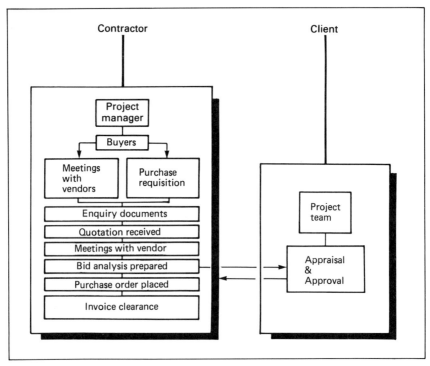

Figure 13.1 Subcontracting procedure for a large contract
This diagram illustrates the respective roles of project manager and client, when it comes to order placement (Adapted from E. A. Stallworthy and O. P. Kharbanda, *Total Project Management*, Aldershot: Gower, 1983)

Once the contract has been signed, purchasing work goes ahead on placing the subcontracts. Very often this has to be done in conjunction with the client, as shown in Figure 13.1. Specifications are prepared, possibly in consultation with vendors and incorporated

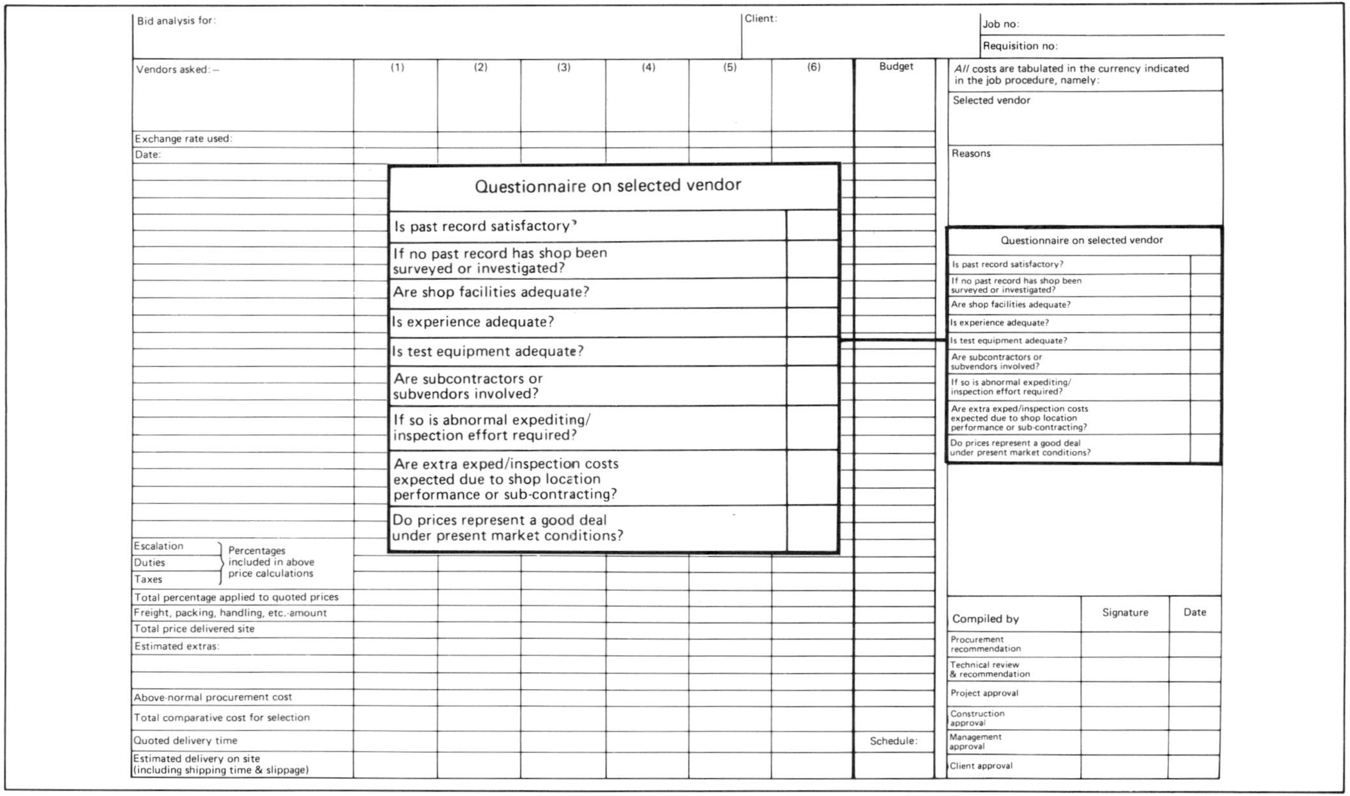

Figure 13.2 Example of a bid analysis form
This form is designed to make sure that all the relevant aspects of vendor selection are reviewed, and compares the bid, or tender price, with that in the budget, or control estimate (From E. A. Stallworthy and O. P. Kharbanda, *Total Project Management*, Aldershot: Gower, 1983)

in the Request for Quotation documents. Normal practice is to allow a month for quotations to be submitted, although on the bigger subcontracts running into millions of pounds worth of work more time may be necessary. Further discussion with suppliers may take place after receipt of tenders, to clarify things, before the bid analysis is prepared for discussion with the client.

An example of a bid analysis form is shown in Figure 13.2. This provides columns in which to list the bids received, allowing comparisons with budget, freight and duty, escalation and other extras. The form also includes a questionnaire on the vendor selected, in which explicit reference must be made to his past record, experience, shop facilities, test equipment and other important aspects of vendor selection.

Whatever procedure is adopted, it is unusual for a bid for a major subcontract to be accepted exactly as made, despite the parity of tender principle. Several meetings between the buyer and the preferred bidder (or bidders) may be required to discuss and negotiate aspects of the specification and commercial terms and conditions. After all bids have been received and appraised, with perhaps only one bidder still in the running, detailed negotiations still continue to establish identity of view between the parties. This should not be seen as an attempt by the buyer to squeeze more concessions out of a supplier who has already put in his final price. Given the timescale, bidders have to concentrate their effort on specification, price, and completion date. Selection of a subcontractor can be made on this basis, but buyers will still want to hammer out the commercial terms and technical people may still want to tinker with the design.

Delay in finalising contract terms or specification details leads to the use of *letters of intent*. These simply say 'we intend to place the contract with you' and in English law they are not binding on either party. Consequently they may not have the desired effect of enabling work to start unless the contractor is able to trust the purchaser.

An unconditional *letter of acceptance* on the other hand sets up a binding contract between the parties. Somewhere between the two is the *instruction to proceed* which authorises the contractor to start work on specified parts of the contract and possibly states an upper limit to the expenditure which the contractor can make on the authority of the letter.

Purchasers usually follow up or accompany the letter of acceptance with an official order form, in order to get the contract into normal administrative and accounting procedures.

PURCHASED MATERIALS AND EQUIPMENT

Projects vary enormously in size, complexity, duration and the nature of their location (a factory in Russia, a hospital in the Middle East, a bridge over the Bristol Channel, a tunnel joining two islands, etc.). Some are far less innovative and more routine than others. But all require the procurement of materials and equipment such as pipe, valves, cables, explosives, none of which was designed specially for the project and the acquisition of which falls more into line with routine purchasing. All must be available on time if delays to the project are to be avoided. All must meet specification. All must be suitably priced if the project costs are to stay within budget.

Even in major projects such purchases may be handled in the purchase department by staff not attached to the project, but who handle these purchases as part of their normal work (although it may be better to second such staff to the project team if the work involved occupies them full time for significant periods). Getting deliveries in on time, product guarantees, and fixed prices, together with the legal, commercial and financial complications of operating on a world scale, can provide a variety of challenges to the purchasing staff affected.

Price analysis and cost analysis

In the consideration of quotations, some form of *price analysis* is always used. Sometimes a more specialised technique is brought into play to support, for example, negotiations about cost-based pricing. This technique is *cost analysis*.

Price analysis attempts, without delving into cost details, to determine if the price offered is appropriate. It may be compared with other price offers, with prices previously paid, with the going rate (if applicable) and with the prices charged for alternatives which could be substituted for what is offered. Expert buyers deal with prices daily and, like their opposite numbers on the other side of the counter, they acquire a ready knowledge of what is appropriate. When considering something like a building contract which does not come up daily they refer back to prices recently quoted for comparable buildings.

When several quotations are received, some will usually be above the average and some below it. Any prices well below the norm should be examined with care. If a supplier is short of work, a price may be quoted which covers direct labour and materials cost without making the normal contribution to overheads and profit. Accepting such an offer can be beneficial both to supplier and purchaser, but it may be prudent to ask why the supplier is short of work. It can happen to anyone, of course, but in this instance have customers been 'voting with their feet' because the supplier's work is not satisfactory?

Low prices may be the result of a totally different position: a seller may have enough work on hand to cover overheads (i.e. expected sales revenue already exceeds breakeven point) and is consequently able to make a profit on any price which is above direct cost. Such offers are not necessarily repeatable; next time round the price quoted may be higher to cover full costs.

Low prices may also be quoted as special introductory offers in order to attract new customers, giving them in effect a fair trial of the goods or services. This can be regarded as a form of compensation to the purchaser for the risk which he incurs in switching to an untried source. Some buyers do not like accepting such offers, regarding the arrangement as opportunism. Building long-term working relationships with proven suppliers matters, of course, more than a single purchase at a cheap price — but this does not exclude acceptance of special offers in all cases.

Management may be pleased with the immediate cost reduction resulting from a one-off low price purchase, but there is a danger that they will expect the buyer to do even better next time. This can be overcome if it is made clear that special offers are, as their name implies, special to the particular occasion: they cannot be made the basis for standard price expectations.

Low prices can also be quoted simply through a mistake of the supplier, or through his incompetence. Suppliers should be given the opportunity to correct such mistakes or withdraw their offers if the price appears to be suspiciously low (say more than 25 per cent below the price which would normally have been expected). Insistence on a contract at low quoted prices has led to bankrupt suppliers and unfinished contracts, and thus to additional costs for the purchaser, when this point has been ignored.

High prices may be quoted as a polite alternative to refusing to make any offer by sellers with full order books. Buyers should not write off such suppliers as too expensive since next time round they could well submit the lowest bid if conditions have changed. High prices may also be quoted because a better specification, more service, prompter delivery, etc. is offered. Obviously such offers should be considered with care. The best buy, not the cheapest price, is the buyer's objective.

Cost analysis examines prices in quite a different way from price analysis. It concentrates only on one aspect, namely how the quoted price relates to the cost of production. When large sums are involved, and a considerable amount of cost analysis needs to be done, full time estimating staff or cost analysts may be employed for the purpose by the purchase department. These people are as well qualified to estimate a purchase price as their opposite numbers in suppliers' sales departments are to estimate a selling price; they have the same qualifications, engineering experience and costing knowledge plus specialist knowledge of sheet metal processing, light fabrication, electronics or whatever is relevant.

Usually suppliers are asked to include detailed cost breakdowns with their price quotations. Some are reluctant to comply, but if one supplier does others find it hard not to follow suit. Differences between a supplier's cost breakdown and the purchaser's cost analysis can then be examined one by one to arrive at a mutually agreed figure. Cost analysis is also used by purchasing management to set negotiating targets for their buyers.

Cost analysis is a useful technique for keeping prices realistic in the absence of effective competition. It concentrates attention on what costs ought to be incurred before the work is done, instead of looking at what costs were actually incurred after the work is completed. This seems more likely to keep costs down (as well as less expensive to operate) than the alternative of wading through a supplier's accounting records after contract completion, probably employing professional auditors to do it.

14
Inspection and Expediting

Bob Chilton

The procurement of materials and equipment for a project is, obviously, not simply a matter which ends when all the purchase orders have been placed. If that were the case, it could be expected that vital items might arrive late, and other consignments could be received with undiscovered damage, specification faults or shortages. The twin processes of inspection and expediting are carried out in order to limit the likelihood of such events.

ORGANISATION

At first sight, expediting and inspection appear to be two different functions. The project management novice might well be justified in asking why they deserve places in the same chapter. The answer lies in the practical approach in carrying out the expediting function. Very often this involves close co-operation with suppliers and manufacturers, to the extent of visiting their premises to view progress and verify claims for progress payments. Since quality is also of paramount importance, it is sensible to arrange that visits to monitor progress are combined with a physical examination of the goods in order that any possible deviation from the specification can be identified as early as possible rather than waiting until the goods have been delivered. Thus it is common for visiting expediters to be technically qualified personnel who can also carry out basic

Inspection and Expediting

inspections. Where the nature of equipment is such that highly specialised engineers should carry out inspection (or witness tests), then the expediter should expect to call upon the project engineering team for support, in the shape of a suitable engineer to accompany him on relevant visits.

Expediting is customarily seen as part of the function of the purchasing department, and it is here where the expediters usually have their base. Sometimes, owing to the international nature of projects, a company will employ a specialist organisation to carry out expediting and inspection for them, either by virtue of the expertise which can be brought to bear, or by the fact that the specialist organisation chosen resides in the same geographical region as the suppliers (which would otherwise be too remote from the contractor's own home base to allow regular visits to take place). In fact, there are many ways in which the functions of purchasing, inspection and expediting can be arranged for a project. In some cases the client's own purchasing department might act as purchasing agent. The matter can be complicated further by the insistence of the client for third party inspections to take place, either to verify conformance with quality and performance standards or to certify that progress achieved is in line with progress payment claims.

For the purposes of this chapter there are three main parts of the organisation, and it is not particularly relevant to be concerned about their corporate positions in the organisation. Wherever they are, the functional arguments and principles are the same. The three main roles (in addition to the project manager) are:

Engineering authority,

which is responsible to the client and to the project manager for quality and performance as defined in the engineering standards and project specification.

Purchasing organisation,

whether an independent organisation, part of the client's organisation, within the contracting company, or a combination of these.

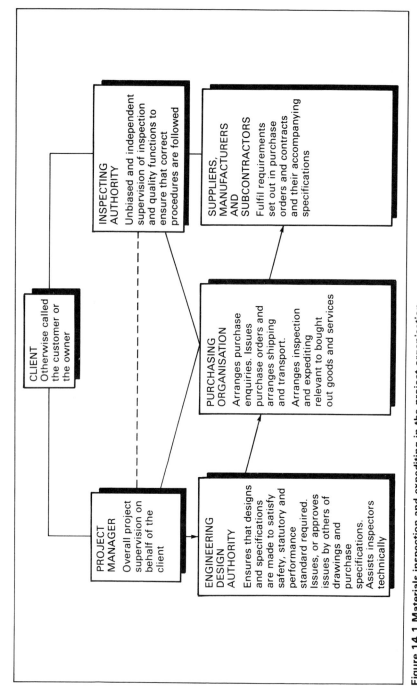

Figure 14.1 Materials inspection and expediting in the project organisation
It is not possible to be specific about what constitutes a typical organisation. There are simply too many possible variations. Apart from the client, any of the roles shown above could be found within the contractor's own corporate group — even including suppliers and subcontractors — or all the organisations could be independent firms linked only for the purposes of one project

Inspecting authority

which again might be within the client's organisation, could include the independent specialists, and would certainly involve the contracting company's own quality control staff.

Please see Figure 14.1 for an amplification of these arguments.

PROGRESSING AND EXPEDITING

Expediting and its closely allied progressing function on which it depends for direction have no internationally agreed definitions and clients often place different interpretations on these processes which tend to confuse the two aspects.

Progressing should be considered as obtaining and verifying information on the procurement position of equipment, which may include the position of ordering equipment on subcontractors and progress on design. The position should be presented to the client in a 'Status Report' which is an integrated report summarising the information determined by the progressing activity.

Expediting is action taken with the manufacturer with the objective of restoring the procurement and manufacturing programme whenever the status report indicates that progress is in danger of being late, or has already failed to achieve the requirements of the programme.

The progressing and expediting activities should be started immediately the contract has been awarded. Of equal importance to the checks on the manufacturer's output are the checks during the initial stages to ensure that the manufacturer has sufficient information to proceed and that the requirements of the contract in respect of the provision of a procurement and manufacturing programme are met. This programme should be critically examined to ascertain that it is in a suitable form for monitoring progress and to determine that the periods indicated are realistic and can be attained. Besides the manufacturing activities the preceding design and drawing work should also be monitored. The margins built into the overall programme to cater for unforeseen circumstances are all too often allowed to be taken up during the design stages with consequent pressure being put on to the construction period from the outset.

As the contract progresses checks should be made to ensure that interface design information is available, orders and requisitions are placed by the due dates, necessary materials and components are received as required and to verify that manufacture is proceeding according to programme. In order to maintain progress the availability of production and test facilities should also be considered and programmes established for any special or type tests which may be required and that adequate arrangements for packing and despatch have been made in good time.

Where the inspecting engineer has discovered that the manufacturing programme is in danger of slipping, or has slipped, and has established with the programmes controller that the overall programme is likely to be in jeopardy, expediting action should be pursued vigorously with the object of restoring the position. This action will vary with the circumstances but would involve a review with the manufacturer to ensure that all possible steps are considered with the aim of optimising recovery of the programme. Such matters as the establishment of additional check points, resolving priorities, overtime working, additional facilities and/or subcontracting work and the possibility of air freighting would be considered in this review.

It is considered that, following guidance from the programmes controller, the inspecting engineer is the best person to initiate such a review as he knows the manufacturer's works and is familiar with the processes involved and the facilities available. If the inspecting engineer fails to get the required results he will escalate the action, firstly by involving his own supervisor or the project engineer. This escalation may well then be taken further to project manager and executive management level, particularly if a solution to the problem is seen by the inspecting engineer but not accepted by the manufacturer. In these circumstances pressure may be brought upon the manufacturer by the inspection authority until a senior member of the project executive management may have discussions with senior executives of the manufacturing company. While such escalation in expediting may not always be certain to succeed, progress on a project is better assured with it than without. It is clearly true that results are obtained only by the adoption of vigorous and active channels of communication.

The client would be given information arising out of the progressing and expediting activities by the status report, which would also give a summary of the position of the assignment as a whole, highlighting important matters. Many clients require regular status reports to give them a proper understanding of progress on their projects and thus enable them to exercise control as may be necessary. In providing status reports the attempt is made not only to state clearly the actual position as it is found to exist, but also to give an estimate of the likely despatch date based on the assessment at the time when the report is prepared and knowledge of the processes to be completed. Status reports should be normally provided at regular intervals (usually monthly at the height of an assignment) and issued to ensure that they are in the client's hands in time for such regular progress meetings as may be held on the project as a whole.

Spares lists and operating and maintenance instructions must not be overlooked by the progressing and expediting functions. Recommended lists of spares should be established early enough in the project period to ensure availability of the spares on site in time to meet operational requirements. Instructions for the guidance of operating and maintenance personnel should be available at least six months before commissioning activities begin at site. For multi-contract projects it is often necessary to prepare overall project manuals particularly directed towards separate groups in the client's organisation. (For example, control room operators are interested in the overall systems and operational regimes rather than in the detailed maintenance aspects).

Programmes should include commitments for the provision of spares lists and operation and maintenance instructions which should be monitored and expedited as vigorously as the procurement and manufacture and erection of the plant itself. Delay in production of such lists and instructions can seriously jeopardise the initial operational intentions for the project.

There is one aspect of progressing and expediting which is not allowed to wait until the routine date for reporting. If in the course of inspection work an item is rejected or the inspecting engineer becomes aware of any other reason why the overall programme may be in doubt, the client should be notified by telex. Thus, with routine status reporting at regular intervals and immediate reporting of situations critical to the programme the client can be kept fully informed as to the progress of procurement and manufacture.

Payment verification

Payment verification is another function which relies on a sound progressing procedure. For large capital cost projects the terms of payment provide for contractors to obtain regular payments at monthly intervals. These payments are related to progress achieved and it is necessary for financial control purposes to ensure that appropriate checks are carried out. Several methods are adopted, and for measured work contracts (such as civil works and cabling contracts) where unit rates are predetermined physical measurement of the work achieved determines the value of each payment.

For other firm lump sum contracts one of the most popular methods is to break down the correct price to identify the value of each of the principal items of equipment. These values are further segregated to show the separate amounts for design, procurement, manufacture and erection. Either financial values or percentage weighting values are used and the payment due is verified by assessing the progress achieved each month against each element of each item. Another method is to establish predetermined payment values which are released when specific key stages in the individual contract programmes have been achieved.

INSPECTION

Inspection work demands a very logical and systematic approach. Assignments to inspect equipment and plant during manufacture require the preparation of product verification plans. Each of these should be compiled from three inputs:

1. The client's operational concern with the proposed design and with the relevant licensing and other mandatory requirements.
2. The inspection authority's design assessment of the equipment and its susceptibility to failure in relation to highly loaded or stressed areas.
3. The inspecting engineer's knowledge of the particular manufacturer's works and of any weaknesses which may exist in them.

Where appropriate, project verification plans should take into

Inspection and Expediting

account the type of quality programme and the extent of quality systems surveillance required (for example, the surveillance of series production standard stock-item components). The plans define in detail any inspections and tests which the inspection authority proposes to witness fully, those of which it is proposed to witness a proportion, and other inspections and tests to be carried out by the manufacturer where it is proposed to accept his test certificates.

During preparation, the product verification plan should be discussed with the client to ensure that his requirements are satisfied. The plan must also (obviously) be discussed with the manufacturer to ensure that it complies with his proposed method of manufacture and to determine that he will be providing adequate facilities for quality control. Once agreed, the product verification plan is used throughout the inspection assignment to cover all aspects of the contract from the inspection of raw materials to the final inspection of packing and shipping (as required by the client).

The overall advantage of a carefully prepared product verification plan is that all parties are agreed on the proposed procedures, and on who will be responsible for the various activities. It often happens that the finished plant or equipment is assembled from components originating from subcontractors or from other factories of the main contractor (sometimes involving overseas manufacture). The product verification plan ensures that, wherever they take place, all inspections and tests are treated similarly. At the end of the purchase contract, the plan forms an index to the inspection reports and certificates produced during manufacture.

The extent of the inspection authority's involvement with any assignment should be adjusted according to knowledge of the contractor's standards and the opinions held of his quality assurance systems. In cases where vendor assessment or vendor rating has been undertaken before the issue of the purchase order, the evidence available has to be considered. Such assessments should be carried out by engineers with particular knowledge of the type of product and manufacturing activities concerned. Visits to the manufacturer should evaluate:

1. The existence and maturity of a quality programme appropriate to that considered necessary for the product.
2. The manufacturer's experience relative to the anticipated order.

3 The manufacturer's history of achievement in quality and delivery.

If the opinion of any manufacturer is low, suggesting poor performance, comprehensive and rigorous (or, at least, additional) cover should be proposed in the areas suspected of weakness. The proposed inspection activity should also be arranged to suit the operational importance of the plant items concerned. The plan can be varied to meet a particular client's requirements: it should always be the intention that the client is clear from the outset on the extent of surveillance to be carried out.

The frequency of inspection visits should not necessarily be related to specific intervals, but should rather be set to correspond with the manufacturing status. As work on an assignment proceeds, surveillance should include periodic checking to ensure that the manufacturer is following the agreed procedures, and that the certificates he is required to provide are always valid.

Design approval

Design approval activities should not be undertaken until the jurisdictional requirement of the country in which the equipment is to be installed is fully understood. Many jurisdictions require the equipment to be inspected during manufacture by an Authorised Inspection Agency appointed by the jurisdiction but themselves retain the right to approve the design calculations. Others permit the Authorised Inspection Agency to perform both the design approval and perform the inspections. In both cases any Inspection Agency must seek the approval of the jurisdiction as an authorised inspection agency.

Approval by a jurisdiction

On the award or indeed in many cases prior to the award of a contract where design approval is required the manufacturer or design agency should ensure that all information concerning design approval is obtained and fully understood. This is particularly important in countries where English is not the official language since the requirements for submission may have to be translated from the official language. Also the methods of calculation may be defined by law and if this is the case alternate methods of performing design calculations may have to be determined and proved.

In many cases the submission to the jurisdiction may have to be in the official language and this can cause problems particularly when translating technical terms. One solution to this problem is to employ, if possible, the services of a firm in the country to which the equipment is being sent, who have experience in the requirements and format of the design submission.

If an inspection agency is appointed (normally by the purchaser or his agent) the manufacturer should ensure that the agency has been appointed as an authorised inspection agency by the jurisdiction. Failure to check on this will unnecessarily cause problems during the latter part of the manufacturing process and could prove extremely costly if fabricated equipment has to be dismantled for reinspection.

Approval by an authorised inspection agency

follows a comparatively simple procedure, the agency having been authorised by the jurisdiction both to approve designs and to inspect the equipment in accordance with jurisdictional requirements. Normally this is termed third party inspection and the manufacturer is responsible for employing the agency. However, the manufacturer must ensure that the agency is authorised by the jurisdiction.

In general design submissions are made to the agency who prove the design calculations generally using a different method of calculation from that used by the manufacturer. When satisfied, the agency approves the design for manufacture and performs the inspection according to jurisdictional requirements.

Reports

Reports should be prepared after each inspection and these should be produced on standard inspection report forms with significant rejection reports clearly identified as such. All reports should be sent to the client at monthly intervals, each batch covering the manufacturing activities of the preceding month. This procedure may vary depending on the particular requirements of the client. Figure 14.2 is an example of a summary inspection and expediting report used by the purchasing organisation of a contracting company.

Managing Project Materials

					DISTRIBUTION	NO. OF COPIES
					CLIENT	
					PROJ. MGR.	
					ACTION FILE	

CHILTON PROJECTS: Purchasing Department — INSPECTION EXPEDITING REPORT

This Report No.	Last Report No.	Date of this visit	Sheet of sheets

ORDER DETAILS

CLIENT ....

PROJECT NO. ....

ORDER NO. .... DATE OF ORDER ....

EQUIPMENT ....

REQUESTED DELIVERY
Wk. No. ....
Date ....

MAIN SUPPLIER DETAILS

SUPPLIER ....

LOCATION ....

SUPPLIER'S REF. ....

PERSONNEL CONTACTED ....

TELEPHONE NO. .... TELEX NO. ....

EQUIPMENT ....

DRAWING DETAILS WHERE APPLICABLE TO BE GIVEN IN TEXT OF REPORT

QUOTED DELIVERY
Wk. No. ....
Date ....

LATEST DELIVERY
Week No. ....
Date ....

NEXT VISIT
Wk. No. ....
Date ....

SUB-SUPPLIER DETAILS

SUPPLIER'S ORDER NO. .... DATE OF ORDER ....

SUB-SUPPLIER ....

LOCATION ....

SUB-SUPPLIER'S REF. ....

TELEPHONE NO. .... TELEX NO. ....

EQUIPMENT ....

DRAWING DETAILS WHERE APPLICABLE TO BE GIVEN IN TEXT OF REPORT

QUOTED DELIVERY TO MAIN SUPPLIER
Wk. No. ....
Date ....

LATEST DELIVERY
Wk. No. ....
Date ....

NEXT VISIT
Wk. No. ....
Date ....

Specification complies	Tests or Certificates	Shipping Released	Ahead Target	Action by:
YES/NO	YES/NO	YES/NO	On Target	
			Slippage .... Wk.	Date .... Inspecting Engineer ....

Figure 14.2 Inspection and expediting report summary
An example of a form used by the purchasing department of a contractor to summarise the results of visits by its inspecting engineers to the premises of manufacturers

Contrary to what is sometimes argued, experience does not lead to the belief that the use of the same man for inspection and expediting produces any conflict of interest in respect of, say, an item of equipment found unsatisfactory in test but known to be urgently required on site. Indeed, it is felt that the reverse is true and that the problems being basically technical, the fact that the inspecting engineer works closely with the manufacturer and is kept fully informed of the programme requirements leads to a good and satisfactory solution in respect of both quality and delivery in the best interests of the project.

GOODS INWARDS INSPECTION

So far, this chapter has been concerned with the activities of manufacturers before delivery of the goods. The functions of inspection and expediting are not finished, however, until the goods are safely in stores, fit for use on the project. Goods inwards inspection is the last link in this chain. Unlike the other activities so far described, goods inwards inspection is more likely to come under the direct supervision of the works or site inspecting team, rather than that of the purchasing organisation. The role of goods inwards inspection is dealt with in relation to the total stores function in the next chapter: here the quality control aspects will be examined in some detail.

Material being received on a site (manufacturing or construction) is normally delivered to the stores receiving bay. An exception to this general rule is when the material is large or heavy and requires handling equipment outside the range of the stores equipment. When this occurs the material should be clearly labelled 'HOLD FOR INSPECTION' and stored in a suitable environment.

The storeman should normally sign the delivery note and relate it to the corresponding purchase order copy before requesting inspection of the material. The receiving inspector (on receipt of the delivery note and copy purchase order) should check through the documents to determine what attributes are to be inspected and obtain the necessary documentation and equipment. Any certification of materials that is required should be requested from the supplier via the purchasing office if it has not already been received. In this case the material may be physically inspected and, if satisfactory, should be held in a bonded area of the stores labelled 'HELD FOR CERTIFICATION' and not released for use. When necessary, assistance should be requested from specialist services (chemical, electrical, electronic, metallurgical laboratories, etc., as appropriate).

Conforming material

can be released for further operations to be carried out and a material release note (MRN) should be drawn up. The top copy should be sent to the purchasing office to enable payment to be made to the supplier, two copies plus the delivery note and copy order to the storekeeper and one copy for file. If supplier history records are kept these should be completed by the inspector.

The storekeeper should then allocate storage space in the stores, mark up both copies of the MRN with the location and forward one copy to the quality assurance/control department, retaining the other copy with the returned delivery note and copy order on file.

Non-conformances

found during goods inwards inspection are covered by a non-conformance report (NCR) which must be drawn up immediately giving full details of the supplier, purchase order number, material description and non-conformance, etc. Since a minimum of four copies is required these NCRs may be of self-carbon copying paper or a single sheet which will be copied. In the former case the sets of copies should utilise a different coloured sheet to enable the top original to be identified. In the latter case a single sheet is used and this should have a coloured identification strip to distinguish the original from any copies. The distribution of these copies should be two to the purchasing office (original for transmission to supplier, copy for file), one to the quality assurance/control department and the final copy for the receiving inspector's files. The non-conforming item should be placed, where possible, within a quarantine section of the bonded area and, in any case, the item should be clearly labelled as non-conforming.

Inspection and Expediting

Resolution of non-conforming items

should be pursued unless it can be determined that the material cannot be used. The supplier should be requested to indicate on the NCR his proposed method of resolving the non-conformance. This could be 'return to supplier', 'repair at site' (manufacturing or construction) or a concession to 'use as is' and to return the NCR. Whatever the resolution is, provided that it is acceptable, the original of the NCR should be completed and copied. The original is sent to the quality assurance/control department, two copies to the purchasing office (one for the supplier, one for file) and a copy retained for the receiving inspector's files, the previous copies of the incomplete NCR being discarded.

Damage in transit

should be recorded by the storekeeper who should annotate the carrier's copy of the delivery note indicating that the goods were received in a damaged condition. The receiving inspector should be advised and requested to make an immediate appraisal of the damage. For raw material (bar stock, tubing, plates, etc.) providing the damage is superficial and can be removed during subsequent operations a transit damage report (TDR) should be made out and submitted to the quality assurance/control department for approval.

Excessive damage to raw materials or damage to proprietary goods (valves, fabrications, etc.) or machined items should be handled in accordance with the procedures for non-conforming items. When crates containing delicate or intricate items are received with excessive damage an initial TDR should be drawn up and copies sent to the purchasing office (one for the supplier, one for file), the quality assurance/control department and one for the receiving inspector's file. The crate should not be opened but stored in a bonded area. The purchasing office should immediately advise the supplier to ascertain whether he wishes to be present when the crate is opened. Following a decision on the parties to be present, the case may be opened paying attention to ensure that no further damage occurs. In certain cases it may be advisable to make a photographic record of the procedure for future reference. If, after examination,

Managing Project Materials

the goods are found to be unfit for project use, a non-conformance report should be prepared in the usual way as the first step towards getting the faulty goods rectified or replaced.

15

Stock Control and Stores Management

Dennis Lock

In a typical industrial project the equipment and materials will account for at least half the total cost. Purchase of special materials, components and equipment usually takes many months — even years — to accomplish, often featuring on the critical path of the project network diagram. Once safely received, all items must be securely placed in store until they are needed for use. Where projects are conducted by manufacturing companies with existing stores facilities, problems arise of ensuring that project goods are separately identifiable from normal manufacturing stocks, so that they can be located readily when the time comes for their issue and use. Another aspect of stores management in manufacturing projects is the correlation of goods which are common to normal manufacturing stocks and to project requirements. These may include simple consumable items, such as screws, nuts, bolts, sheet metal, and so on. They can also involve more complex components, such as motors, control valves, hydraulic cylinders, bearings, and the like. Projects, on the other hand, carried out on remote sites raise the problems of setting up secure stores from scratch, solely for the duration of the project construction or erection phase. It is to these problems of stock control and storage that this chapter is addressed.

PROJECT STOCK CONTROL

Consider the two extremes of stock practice. On the one hand, materials ordered specially for a project are ordered once only, according to a 'shopping list' contained in bills of material, parts lists, purchase schedules or some other form of control document. At the other extreme is the stock provisioning system used by a manufacturing company engaged in batch or process production, where a range of materials and components is always held in stock, with regular issues to the manufacturing organisation which have to be replenished from time to time. In many manufacturing projects, these systems have to mix. It will be convenient first to review what happens in a typical batch or process stock control system, and then go on to examine how the project system fits into the same stores organisation.

Manufacturing stock control

In a typical materials and stores control organisation, the objective is to ensure that the manufacture of products, and the supply of spare parts to customers from stock, can all take place without undue shortages ('stockouts') occurring. To maintain stock levels which always cover all possible requirements would be expensive in terms of the space required, the money tied up in those stocks, and in the risk of stocks being left over as obsolete and valueless when product lines are withdrawn from production. In order to cope with such problems, materials controllers have evolved a number of rules and practices over the years which, more recently, have lent themselves readily to adaptation for computer control.

It is convenient to consider three categories of stocked supplies. The simplest of these is the range of consumable, low cost items. These can include such things as cleaning rags, lubricants, and small components. Because of the low value of such items, it is less necessary to exercise rigid control in their use and issue than that needed for high value goods. Stock control is typically conducted by the 'two bin' method, where the items are issued from a container which, when empty, is replaced by another which has been held in reserve. New supplies are then ordered to refill the first bin. The only stock control decision necessary is to determine the size of the bin (possibly a little over-simplified, but that's the general principle).

Stock Control and Stores Management

There is a statistical technique, known as Pareto analysis, which can be applied to goods held in stock. The method examines the relationship between the number of different items held, and their relative values. It is commonly found that 80 per cent of the total stock value is represented by only 20 per cent of the items (sometimes called the 80/20 law). Clearly those 20 per cent of the goods which represent so much money invested demand the closest control. Their re-ordering will almost certainly be subject to scrutiny and senior authorisation. Indeed, the purchase of such items (which might include instruments, bought-out assemblies, motors, and so on) might be regarded as similar to project purchasing since they are likely to be ordered against specific, known requirements rather than for general stores.

If the relatively cheap consumable items are regarded as class 'C', and the most expensive as class 'A', then to complete the picture there are the class 'B' mid-range items. These will be controlled by some agreed formula that takes into account their purchase price, the rate of usage, the cost of storage, other overhead and administrative costs associated with their storage and re-ordering, and the importance of ensuring that the items do not run out of stock. Then, an automatic re-ordering system is implemented. The idea is that new orders are placed when stocks fall to some pre-determined level, giving rise to planned minimum and maximum holding levels with the actual quantity ordered each time (derived mathematically) known as the economic order quantity for the particular item. As with other stock control procedures, the control of maximum and minimum levels is very suitable for control by computer. The only real problem is to gauge the level of usage correctly against future production forecasts, and especially to ensure that goods are not re-ordered when a particular product range is planned to end.

These routine stock control methods, when applied as outlined here, are known as the 'ABC' system, obviously as a result of the A, B and C classes of stocks identified. The method is summarised in Figure 15.1.

Identification of common parts

A company which purchases stocks specially for a manufacturing project will almost certainly find that the materials needed include

Managing Project Materials

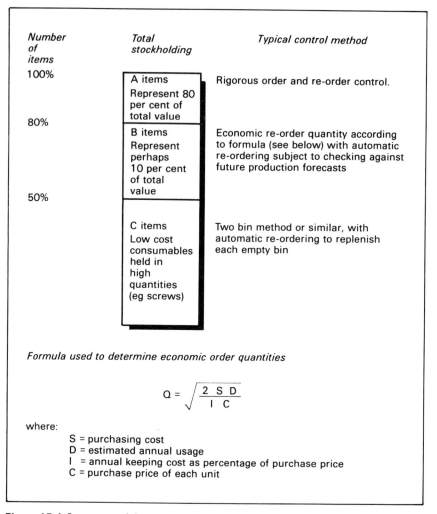

Figure 15.1 Summary of ABC stock control principles

some items which are commonly held in the general manufacturing stores. The purchase of those items should be correlated with the purchasing for stock, since by this means the quantities ordered are more likely to be large enough to attract suppliers' discounts.

There is a similar need to identify parts and materials which, although they may not normally be carried as stock, crop up in more than one assembly in the finished project, or in more than one batch

Stock Control and Stores Management

where the project comprises the supply of a number of pieces of equipment.

A sensible classification of parts by a standard numbering system is one way of identifying common parts. For things like nuts and bolts, classification by description may suffice, provided that the descriptive data are always expressed in the same units and in corresponding format. Computer analysis of parts lists and checking against a stock control data base are advantages which enable the project manufacturing management greater facility in carrying out this task than was the case a few years ago. The process used to involve compilation of index cards for all assemblies and sub-assemblies, from which common parts had to be identified manually.

In order to implement a common parts identification it is essential not only that a sensible parts numbering system is used, but also that an engineering standards manual is produced and kept up to date which lists all parts likely to be common. Again, computer listings provide a useful management tool: at their simplest these lists could be generated from the stores stocklists.

It should be noted that common parts can include parts, sub-assemblies and assemblies manufactured within the factory.

Quantifying common part requirements

It is not sufficient simply to be able to recognise the coincidence of parts common to two or more assemblies, or to assemblies and regular manufacturing stocks. In addition to calling 'Snap' the clerical or computer exercise must identify the total number of each part needed to fulfil all needs, and also determine the rate at which usage is likely to take place (purchase orders may have to be phased for bought out common parts and, more important, production control schedules for internally made parts have to be established).

The calculation of production or purchasing plans for common parts is a matter of correlating the total number of items needed, using parts lists, bills of material and other usage data from manufacturing stock records. There is a form of line of balance which is useful in this application (see Dennis Lock, *Project Management*, third edition, Gower, 1984).

Some aspects of common parts scheduling are illustrated in Figure 15.2.

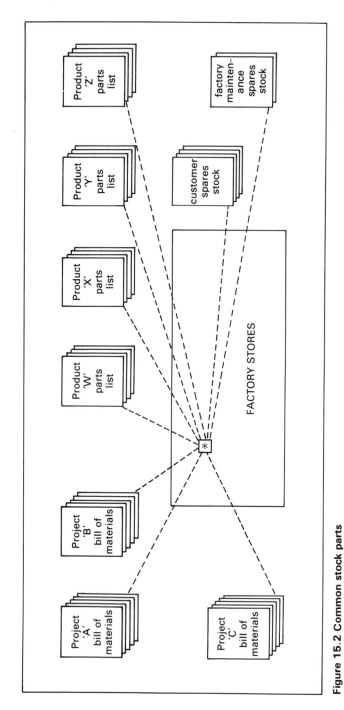

Figure 15.2 Common stock parts
The large rectangle represents total stocks held in the stores of a company engaged in batch manufacture and engineering projects. The small square marked * is just one of many thousands of items held in manufacturing stocks. This item may be required for several products, in which case it will feature on the relevant parts lists. The same part could also be stocked for the purpose of spares orders received from customers, and for the company's own maintenance department. When the same part also appears in the bills of material for complex projects, each with its own needs in terms of timing and quantities, total economic scheduling of stocks for just that one common part becomes quite an exercise, fortunately made easier by the use of computerised stock control. The problem is seen to be even more complex when it is remembered that many hundreds of parts could be common stock items

Stock Control and Stores Management

Pre-allocation of project stocks

Comprehensive stock control records in any well managed manufacturing company will show not only the level of stocks held and criteria for re-ordering, but also the assemblies and products on which each item is used. Again, computerised techniques are invaluable (especially when products are changed, added or deleted, in which case the stock lists can be searched by the computer to identify parts used on the affected products and amend the control data).

In the situation where one or more manufacturing projects are being conducted along with other manufacturing, the stores intake (and therefore the total stockholding) will include common items and goods bought or made to special drawings for specific projects. It is possible to introduce management controls in the stock records which prevent the issue of any materials needed for a project. This is simply a matter of listing the specified use in the stock records, and these should prevent wrongful issue for non-project use if the storekeeper scans the lists before fulfilling each stores issue requisition. This subject is discussed again in the following section on stores management, when it will be seen that pre-allocation in stock records may not be enough to prevent wrongful use of goods.

MANAGEMENT OF FACTORY STORES FOR PROJECTS

A typical materials handling function for manufacturing, which can include manufacturing projects or batch production or a mixture of the two, is shown in Figure 15.3.

Location and retrieval

It is very easy to lose stock items in even a small factory stores. Having to re-purchase goods that cannot be found, only to have the missing bits turn up later when they are no longer needed, is not a very edifying manifestation of efficient stores management. This problem is overcome by allocating every part of the stores a unique 'address'. These addresses are almost always known as bin numbers, whether or not the goods are stored in bins. A bin number will identify the stores bay, the rack, the shelf and the position along the shelf for each item.

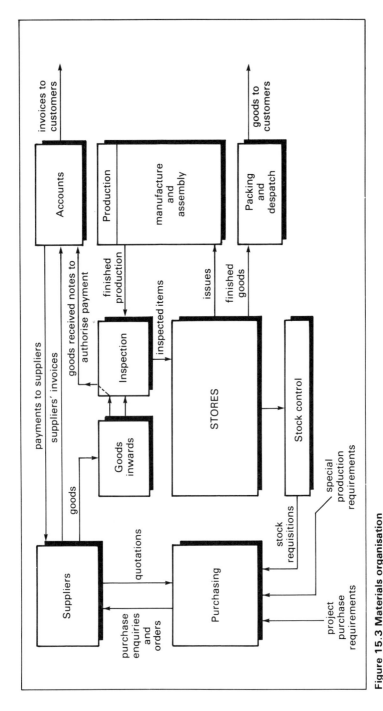

Figure 15.3 Materials organisation
This chart shows some of the principal activities and flow patterns associated with a stores and purchasing organisation which has to supply both batch production and project manufacturing needs. Note that all stores receipts have to pass through inspection (or quality control) to ensure that only materials and components in good condition are taken into stock. Any defects should be detected on receipt, and not when it is too late at the time of issue to production. The same quality control checks are also applicable to goods surplus to production which are returned to stores

Stock Control and Stores Management

Goods stored outside the factory, for example in a yard full of castings and weldments, will be included (the yard can be marked out in a numbered grid, with each small grid segment having its own bin number).

In very large warehouse facilities the location and retrieval of parts is automated, with 'order picking' machinery able to find items and deliver them to despatch bays without any need for handling by the storemen. Such systems are, however, likely to be outside the scope of firms engaged in mixed manufacturing with projects included.

Whatever the size and complexity of the stores organisation, the fundamental principle for ensuring tidy storage and subsequent retrieval is that the bin number for each item is tied to the part number in the stocklist.

Figure 15.4 illustrates the concept of bin number allocations which ensure that even the smallest and darkest corner of the stores can be identified by means of a simple number.

Security of project stocks

The most obvious aspect of stores security is to ensure that the whole stores area can be securely locked up when stores staff are not in attendance to keep their eyes on the goods. If especially valuable items are held in stock, particularly where these include readily saleable goods, simple locks may not be enough. Sophisticated alarm systems, designed to detect intruders, may be necessary, connected to a guard house, or by telephone line to a specialist security company's monitoring station (the system being known as a central station alarm). Automatic alarms can also be installed to detect and signal the presence of smoke or fire (again with central station involvement where this is considered to be desirable).

The usual procedure for the release of goods from stock is that the person requesting the goods presents either a properly authorised stores requisition to the storeman, or the production control department issue production documents which list the goods to be 'kitted' or 'kit marshalled'. Such lists are typically the parts list for the particular product line or, for projects, a more substantial bill of materials (one for each subassembly and for each main assembly). Provided that purchasing and stock control have been successfully managed in order to schedule goods deliveries into stores at the right

Managing Project Materials

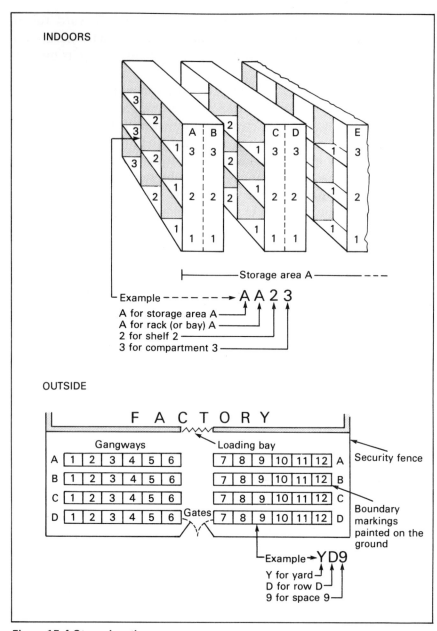

Figure 15.4 Stores location
Wherever goods are stored, it must be possible to find them again by means of a unique and unambiguous 'address'. This is achieved by the allocation of bin numbers, the principles of which are illustrated here for goods stored inside the factory on shelves or racks, and in external yards

Stock Control and Stores Management

times and in the correct quantities, then there should be no problem. Life is not so simple in practice. Too often unsuspected needs crop up, leading to unscheduled issues of items that are really reserved for other use. This can lead to shortages and consequential production and project delays. Project managers will usually suffer quite enough from materials shortages caused by late deliveries, without the added complication of shortages arising from unscheduled issues.

The only certain method for ensuring that goods received for a project are still available in stores when the time comes for their use is to pre-allocate them. Pre-allocation is done in two ways. The goods can be left in the common stores area, with the pre-allocation instructions marked up in stock records. In practice this will not prevent issues for other use, especially when the alternative use is demanded by a manager, not connected with the project, who is of large and intimidating appearance, with a voice and choice of language to match. The only safe and secure method of pre-allocation is to set up a special store for the project. The goods are then held under separate lock and key, and issues require the authority of project management staff. Even common stock items are withdrawn from the normal stock bins and transferred to the special project store.

When a special project store is established, this constitutes a form of bonded store. The goods are bonded in the store until needed. Such a bonded store may be a condition of contract where the project is for military purposes, or for aviation. In such projects inspection requirements are stringent, and demand that every item in stores (even down to single nuts and bolts) are traceable back to the original supplier and to the actual production batch. These conditions are imposed so that, in the event of a failure in service or a plane crash, all suspect components can be traced back to source: then future supplies can be modified or improved and military equipment, ships or aircraft fitted with the same suspect components can be traced and checked.

So now, by means of efficient purchasing, pre-allocation and (if necessary) the provision of bonded stores and special security alarms, it should be possible to make certain that the goods really will be available when they are to be used on the project. There still remain problems. One is that the goods will simply be lost in some dark corner of the stores. This is possible, even in a stores of modest size.

Location and retrieval problems will not arise if the bin numbering system is clear and unambiguous, provided that the storemen do not make mistakes, and that the stores management of stocks on the shelves is carried out in an orderly and tidy fashion.

The final problem faced by project managers attempting to have goods withdrawn from stores is that, although the goods are available, they have been damaged or have been allowed to deteriorate through inappropriate storage methods. Certain plastic raw materials, for example, should not be stored in the proximity of others. Some commodities could be affected by damp, while others might be spoiled by light, heat or excessive dryness. These are all matters for the stores manager, but the project manager should maintain an interest, at least regarding any items of known special risk.

Allocation of stores space

While the management of project stores may not be a function under the control of the project manager, whenever a project is going to demand the storage of materials in a factory or area shared by others the project manager must ensure that space will be available when needed. The space taken up by stores is a resource, and needs some form of planning, along with all other project resources. This is not to suggest that space planning should be included in networks and computerised resource allocation (although this has been done successfully). What is essential is that the project manager confers with production management, giving estimates of the amount and type of storage space that will be required, and a sensible estimate of the timing of goods deliveries.

The author remembers one particular occasion from his own project experience when a very large lorry, loaded to overflowing with a huge tarpaulin-covered batch of specially made wallboards, arrived at the factory in London after a long journey from the Clydeside area of Scotland. The driver was tired, and not amused by being kept waiting for a whole morning while the factory stores management attempted to find somewhere dry and secure for this load to be placed. The load was expected, and storage space should have been made available in advance. The lorry driver was able to express himself very well on this occasion! And some of the names which he called the stores management were well deserved.

Shortages

Shortages can occur through a variety of causes. Perhaps a common stock item has not been re-ordered in sufficient time to replenish stocks as they are used. Any stock controller knows that to guard against any possibility at all of stock shortages (zero stockouts, to use the awful jargon) investment levels in stocks would simply be uneconomic. Stock control systems aim to reduce the possibility of shortages to a low, acceptable level. Statistical methods are used to achieve this aim. So, there will almost inevitably be shortages in common stock items from time to time in a manufacturing company.

Project purchasing should not result in shortages through under ordering. There is no economic problem to work out on quantities and levels of stocks. There are bills of materials or purchase schedules which spell out what is required, with specific quantities known. All that should be necessary is to order everything at the right time, and there should be a complete stock of all bits, pieces, components and materials when the project has to be built. Well, of course, there are many reasons which get in the way of this ideal.

Suppliers may default on their delivery promises, through incompetence, strikes, genuine problems and through failures of their own suppliers. The next snag comes when goods are transported. It is not unknown for goods to be lost or damaged in transit. Items shipped or airfreighted from overseas sources can be delayed by port or customs formalities. Upon arrival at the factory, the goods have to be inspected. This can be a simple visual check, or it might be a full inspection and testing of some instrument against a carefully prepared set of inspection instructions and drawings. Only when the goods received are declared fit for use on the project should they be passed into stores. That is still not the end of the story. It has been known for items to be lost in the stores area, or damaged by careless handling. Indeed, upon reflection it is rather surprising that any goods at all ever overcome all the obstacles along the way to their inclusion in the final project assembly.

For really large items of equipment, the project manager will almost certainly be aware of any delays in their supply, since they will certainly be the subject of regular inspection and expediting action. Many smaller items can, unfortunately, come as a nasty surprise through their absence on the day when the storeman attempts to

Managing Project Materials

gather together all the items needed for a particular project sub-assembly or main assembly. This process of 'kit marshalling' (or simply 'kitting') is usually controlled from the relevant parts list or bill of materials, presented to the storeman by production control.

Whenever the storeman is unable to complete a kit through the appearance of shortages, he must immediately inform the project manager (or at least the manager responsible for manufacturing) by means of a document which gives details of every missing item. This document is, not surprisingly, known as a shortage list. By passing copies of this list to various people in the organisation, the storeman effectively stirs up quite a lot of activity in order to get the missing items produced in the shortest possible time. One copy of the list goes to the buyer or purchasing expediter. Another goes to the project manager, and he will then be warned to keep an eye on the purchasing department. Another copy of the shortage list goes to production control (or to production management) where a decision can be made on the desirability or otherwise of issuing the kit to the factory for production to start. It is often possible to assemble part of a project without all the materials, in which case the incomplete assemblies have to be tagged as having shortages, and placed on shelves together with their relevant shortage lists. Starting project assemblies with shortages is an undesirable and untidy business, to be avoided if possible. In a badly run factory it is an unpleasant sight to see quantities of assemblies on shelves (or standing about on the floor) waiting for parts. It does happen.

While shortages should not occur in any number in a well run project organisation, they obviously cannot be avoided altogether. The shortage list procedure is an effective method for rectifying problems when they do occur. It is, indeed, a very good example of the principle of management by exception.

Stores documentation

In Figure 15.5, some of the most important documents used in stores management are shown. Please do not pay too much attention to the flow patterns indicated, since these will vary from one company to another depending upon the particular organisation and procedures. For example, it is quite likely that parts lists and bills of material would be issued to stores via production management, rather than

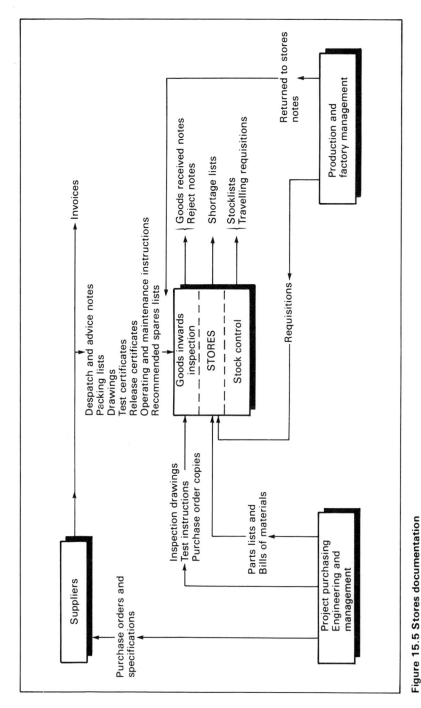

Figure 15.5 Stores documentation
Some of the more important documents which are likely to be handled by a factory stores unit which also has to support engineering projects

directly from project management. The aim of this section is to explain the purpose of the various documents that control the management of stores materials.

Purchase orders

are obviously the documents which authorise suppliers to start the manufacture or provisioning of materials, and they contain all technical and commercial information relevant to each purchase contract. A copy of each purchase order is relevant to the goods inwards inspectors, since this gives prior warning of deliveries to come and enables the inspectors to check that quantities received agree with the order.

Inspection drawings,

possibly accompanied by test instructions, give the goods inwards inspectors information against which they can check or test incoming goods to ensure that they conform to requirements and are fit to pass into stores for subsequent project use.

Despatch or advice notes

are issued by suppliers to indicate when they are about to send goods, or they actually accompany the goods. These come typically as copies of the suppliers' invoices, except that price information is blotted out by overprinting. Despatch and advice notes can carry useful information such as the mode of transport arranged (useful sometimes for expediting deliveries held up or lost in transit) and they give notice of part shipment of orders where the supplier has been unable to fulfil all the obligations at one delivery.

Drawings

from suppliers are important for project records. They may be needed for goods inwards inspection, but they have to be retained by the contractor on behalf of the client or project customer in order that the contractor can continue to give technical back-up to the project long after the initial construction, erection, installation or delivery has taken place. Drawings may need engineering approval.

Test certificates

from suppliers may be necessary for pressure vessels and other equipment where safety is to be ensured. This category would also include lifting and hoisting equipment.

Release notes

are essential before goods can be accepted into stores for certain military and aviation projects. These show that the goods have been produced according to quality control and inspection standards approved by the relevant government inspectorate and enable the source of the goods to be traced in the event of any kind of failure during service.

Operating and maintenance instructions

for bought in equipment and components are obviously necessary for project management to ensure the commissioning engineers are fully briefed. In all probability the operating and maintenance instructions will have to be passed on to the customer at the end of the project, although (because of the project contractor's long term obligations to his customer) the contracting firm should file at least one copy.

Recommended spares lists

should accompany some of the more complex items received into store. These are the suppliers' recommendations for spares stockholdings. These lists are usually passed on to the end user of the equipment in order that he can assess stock quantities.

Goods inwards receipt notes

are issued by goods inwards inspectors when they are satisfied that goods comply with purchase order needs. One copy accompanies the goods into stores, where (acting as an inspection clearance certificate) it tells the storemen that the goods as received are fit for use on the project, and can be accepted into stock. Other copies go to stock records and to the accounts department (to release payment against suppliers' invoices). Although goods inwards received notes may be specially printed forms on pads, it is possible to shortcut paperwork by simply photocopying the suppliers' own delivery or despatch notes (if necessary on to colour coded plain paper sets in order that the receipt note copies can be recognised clearly for the purpose of distribution to the various departments who need them).

Reject notes

are produced by the goods inwards inspectors when deliveries are deficient or damaged or otherwise unacceptable. These notes hold up payment of invoices and, by means of the copy sent to the purchasing organisation, ensure that replacement goods are obtained quickly.

Parts lists and bills of material

are 'shopping lists' prepared by project engineering personnel, which list all items needed for each project assembly. The quantities of each item are given, and the goods are described clearly by means of both descriptions and part numbers. The storemen are expected to produce kits of parts for each bill of material received. Purchasing department will have received each bill of material earlier for the purpose of ordering the goods from relevant suppliers. When issued through production management or production control, bills of materials are the authority against which the stores release goods for production.

Shortage lists

are compiled by storemen to highlight any stock deficiencies which prevent them from making up full production kits. The use of these has already been described in an earlier section of this chapter.

Stocklists

produced by the stock control section of the materials and stores organisation, are useful in many ways. They are valuable to engineering design staff, and help to ensure that new bills of material and designs are made without calling for new stock items that would duplicate alternatives which would be just as satisfactory and which are already stocked. Stocklists perform all sorts of other functions, from the provision of information to salesmen about goods available for sale to assisting the accounts department with inventory valuations.

Travelling requisitions

are documents which form part of stock records. They are detached from the stock records whenever the number of items held in stock falls to a pre-determined re-order level. The relevant travelling requisition (which is really a pre-prepared purchase requisition) is sent to the purchasing department to generate an order for replenishment stocks. The travelling requisition is returned to stock control on each occasion for re-use. Hence it travels back and forwards between purchasing and stock control. The only relevance to project stocks for travelling requisitions is in the maintenance of common stock items — that is items used for normal manufacturing in the factory and in project assemblies.

Stores requisitions,

which authorise the release of items from stores other than those called for on bills of materials and parts lists, may be generated by factory management. Typically these will be used for items needed for maintenance, for replacements when parts are lost or damaged, and for consumables such as oil, rags, and the like. Another typical use of stores requisitions is for parts needed by the engineering department for building prototypes or test rigs.

Returned to stores notes

are raised by production management whenever items are found to be surplus to requirements on the shop floor. It is essential that any goods returned to stores are re-inspected to ensure that they are fit for later use, and for this reason the goods and the returned to stores notes are sent back through goods inwards inspection. Returned to stores notes, once approved by the goods inwards inspectors, are distributed rather in the same way as goods received notes. They correct stock records and cost control records.

Managing Project Materials

SITE STORES MANAGEMENT

Many large projects involve the establishment of storage facilities at sites remote from the contractor's own premises, and staffed by a team outside the immediate control of head office staff. The arrangements can vary considerably, from the relatively simple set-up in which goods are delivered to a site controlled by the customer or client (where the client already has adequate storage facilities) to the other extreme of a location in some remote part of the world with no roads, and where the only inhabitants are wild animals, or poisonous reptiles, or hostile human beings, or some combination of all these.

All the usual stores requirements are needed, such as racking with proper location coding, security, goods inwards inspection, formalities to ensure proper authorisation for issues, shortage control, and so on. But, removed many thousands of miles from home base, these functions become considerably more difficult. It was seen in the previous section on the receipt of normal manufacturing stocks that every item has to undergo a series of obstacles which could jeopardise final receipt into stores. For a remote site, the obstacles are more numerous and more hazardous. For example, it is not unknown for consignments to suffer theft for the very packing case materials which were designed to protect them. Packing cases contain wood which is very suitable for a number of purposes, especially where the local inhabitants live in shanty towns.

The situation will most probably be further complicated by the fact that sources of supply will include shipments ordered from head office, together with bulk materials and other commodities ordered locally. The stores will be dealing with shipping agents and a purchasing network which is generally more complex than that needed for a factory. Documents also will be more difficult to manage and comprehend, involving international shipping documents, customs documents, and the like. The project manager must ensure that those responsible for managing and operating a remote site stores are fully experienced, competent, trustworthy and resourceful.

Warehousing and storage facilities

The siting and arrangement of external and covered storage areas must be arranged carefully so that the passage of materials and supplies into and out of the stores can proceed during the course of the project in the most efficient manner possible, with short routes and with as little risk as possible of those routes being interrupted through excavations and the like. Provision of roadways, gates, fencing, yard and road lighting are all considerations essential to the secure storage of goods and their subsequent transport.

Construction

methods used in warehouse buildings will depend upon the life of the project and whether or not the stores are to remain as part of the operating project. Ideally, stores buildings should be of permanent construction, totally weatherproof and secure against unauthorised entry.

Floors

must be capable of carrying the loads expected, including the weight of racking and any handling equipment or fork trucks. They should also be level, especially where high racking or stacks are envisaged. The floor surface should be capable of withstanding the kind of rough wear associated with a project site store.

External doors

must be of sufficient width and height to permit the passage of the largest loads expected, if necessary including transporting vehicles.

Material handling equipment

may have to include hoists, overhead travelling cranes, lift trucks and, for external use, rough terrain mobile cranes and trucks.

Lighting

must be adequate internally and externally to allow efficient and safe working, the outside lighting having also an important use as a deterrent to night-time intruders.

Environmental control,

including ventilation and possibly heating (depending on the climate) must be designed to make certain that stored goods do not deteriorate sooner than their normal shelf life expectancy.

Risk of fire

is real, and must be guarded against. Smoking should be prohibited within stores buildings and all equipment and electrical installations must be maintained adequately to avoid fire risk.

Covers

for externally stored supplies must be made available, such as tarpaulins. Also available should be items such as sleepers (so that equipment can be kept raised off the ground) and spare pallets.

Tools

must be provided for stores staff, including those necessary to open (and, if necessary re-seal) packing crates.

Offloading and receipt of goods

It is obviously important that offloading facilities for goods are provided right at the start of a project in order that the first deliveries of heavy items can be handled. Responsibility for offloading and initial handling must be clearly established: it is assumed here that the site management team will be responsible, through its stores staff.

Those offloading and receiving goods at site have a responsibility similar to that of the goods inwards staff described in the earlier parts of this chapter for an engineering factory. Goods must be checked against the accompanying documents to ensure that they are present in the correct quantities, and that they tally with the descriptions. Any deficiency, sign of damage, or other discrepancy must be noted on the receipt copy of the shipping documents or other despatch note, and a separate report made to the appropriate shipping or purchasing agent.

Identification of goods for subsequent retrieval is vital, and the receiving personnel have to ensure that cases bear suitable identification. Usually this is the purchase order number, but it could also be the project area code for which the supplies are intended. The time to ensure that this marking is clear and correct is at the time of receipt, and not after the goods have been stored and their purpose forgotten.

Where supplies are received in mixed lots, it may be necessary to unpack them and re-group so that they are arranged according to the project usage requirements.

Site stores documentation

In many respects the control documents at site correspond to those needed for a factory handling projects internally (these were described earlier in this chapter). At site, it is probably practical to file all documents in numerical sequence of purchase order numbers. These documents will typically include:

1 Purchase order copies.
2 Specifications (associated with the purchase orders).
3 Suppliers' drawings and other technical documents.
4 Goods received notes.
5 Requisitions for stores issues.

Documents which are especially connected with remote (rather than home-based) stores include:

1 Shipping documents, including bills of lading and airwaybills.
2 Discrepancy reports, which report goods received short supplied, over supplied or damaged.
3 An overall materials status report, for circulation among site management and transmission back to home office. An example of this report format is given in Figure 15.6.

Stock control of site materials

It may be necessary to arrange for stock control procedures to govern the procurement and stockholding levels of certain construction bulk materials and consumables. The system can be set up using stock

MATERIALS STATUS REPORT

Project No. ....
Report date ....
Sheet No. .... of .... sheets

Purchase order No.	Description	Vessel/flight	Notes and references	Arrival date	
				Planned	Actual

Figure 15.6 Site materials status report
One method for recording shipments planned and received at site. Late deliveries, or those in danger of being received too late, can be highlighted in the final column. Reports such as this are circulated to relevant site managers for information on progress, and one copy is transmitted back to home office for action to expedite any overdue items

record cards (for example Kalamazoo) with information on acquisitions given by goods received notes, and withdrawals notified by stores requisitions. Naturally, it will be necessary to carry out physical stock checks from time to time, and not rely upon the records alone.

Storage and maintenance of equipment

The following guidelines apply to project supplies which are to be held in storage for significant periods:

Mechanical equipment

such as pumps, compressors, turbines, should be:
Stored off the ground.
Protected from rain and moisture.
Kept lubricated.

Piping

should be stored with ends covered and on suitable racks, grouped in the various sizes and specifications.

Valves

and other flanged components should be protected with grease. Where provided, wooden covers should be kept bolted in place.

Instruments

must be stored under cover, indoors, away from any risk of damage through shock or vibration.

Electrical equipment

must also be stored indoors wherever possible but, where items are too large for accommodation indoors, they must be well covered for protection against the elements and stored off the ground.

Managing Project Materials

THE SITE MATERIALS CONTROLLER

To round off this chapter, here are some of the principal duties and responsibilities of a site materials controller. These have been summarised from a job description used by a construction company.

Key duties and responsibilities.
> Controlling all materials required for construction.
> Ensuring that the status of all materials is always known and communicated to other members of site management.

Site establishment.
> By co-operation with cost and planning engineers, determine the expected quantities and volumes of materials that the stores organisation must handle.
> Specify storage areas required, whether outside or covered, together with fencing, materials handling equipment, security arrangements and other equipment and tools.
> Estimate the staffing required to operate the stores and specify the timing of recruitment and release of staff according to programme.
> Work with the client's own stores organisation and local purchasing agent to ensure good liaison during the project construction and proper handover of remaining stores when the project is commissioned.

Material orders.
> For materials requested by site engineers, establish first that these have not been ordered by head office and then obtain the materials by means of a local purchase order, or by requesting head office or the relevant purchasing agent to order the goods. Understand and record the delivery programmes for all materials and follow progress through receipt of telexes, inspection reports and other correspondence.
> Collaborate with the local planning engineer whenever material or equipment delays are forecast in order to determine the effect on the construction programme.
> Co-operate with shipping agents and be aware of all shipping routes to be used and the timings of all consignments due.
> Inform head office of any special site requirements concerning packing, maximum loads, etc.

Stock Control and Stores Management

Where special urgency demands, make special arrangements with head office for transport to be expedited, using airfreight where necessary.

Follow up and arrange for action whenever delays are apparent, if necessary visiting local ports or railheads to carry out personal on-the-spot investigation.

Damaged materials.

Arrange for immediate inspection of goods received damaged by the relevant field engineer.

Estimate the costs of damage and institute an insurance claim. Arrange reinstatement or replacement or damaged items in order to safeguard the project progress.

Take similar insurance and replacement action for goods lost in transit.

Storage.

Arrange regular examination of stored goods to guard against deterioration.

Carry out regular stockchecks.

Stores issues.

Ensure that issues are properly authorised.

Record all issues and ensure that they are correctly allocated to project cost codes.

Surplus materials.

At the end of the project, make an inventory of remaining stocks and arrange for disposal as directed by the client or by the project manager.

Ensure that cost allocations are made correctly for the values of surplus material disposals.

Safety and welfare.

Learn and follow the client's own regulations concerning the site together with all local statutory regulations, particularly concerning the storage of explosives and construction safety.

Be on the lookout for any failure to meet such regulations by contractors and subcontractors on site, and report any such failures to the relevant field engineer.

Learn and obey all local labour legislation.

16
Packing and Shipping

Graham J. McCleery

Project shipping is the function of delivering all the equipment and materials necessary to fulfil a project. A good example of a major international project involving the delivery of supplies is seen when a country suffers a natural disaster such as an earthquake or a famine, and international aid has to be organised on a grand scale at short notice. This demands the rapid movement of supplies from source to the disaster site, often against the handicap of difficult communications and poor transport routes. From the initial procurement of supplies to their delivery at the scene of the crisis, every element of the support services plays a vital role. One weak link in the chain, whether this is the failure to package the supplies carefully or the absence of a suitable truck to deliver 10 tonne loads of grain over the last few miles, can spell failure for the whole venture. Similar considerations apply in the field of commercial projects, and this chapter deals with the planning and teamwork needed to ensure that project capital equipment, pipework, steel, electrical and all other components and materials are delivered to the project site in good condition and at the right time to meet the project construction schedule.

FEASIBILITY

Depending upon the location of the project (but particularly if it is upcountry in an undeveloped part of the world) a full evaluation of shipping services and the means of final delivery is advisable, as existing road, rail and port facilities may be inadequate. As an example of the unexpected findings which such a study could reveal, the curve inside a railway tunnel was found to be too sharp for the transit of a 25 metres long cylinder so that alternative discharging and delivery routes had to be arranged just for this item. Far better to discover such restrictions before, and not during, the shipping programme.

A feasibility study can be a costly affair in terms of qualified personnel, travel and accommodation. Savings can be achieved, however, by involving a specialist freight forwarding agent at an early stage. His local office or agency in the destination country provides an obvious source of up-to-date information, including awareness of local official regulations. Clearly in a competitive situation there is merit in inviting more than one forwarder to submit a report and quotation. Those approached should be made fully aware of the probable shipping programme (with dates and tonnages) and the weights and dimensions of large individual items. Limits of responsibility would also have to be defined, including customs clearance and delivery to site.

The essential features of a feasibility study can be summarised as:

1   Shipping services (covering both liner and non-conference sailings).
2   Alternative ports of discharge.
3   Ability of vessels on the route to accommodate non-containerisable items.
4   The maximum size and weight acceptable for loading and discharging by ship's gear, and with port equipment.
5   Port facilities. Capabilities of lifting gear, forklift trucks and mobile cranes. Availability of lighters for direct overside delivery from vessels. Details of open and covered storage areas. And, of course, the cost for each of these services.
6   Clearance and delivery. The attitude and degree of co-operation expected from local customs. The effect of any import licence regulations on the release of cargo by the customs. Availability and suitability of vehicles or railway rolling stock to convey materials (including long containers) from the port to railhead or project site. The provision of special trucks for long lengths, heavy lifts, flammable or corrosive liquids and explosives.

7   Transportation and handling costs from port to site.
8   Transit formalities if the project site is in a land-locked country.
9   Documentary requirements for local and transit customs processes.
10 Security recommendations.

From the main contractor's point of view, the above summary is somewhat abbreviated as it excludes such essentials as temporary office accommodation, housing, catering, supply of construction materials (whether sourced locally or imported) and local personnel transport. However this chapter seeks to concentrate on the considerations surrounding the shipping of goods from country of manufacture as distinct from local domestic forwarding, but overall planning does of course encompass delivery of local commodities.

A feasibility study would normally be conducted well in advance of any firm commitment and, on the assumption that a reasonable period of time would be available between the evaluation and commencement of the shipping programme, steps can be taken to effect alterations or improvements to the handling or transportation system. This may involve re-grading roads, strengthening bridges, widening port gates, etc., all of which will require official sanction. Here again the project forwarder's local contacts may prove useful.

PLANNING

In project shipping, planning and teamwork are the recipe for success. Planning will have been developed from the results of the feasibility study and can be subdivided into:

1 Schedule of constuction site requirements and deadlines.
2 Procurement lead times.
3 Inspection and expediting requirements.
4 Forwarding to the country of destination.
5 Final delivery to site.

The team which will co-ordinate the operation will have individual responsibilities and reporting lines but ultimately is accountable to the project manager. He will probably appoint a senior person to

Packing and Shipping

administer all aspects of supply and delivery with appropriate authority on decision taking. Normally the administrator will chair a committee composed of delegates from the purchasing department (with professional civil, electrical and mechanical engineering back-up) from the site contractors and from freight forwarding (which could of course comprise an 'in house' shipping department, although frequently agents specialising in project shipping are nominated to attend, not least because of their established connections with international carriers and on-ground presence in the country of destination enabling them to identify problem areas).

The freight forwarder included in the team will be either the successful bidder for the transportation element or a retained agent with whom the project manager has had a successful working relationship for a period of time. The latter category will probably achieve better results because in a complex sequence of production and handling there will inevitably be numerous occasions when lines of responsibility have to be crossed in the interests of the enterprise as a whole, and proven contacts are usually hard to substitute.

In this sequence of events, the project forwarder acts as an extension of purchasing and the following review concentrates on the considerations arising therefrom. As the objective is the efficient transport and delivery of materials to a predetermined schedule, the forwarder will usually be made responsible for ensuring that adequate shipping space is prebooked. Steamship services to many areas of the world are advertised by conference lines (who offer regular scheduled sailings) and by outside operators who may have comparable equipment but are not subject to regulation in the traditional sense (hence these are termed non-conference, and have the reputation of being more competitive). The forwarder must satisfy himself that either option (scheduled or non-scheduled) offers acceptable prospects of cargo space being held for his principal's requirements throughout the duration of the shipping programme. It has further to be established that vessels on the route are capable of accommodating outsize pieces, long lengths and heavy lifts requiring deck stowage or loading to a break-bulk hold if unsuitable for container shipment. It is also usual for the forwarder to be a party to negotiations with the carrier for an agreed project rebate on the freight rate. On both these issues it is essential that the maximum information on shipping tonnage and expected dates of availability of cargo is made available

Managing Project Materials

by the operating committee, and that all offers are confirmed in writing.

In exceptional cases, at ports or terminals which are operated on a competitive basis, preferential handling charges can be negotiated for a project tonnage over a fixed period, and the successful outcome could of course influence a decision on the choice of carrier. Supplementing the shipping programme, the forwarder is well advised to have access to estimated shipping specifications of individual orders. These details usually are indicated in supplier's data and can be incorporated in purchase orders copied to the forwarder. He can introduce them into his own systems for processing by his own dedicated team, who will later be involved in calling forward ex works and arranging the export shipment. The project manager will doubtless identify all related work and material orders with a common reference number or code which should be used as the prefix for all communications and master references on documentation. This is particularly advisable if the project manager has existing plant already operating in the same area and should help to prevent goods being incorrectly delivered.

Decisions will be taken at the planning stage on the terms of supply. These may vary depending on the nature of the materials and on the practicability of the buyer taking delivery ex works or free on board (fob) at a nominated port of loading. In many instances the quoted cost of the goods may determine the terms. The forwarder must obviously be advised of these terms in advance, and copies of purchase orders are an ideal way of meeting this standard requirement.

The need to advise the freight forwarder on order terms should perhaps be described further. Ex works sales place the responsibility for collecting the goods from the manufacturer or supplier on the buyer. He has to make his own arrangements to take delivery through the project freight forwarder or preferred transport contractor, and the buyer can therefore exercise cost control. Sales on fob (free on board) terms defer the passing of title to the goods from manufacturer to buyer until they are delivered to the ocean or air carrier (or carrier's agent) and so far as the forwarder is concerned responsibility for delivery rests with the supplier and he is not

Packing and Shipping

required to arrange collection. In practice however, many manufacturers are prepared to delegate collection arrangements of fob sales to the project forwarder (but for supplier's account of course). This interchange of services, subject to a clear distinction of responsibility for payment, assists the orderly flow of materials to the port of loading.

In the planning context, the gathering and distribution of documents including purchase orders, shipping specifications, suppliers' invoices and receipts given for goods, has to be considered. Although control should be with the shipping or progress department of the project management, the forwarder can make a contribution by undertaking certain work associated with his function. As an example, the forwarder can undertake to produce sets of shipping forms specifically designed for a particular project which could incorporate:

1 Shipping instructions to the supplier to deliver to the forwarder's depot.
2 A copy of the shipping instructions for the shipping and progress department as evidence of action.
3 A warehouse receipt copy of the shipping instruction documents for the shipping department to use in providing evidence of delivery for goods supplied on terms other than ex works, thus facilitating release of payment for the goods.

In support of such a document system the freight forwarder can provide inland courier services between the various organisations concerned (such as the shipping department, engineering inspection authority, receiving warehouse and the forwarder's own offices). If the volume of paperwork so dictates, the courier could be a dedicated service, with the documents carried in pouches which are colour coded to ensure transmission to the correct parties. Prompt distribution of shipping documents is vital to any shipping programme, but it assumes even greater importance when all the procedures are required for a strict delivery schedule in which the elements are interdependent. Equally important is the availability of adequate telecommunication links between the shipping department and the forwarder's relevant offices.

FREIGHT FORWARDING

Packing standards

Packing goods for shipment overseas has two basic objectives:

1. To protect the goods from physical and climatic damage.
2. To afford the means of handling individual pieces in the interests of achieving correct delivery to the final destination.

The range of packing methods is very wide indeed, and can depend on the method of transport. Lightweight tri-wall cartons can be used for airfreight in preference to heavy wooden cases in order to keep down the weight of the consignment and ensure that the freight costs are confined to the goods, without paying also for the carriage of heavy packing materials. On the other hand, for heavy pieces the load-bearing capability of the aircraft floor will be the determining factor, requiring (for example) that a heavy casting or awkwardly shaped steel fabrication must be mounted on wooden skids or flat platform to spread the load. At the same time, the base of the load has to be compatible with the fork trucks and other ground handling equipment which exists for loading and unloading.

Items for delivery by sea freight which at one time would have been wood cased or shipped unpacked might nowadays be transported to the project site or its nearby port by container, in which cases it is often possible to reduce the packing specifications.

It is seen, therefore, that there are many permutations of the ways in which project materials can be packed. The project manager's shipping department must obviously issue guidelines on packing standards to manufacturers and suppliers of goods. In liaison with his freight forwarder the project manager must take into consideration all the handlings to which the goods will be subjected over the entire route from factory to project site, including the various means of conveyance, climatic conditions likely to be encountered en route and the handling equipment availability and type, always bearing in mind that these conveyances and the associated materials handling equipment might not be ideally suited to the project needs or up to standard.

If the shipping services and connecting transport and facilities allow the use of standard containers delivered right to site, then these

Packing and Shipping

packing guidelines become less rigid. The considerations are:

1. Will the piece fit into the container? (If so, mount it on a pallet, and give special protection to any delicate parts.)
2. Is the size and shape of a piece such that it might have to be overstowed by other cargo within the container? If so, and it is likely to be damaged by being overstowed, then it is clearly necessary to provide strengthened packing.
3. Are the goods themselves vulnerable? Steel plate takes care of itself but electrical equipment requires protection against accidental damage and excessive humidity.
4. If not strongly packed will it survive the journey from the manufacturer to the freight forwarder's depot or to the carrier's inland container depot (ICD) for stuffing into the container? Many a package has come to grief by falling from a vehicle, or from a forklift truck.

For projects at destinations not served by door-to-door container facilities, the packing criteria can be summarised as follows:

1. Drums — designed to carry liquid. These are often reused so care must be exercised to check for leakage.
2. Fibreboard cartons — widely used and suitable for most goods.
3. Wood cases — constructed from softwood boards or plywood panels.
4. Cardboard cartons — goods of a robust nature such as floor tiles, nuts and bolts, canned provisions etc. can remain in this original factory packaging but would normally be polythene draped and strapped to a pallet.

Large fabrications may be impracticable to pack but should be on timber ties of sufficient gauge to protect the transportation floor, and to facilitate handling. If movable only by overhead gear, lifting points must be shown.

Goods of a hazardous nature, for example chemicals or other products with flammable, corrosive or explosive characteristics, are all subject to international transport regulations which define the quantity permissible for carriage per individual receptacle or overall case. Most manufacturers will be familiar with these stipulations but if in doubt should refer to the official regulating body of the exporting country. In the United Kingdom, the 'Blue Book' issued by the Department of Trade & Industry is the standard work of reference for surface freight movement of dangerous goods, and its airfreight counterpart is the *Restricted Articles Manual* issued by the International Air Transport Association (IATA). All those concerned with export shipping should be aware of the basic restrictions as failure to advise port authorities and the carrier of the nature of hazardous goods can result in prosecution under United Kingdom legislation.

Airfreight

Generally speaking it will be mainly lightweight goods or those of a particularly fragile nature that will be intentionally programmed for airfreight despatch. The tare weight of the packaging has to be kept to a minimum in order to avoid unnecessarily increasing the total weight on which the freight costs are calculated. At the same time, the packaging has to be consistent with safety and able to withstand the handling to which the package will be subjected throughout transit.

To this end many types of standard size cartons are marketed. These are constructed of two or three ply corrugated cardboard and have immense integral strength but remain vulnerable to an external blow such as an ineptly operated fork lift. Lightweight plywood panel cases built on to a strong base are a more expensive alternative with a higher survival rate, particularly on the final leg from airport of discharge to the project site, and are more likely to deter the pilferer than a carton which can easily be opened up with a knife.

Care should be taken to ensure that case dimensions are acceptable by the air carrier. On most international routes there are freighter aircraft operating but occasionally there will be a requirement to move a consignment at a time, or to a place, served only by passenger aircraft where cargo has to be stowed in the belly-hold. Even with freighter aircraft, the loading of a large case can present problems. The door size may permit access but the other case dimensions have to be within the limits dictated by the curved fuselage otherwise it would not be possible to turn and manoeuvre the case down inside the cabin to the required stowage position.

Packing and Shipping

Case markings

Cases can be specially marked for a variety of reasons but markings are essentially used to identify:

1. The port of offloading together with the final destination.
2. The contents of the case through the medium of an order number with project prefix reference. For goods which may be potentially attractive to villains there is merit in avoiding declaring the contents on the exterior of packages.
3. The hazardous nature of the contents, supplemented by obligatory warning labels.
4. Dimensions, and gross and net weights. Not always shown but nevertheless very useful for checking packages against a written specification, also to indicate the appropriate capacity of handling gear to be used.

In a project shipping programme, where goods are being despatched to a destination already used by the same company, it is advisable to instruct suppliers and forwarders to give prominence to the project reference and to apply an additional distinguishing mark which will be unique and immediately recognised by port workers, transport contractors and all others concerned. This mark would usually be in colour in the form of a diamond, square, circle or cross, and the project reference is frequently shown within this symbol.

Specially printed labels, bearing the project reference prefix with space to insert the purchase order number, are also recommended and these can be colour coded in agreement with the project manager to provide for segregated delivery of varying categories of materials to the required locations on the construction site. Such labels are always useful to have for dealing with the occasional case which is found to be insufficiently or incorrectly marked prior to shipment.

These persons involved in handling freight also appreciate an indication of unusual centre of gravity. The wording 'Heavy This End' can help to avoid accidents, quite apart from damage to goods.

Transport arrangements

Upon being told by the purchasing or shipping department that a particular order is ready at the supplier's premises, the freight

Managing Project Materials

forwarder initiates one of the following processes, depending upon the terms of purchase:

1. *Ex works* — he arranges for transport to collect the goods for delivery to the port of loading, inland container depot (ICD) or forwarder's warehouse for grouping with other goods for the same project.
2. *Free on board (fob)* — he instructs the supplier to deliver the goods to the port or depot (having first obtained confirmation of space booking on the required sailing) or to the warehouse for groupage.

For goods delivered direct to the port or ICD the supplier is given a booking reference to include in his own delivery documentation. This is normally a standard shipping note, the format of which is multi purpose and contains many details which will be repeated on the bill of lading.

Goods received into the forwarder's warehouse would generally be relatively small items for re-packing into larger containers prior to re-delivery to the port or ICD, or for airfreight despatch, or to be held for examination by an inspecting agency. It is quite common for such inspection to be made a pre-condition of shipment by overseas parties who require to be satisfied as to the quality and/or quantity of goods, and this is particularly the case where a government has some interest in the enterprise.

On delivery of goods to the ocean or air carrier, the forwarder compiles a bill of lading or an airwaybill. This shows the names and addresses of the exporter, final consignee and (usually) the clearing agent at the port or airport of discharge. Also shown are the description, weight and measurements of the consignment and the case markings. These would include the project order numbers and such other item references which may be required by the shipper or consignee to ensure correct identification of specific packages or crates. These documents constitute a contract of carriage, when signed on behalf of the carrier as confirmation that the shipment has been duly loaded on the nominated vessel or flight. The documents therefore give title to the goods when presented to the carrier's agent at the destination.

In liaison with his principals, the forwarder is frequently required to transmit shipping documents to the consignee or his clearing agent. A typical set of such documents would comprise:

Packing and Shipping

1. Original bill of lading.
2. Original supplier's invoice, plus copies.
3. Packing specifications.
4. Certificates of origin, as required by the customs authorities at the port of discharge. (These certificates can be prepared by the freight forwarder from particulars given in the supplier's invoice. Depending on the statutory requirements of the destination country these particulars are certified by an approved chamber of commerce, and then 'legalised' by the appropriate consulate or embassy).
5. Insurance certificates, or other acceptable evidence that the goods have been covered, together with the premiums paid.

On discharge of the consignment at the port of destination declared on the bill of lading, delivery will be given to the carrier's agent against presentation of the bill of lading and payment of any landing charges. Release of the goods from the port area, however, remains subject to the approval of the customs entry document. This is normally prepared and lodged by the consignee's clearing agent, who probably also has the responsibility for forwarding the goods by road or rail to the project site.

Customs formalities vary considerably and many countries have complicated entry and clearance procedures. These are best delegated to an import broker or to the import clearance department of the consignee's agent.

On taking delivery, the clearing agent must satisfy himself that the goods covered by the bill of lading are correct in all respects and undamaged. If not he must qualify the receipt given to the carrier with details of any visual damage and notify Lloyd's local surveyor. The operation of taking delivery, examination and transfer to the customs area for clearance would be observed and reported on by the shore superintendent. Details of the materials received would be sent to the project site in preparation for their subsequent arrival.

Onforwarding to final destination is undertaken either by project site management, using their own or hired transport, or is delegated to the clearing and forwarding agent at the port of entry to organise. If onforwarding is by rail a series of additional handlings may be involved in transferring goods from the port area to railway depot, with subsequent handlings from rail wagons to vehicles for eventual site delivery. At all handling stages goods will be at risk of damage or pilferage. Maximum supervision is necessary to ensure that correct receipts are given so that the appropriate party can be held responsible in case of need. The forwarding agent's duties would be to arrange for transport to remove goods or containers from the quay or the ocean carrier's inland depot, to prepare road waybills or rail consignment notes, to supervise the loading of vehicles or rail wagons, to prepare transit customs documents and manifests (if the project site is across an international border) to defray inland freight charges, and to advise the site management in advance of the delivery, with full details of the goods by quantity, weight, description and order number.

In undertaking these duties the freight forwarder is at all times acting on behalf of his principal who is ultimately responsible for paying charges. The freight forwarder's liability is limited by his terms of trading. These include provisions to protect himself from the consequences of actions by carriers, subcontractors or others involved in the transit of goods over which he does not have direct physical control. Frequently the freight forwarder finds himself caught up in disputes between the cargo interest and the carrier, but his allegiance must be to his principal.

The freight forwarder can be remunerated through varying arrangements. He can make agreed charges for the specific services provided (for example, booking cargo space, compiling shipping documents, and so on). Under arrangements which are possibly more suited to project shipping he could negotiate a lump sum payment, or a fixed charge for each individual purchase order handled (with disbursements recovered at cost). The laws of fair trading prevent the operation of any cartel regulating charges made by UK freight forwarders, and as a consequence this section of the business community has become highly competitive.

COMMUNICATIONS

Communications are vital to the whole process of project shipping, not simply during the passing of telex messages between the forwarders and their opposite numbers at the destination, but over the whole programme of events from the initial ordering of goods to their arrival on site.

Packing and Shipping

The project freight forwarder will probably find that he is obliged to match his principal's systems. This is logical, since he acts as an extension to the ordering process. Most such systems are computerised, so that the project manager can communicate via a terminal to his forwarder to arrange constant updating of the status for each individual order. Similarly, by telex such information can be relayed to the site manager or contractor overseas, and repeated to the shore superintendent who acts for the project manager at the port of discharge.

The shore superintendent is a key link in the communication chain. His is an appointment that any project manager would be well advised to make. Ideally his background should be a combination of merchant marine and freight forwarding experience, since his assignment will bring him into daily contact with people from ship to quayside, in the warehouse and, finally, in rail or road transport. Bearing in mind that he will be receiving consignments of loose or containerised goods from the ocean carrier, and taking control on behalf of the project manager, it is essential that he is advised in advance of all the particulars of each consignment (order numbers, item numbers, weights and dimensions of outsize pieces, etc.) to facilitate correct scheduling of deliveries to the site and to organise any special materials handling equipment or transport. Depending on the efficiency of postal services over the relevant routes, and the voyage times, the project manager and his freight forwarder must agree on how best to ensure that full specifications are available to the shore superintendent some days before the arrival of each ship. If normal airmail services are unreliable it will be advisable to use airfreight or courier services to carry the documents. Certainly telex or facsimile transmissions can prove suitable for relaying the information but, unfortunately, there are still some parts of the world where telecommunications cannot be relied upon, and other suitable provisions must be made.

Telecommunication links between the project manager's shipping department and the project freight forwarder are likely to be used intensively. Cost savings may be possible through installation of direct, private wires (tielines). Such lines are very convenient, since they relieve pressure on other exchange lines, allow all calls to be made without charges and guarantee that the line will be open and not engaged when it is needed.

For messages received from suppliers or manufacturers it is usually preferable to use telex or facsimile, so that written proof is generated. In the world of shipping and forwarding it is paramount that the written word is kept on file.

At all levels of the production, packing, shipping and final delivery stages good communications can speed the flow of work, minimise delays and allow corrective action to be taken when necessary. The aim must be to keep all parties fully informed, even when the news is bad. It is better to be advised of a production delay, short shipment of a piece of equipment with a critical delivery deadline, or the dropping of a crate into the waters of the harbour rather than have everyone find out the hard way.

CONTINGENCY

Regardless of planning and the best professional control throughout the operation, there will be occasions when one or more points in the delivery cycle are interrupted, usually with minimal warning. Industrial disputes at source of supply or at the construction site, or misadventure in transit, can have a serious effect with imponderable knock-on consequences. Although the circumstances are generally outside the control of the project management, the heavy commitment in terms of finance and manpower dictates that a contingency plan should be agreed in basic form in advance, be it additional storage space for goods supplied ex works, or alternative means of export shipment.

The decision to put a contingency plan into operation is never easy as invariably it attracts higher costs. The tendency is therefore to sit out the dispute for a while and wait on developments. Unfortunately such a policy can aggravate matters and the freight forwarder finds himself seeking shipping alternatives in a carrier's market at inflated rates.

Airfreight is an obvious alternative as means of delivery if the dispute affects ports or deep sea shipping services and, from the wide selection of freighter aircraft employed across the world, an air broker can obtain price indications and take out options on whatever availability may be on offer. The aircraft finally 'fixed' must of course be suitable for the task which the freight forwarder and air broker can evaluate between them. The weights and dimensions of pieces, their 'stowability' within the aircraft, equipment necessary to load and offload the cargo, and the availability of suitable handling equipment at the airport of destination are all elements requiring detailed examination before commitment to an air charter. The project forwarder, either directly to the air carrier or through an air broker, can establish the availability of aircraft in a matter of minutes via modern communications systems. A telex confirmation by the carrier and the cargo interest forms the basis of an Air Charter Agreement which, by universal custom, calls for payment prior to flight departure.

The short notice at which a flight or series is arranged in support of an emergency normally dictates that the project managers resign themselves to paying for the round-trip. But occasionally there are opportunities to broke the return 'empty leg', subject to there being no objection raised by the national carrier of the country concerned, thus facilitating the granting of traffic rights. However, generally speaking, revenue derived from an empty leg makes only a small contribution. The organisational effort is regarded by many as disproportionate to the benefit and possibly jeopardising the performance of the succeeding flight.

Contingency planning should also take into account the otherwise orderly processes that stand to be disrupted. If goods are being supplied by the manufacturer on fob terms and he has elected to arrange his own delivery to the port, the shipping departments of the manufacturer and the project manager must be able to pre-empt the situation and implement alternative delivery instructions. These may call for diversion to a different port of loading, to an inland container depot for movement to the continent, to an international airport, or to the freight forwarder's storage facility depending on the decision taken and success of alternative fixtures. For goods supplied on ex works terms, the project forwarder may find himself required to organise additional storage space, regardless of the overseas despatch method, because the manufacturer is unwilling to allow the goods to remain on his premises in space needed for other purposes, or because he wants to realise payment for the goods against their delivery.

There are, of course, endless permutations of the circumstances and of the remedial actions which can be taken. As with planning, the essential feature is close liaison between all the parties concerned

Managing Project Materials

coupled with a clear mandate from the principal defining areas of responsibility and lines of communication. An emergency air charter might be organised in exemplary fashion but, if the freight controller in charge of final delivery at the destination has not been properly advised in advance, time will be lost while road transport and materials handling equipment is moved to the arrival airport. If such delays hold up unloading of the aircraft high demurrage charges could be incurred.

INSURANCE OF GOODS AND INSURANCE CLAIMS

Marine insurance is a vast and complex subject. The following account describes its application to project shipping.

Responsibility to insure

For goods purchased on ex works or free on board terms the buyer arranges transit insurance of the goods. Goods supplied on cif terms (cost of goods, insurance and freight) are insured by the seller unless otherwise agreed.

There is an anomaly with fob sales because legal title to the goods does not pass to the buyer until they are loaded on to the vessel or delivered to the carrier's shore based facility. The supplier should, therefore, insure the goods fully up to the point at which the risk technically passes to the buyer.

Many foreign governments are able to insist that the insurance of goods delivered to their countries is placed with locally registered insurance companies (usually state controlled). This frequently dictates that purchases are made on ex works terms, as a supplier would not accept the risk of insuring outside his own country.

In Chapter 7 the subject of insurance is treated in its wider application to project work, and we repeat here the advice that there is an advantage in placing transit insurance with the same insurer who covers the risks of construction and erection at the project site. Should any damage be discovered to equipment during erection, it may not be possible to determine exactly when the damage occurred. The project manager will want to avoid a situation where two insurance companies, one responsible for shipping and the other for

Packing and Shipping

erection, each refuse to meet a claim on the grounds that the damage cannot be proven to have taken place while the goods were covered by their policy.

Scope of insurance

For most project accounts, an 'all risks — warehouse to warehouse' cover is contracted through an insurance broker who places the risk with an underwriter at Lloyd's. The total amount held covered must not be less that the insurable value of goods destined for the project on board any one vessel, or aircraft. Otherwise only a proportional settlement can be obtained in the event of total loss.

The contract of insurance will be given a reference specifically identifying the cover with the project, and will probably have an agreed schedule of percentage rates regulated to the nature of the various commodities to be shipped. High risk goods such as fragile electronics will be charged at top rate, steel girders at a low rate, and (depending on the location of the project and the route) the underwriter may encourage specialist packing in exchange for a reduced level of rates.

The 'warehouse to warehouse' scope is intended to cover every aspect of transit through to the project site, including retention of cover whilst goods are held in a forwarder's warehouse or carrier's depot. There is normally a time limit placed beyond which the cover would expire unless the insurers were notified. Declarations of individual consignments despatched against such all risks cover are usually made in summary form 'per vessel' or 'per flight', detailing:

1. Purchase order number.
2. Class of goods, as defined in the contract of insurance (for example, 'fragile' or 'hazardous').
3. A brief description of the packing method.
4. Value for insurance purposes.
5. Name of the vessel.
6. Sailing date.
7. Intended port of discharge.

Inaccuracies in particulars given on the declaration could lead to a disputed claim in the event of loss or damage. Care must be taken to make a full and correct entry for each consignment. Responsibility for lodging declarations with the insurer could be assumed by the project contractor, acting as overall exporter, or it could be delegated to the freight forwarder. The forwarder already has the necessary information from the documents in his possession and from the shipping or flight arrangements which he makes.

For some overseas destinations the customs at the port of discharge require a declaration of the cif (cost of goods, insurance and freight) value to supplement the import entry. This declaration can be in the form of a cif certified invoice, which the exporter (or forwarder) would compile. The insurance element would be calculated from the agreed schedule of rates. This system is often required when the insurance cover is contracted abroad, and under these conditions the insurance declarations themselves have to be filed abroad. Here again is a service which can be performed by the freight forwarder's office or agency in the destination country.

The current cargo insurance policy is known as the 'MAR' policy. This incorporates the findings of the technical and clauses committee of the Institute of London Underwriters, following the *Report on Marine Insurance*, United Nations Conference on Trade and Development, 1978. The MAR policy became obligatory in 1983.

Cargo insurance claims

There are three distinct aspects of cargo claims. These are:

1 Total loss.
2 Partial loss.
3 Damage in transit.

Settlement of a total loss claim is the insured value of the goods, whilst partial loss claims are dealt with on a proportional basis. Claims for damage in transit can be time consuming and require that precise attention is paid to the collation of supporting documents as the onus to prove damage rests with the claimant.

If there is visible evidence of damage when the goods arrive at the clearing agent or final destination, the receipt for the goods given to the carrier must be qualified by a written statement to the effect that the goods are damaged. A copy of the receipt must be retained by the recipient of the goods. Unless this is done, the carrier can maintain

Packing and Shipping

that a 'clean receipt' was given, which would limit his liability and impede the settlement process in the event of a claim.

If goods are found to be damaged on receipt they should be surveyed as prescribed in the terms of the insurance cover or policy and a report obtained. The consignee must concurrently address letters of reserves to the carrier (or carriers, if ocean and inland transport were employed to achieve delivery). These letters hold the carriers responsible for the damage caused, and reserve the right to claim from them in due time. The carrier, in order to protect his position as required by the insurers, will probably reply repudiating any liability.

A typical claim for damage to goods against a cargo insurance policy would require the following documents:

1. The insurance policy or copy of memorandum.
2. The invoice relevant to the damaged goods.
3. The original bill of lading, or consignment note, or waybill.
4. The survey report (described above).
5. A copy of the claim sent to the carrier, together with his reply.

The insurance underwriter will settle the insured value (or a negotiated proportion if there is a discrepancy in the proof supplied) through the broker's claims department. Most project managers will elect to stipulate 'claims payable in the United Kingdom' (or in their own country) as this simplifies the re-ordering process. A 'claims payable abroad' basis is obviously undesirable but this occasionally has to be accepted if the insurance cover is held (by decree) in the destination country. Technically the re-ordering or replacement of damaged goods would have to proceed regardless of the prospects for settlement by overseas insurers in order to get the project finished. Another difficulty in using overseas insurers is the possibility that fluctuations in exchange rates could put true settlement figures at risk.

CONCLUSION

Packing and shipping form the last links in a chain of procurement activities which begin with the specification of goods and equipment needed for the project and end with their safe arrival on site. Being at the end of the procurement chain, shipping dates are subject to the cumulative delays and programme slippages of all preceding activities. There is often a degree of urgency needed to get the goods transported as quickly as possible to their destination. And yet any haste in packaging, or in the preparation of vital shipping documents can, if carried out wrongly, put the safety of goods at risk and lead to avoidable delays at ports, airports and frontiers. International shipping has to be a team effort, and the project manager will want to be reassured that the members of that team, wherever they are, are properly experienced and competent.

As part of the project shipping team, a freight forwarder in the exporting country, complemented by his counterpart at the destination, can make a very important contribution to the efficient delivery of goods and materials. The freight forwarder therefore makes a positive contribution to project progress and efficiency. There are over 3000 freight forwarding companies in the United Kingdom, many of whom are equipped to handle complex shipping programmes through world-wide connections. Many are specialists in their own fields, or in the range of commodities which they handle. One thing which they all share is enthusiasm for their chosen profession, which is (without doubt) one of the most absorbing possible.

FURTHER READING

Croner's Reference Book for Exporters, Croner Publications, New Malden, Surrey, UK (by subscription, updated monthly).

Croner's Reference Book for Importers, Croner Publications, New Malden Surrey, UK.

Croner's World Directory of Freight Conferences, Croner Publications, New Malden, Surrey, UK (by subscription, updated monthly).

Export Education Packages, Formecon Services Ltd, Crewe, CW1 1YN, UK.

Packing and Shipping

ORGANISATIONS

Technical Help to Exporters, British Standards Institution, Maylands Avenue, Hemel Hempstead, Hertfordshire, HP2 4SQ, UK.

Export departments of the major clearing banks.

The Institute of Freight Forwarders, Suffield House, Paradise Street, Richmond, Surrey, UK.

Part V
PLANNING AND SCHEDULING

17
Planning with Charts

A. G. Simms

The human eye is very good at recognising patterns, and management science makes good use of this by presenting complicated facts in the best form. Charts and figures can be made to convey a good deal of such information. In verbal descriptions words necessarily follow one another, so that cross-connections cannot be shown clearly by words alone, and this is where charts are most powerful. If a chart models reality well, all sorts of connections are made evident.

BAR CHARTS

One of the oldest and most familiar management aids is the bar chart. This shows all relevant jobs, operations, activities, processes, etc. in the form of bars. The length of each bar is proportional to the duration of the activity being represented, and it is shown against the same timescale as all other activities. Such a chart illustrates at a glance what jobs are to take place at any one time, how starts and ends of different jobs are related, and so on. A Gantt chart, named after Henry Gantt who introduced it in the 1900s, is basically a horizontal time bar chart.

To appreciate the immediacy of understanding which a bar chart can give, compare the listing of jobs to be done when developing a new office building (including their start and end dates) with the corresponding bar chart (Figure 17.1).

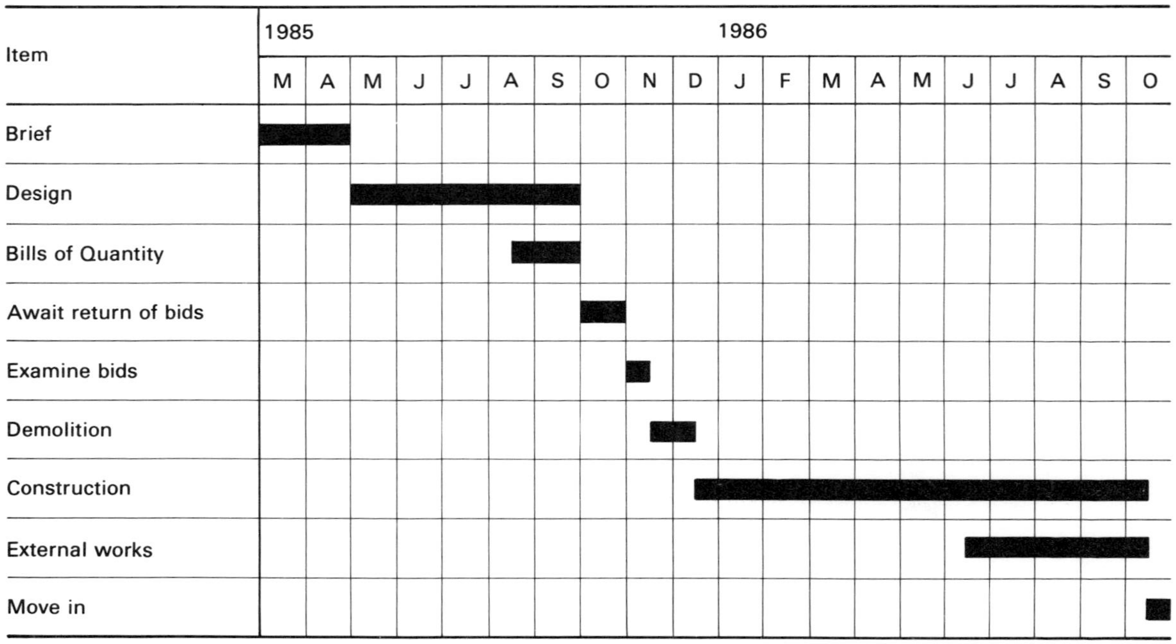

Figure 17.1 A project plan in bar chart form

Planning with Charts

Item	Start	End
Prepare brief	1 March 1985	30 April 1985
Design	1 May 1985	30 September 1985
Bills of quantities	15 August 1985	30 September 1985
Await return of tenders	1 October 1985	31 October 1985
Examine tender bids	1 November 1985	15 November 1985
Demolition	20 November 1985	4 December 1985
Construction of building	5 December 1985	5 October 1986
External works	5 June 1986	5 October 1986
Move in furniture and equipment	6 October 1986	31 October 1986

Time scale for new office building

The bar chart (Figure 17.1) has a horizontal timescale, in this case a calendar, and each of the nine items is shown against the listed dates. Note that one of the items does not represent any action by members of the project team, namely waiting for the return of the bids.

This form of a bar chart is quite typical in that it gives an outline plan of the timescale of a project broken down into a relatively small number of project components, some of which represent a collection of many activities. If necessary, any major component can be broken down into suitably detailed jobs to provide a guide for supervision at a lower level. For instance, the foreman in charge of external works would be given a plan in the form of a bar chart of all the separate jobs summarised here as 'external works'. Long experience on the working site has proved that such a chart is more easily used than a list of start and end dates of activities and their durations.

It may often be convenient to give the timescale relative to the start date of the project (whenever that may be) starting with zero, so that there would be no need to change all the dates if the project start is changed.

Bar chart for project control

The progress actually achieved can easily be entered on the bar chart. For example, the bar showing the plan of the job can be in the form of an open bar or box, which can be filled in for the time during which work is being carried out. Alternatively, the bar representing work reporting back from the working site can be shown in parallel. Figure 17.2 shows the position of the project described above on 5 December

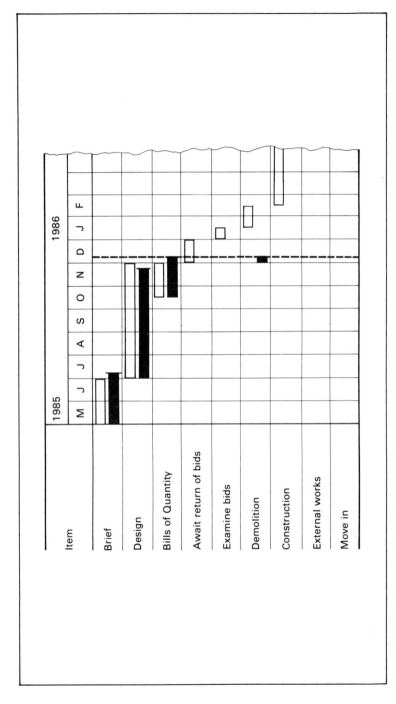

Figure 17.2 Bar chart used for project control
The chart shows the state of the project on 5 December 1985. Open bars are the planned operations (revised if necessary to accommodate programme changes). The filled-in bars show dates actually achieved, with the completion of each phase indicated by a vertical line at the right hand end of the appropriate bar

Planning with Charts

1985. We note that there has been a change in the time table, as the go-ahead for the project was given on 1 May instead of 1 March 1985. This means that all dates are 2 months later than planned, unless there has also been a change to the plan itself. It might have been easier for the planners to use a timescale relative to the start date — whenever that took place — but at working level it is much better to show actual dates or week numbers.

No changes of plan (other than the start date) have been made to the first jobs of the project, and both the design and the preparation of the bills of quantities should have been finished by 25 November. Figure 17.2 records the reports from the work and this shows that the drawings have been completed on time, but the bills of quantities are not yet to hand. On the other hand, demolitions were not expected to start until well into 1986, but in fact they were reported to have started on 1 December 1985. The bar chart in itself is quite incapable of showing what has happened, or indeed of indicating what actions are open to the planners to make such a change. In this case, when the project was planned demolitions were intended to be part of the main contract, and that was the reason for their start to be planned immediately after the contract had been awarded (at the end of the activity: 'examine bids'). Instead of this the project team decided to award a separate contract for the demolitions. As a matter of fact these could have been done at any time, but the bar chart cannot show which jobs, if any, must precede demolitions. Figure 17.2 does not show either whether the plan has been changed in other ways: it seems likely that construction of the building could start sooner; at least one can assume that that was the reason for the early start on the demolitions.

Adding information on the bar chart

The information on a bar chart can be enhanced in a number of ways. For example, the bar symbol itself can be labelled. Such a label could be used to indicate who is to carry out the job, or the responsible department. On manually drawn charts a colour code can be helpful, but for reproduction it is better to use shading. A further refinement is an indication of the resource loading. For example the number of tradesmen needed for an activity can be shown on the bar symbol. Figure 17.3 shows two different grades by their shading, and it gives

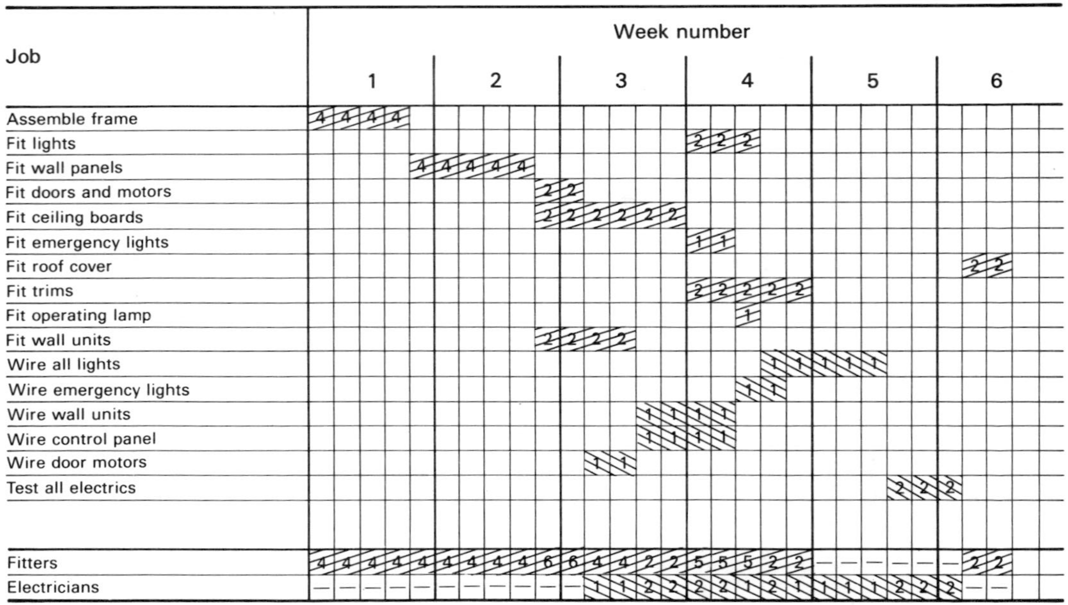

Figure 17.3 Bar chart with resource scheduling
The total number of men in each trade needed for each day are shown at the foot of each column. If the chart is constructed on an adjustable board, so that the bars can be moved or slid horizontally, then it is possible to adjust the planned timing of jobs to achieve a sensible and practicable rate of usage for each resource

the number of each that is needed. The manager can see how many tradesmen are needed day by day from the totals shown on the bottom lines. In this way the chart makes it simple to allocate resources efficiently.

It is most important, however, never to lose sight of the greatest advantage of the bar chart, namely the directness and power of its message. Any secondary information that is added should never obscure the main point, namely the timing and duration of the depicted activities. 'If in doubt, leave out'.

Uses and limitations of bar charts

The purpose of the bar chart is to aid the timescale planning and sequencing of tasks, and to present timing information to the manager in a form that is grasped easily. Too much detail can be a hindrance. Thus a bar chart with more than 50 activities or so becomes little more than a list, and it loses its point of clarifying the structure of the project. This does not mean that bar charts cannot be used on projects consisting of many activities. For such projects one could simply use single bars for groups of jobs or processes. That would enhance its use at the top level, that of project supervision, wherever an overview is needed with sufficient (but not too much) detail.

It is at the work level that the bar chart is the most useful management tool. Foremen and supervisors in charge of jobs actually being carried out need to see precisely the timing of that part of the whole project for which they are responsible.

The main drawback of the bar chart is that it does not show directly how the jobs are connected, in particular how far the start of any job is constrained by the completion of one or more other jobs. For instance the activity: 'move in furniture and equipment' in Figure 17.1 is planned to start when two other jobs have finished. It is not possible to tell from the chart alone whether there is any connection between the end of one or both of these jobs, and the start of the subsequent one. While such connections may seem obvious to the person who drew up the plan, or to anyone familiar with such building projects, they are simply not represented on the bar chart. It would be possible to enhance bar charts by showing connections, but

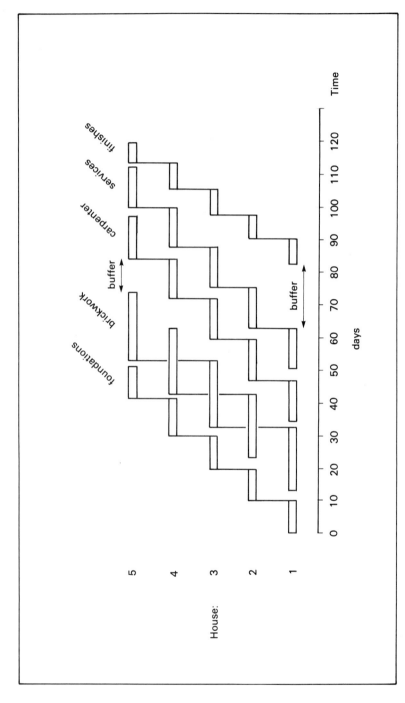

Figure 17.4 A line of balance chart for the construction of five houses
Each horizontal bar represents an operation on a house. The vertical lines show how a gang of tradesmen moves from one house to the next as the jobs progress

they were not devised for that: it is much better to use diagrams designed for that purpose. These are discussed in Chapter 18.

To sum up, it is not so much the size of the project that limits the use of bar charts, as the amount of detail that can usefully be shown. For the beginner, bar charts with more than 20 or 30 bars are not so easy to handle, and even experienced practitioners rarely employ such charts with more than 50 bars (except possibly as a form of list). Provided that bars represent appropriate sections or components of a project, a bar chart can be a useful and productive aid to management of large and small projects.

THE LINE OF BALANCE CHART

The bar chart concept has been extended to deal with some kinds of repetitive projects, for instance the manufacture of a number of units, or the construction of identical houses on a housing estate, or floors of multi-storey buildings. Successive units go through the same stage, and after one unit has passed through a stage, the next one can start to go through it. The bar charts for each unit are the same, and all of them can be drawn on the same figure. Conventionally one draws them one on top of another, with the first unit at the bottom.

There is a time lag between the start of one unit and that of the next, and at the end of the process units are completed and handed over at a similar rate. Figure 17.4 shows the five bar charts for building five houses successively on the same figure. For each house the construction process is broken down into a simple succession of jobs. As an illustration, the whole process is broken down into: foundations, brickwork, carpentry, services and finishes. Each of these stages is done by a different gang, so that any one of them can only start its work on one of the houses when the previous gang has finished its work there. A brief interval of time is allowed on the plan between one gang finishing its task and the next starting. This arrangement can deal with minor hold-ups as well as the planned change-over between gangs. These periods of no activity are called buffers. It is quite economic to be reasonably generous in allocating buffers, as it is much cheaper to have a unit not being worked on than to have to pay men employed on the next for unproductive idle time after small hold-ups.

A brief look at Figure 17.4 shows that four of the five operations take about the same time, and that the brickwork takes about twice as long. By having two gangs of bricklayers it is then possible to plan the work in such a way that all gangs work at about the same rate, namely about 12 days per house; some more and some less. The second bricklayer gang starts working on the second house as soon as the foundations are finished, and whilst the first gang is still working on the first house. When the first has finished the brickwork on the first house, it starts on the third, the other gang goes from the second to the fourth house. The carpenters take a little longer than the bricklayers with their work, so that the gap between them increases with each house. On the other hand, the finishes take less time than the services, and they must therefore not be planned to follow on immediately, otherwise they would have to stand idle each time. Instead, a correct gap is calculated for the first house, and the finishing gang is not scheduled to start until day 83. However, they catch up with the previous gang until the fifth house when the gap has disappeared.

For schemes with a large number of units, for broad-brush planning and discussions, it is sufficient to draw straight lines instead of the stepped ones of Figure 17.4. The term 'Line of balance charts' is used. Thus, in Figure 17.5, the strategy for a housing estate of 80 houses is shown. At this level of discussion, one can immediately appreciate with the help of the chart that ideally all lines should be parallel. If they are not precisely aligned, one can assess the effect, and make adjustments to the size of some of the gangs, for example. One such adjustment is shown in connection with glazing. For the first 40 houses, two glaziers are used, rapidly making the working site available for the following gangs. At that rate they get nearer and nearer to the previous operation, roof tiling, until they have caught up. This is shown in Figure 17.5 by the minimum buffer that has to be allowed. At this stage, one of the glaziers is released (to another project), and the other one completes all the remaining houses. This means that glazing now falls behind roof tiling, and joinery first fix gets closer and closer but does not catch up until the last house.

The line of balance chart in use

Like the bar chart, the line of balance chart is most useful as a control

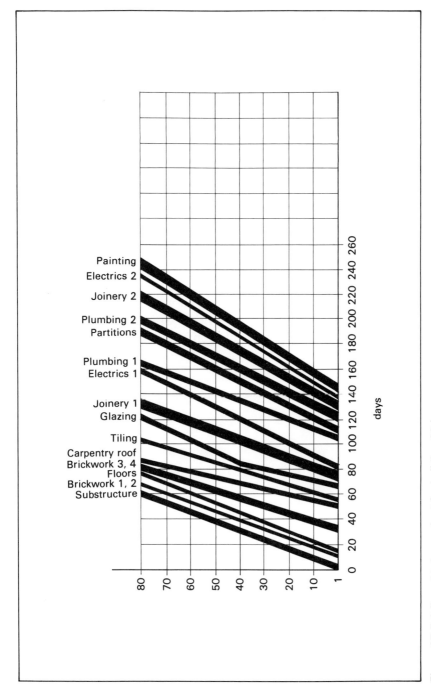

Figure 17.5 A line of balance chart for building 80 houses

355

tool on the working site. It allows actual performance to be monitored, so that deviations from the plan can be detected as quickly as the information feedback allows. This enables the supervisor to judge whether such a deviation is likely to have serious effect, or can be dealt with routinely (that is: within the buffers of the line of balance chart). If the deviations shown by the review threaten to encroach on other operations (i.e. if the buffer is not large enough) then the chart can be used for re-planning, and for taking the most suitable action.

Line of balance in general

The technique originated in the manufacturing industries for controlling the manufacture of components in repetitive production. As a graphical technique, such as that outlined above, it has been used in multi-project situations, particularly in construction.

The techniques in these two situations are similar but not identical and terms may be used in slightly different ways. It may be necessary to consult a reference such as British Standard BS 4335:1985 (Appendix C) to avoid any possible confusion.

18
Critical Path Methods

A. G. Simms

A project consists of activities. When all activities have been carried out, the project is completed. In a very real sense, therefore, project management is the management of all activities which comprise the project.

Methods for planning project activites were, at one time, limited by the notation available. Visual representation in the form of bar charts afforded a useful scheduling and control tool, but (except in the very simplest cases) it was never possible to indicate all the complex relationships and sequence dependencies between activities. The introduction of network diagrams overcame this problem, and introduced a powerful notation which allows all activities to be displayed in charts which clearly indicate all the interrelationships.

Basic ideas of project network techniques were formulated at about the same time in the 1950s by a number of managers in different, independent organisations. Two of these were in the United Kingdom, at ICI and the Central Electricity Generating Board. One was in France, and another group was in the US. The US group published a full account of their method and of their experience with major projects in 1958. By 1960 project network methods had spread to many of the larger public and private organisations. In the UK, many of those working in this field came together in the Network Study Group of the Operational Research Society.

It was found that a proliferation of symbols and terms had been developed by different groups. Efforts to rationalise practices resulted in the first British Standard *Glossary of Terms used in*

Project Network Techniques in 1968. The notation used in this chapter is that recommended in the 1985 edition, which bears the reference number BS 4335:1985.

PHASES OF PROJECT NETWORK PLANNING AND CONTROL

Project network analysis can be seen as divisible into four phases. A typical project network will undergo development through each of these phases, which are as follows:

1 Project Planning,

   in which the network is drawn to show all the activities necessary for project completion, together with their logical interrelationships

2 Project timing,

   where estimates of durations are added to activities, and calculations determine the likely project duration and identify those activities which are likely to prove critical to the programme

3 Resource allocation,

   in which the information derived from the planning phase is used to produce a practicable schedule of resource usage (techniques for resource allocation are dealt with in Chapter 19)

4 Project control,

   where project progress is measured against the network plan and deviations noted and used for corrective action. During this phase the network will almost certainly need to be changed ('updated') in order that the schedule for all activities in progress or not started remains valid and acceptable.

Critical Path Methods

ACTIVITIES AND EVENTS

An activity

(also sometimes called a job) is an operation or process consuming time and possibly other resources. In order to build up a picture of the project in terms of its activities and their relationships to one another, it is convenient to symbolise an activity by an arrow. Since in the planning phase it is only connections that matter, the direction, length and shape of the arrow have no significance, although conventionally it is always drawn from left to right.

An event

is defined as a state in the progress of the project after the completion of all preceding activities but before the start of any succeeding activity. The event symbol used to show the connection between activities is a circle. Each event has to have a unique label which is shown in the left half of the symbol. The two pieces of information that go into the right half will be discussed later.

Figure 18.1 shows an activity, symbolised by the arrow, with the direction of the arrow showing the flow of time as the activity is being carried out. It also shows the start event of the job (labelled A27) and the end event (labelled A42). The nature of the job is briefly described on the diagram. Each activity is identified uniquely by its start and end event labels, so that the activity: 'Evaluate proposals' would be called 'activity A27,A42'.

RELATIONSHIPS BETWEEN ACTIVITIES

There are only a few kinds of relationships and these suffice to circumscribe completely the most complex project.

1 *Independence*. Two activities are not related to one another. For example, in Figure 18.2, the activity 'engage computer staff' is not directly related to the activity 'move filing cabinets to the new building': neither the start nor the end time of each job is affected by what happens to the other.

Planning and Scheduling

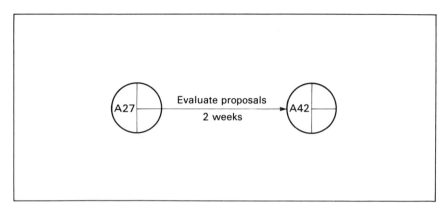

Figure 18.1 An activity with its start and end event
The estimated duration of this activity, which is to evaluate proposals, is two weeks. The start event has been numbered A27 for reference, and the end event A42. Event numbering becomes significant when a computer is used for network analysis, and this activity would be known as activity A27, A42

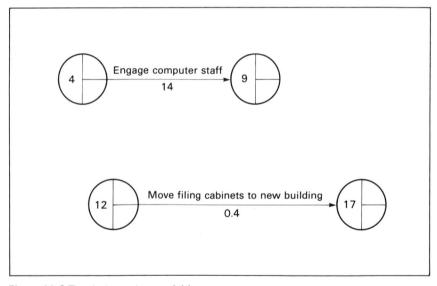

Figure 18.2 Two independent activities

2 *Sequence*. One job cannot start before another is finished. For example, a wall cannot be built until its foundation is finished. The end event of the earlier activity is the start event of the later one (see Figure 18.3)

Critical Path Methods

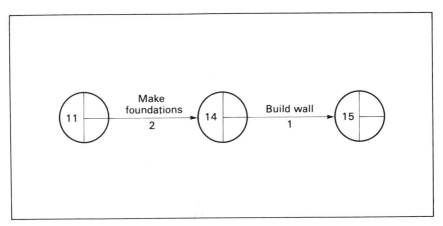

Figure 18.3 Simple sequence of two activities
Activity 14, 15 cannot begin until activity 11, 14 has been finished or, in other words, until event 14 has been achieved

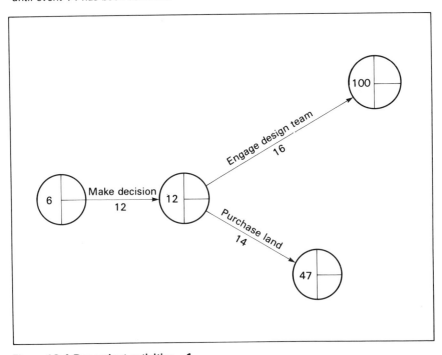

Figure 18.4 Dependent activities - 1
Neither activity 12, 100 nor activity 12, 47 can begin until activity 6, 12 has been finished

361

Planning and Scheduling

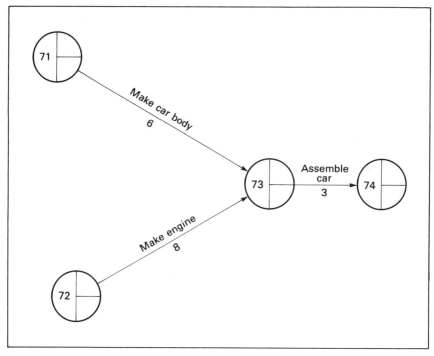

Figure 18.5 Dependent activities - 2
Activity 73, 74 cannot logically start before both preceding activities (71, 73 and 72, 73) have been finished

3 *Burst*. As soon as one activity is finished, two or more others can start. In Figure 18.4, for example, as soon as the board has decided to go ahead with building a new office the design team can be engaged and the building plot can be bought

4 *Merge*. An activity cannot start until two or more immediately preceding activities have been completed. This is illustrated by the example in Figure 18.5. The motor car assembly cannot start until the body and the engine are made

5 *Combined burst and merge*: several activities cannot start until two or more immediately preceding activities have been finished. This situation has to be examined carefully. Consider, for instance, the example in Figure 18.7. The first two activities 'Dismantle machine' and 'Fetch new component' must evidently take place before the jobs 'Repair old component' and 'Fit spare and reassemble machine'. It would be quite wrong,

Critical Path Methods

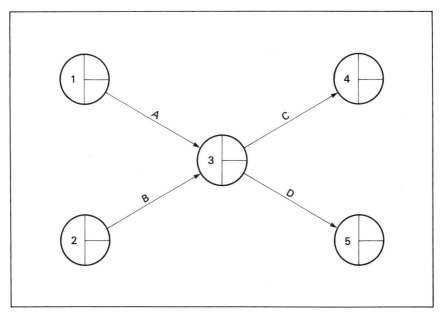

Figure 18.6 Dependent activities - 3
In this example, both activities 1, 3 and 2, 3 must be finished before either activity 3, 4 or activity 3, 5 can start

however, to picture the situation as in Figure 18.6, since the completion of all the earlier jobs is not necessary to start at least one of the later jobs. D can be started as soon as A is finished, regardless of what happens to B, whereas C requires that both A and B have finished. In other words, while it is true that job D follows job A (so that the start event of D is end event of A) it is not enough to allow C to start when B is completed. The logical link from the end of A to the start of C is also necessary. The end of B is then shown correctly as the start of C. Figure 18.7 shows the situation correctly, including the additional dotted link. This dotted link is called a dummy activity.

Dummy activities

Dummy activities (usually called, simply, dummies) are activities which do not in themselves represent time or work. They are put in the network to show logical links between other (real) activities. Dummies are shown as dotted arrows. As with any other activity arrow, they are not drawn to a timescale (if they were they would have

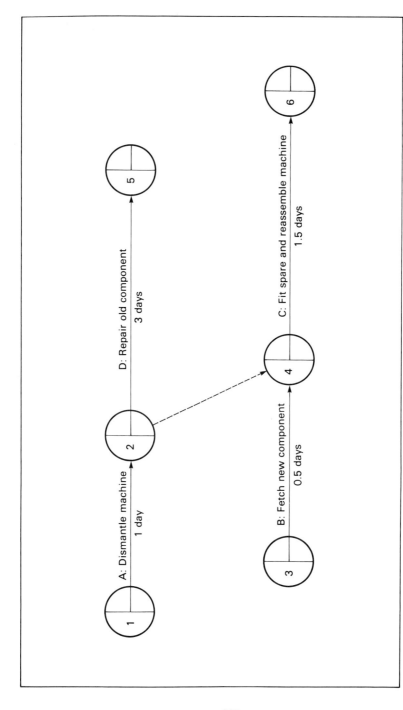

Figure 18.7 Use of a dummy activity as a logical link
The dummy activity does not represent any work and has no duration, but is used to show a logical link. In this case the dummy denotes that activity 4, 6 is dependent not only on activity 3, 4 but also on the completion of activity 1, 2

Critical Path Methods

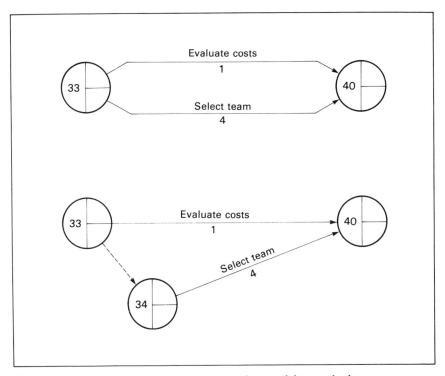

Figure 18.8 Dummy activity used to ensure unique activity numbering
Without the dummy, two activities would both be numbered 33, 40. This would confuse any computer used to process the network, and the dummy avoids this situation, without affecting the logical intention depicted in the top diagram

zero length!) but their direction is important. Figure 18.7 illustrated the use of a dummy to show a logical link, and there is another such example in Figure 18.12.

Another use of dummies is to ensure that two or more activities which share the same start and end events (known as parallel activities) can be isolated and given their own unique start and end event numbers. This is illustrated in Figure 18.8. If it were not for the dummy 33,34, both activities would be in parallel and both would be labelled 33,40. This becomes very important when a computer is used to list and analyse network activities, since the computer uses the event numbers (not the descriptions) to identify activities uniquely.

In cases where it is necessary to show a time lag between the end of one activity and the start of the next, this could be indicated by the use of a dummy to which a duration has been added. However, it is not advisable to use dummies for this purpose: it is better to use a full activity arrow, and either put in the description the reason for the delay or, simply, write 'Delay' for the description.

THE ARROW DIAGRAM

The project network that shows all the activity arrows and event circles is called the arrow diagram. It pictures the interrelationships explicitly, and this is essential at the planning stage. Every project has a definable start, and this is shown by the existence of the project start event, the only event symbol with outgoing but no incoming arrows. The definable project completion is shown by the finish event which has arrows entering it but no outgoing ones.

The arrow diagram is the project team's first complete project document. As such it forms the basis for informed discussion of strategic methods for carrying out the project. It can point the way to improvements, for instance by changes so that more activities are done in parallel rather than in sequence.

Detail and complexity

In small projects, all activities may be under the direct control of a single person. The supervision of larger ones often involves several levels of management, or indeed several independent organisations. The manager in charge of the whole project needs to know its overall shape and the relation of major parts to one another without having to go into the kind of detail appropriate for a subordinate in charge of a small portion. If all the detail needed by everyone were to be shown in a single network, there would be the danger of not seeing the wood for the trees. The problem of not obscuring the structure and yet showing adequate detail can be solved by using the concept of a hierarchy of networks. When planning a large project, a master network showing a relatively small number of major activity groups or sub-projects gives a level of detail or subdivision appropriate for the level of control exercised by the project manager. Each activity group under the control of an immediate subordinate is then prepared in greater detail, breaking up a single arrow (or just a few arrows) on the master network into a whole subnetwork. Such a second-level subnetwork could be further subdivided into third-level networks and so on.

This way of planning reflects levels of responsibility, draws attention to the correct level of detail and highlights interactions between activity groups under different supervisors, or between different organisations taking part in a large project. Communications between different levels are facilitated, since interface events (events common to two or more subnetworks) are a firm guide.

PROJECT TIMING

The timing phase of project planning produces the project programme, namely start and end times for all activities. Its basis is the project plan, as pictured by the arrow diagram, together with estimates of the duration of every activity.

The timescale

There are projects with a timescale running to many years, whilst on the other hand project planning has been applied to special small projects, such as the evacuation of a building on receipt of an alarm, where the timescale is minutes. For most usual projects the most convenient units for activity durations are weeks, days, shifts or hours. A convenient rule is that the basic unit should be of the order of 1 per cent to 2 per cent of the timescale for the whole project (e.g. weeks for projects lasting up to 2 to 5 years). The unit used should relate to the time span of routine control: there is no point in using hours when the reviews are only once a week.

It is essential that the same unit is used for all activity durations, and this unit is then also the unit for the event times.

Estimating the durations

Duration estimates should be free from bias and have the smallest possible estimating errors. The smallest errors are likely to be made by those closest to the job to be estimated, namely those who will carry it out when the project gets under way. They are the ones, however, who could easily misunderstand such estimates to be promises. It is only human nature that they would try to ensure being able to keep each 'promise' by over-estimating the time that job would take. Such a bias would defeat the objective of realistic timing, in which over-estimates and under-estimates should average out.

Many jobs are relatively easy to estimate with acceptable error margin, but others are more difficult. For instance innovative or exploratory projects, such as search, research or development, basic changes of existing systems and the like, often have a few activities which are difficult to envisage fully beforehand in sufficient detail to allow reasonable duration estimates.

Difficult estimates

When dealing with activities that are difficult to estimate, it has been found that it is often easier to give three estimates than to commit oneself to a single one. For example it may be quite easy to find a minimum time for the job, a time that cannot be undercut even if everything goes well: the optimistic estimate. Similarly, the longest time for the job, a duration that can be guaranteed not to be exceeded even if things go wrong, namely the pessimistic estimate, can usually be agreed without too much difficulty. Having guarded his reputation by these two values, the estimator is much happier to estimate a most likely duration. A weighted average of the three estimates gives the expected duration, which is then used in time analysis. A weighting of optimistic : most likely : pessimistic in the ratio 1:4:1 is the most popular, but 1:3:1 or 1:5:1 could be used equally well. One of the first projects for which project network techniques were developed contained several innovative activities which were troublesome to estimate and the psychological advantage of the three estimates was incorporated into the project network technique known as PERT (Program Evaluation and Review Technique). It does not otherwise differ from other activity-on-arrow techniques.

In practice it is invariably found that the three estimates are quite useful in overcoming resistance to the introduction of network methods. As soon as project teams appreciate the need for unbiased estimates, they tend to give good single estimates.

Consider the example of a task where 600 files have to be checked in a records section. The total activity must depend upon how many queries arise, and on how long each takes to sort out. The supervisor

Critical Path Methods

reckons that it takes about 5 minutes to go through a file if no queries result. This would give a total time for the job of 50 hours for one clerk working continuously. But clerks do not work continuously. They are not robots. They need to sleep, eat, take breaks. Their hours in the office may amount to 40 (say) in a week, of which only a proportion are used effectively. However, in its simplest interpretation, at the most optimistic estimate of 50 manhours, the activity duration would come out at 1.25 weeks (assuming a 40-hour week).

A better guess in this example (perhaps made after looking through a small sample of files) might be that some 100 files are likely to contain queries or problems needing half an hour each to sort out. This would give a total time, in manhours, of 50 hours basic work plus another 50 sorting out the problems: 100 manhours total. Again assuming a 40 hour working week, this is 2.5 weeks. If the supervisor is trying to be realistic, he or she will add on a factor for lost time (short breaks, mistakes, and other causes).

A pessimistic estimate would assume that half the files were going to prove troublesome, adding an hour each to the work. This would make a total estimate, in manhours, of $(50 + 300) = 350$. At 40 hours per week, and with the clerk possibly being the only one available, and with a record of time off for illness (or feigned illness), this job might run to a duration of 12 weeks.

Using the PERT formula, with a weighting of 4 given to the most likely estimate, we have:

$$t_e = \frac{t_o + 4t_m + t_p}{6}$$

where

t_e is the expected time
t_m is the most likely time
t_o is the optimistic time
t_p is the pessimistic time

Substituting the values from this example we get:

$$t_e = \frac{1.25 + (4 \times 2.5) + 12}{6}$$

which is 3.875 (4 weeks for practical purposes).

Planning and Scheduling

This example illustrates one important aspect of time estimates for activity durations. The concern is with *elapsed time* and not simply with the manhour content of the job.

Calculating event times

Two sets of calculations are needed in order to determine the timing of all the network events (and consequently their associated activities). By working from left to right through a network, adding the durations of activities leading to an event will give the earliest possible time at which the event can be achieved. Where more than one path is possible through to the event, then the longest path, in duration terms, will provide the answer. The result, for each event, is written in the top right hand quadrant of the circle (see Figures 18.9 and 18.10). An illustration of earliest event time calculations is given in the (very simple) network of Figure 18.12. This network starts on day 8, so that if this is considered to be 8 May, then taking event 6 as an example, it is seen that the longest path to this event lies through events 1, 2, 4 and (through the dummy) to 6 itself. The durations are $1 + 8 + 0$ (dummy) $= 9$, which added to the 8 May gives 17 May. The path through 1, 2, 3 and 6 is shorter by one day, and does not count in this calculation.

By reversing the process, and working back from the earliest possible time of the final event, subtracting durations gives the latest permissible time for each event to be finished if the earliest possible time of the final event is not to be exceeded. This, again, can be examined by looking at Figure 18.12. The notation conventions are illustrated in Figures 18.9 and 18.11.

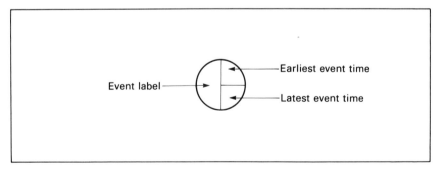

Figure 18.9 The event symbol

Critical Path Methods

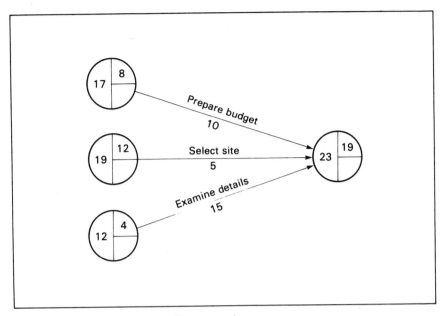

Figure 18.10 Convention for earliest event times
The earliest possible completion time for each event is written in the upper right hand quadrant

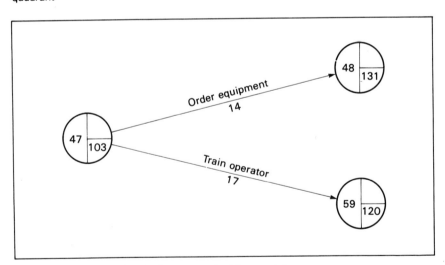

Figure 18.11 Convention for latest permissible event times
The latest permissible event times are written in the lower right hand quadrant

Planning and Scheduling

Whichever pass is done first, the forward or the backward, depends upon circumstances. In most cases, where the final end date is not known, but the start date is, then a forward pass is done first, followed by the backward pass. This yields the earliest possible time for project completion which, because it is normal to want to finish a project as soon as possible, is also taken as the latest permissible time for the final event. Conversely, if the backward pass if done first from a specified completion time dictated by external circumstances, then the latest time at which the project may be allowed to start is discovered (this could be the case, for example, where a school refurbishment programme has to be finished before the first day of the next term).

Event times can be given and calculated in one of two ways. Either they can be specified in units (hours, days, weeks, etc.) from the start event (usually at zero) or (as in Figure 18.12) dates or times can be used. The former method is used when the start date is not known. The latter method can be used to work ahead from a known start date or time.

The critical path

When the forward and backward passes have been carried out through the network diagram, and the earliest and latest dates are known for every event, then the initial part of programming the project is complete. This process is called, for obvious reasons, time analysis. The most important result is that the total project duration becomes known, namely the difference between the times for the project start and finish events.

Note that a study of the network in Figure 18.12 reveals a number of events which each have identical earliest and latest times. These are called critical events, since at least one following activity must take place immediately after completion of each critical event if the total project time is not to be extended. The project start and finish events are always critical events. In the example of Figure 18.12 events 1, 2, 4, 6 and 7 are critical. Events 3 and 5 are not.

Critical activities can also be identified. These are important in project management because, if they are delayed or exceed their estimated durations, the whole project will be delayed by that amount. A critical activity is an activity which:

Critical Path Methods

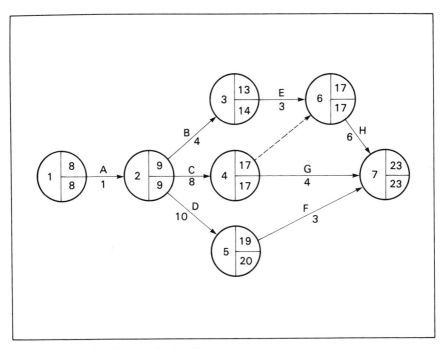

Figure 18.12 A simple critical path diagram
In this very simple network diagram, the 'project' is shown as starting on day 8, with the earliest possible finish time at day 23. The critical path flows through events 1, 2, 4, 6 (via the dummy) and 7

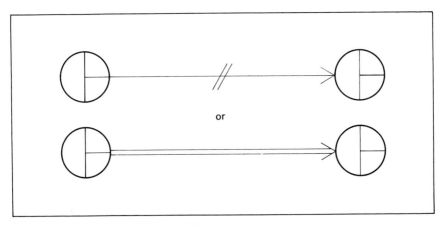

Figure 18.13 Depicting critical activities
The two methods shown here can each be used to mark critical activities in order to highlight the critical path on the network diagram

1 Joins two critical events.
2 Has a duration which equals the difference between the times of these critical events.

For example, in Figure 18.12 activity F is not critical because only its end event is critical. Job G is not critical either, even though it joins two critical events, because its duration (4 days) is less than the difference between the times of its two end events ($23 - 17 = 6$). On the other hand C is critical, as it joins the two critical events 2 and 4 and its duration is equal to the difference between the times of these events. Similarly A and H are critical activities. It is also clear that the dummy is critical, since it joins two critical events, and the difference between their times is zero, which equals the duration of the dummy.

Whilst there is usually no need to mark critical events, it is very useful to highlight critical activities and dummies on the diagram. Figure 18.13 shows preferred ways of doing that.

Every critical activity (except a final one) has at least one critical successor, and it also has at least one critical predecessor (except for initial activities).

In a network, an arrow or unbroken sequence of arrows is called a path; the most important paths are those which join the project start to the project finish. Examples of such paths are 1, 2, 3, 6, 7 or 1, 2, 4, 7 in Figure 18.12. A critical path consists of critical activities only. Every project has at least one critical path. If it has more than one, they all have the same duration. In the example there is a single critical path, namely 1, 2, 4, 6, 7. Its duration is 15 days, the total duration of the project.

The arrow diagram obtained from the timing phase and showing the critical path is usually known as the critical path diagram. Other timing information, such as event times, is also usually shown.

Float and slack

An event that is not critical is said to have slack. Slack is the calculated time span within which the event must occur. The term 'slack' is used only in referring to events.

Of greater practical importance is the concept of float, the time available for an activity in addition to its duration. Non-critical activities have float. There are different kinds of float, and their measure has the form:

Critical Path Methods

Float = end time − start time − duration

Since both the start and end events of an activity have earliest and latest times, there are four kinds of float possible. In practice only three of these are used, namely:

Total float

This is the time by which an activity may be delayed or extended without affecting the total project duration.

Total float = latest end − earliest start − duration

Free float

This is the time by which an activity may be delayed or extended without delaying the start of any succeeding activity.

Free float = earliest end − earliest start − duration

Independent float

This is the time by which an activity may be delayed or extended without affecting preceding or succeeding activities in any way.

Independent float = earliest end − latest start − duration

Calculation of floats

Figure 18.14 illustrates the different kinds of float and their calculation. It shows just one activity and its two events against a time scale.

The slack of event 74 is 7 days: that is the meaning of the time interval marked 74. Similarly the slack of event 92 is 63 − 54 = 9 days. The total float is 63 − 31 − 10 = 22 days. The (early) free float is 54 − 31 − 10 = 13 days. The late free float is of little use, its value is 63 − 38 − 10 = 15 days. The independent float is 54 − 38 − 10 = 6 days.

The importance of the float for project management decisions is considerable. For example, the person in direct charge of one activity can (usually) be allowed to make use of any independent float, since it would not affect anyone else if he used it all up. Total float, on the

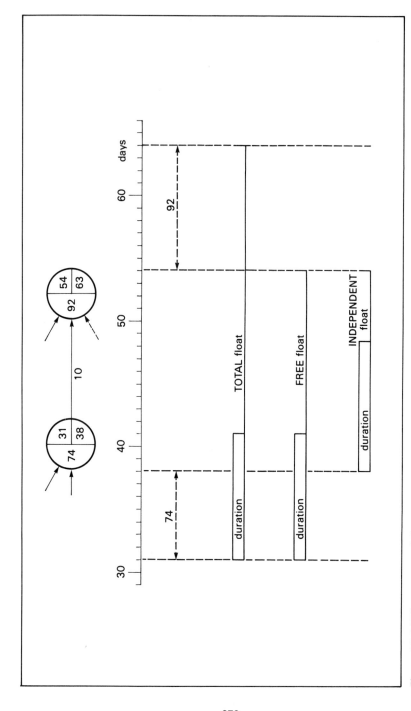

Figure 18.14 The concept of float
If the activity shown here is part of a network, and has the early and late event times shown, then there are three different kinds of float as shown in the time-scaled diagram

Critical Path Methods

other hand, is shared with other jobs, and it should not be used by one activity at the expense of others. It is quite usual to leave the allocation of total float to a higher level of management than that of single activities.

Another important application is using float to achieve a more economic allocation of resources. This is discussed in Chapters 19 and 20.

More than one imposed date

Sometimes both the start date and the completion date are fixed for a project before the planning phase. During the planning and timing phases more information becomes available, and it is often found that the time allowed by the imposed dates (the difference between the completion and the start) differs from that found with better information. Usually more time is needed than was first thought necessary.

In such a case, the forward pass is based on the imposed start date, and the backward pass on the imposed completion date. It may then happen that when the slack of every event is calculated, the smallest value found is not zero but some negative number. In such a case, the definitions of criticality need to be slightly modified: a critical event is one with the smallest difference between earliest and latest time. This difference may be negative. The start event and the finish event of the project are always critical events. All events having the same slack as these two are critical events. In such a case, all critical activities will have the same float, namely a negative one rather than zero.

The managerial implication of such a situation is that it cannot be resolved at the level of the management of the project. A higher level of management has to make suitable decisions: to relax one or both of the imposed dates or to allocate more resources so that some of the critical job durations can be reduced, or a combination of both.

PROJECT CONTROL

Whilst the project is being carried out, the task of project management is that of control. A powerful aid for that purpose is a modified form of the critical path diagram.

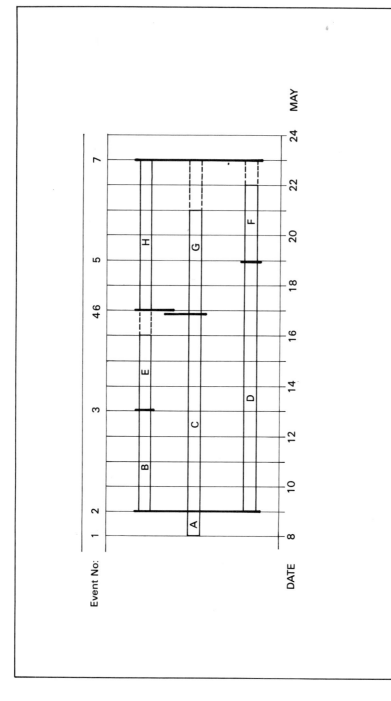

Figure 18.15 Time scaled network diagram
Although not normally drawn to any time scale, it is possible to redraw a network to a time scale. It then resembles a linked bar chart. The dotted bars indicate float. This example is derived from the simple network of Figure 18.12

The time-scaled diagram

Whereas previously the length of the arrow symbol in arrow diagrams or critical path diagrams had no significance, the critical path diagram can now be modified by making the length of each arrow proportional to its duration, with all arrows horizontal, and events indicated by vertical lines (the middle line of the event symbol). This form of the project network is a time-scaled diagram. At the same time it can be regarded as a bar chart, but a bar chart showing the way activities are linked to one another: a linked bar chart.

Figure 18.15 is the time-scaled diagram, the linked bar chart of the project whose critical path diagram was shown as Figure 18.12. Events with slack are normally shown as occurring at their earliest event times, but critical events and critical jobs can only be placed in one position. Non-critical activities however have float, which is shown on the time-scaled diagram in the form of a dotted line.

Note that the critical path is a solid line from project start to finish, whilst non-critical paths have float. The critical dummy is represented by the way events 4 and 6 are connected. If the paths were railway lines, and the activities were wagons, it is apparent immediately that a small push from either end would be transmitted to the other only by wagons on the critical path.

Being a bar chart, the time-scaled diagram is immediately understood at the working site where the project activities are being carried out. In effect it shows the project programme directly in the kind of graphical form that has been in use for many years.

The time-scaled diagram as a control tool

Contrary to superstition, projects will not automatically finish on time just because they have been networked! But networks are indeed a powerful aid for project management, enabling those in charge to identify actions most needed for success. At this point, the tool will be described, and a more detailed account of managing progress will be given in Chapter 22.

Two kinds of input form the essential basis for any effective project control.

Planning and Scheduling

1 A sufficiently detailed programme has to be shown in a convenient form.
2 Information about the progress achieved to date has to be acquired, transmitted and presented reliably, timely and completely.

These two elements are the essence of project monitoring, the comparison of the current project status with the programme, to identify and explain any deviations.

The time-scaled diagram shows the programme as a whole, and a vertical line corresponds to a given date. Such a vertical line can be used as a cursor; it cuts the bars corresponding to all activities in progress on that date. The role of the progress information is then to report on the status of each activity in progress on that particular review date, and all activities that were programmed to be completed since the previous review.

In its simplest form, the progress record is the time-scaled diagram with a movable cursor marking the current review date. The most reliable and incontrovertible information about any activity is whether it has started or not, and whether it is completed or not. Such a report can then be marked visibly on the diagram and compared with the cursor: any unmarked event to the left of the cursor is a danger signal showing that the event has not yet occurred although it was supposed to. It is more difficult to measure jobs in progress. In practice it has been found that estimates of what percentage of the job has been completed tend to be unreliable. A slightly better measure is to estimate what percentage of the job still remains to be done.

Another way of picturing progress is to stick pins into achieved event symbols on the chart and to use a thread to mark all the pins furthest to the right: ideally that thread should lie on the current cursor line, and any parts of it on the left indicate delays.

PROJECT NETWORK ANALYSIS AS AN AID TO PROJECT MANAGEMENT

Advantages over the bar chart

The various forms of the project network are well suited to the phases of project management. The arrow diagram brings out one of the

Critical Path Methods

aspects that a bar chart fails to picture, namely that of the inter-relationships between activities. This important aspect is fundamental during planning, when alternative methods of proceeding are discussed and the best choice refined and amended. Since bar charts do not show relationships, they are not suitable for the planning phase of any but the simplest projects.

As originally conceived, the bar chart was used on well-known types of project only, such as the manufacture of products, building projects and the like, where most jobs follow one another in sequence with little paralleling. This inability to show connections makes it quite difficult to handle large numbers of jobs within a project. Very few pre-network planners were able to deal with projects that were broken down into more than 30 to 50 jobs. This in turn shows that, even for projects of moderate size, each 'activity' represents a fairly large work package rather than a well-defined job sufficiently small for work on it to proceed without interruption from other tasks.

The bar chart clearly shows the timescale of jobs, but the lack of connections makes all the difference, since it is impossible to identify critical jobs or the critical path. On a bar chart there is no means of checking automatically whether a job can be started earlier than planned (other than from a knowledge of its nature), or what would be the effect on subsequent activities of a delay.

The bar chart in its long history has proved invaluable as a control tool, as a means of indicating start dates of jobs and showing durations, even though the scheduling of dates was done by other methods. The time-scaled network diagram is in the form of a bar chart and therefore it can be used wherever bar charts have been well-established. This avoids the complication of introducing unfamiliar innovations. The additional facility of showing connections brings more benefits; for example in helping co-ordination and in assessing the likely consequences of delays.

Disadvantages of project networks

Project networks methods were first developed in environments where time was of over-riding importance (a complex routine maintenance operation during which a highly productive oil refinery had to be shut down, and a large military project to develop and deploy a new missile system vital for defence). The primary objective of the management of projects where the value of time is very much greater than that of the resources involved is to reduce the total project duration as much as possible. This includes dealing with emergencies, interruptions of costly processes, re-organisations and introduction of new administrative procedures. For these, project network techniques based on time analysis alone is adequate.

In a commercial environment, however, the economic use of resources is at least as important for the management of the project as the need to complete it quickly. The methods described above are not directly capable of scheduling more than one resource in the best possible way, though the arrow diagram of all activities and their interrelationships can, after time analysis, provide the information on criticality and float upon which effective resource scheduling can be based.

PRECEDENCE NOTATION

A project network consists of arrows (that is links having direction) and of nodes. There are two equivalent ways of representing activities on a network: the activity-on-arrow form described above, used extensively in the USA, the UK and many other countries, and the activity-on-node form. This latter form is quite popular in France, Germany and some other continental countries, and it is used in some industries in the United Kingdom.

The activity-on-node network

In the basic form of the activity-on-node network, each job is represented by a rectangular box. A descriptive label and the duration of the activity is written into the box, the left edge of which represents the start and the right edge the completion of the activity. Sequence arrows represent the relationship between the completion of preceding activities and the starts of succeeding ones. Figure 18.16 shows the project of Figure 18.12 in this alternative representation.

The time analysis of a project shown in this form is identical with that of the activity-on-arrow diagram. The only slight difference is that instead of event times, it is the job start and end times that are calculated. The total float of each activity can also be derived

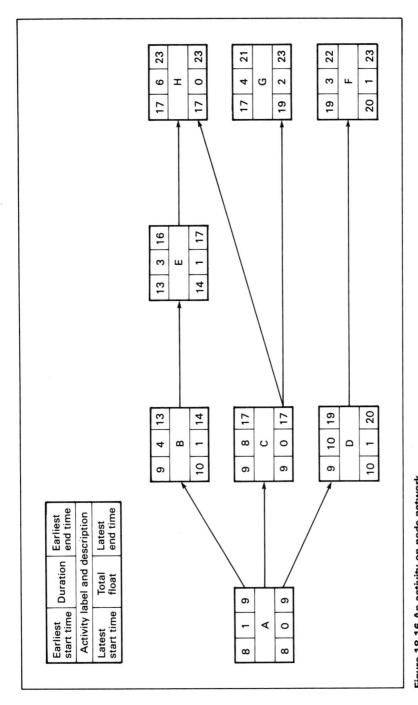

Figure 18.16 An activity on node network
An alternative to the activity on arrow network. Each box represents an activity and the arrows are merely logical links. This notation is the basis of the precedence method

Planning and Scheduling

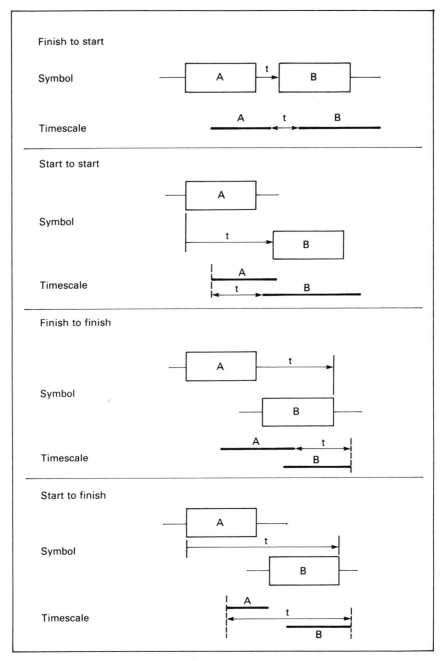

Figure 18.17 Precedence logic notation
The four kinds of precedence dependency are illustrated here

Critical Path Methods

immediately, and all jobs with zero float are critical. Critical sequence arrows are those which join critical activities, and they can be marked to show up the critical path clearly on the diagram.

The precedence diagram

A slightly more elaborate form is the precedence diagram, also known as the multi-dependency network. It is an activity-on-node network in which a sequence arrow represents one of four precedence relationships, depending on the positioning of the head and the tail of the sequence arrow.

The precedence relationships

1. *Finish-to-start*. The start of an activity depends on the finish of the preceding one. The notation is able to specify if the second activity can start immediately after the predecessor, or if there must be a delay.
2. *Start-to-start*. The start of an activity cannot take place until a stated lapse of time after the start of a preceding one.
3. *Finish-to-finish*. An activity cannot finish until a given time after the finish of the preceding activity.
4. *Start-to-finish*. An activity cannot finish until a given time after the start of the preceding activity.

Figure 18.17 shows the symbols for these four precedence relationships, with a time lapse t in each case. An explanatory bar chart (because it is drawn to a timescale) shows the real time equivalent. The time value t of the dependency arrow must be equal to or greater than zero. It cannot be negative. It is possible to use different kinds of dependencies in combinations.

When obtaining rules for calculating start and finish times of activities, note that the first relationship (finish-to-start) is the one discussed so far in this chapter in the arrow diagrams (but with t always equal to zero).

To find the earliest possible activity times in a precedence network, a forward pass is made (from left to right, as in the arrow diagram). The general rule for calculating the early start and early finish times during the forward pass is:

Planning and Scheduling

> To the activity time at the tail of the sequence arrow add the time lag t and enter this value at the activity time to which the arrow head points. The other time of the activity is obtained by adding the duration if the arrow head points to the start, or subtracting if the arrow head points to the finish of the activity. If there is more than one preceding activity, calculate the start time from each of the arrows but enter the highest value as the actual start time on the symbol.

The corresponding form for the backward pass is:

> Each latest activity time is found by subtracting the time lag from the latest time of the succeeding activity on the arrow head. This gives the latest time of the preceding activity at the arrow tail. The other time of that activity is found by adding or subtracting the job duration. If there is more than one succeeding activity, calculate the latest start time from each of these outgoing arrows, but enter on the symbol the lowest of the calculated latest start times.

USING NETWORKS IN PROJECT MANAGEMENT

Having presented the methods of project networks, a few practical guidelines will now be given to help those who have not used networks before. The British Standards Institution has published a four-part guide to the use of network techniques in project management, BS 6046:1984. Its first part, *Guide to the use of management, planning, review and reporting procedures*, is particularly relevant at this point. Only points referring to networking will be discussed here; more general aspects of project management are dealt with in other chapters.

Starting to plan a project using a network

At the start of project planning, one or more meetings are necessary to produce the first network diagram. The initial planning meeting should not be too large, six to ten people usually being enough to allow discussion while avoiding speechmaking. All aspects of the project need to be represented by experienced managers who have sufficient seniority to make decisions and accept commitments.

The job list

This is often the starting point at such meetings. All members contribute to this list, which must eventually include every significant activity of the project.

At first, very little is known about the sequence of the various activities, and they can be written down in any order, as they are mentioned. A useful method for ensuring that the discussion is conducted at a suitable level of detail is to identify a few key operations, after which it is quite easy to find a level of detail which appears correct in relation to the project as a whole and to the degree of supervision and control envisaged. The jobs listed should not be too small (making the list too long, and obscuring the overall shape of the project plan). On the other hand the jobs must not be so large that significant details of co-ordination or opportunities for rationalising progress are hidden. Such a key forms an obvious start for formulating a planning strategy for the project. By writing down jobs connected with those already mentioned, each member of the meeting can satisfy himself that he has covered all aspects for which he is going to be responsible.

The rough first draft will probably consist of some 50 to 100 jobs, and it forms a good basis for more detailed probing. During discussion, the list is refined. Particular attention should be given to completeness and to the boundary areas between different responsibilities (for example between co-operating departments or organisations). The discussion is made more effective if, for each job, a note is made of other jobs which must immediately precede it. This can help to highlight omissions and clarifies the relationships between activities to assist in drawing the network logic.

The arrow diagram

This can now be drawn. For the first draft, pencil and eraser are the best tools, as there will be plenty of changes. The starting point will be the event common to all activities for which no predecessor is needed: the start event. The rest follows in succession.

Drawing up the arrow diagram could be a simple routine if all the activities had been listed with their precedences correctly and completely noted. However, such perfection rarely happens, and the first attempt at an arrow diagram gives all the main participants their first opportunity of seeing an outline of the whole project. This joint effort usually gives considerable and valuable insights. In the first place it allows amendments and revisions of the job list but, most importantly, it points to improvements in methods of execution and of co-operation in boundary areas.

Another function of such a draft is the detection and avoidance of logical inconsistencies. There are two kinds of such logical faults that must be dealt with. The first is the 'dangle', an activity represented in the network where its head or tail does not connect either with any other activity or to a start or finish event. The second kind is a 'loop', an error in a network which results in a later activity imposing a logical constraint on an earlier activity. Loops can be detected if a simple numbering rule for events is followed: the end event of any activity must have a higher number or label that that of its start event. If it is found impossible to label at least one of the events, even after attempts to re-number the events of the network, then the network contains a loop.

Dangles can usually be rectified by finding the missing relationship, but loops often require a thorough re-examination of the whole project plan.

It is good practice not to allocate consecutive numbers to all events, but to leave some gaps, in case re-numbering is made necessary by insertions or amendments. One could leave out one number in five, or use only the even numbers at first.

Hierarchies of networks

These can be discussed at any stage, for instance at the outset of planning large projects. For smaller projects the first arrow diagram may suggest the convenience of subnetworks, but sometimes that need is not felt until a later stage. It may be convenient to use as event numbers for the top level network only multiples of 1000, and multiples of 100 for the second level, and so on.

Time estimates

Time estimates for the durations of all activities are the next task. The project manager may wish to arrive at the more important ones in a project meeting, but more specialised subordinate jobs, and those in subnetworks, will normally be estimated at a lower level. All duration estimates are then collated for the purpose of the time analysis. Those experienced in the use of networks for project management usually do not need the three-times estimates of PERT. These have been found quite useful however for the inexperienced. Involvement with two or three projects provides sufficient experience to enable unbiased duration estimates to be made.

The time analysis

The time analysis of smaller networks is straightforward, and even a beginner can handle projects with 50 or so activities. Before computer methods became widespread experienced project engineers had no difficulty with much larger networks of 1000 or more jobs. Such large projects are almost invariably broken down into subnetworks of more manageable size, making it quite feasible to do time analysis by hand. One great advantage of hand analysis is that it gives a better and deeper understanding than looking at a computer print-out. The flexibility of computers (for instance in coping with changes) is one of their main advantages. In recent years there has been a dramatic improvement in the availability of 'user friendly' project management programs and packages (even on microcomputers) in parallel with the fall in price and increase in power of computing. It is probably true that a large number of project networks, particularly those needing regular updating, will be on computers. It is equally true that a rough draft network is best analysed by hand at some early stage, not only providing a check on the computer but also because it is quicker to do than to input all network data and checking these.

Resource allocation

This is not recommended to project teams inexperienced in the use of project network techniques. Project management using networks requires a substantial degree of discipline which has to be acquired through experience with a few projects networked for time-only analysis. Only when such discipline is firmly established should resource allocation be attempted.

Reviews of plan and programme

These, whether in response to instructions by the controlling authority (for instance changes in specification or imposed dates) or because of a need to shorten the programme, can be made at any time before the execution of the project. Small changes may have relatively few consequences, but should major time savings be required, changes may be needed in the basic method. For instance jobs hitherto shown as single arrows may have to be broken down into several components so that some of them can be carried out in parallel. In any case, a minute checking of relationships may reveal refinements in the logic; for example, a job could possibly be started when the preceding one has reached some intermediate stage rather than waiting for its completion.

Checking the durations is not a paper exercise. It might seem quite simple for higher management to shorten some duration arbitrarily, but this should never be done without a careful examination of the implications at the work place and on the number and quality of the available resources. A change in plan means the re-calculation of the programme.

Completion of planning and timing

This is signalled by the preparation of the time-based network. This can be broken down conveniently by work station, so that each of these has its own bar chart. A list of all activities in earliest start date order is an essential document for the management of the whole project and of sub-projects, activity groups and single activities. Rules for the disposal of float need to be made.

Arrangements for information collection

These arrangements are central to any project control. To this end the length of the project review cycle has to be decided and arrangements have to be made to ensure that project information is collected rapidly and accurately and transmitted regularly and reliably to the monitoring centre. Unless this link is dependable control is lost, and it is well worth checking all data collection points and links and rehearsing the operation of the system before the project gets under way.

19
Resource Scheduling

David A. Barrett

A critical path network is not an accurate representation of reality. It predicts the start times of tasks from estimates of the time necessary to carry out preceding tasks; a schedule derived from such predictions might be quite unrealistic. There are many reasons why a time schedule can prove to be unrealistic, but the most common is that tasks which are scheduled by the planner to run in parallel cannot in fact happen simultaneously. The most common reason for such problems is that there are not enough resources to carry out all the tasks which could be in progress at any one time. Many different kinds of resource can produce this sort of limitation.

There may be limited manpower, equipment, space, money or material assigned to the project being planned. If two activities involving (say) the installation of instruments in the cockpit of a single-seater aircraft could both start at the same time — perhaps as soon as the control panel has been installed — there will not be enough space for the two technicians to carry out this work simultaneously. This is an example of a 'space' resource being required. One of those tasks will have to be delayed until the other is finished.

This could be represented by the planner in his network. He could select the task he considered to be more important and run a dummy activity or a precedence relationship from the end of that activity to the start of the less important activity. This might lengthen the project or change the criticality of that area of the network, but the plan would become more realistic.

Resource Scheduling

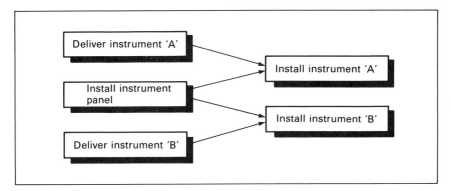

Figure 19.1 Simple example of resource conflict
Only one instrument can be installed at a time in the confined cockpit space of the aircraft. The planner could signify this by adding a dummy which would put the installations into a sequence (A followed by B for example). However, this would be an artificial constraint, and the network logic too inflexible to cater for the likelihood that instrument B would be received before instrument A, in which case it would make practical sense to fit instrument B first

NETWORK LOGIC METHODS FOR INDICATING RESOURCE CONSTRAINTS

There are two main objections, (and one advantage), to adding such artificial constraints to a network. The most important objection is that the sequence of activities has been artificially predetermined. This is less important in the initial planning stage. The planner has exercised his judgement to alter the schedule.

Nothing ever goes according to plan. When a project actually starts, some items will come in ahead of schedule; others, sadly all too often in the majority, will come in behind schedule. It will become necessary to re-plan. When the project is in progress, additional constraints can distort the network, which has become less flexible.

To return to the example of two instruments in an aircraft cockpit, the start time of installation of each instrument may depend not only on the presence of the control panel, but also on the delivery of the instrument in question (see Figure 19.1).

Suppose the planner had, for good and sufficient reason, chosen to install instrument A before instrument B. If there should be an unexpected delay in the delivery of instrument A, it would be better to install instrument B first. In order to do this, the planner has to remember why he added to the network the constraint that B should follow A, and then has to replace it by a constraint that A should follow B. This is by no means an automatic process, and at the very least it gives the planner a lot of additional work.

Detection of resource constraints

The second objection to resolving such problems by adding network constraints is that resource conflicts may not be easy to detect, particularly if the resource in question can handle a large, but limited, number of simultaneous tasks. It can be difficult to decide which tasks to delay in such a situation.

Overloads can be detected by a technique known as 'resource aggregation'. This method implies that each task should have its resource requirements annotated against it. Such requirement will consist of a series of codes identifying the resources required by the task, together with a series of matching quantities.

When the resource scheduling is done manually, the next step is to prepare a sheet of paper for each resource. The sheet is squared, with a vertical division for each day of the project (or each working time unit of the project). There should be a horizontal division for each available unit of the resource.

The planner then takes each activity in turn and marks the resource sheets of every resource used by that activity. He shades in a number of divisions on the resource sheets. The number of divisions shaded should correspond to the level of requirements of that resource by that activity between its earliest start and finish. Overload situations will be obvious as soon as it becomes necessary to shade in areas over the top of the resource line. This is an oversimplification of the technique, which can be refined in many ways. One can allow for varying availability of each resource over time, for example, by marking availability lines on the resource sheets. One can use a computer instead of using sheets of paper for the resources, and so on.

The planner can use this tool for a limited amount of resource scheduling. It can be helpful to take the most critical activities first when filling in the resource usage. Activities which would use more resources than are available can be artificially delayed. If activities are taken in order of increasing float, the activities considered later in the process will be more likely to be the straws to break the camel's back as far as resource loading is concerned. If those are also the activities

Resource Scheduling

with the greatest float, they can be delayed further without delaying the entire project, and so give the greatest flexibility for scheduling. Note that when any activity is delayed, at least the same amount of delay must be applied to all its successor activities.

Such artificial resource delays can be imposed by adding dummy activities containing time durations to the beginning of each activity to be delayed, by adding a 'transit time before' to these activities, or by adding elapsed time to the precedence relationships connecting the preceding activities. This depends on the kind of network the planner is using, and what conventions he prefers. Alternatively, one can add imposed start dates to the activities in question, or add constraints such that the activities to be delayed follow some or all of the activities already scheduled to use the resource being loaded. All these techniques are time-consuming, and difficult to manipulate when a project is in progress and needs to be rescheduled.

Resource overloads and criticality

Surprisingly, there is one advantage in the addition of artificial constraints to a network so as to keep within resource limits. That is, the lack of resources shows up in the critical path floats of the activities which have caused the delay, as well as of those which have been delayed. One of the drawbacks associated with computer-generated resource schedules is that activities which have been scheduled early in a resource conflict situation still may show float. This float can extend over a time period where other activities must use the resources the activity needs. Such float is, of course, largely imaginary. Nevertheless, the manager in charge of executing the job may still see it in the network results, and try to make use of it.

SCHEDULING GOALS: TIME LIMITS AND RESOURCE LIMITS

Early in the history of critical path analysis methods, attempts were made to automate the resource scheduling process. The purpose of this was to enable a computer to add up the usage required for each type of resource, taking into account all activities in the network, on a day by day basis. The computer would then be used to compare this estimated total requirement with the numbers of resources expected to be available each day. Should there be insufficient resources available for all the tasks on a given day, some of the tasks would be rescheduled (delayed) in order to shift the timing of resources needed. If the float available for delayed activities were sufficient, then it would be possible to give these jobs scheduled start dates lying somewhere between their earliest and latest starts. These would be the dates at which each activity should be started from the point of view of sensible resource usage. If this were possible to achieve for all resources, then the project could be scheduled for completion within its critical path duration using the available resources.

Unfortunately, this kind of happy outcome is rare. Frequently target dates are assigned to projects on the basis of customer pressure and competitive bidding, with little thought to how the date is to be achieved. The planner will have a difficult enough time to create a time analysis schedule which will bring the critical path down to the desired length. During the process, he will probably make a number of sub-critical paths critical also, by overlapping operations where possible, shortening pessimistic duration estimates, increasing resources applied to tasks, and so on. The more the time analysed network is squeezed down, the less flexibility will remain for the resource scheduling algorithm to play with.

More frequently one will eventually arrive at a point where an activity cannot be squeezed in, even by delaying it right to the end of its float. When this happens a decision has to be made. Should the resources be exceeded? Should the project be delayed past its planned end date? One question a planner may wish to ask is: 'How long will the project take if I keep within the available resources?' If more resources can be acquired for the project, either by adding more men and equipment, or by working overtime, then it may be necessary to have a 'threshold' level specified for each resource. The objective is to keep within the normal availability of a resource if possible, but use the additional threshold level if it would otherwise become necessary to delay the project. This is particularly appropriate for overtime working, which one would prefer to minimise, for reasons of both cost and efficiency.

Another situation which automatic resource scheduling can help to resolve is the one where an essentially unlimited workforce is available to carry out a job. In this case, the job could be accomplished at

Resource Scheduling

its critical path time analysis duration, by starting every activity at its earliest start time.

There would then be large peaks and troughs in the usage of manpower causing much hiring and firing of personnel. It is not easy to hire manpower for a few hours at a time. One would prefer to hire a fixed number of men for the entire project, or at least only change the level of workforce occasionally. Resource scheduling can help by carrying out a 'resource levelling' process. The purpose of this is to give a fairly 'lean' availability of the basic resources to the project, allow activities to use their total float in order to keep within this smooth usage, and when the float is used up, to start using another 'layer' of availability of the resource. The result is a smooth recommended resource utilisation, which minimises hiring and firing.

Figure 19.2 shows how a computer has been used successfully to schedule activities within network constraints to achieve smooth resource usage, without the penalty of delaying the project. In part A of the figure all activities have simply been allowed to start at their earliest possible network start dates. Part B of the figure shows the effect of rescheduling the activities, each within its total float, so that the maximum availability of this resource (5 units in this case) has not been exceeded. The accompanying bar chart, also drawn by the computer, shows the timing of activities before and after resource scheduling. The same computer program also plotted the network diagram.

There is some advantage in carrying out resource scheduling backwards from the end of the project. The question being asked is 'When must I start in order to carry out this project?'. The answer being given is usually 'Yesterday'. Projects involving assembly processes are sometimes best handled in this way. One important criterion is the value of investment made in the project whilst it is in progress. If the delivery of some costly item can be delayed until near the end of the project (and the payment date), this can be valuable in terms of interest charges for the money involved. If work is delayed until near the payment date, any variable costs involved in the work, particularly if subcontractors are involved, can show a financial gain of the same kind.

The main objection to scheduling projects backwards from the end, as far as resources are concerned, is that the high priority items tend to be considered first in the process, to be sure of fitting them in.

Planning and Scheduling

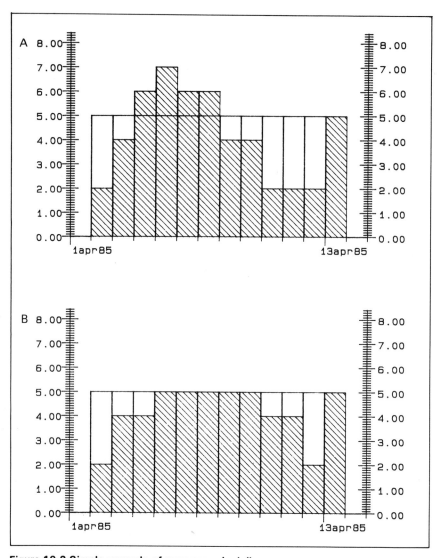

Figure 19.2 Simple example of resource scheduling
In part A the histogram shows the effect on resources of attempting to start every activity at the earliest possible network start date (resource aggregation). Part B shows the histogram after rescheduling by computer (calculation and plotting by K and H Project Systems 'CRESTA' system). Part C is the corresponding bar chart (which the computer is also capable of plotting)

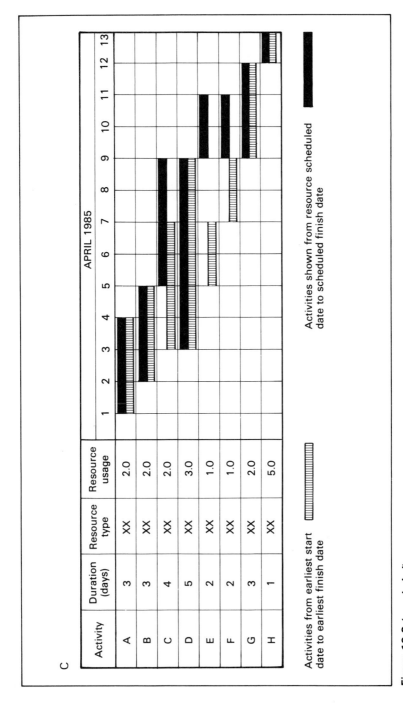

Figure 19.2 *(concluded)*

If they are considered first in a backwards scheduling process, then they occur towards the end of the project. This means that there is not very much margin available if there is a delay on one of the high priority items.

It may be preferable to schedule such projects forwards from the beginning, but use 'order/delivery' activities for high-cost materials, or for any items which do not use resources and which can be put off until later in the project.

Parallel and serial scheduling

Considerable effort has been expended in the search for mathematically ideal project scheduling methods. Theoreticians have tried to apply many of the popular techniques of operational research to resource allocation, with some success. Linear programming approaches exist which will find the optimum solution to networks of up to five activities. Mathematical optimisation algorithms tend to over-kill the problem, and use more computational resources than is practical.

In any case, even if one could slot activities into the resource schedule with watch-maker precision, this has certain disadvantages. The estimates of activity durations are approximate. Reality varies from the estimate, the beautifully fitted pieces turn out to be a different size from that imagined.

For most practical systems, then, the goal is to provide a 'good', usable schedule — not necessarily the mathematical optimum — without using vast amounts of time or computer resources. There are two main approaches which have been popular. Nearly all resource levelling methods are based on either a 'parallel' or a 'serial' approach. Both are 'heuristic', common-sense techniques.

Parallel scheduling

This can be visualised as follows. Imagine a network with several possible start points. This network is to be scheduled on a day-by-day basis through the project. First we consider day one. Take all the start activities of the network. Those are all the activities which could start at day one. Build an 'eligibility list' consisting of those activities. Take the activity with the highest priority from the eligibility list. Can it start yet? Is its earliest start less than or equal to the day we are considering? If so, compare its resource requirements for its next day with the resource availability on day one of the project. If all relevant resources are available in sufficient quantity, schedule the first day of that activity to occur on the first day of the project. If that completes the activity, then include all successor activities into the eligibility list. Repeat the process for the activity with the next highest priority from the eligibility list, and so on until all eligible activities have been considered for that day.

Then move to the next day of the project. Any amounts remaining of 'pool' resources are rolled over to day two. The actions described in the above paragraph are repeated for day two ... and so on until all activities in the project have been scheduled.

Notice that this process works more naturally when the resources available to a project are limited, and the time available to complete it can be extended indefinitely.

Serial scheduling

This considers each activity in turn, rather than each day of the project in turn. It can be visualised as follows. Consider a two-dimensional table of resource availabilities. It will have an amount available for every resource for every day of the project. Against this, there is a pre-sequenced list of activities which comprise the project. In addition to its time analysis results, each activity will have an 'earliest feasible start' figure, which will initially be the same as its earliest start.

Each activity is taken from the list of activities in turn. The section of the resource tables between the activity earliest feasible start and the activity late finish is scanned to see if the activity can be scheduled as a whole. If so, it is scheduled at the first available point. If not, then if the activity is splittable, an attempt is made to fit the activity in between its earliest feasible start and latest finish in sections. If this is impossible, an extra layer of resource availability is called in for any resource which was in inadequate supply, and the process is repeated for the activity, until it can be fitted in. If an activity is scheduled at a point later than its early start, the earliest feasible starts of all successor activities are updated to be greater than the finish of the activity that has just been scheduled. When all this has been done for every activity in the network, the project has been scheduled.

Notice that this process works more naturally if there is a fixed end date to the project, but the resources can be exceeded if necessary.

Serial methods are now more popular than parallel methods, for a number of reasons. Parallel scheduling tends to split activities rather more than serial. Ideally, a parallel scheduling algorithm would like to be able to split any activity into one-day sections, particularly if activities have complex resource requirements, or if resource availability changes during the project. Parallel schemes are typically heavy users of computer resources, both in the time taken to carry out a schedule, and in the amount of computer memory required per activity (which can limit the size of network that can be calculated on a given computer).

Special features in resource levelling

The above descriptions of the parallel and serial techniques show the basic method involved in each case. There are many refinements and special features which can be added to both processes.

A 'threshold' amount can be associated with each resource, as mentioned above. This is an additional emergency allocation of the resource which can be used if the project is about to run behind time. The threshold resource level cuts in when activities would otherwise be delayed past their latest finish.

Serial levelling schemes sometimes have a feature whereby two project end dates are specified — a desired project end and a maximum project end. Resources are classified into two sections — 'important' and 'exceedable'. If the scheduling system would have exceeded the availability of an 'important' resource, (and its threshold level, if there was one), then the activity is allowed to delay itself past its latest finish. It is not allowed to delay past its secondary latest finish — that is, the latest finish relative to the maximum project end date.

Alternative and 'summary' resources

In practice in project management, resources in short supply can be compensated for by substituting other resources.

For example, in a project using both senior and junior engineers, senior engineers might well be substituted for junior engineers to ease a temporary overload.

One can attach an 'expansion factor' to the use of alternative resources. The expansion factor is multiplied into the resource requirement of the primary resource to determine how many of the alternative resources are required to complete the task. Two different kinds of tool may be capable of carrying out a given process. One type may be less efficient than another for this purpose, so that larger numbers of that particular type may be required, if it is used as an alternative.

'Summary' resources act in a similar way. If a given resource is used, a corresponding amount of the associated summary resource must be available too. For example, if there is a limited pool of machine operators, each capable of operating any of three types of machine, then the operator might be specified as a summary resource associated with each machine. Using expansion factors, money can also be treated as a summary resource associated with any or all other resources in a project.

MULTI-PROJECT SCHEDULING

Most organisations work on several projects simultaneously. The projects may be at different locations and may be represented by logically independent networks.

They frequently require some of their resources to be provided from a common pool. Engineers, draughtsmen, laboratory facilities, corporate resources are all examples of this.

Multi-project scheduling has to allow for scheduling some or all of the projects based on the resource availabilities in the common resource pool, and also on the resource availabilities assigned to specific projects. When several projects are being scheduled against resources which are common, one has to consider the question of the relative priority of these projects.

It may be enough to consider the total float of the individual activities in the projects as being the criterion upon which they are scheduled. This is adequate if the projects are of roughly equivalent importance, so that a critical item in project A is 'worth' the same as a critical item in project B. If this is not so, a process known as 'residual scheduling' may be appropriate.

Planning and Scheduling

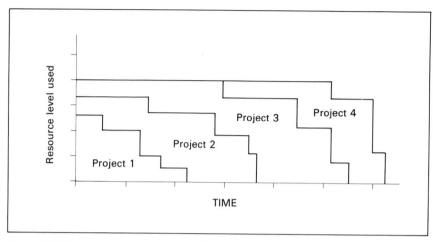

Figure 19.3 Resource usage pattern typical of residual scheduling
This pattern results from considering projects one at a time in a multi-project resource scheduling calculation

In residual scheduling, the projects to be scheduled are taken one by one. All of the highest priority project is scheduled before any of the second priority project. The second priority project uses those resources remaining after the first project has finished, and so on down the list. This tends to produce a resource utilisation pattern like that shown in Figure 19.3.

This is the opposite extreme from the first strategy of giving each project essentially equal weight. The ideal situation often lies in between these two extremes. Compromise solutions can be obtained by allocating only part of the total resource pool to the highest priority project or group of projects. When they have scheduled themselves against their allocation, an additional allowance of resources can be added before the second priority projects are considered. Strategies of this kind tend to spread out the projects considered earlier in the sequence more or less in inverse proportion to the size of the resource share allocated to the earlier projects. It may be necessary to try a few experiments. One possible approach is to carry out two calculations, one of which mixes all the projects together with the same priority, the second of which treats the projects in strict priority sequence with no secondary allocation. The comparison between these two extremes may suggest what compromise answer will give the most acceptable solution for the particular case under consideration.

20
Computer Programs for Network Analysis — 1

David A. Barrett

It is not easy to carry out the amount of calculation implied by the resource allocation techniques described in the previous chapter without enlisting the aid of a computer. If one is going to use a computer, one might as well make full use of it and allow it to suggest a complete resource schedule. Computerised resource levelling carries out a process similar in principle to the aggregation described in Chapter 19 but can make decisions of greater complexity and sophistication, depending on the calculation method used and the user's instructions.

The time analysis of networks above a certain size and complexity can be handled faster by computer equipment. The results will tend to be more reliable. They will be free of calculation errors (although the planner will still have to watch out for data errors). A computer program will apply a consistent set of rules to a project network. Providing that the planner can predict how his program will react to any given combination of circumstances, he can use it as a precise tool for evaluating initial network plans. More importantly, it can be used to show the effect of progress when the project is under way, and the effect of variations and additions when the project scope changes.

There is a wide range of computer programs on the market capable of carrying out these kinds of calculation. The programs vary enormously in price and in usefulness. These two aspects are not necessarily co-related.

Planning and Scheduling

Programs vary as to which computer equipment they require. Such machinery itself varies dramatically in price and capacity. It is possible to obtain a computer program for a few hundred pounds to carry out critical path analysis; at the other extreme, products exist which are marketed at prices of more than one million pounds.

Computers capable of carrying out the necessary calculations have an even greater price range, starting at about one hundred pounds, with practically no upper limit to the price that could be paid.

Such vast price ranges imply great differences in the characteristics of the products in question.

COMPUTER HARDWARE

Factors affecting hardware costs

The main factors affecting the cost of the computer equipment will be:

1. How many simultaneous users can be handled.
2. Memory size — possibly affecting the maximum network size which can be computed.
3. Speed of peripheral devices. Disk storage access speed will affect calculation speed. Printer speed will affect report production speed.
4. Number of specialised display devices available: automatic drawing equipment, colour screen displays.
5. Size of disk storage. This affects the amount of information available 'on-line' with minimal delay.
6. Communication capability with other computers.
7. Hardware maintenance costs and reliability.

Hardware performance per unit cost is increasing all the time. It is, however, possible to use up additional hardware capability by careless or inefficient software design much faster than engineers can produce faster computers. Do not believe the 'just get a bigger machine' line, particularly if it is the hardware manufacturer who is persuading you to use inefficient software. He may have an ulterior motive.

Every company has a different view of the relative advantages of central and of local computing. At one extreme there is the gigantic number-cruncher buried beneath a mountain in Wales, with large numbers of wires leading from it to hundreds of users scattered over the country or, via satellite links, the world. At the other extreme is the micro computer sitting on the desk of every user.

A single central computer makes integration of information and systems easier. Individual machines give each user control of his own facilities, and avoid conflicts in the assignment of priorities for the use of machine time. Various compromise solutions are possible. Local machines may be able to handle a few simultaneous users, and so allow more than one person to access the same body of information at one time. The local machines may be able to pass information down a wire to the central facility.

The larger the memory of a computer, the larger the network a given piece of software will be able to handle, up to a certain limit determined by the software itself and by the addressing structure of the computer. Memory comes in two popular flavours, 'real' and 'virtual'. The more of the computer's memory that is real and the less that is virtual, the faster will be the computation speed of the machine. Some machines provide memory to multiple simultaneous users by using virtual instead of real memory, others do not have the possibility of using virtual memory, and need enough real memory to be able to service the maximum number of users envisaged at any one time. Different computer programs need different amounts of memory when they are in use, so that both the number of users and the efficiency of the software as regards the use of memory must both be considered when deciding how much memory is required by a particular installation.

Disks

Disk speed has a strong influence on the time necessary to perform a calculation. In the terms used in this chapter, the word 'disk' refers to 'hard' disks, which are used for the storage of online information rather than to 'floppy' disks, which should only be used for information transfer between computers, or to hold information copied from a hard disk for security purposes.

The speed of the disks seems to be one of the important dividing points at the moment between so-called 'mini' and 'micro'

Planning and Scheduling

computers. The time taken to fetch a piece of information from the disk, which is used to store network information, and also for intermediate working storage during computation, directly affects the time elapsed for computer operations. In addition to this effect, virtual memory (mentioned earlier) is implemented by rolling information in and out of main memory from and to disk. The disk speed therefore affects the processing speed if virtual memory is being used. The number of reading mechanisms on the disk equipment can be critical when many users are active on the computer at the same time. These arms can be constantly in motion from the areas of interest to one user to the areas of interest to another. Such 'thrashing' of disk arms can slow down processing for all users dramatically.

Printers

Printers vary greatly in speed and in price. The speed of slower models is generally measured in characters per second. Faster printers are often quoted in lines per minute. The very fast laser printers now available usually have their print speed quoted in feet per second of output.

Amongst the slower printers, the most popular printing methods are by 'dot matrix', whose quality tends to be inversely proportional to its speed, and by 'daisy wheel' which tends to produce slow but high quality output.

The speed of printing can be a significant factor in the delay between a planner ordering a recalculation of a network, and his receiving the results. One user, having switched from K&H Project Systems' IBM mainframe program PREMIS to the K&H CRESTA system on a super-micro computer complained about the relatively slower speed of the second system. Upon investigation, it turned out to be the slower speed of the printer on the small computer, compared with the very fast printer on the mainframe that was the cause of the problem. The answer was to find a faster printer for the super-micro and attach two of them to the machine, so that two reports could be produced simultaneously.

Screens

Visual display units (VDUs) used for the input and display of information have a range of capabilities and features. Very simple screens may not be capable of operating in full-screen mode — only one line may be entered at a time. Others may or may not have the capability for reverse video display, making fields blink, and the like. Some screens have colour capability. Both the screens themselves and the program driving them must have the particular feature for it to be usable by the planner. Some of the most powerful terminals are almost small computers in themselves, and can for example accept a network drawing, and from that point onwards carry out automatic panning, zooming and windowing to display parts of the network on request without further troubling the main computer, until a new network or network section is requested.

After allowance has been made for the operating system of the computer, any virtual memory paging areas that may be necessary, and for the project management programs themselves, enough disk space must remain to be able to store the network information.

Different project management programs use very different amounts of disk storage to hold each activity. Database systems also vary considerably in the amount of disk space taken up for a given amount of data. One must allow room for the maximum likely amount of network data, and should bear in mind what must be C. Northcote Parkinson's nth law ... that information grows to fill and overflow the disk space allocated to it.

It is not always easy to transmit information from one computer to another, especially if they come from different manufacturers. Even the 'standard' interfaces such as RS232 are less standard than one would wish, and the programs which are used at each end of the connecting wire to send and to receive information often use different protocols. If one program passes some information and says: 'After you, Cecil.' where the receiving program is expecting 'After you, Claude.' an uncomfortable silence will ensue.

The speed of passing information down a wire from one computer to another is measured as a 'baud rate'. Typical rates are 19200, 9600, 4800, 2400, 1200, 300, 100. The faster the rate, the greater probability of error. The greater the amount of error checking that is carried out by the computers at each end of the wire, the slower the transmission process. Satisfactory error-free transmission procedures can make the passing of data a very slow and painful process.

If the two computers in question have removable disks, tapes or cassettes which are compatible in their data recording methods, it may be more satisfactory to send such media through the post rather than to attempt direct transmission.

Plotters

Automatic drawing equipment also varies tremendously in speed and price. Electrostatic plotters are much faster than other models, but their quality is not always as good. They do not produce coloured output, and may need special paper. Pen plotters may have multiple pens of different colours; they vary in speed and in precision. Precision is not generally an important factor in project management outputs, which are generally not drawn to scale.

The drawing area of cheaper plotters may be limited, so that a network has to be drawn in several sections and glued together afterwards.

Hardware maintenance

The costs of maintaining the chosen computer should not be forgotten. Typical rates vary around ten per cent per annum of the list price of the equipment. It is worth checking with existing users of the equipment what speed of response is provided by the agent or manufacturer in case of operational failures, and how often such problems occur.

Is it blue?

Some companies suffer from centrally decided policies which dictate that computing hardware should only be purchased from one particular manufacturer. This will obviously subject the user's choice of equipment to very constrained limits.

GENERAL FACTORS CONCERNING SOFTWARE

Practical considerations can short-cut the software selection process. If computer facilities already exist, and are easily accessible, it may just be a matter of discovering whether a program has already been acquired. If not, or if that program is inadequate, the first step might be to find out what programs are available for the computer equipment which is currently installed.

Computer manufacturers maintain catalogues of programs which have been made commercially available for their equipment. Organisations such as INTERNET in Europe or PMI in America can advise on what may be available, or point out the major companies who supply software for project management.

Even if the planner does have access to a large company computer with an appropriate program, he should consider that he will be sharing a facility with other users. He will not necessarily have the highest priority among them. Before committing himself to use the locally available facilities, he should experiment to see whether delays in computer access or in calculation time when using this equipment are acceptable in the context of the project he is controlling.

It may be better to acquire a small computer completely under his own control, rather than to rely upon a large shared facility. The wider range of possible machines under these circumstances will imply a wider selection of computer programs. Many programs are only available for a restricted range of computer equipment. The planner will wish to choose a combination of hardware and software appropriate to his situation.

Consider in a little more detail some of the factors which affect the choice of software package. Many of the categories already summarised will overlap a little. Capacity and speed, for example, are interrelated in that a theoretical ability to handle networks of many activities may in fact be unusable because long calculation times make the analysis of large networks undesirable.

The maximum network size which a computer program can handle may vary from a few tens of activities to millions. The limitation almost always applies to a single network. The user is allowed to have many independent networks, but no one of them may exceed (say) 2000 activities. The limit on the number of activities per network is generally determined by the computational algorithm used in the program and by the memory capacity of the computer. The larger the memory, generally, the larger the network which can be handled with a given computational method.

Sometimes, programs with a relatively low limit of network size will calculate network sections independently and then combine the

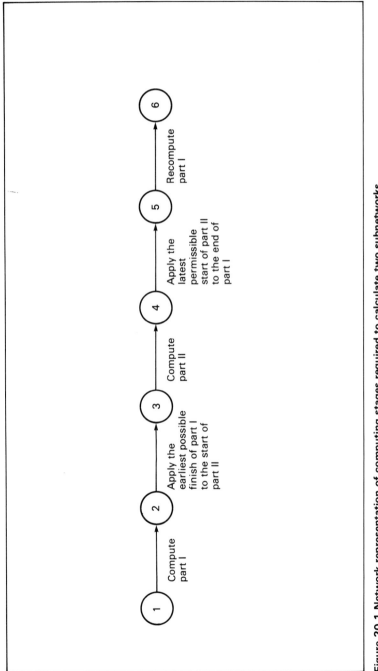

Figure 20.1 Network representation of computing stages required to calculate two subnetworks
By splitting a network up into a series of separate subnetworks it is possible (given suitable divisibility of the main network) to overcome limitations of a computer program which can only cope with a relatively small number of activities in any one network or subnetwork. But this arrangement increases the amount of computational work for the computer, as shown in this example of just two subnetworks, I and II, which together form one larger network

results. Taking a very crude example, consider a network which divides itself into two distinct halves — say phase I and phase II of a project — whereby the connections between one part and the next run entirely through a single activity (perhaps a decision point as to whether or not to commence the second part at all). Then it is very easy to compute part I first, and then use the earliest finish of the end of part I as the project start of part II.

If there is a definite required end date to the project, as is so often the case, then that end date can be applied to part II of the project. The latest start of the first activity of part II can then be applied to part I as a required finish date. To express the computation of the network in critical path terms, please refer to Figure 20.1. Notice that three computational passes are required to calculate the two networks.

If a program must resort to this kind of 'subnetting' or 'interfacing' in order to be able to calculate a network of the required size, it will probably not be operationally efficient.

The number of passes of the data tends to grow rapidly as the number of independent network sections increases, and as the number of points of contact between them increases too. In general it is unwise to attempt to stretch the capacity of a program in this way. Better use a tool that will be adequate for the maximum network size envisaged. Allow an appropriate safety margin for the fact that networks tend to grow, particularly if there is a computer available to solve them (yet another of the countless corollaries of Parkinson's first law).

The above comments should not be taken as advice to avoid subnets and interfaces in general — only in those cases where they are forced upon the user by computer-related limitations. It may well be convenient to divide a project into subnets, provided that the computer program being used can take them in a single mouthful for calculation purposes. Generally, subnets can be numbered independently, so that the same activity number or event number can be used in two separate subnets without fear of confusion. This is particularly helpful when the same general pattern is repeated in different parts of an overall network — for example the installation of pumps occurs many times in networks describing the construction of an oil refinery. It may be possible to duplicate one network and include it in many different places.

Planning and Scheduling

It may be convenient to assign responsibility for different network sections to different individuals, particularly if the network is large. Normally one will allocate a different range of possible activity numbers to each person responsible for a network section, but such schemes have been known to go awry. When they do, the logic is sometimes difficult to disentangle.

Where subnets are used, they must be able to connect at one or more points into the main network. These connection points are commonly called 'interfaces'. The activities which are identified as interfaces do share a common numbering system with the overall network, and so provide connections with it.

The fewer connection points for each subnet, the simpler will be the evaluation of paths which cross several subnets and hence perhaps more than one area of responsibility. If each planner working on a project has activities separated into his own individual subnet or subnets, he can more easily update the tasks under his control with progress information, without needing close co-ordination with his colleagues.

Many computer programs have a quoted limit of 32 000 events for activity-on-arrow networks, or 32 000 activities for precedence networks.

This particular figure is a common one because it arises as a consequence of a popular type of computer design. This design tends to group the fundamental 'binary bits' of which computer memory is constructed into sets of eight at a time. Two sets of eight make a conveniently sized storage medium for holding a sequential activity counter. Such a counter can count up to 32 767 easily, and with some difficulty can be persuaded to count up to double that figure. This is why many programs quote a theoretical limit of 32 000 or 64 000 activities. Nevertheless, the practical maximum network size may be well below this figure, either because a very large computer memory could be needed for the program in question to attain such a maximum, or because calculation time might be unacceptably long.

There may well be several capacity limitations to a given computer program. There may be different limitations on the network size which can be handled in resource analysis as opposed to time analysis. This is because different computational methods will be used for these two functions. There may be limits to the number of resources which can be processed per project, and limits to the number of resources which any one activity can be specified as using.

SOFTWARE PRICE FACTORS

The main factors affecting the prices of computer programs are:

1 The maximum network size which can be computed.
2 The kind of data which can be handled (arrow, precedence, arrow and precedence, resources, costs, materials and other associated data).
3 The calculation features (time analysis, resource aggregation, resource smoothing, probabilistic analysis, cost performance analysis, and so on).
4 Flexibility of output reports, graphical presentation of results, and the like.
5 Ease of use (screen input, menus, special updating methods).
6 Speed (calculation speed, updating speed, report production speed).
7 Level of support provided to the user (documentation, training, 'hotlines').
8 Software maintenance costs and enhancement schemes.

CHOICE BETWEEN ACTIVITY-ON-ARROW AND PRECEDENCE NETWORKS

When planners get together, a favourite topic for discussion is 'Which is the better technique — arrow or precedence?' Despite the many man-hours spent arguing this question no clear answer has emerged. An analogy could be drawn with different systems of religious belief. It is rare for a believer in one system to convert a believer from another system to his own faith.

If there is a clearly defined policy in an organisation as to which planning technique must be used, then the computer program must be able to compute networks of this kind. Some programs are able to compute either precedence or arrow networks, at the user's option. A few programs are capable of calculating arrow and precedence networks simultaneously, or of computing 'mixed' networks, which may become more popular in the future. If a company contains strong believers in precedence networks, and also contains strong believers in arrow networks, it may avoid bloodshed to acquire a program capable of handling mixed networks. A main contractor may be able to accept all the different forms of network diagram used by his subcontractors if he can process mixed networks.

One should look for possible limitations in the numbering schemes that the program allows for either precedence activities or for arrow events. Some programs will accept only numeric input for these fields. There are even still some programs which demand that a succeeding event has a higher number than its preceding events, so that a network must be numbered from left to right sequentially. This requirement produces less than ideal results when it is necessary to insert a new network section, or to expand an existing activity into more detail. It may also be relevant to look for limits to the number of characters which a program will allow the planner to use for an activity number. If this is small compared to the network size contemplated, then there will be a danger of using the same number twice inadvertently. If it is necessary to match the activity number with any existing numbering scheme — say, cost coding structures, work breakdown structures, or work-order numbers — then the activity numbering scheme must allow of enough characters of information to accomplish this.

RESOURCE AND CALENDAR FEATURES

If the planner wants to use automatic resource levelling, then the program chosen should be able to do this. Look for limits on the size of the resource code. Is it large enough to be meaningful, and instantly identifiable amongst the set of resources that might be used? Some programs insist that the amount of a resource used by an activity be expressed as a 'rate constant'. This implies that the amount of a resource used is broken down into a daily rate, and associated with the activity in this form. This is ideal for skilled trades, labour, machinery and the like, where it is easy and natural to say that a given activity requires 10 carpenters or 3 labourers or 1 crane throughout its duration. It is less natural to express a need for 1000 cubic yards of concrete, or 100 man-hours of effort in these terms. Other programs demand that resource requirements be expressed as 'work-content' — that is, a total amount used by the activity. This is excellent for volumes of material, for example, but not a natural form for labour and machinery. The planner should be able to express the resource requirements in either way for each resource for each activity. Some computer programs allow for this.

Fractional resource amounts

Fractional resource amounts can be used when scheduling individual people who have different skills. A particular person may be required to attend to a given task which will only take up a certain percentage of his time. One way of dealing with this is for the different tasks needing the person's attention each to ask for a fraction of his time — his initial availability will be either one or zero at any one time unit. The same technique can be extended to handle a number of individuals with similar skills included under the same resource code. If the computer program will not accept fractional or decimal resource requirements, one can always scale up by a factor of (say) 100, so that the resource requirement is in terms of one percent of a person per day (or time unit). Approximate planning for overtime can be carried out in this way — in the case of an individual, if he ends up being used at the level of 1.1 in a day, this can be interpreted as a need for about one hour's overtime on that day.

Complex resources

Activities are described as complex when they do not require a constant rate of resource usage throughout their durations. For example, an activity could need two bricklayers for 7 days, and then only one bricklayer for a further 3 days, so that the resource requirement throughout its 10 day duration is not constant. The planner may wish to plan in great detail, so that any change of resource usage during a process is taken care of by ending each activity and starting another every time there is a change in the resource usage. In such a case there is no need to be able to tell the program at what point in an activity a resource is required, or for how long. This kind of detailed planning tends to increase the number of activities in the network, but it keeps each activity much simpler.

Splittable activities

It is preferable to be able to define a process as one complex activity, rather than a series of sequential operations. One reason for this is associated with whether an activity can be discontinuous. If a complex task is expressed as a series of sequential operations, each of which uses resources, then an automatic scheduling system might well schedule one section of the task to start long after the end of the preceding section, if resources were not available in the mean time. The planner may wish the process to be carried out as a continuous sequence, either to avoid moving labour from one location to another, to avoid the loss of concentration involved in the workers starting a task, stopping it, and restarting later, to minimise the amount of work or investment in-process, or for a variety of job-dependent reasons. Some programs allow an activity to be 'tied' to its predecessor as a way of producing this effect. Such features have drawbacks in that the sequence is not considered as a whole for scheduling. The tying of activities will sometimes cause resources to be used badly.

Many computer programs allow the user to mark each activity as 'splittable' or 'non-splittable'. A process to be carried out as a continuous sequence would therefore be coded as non-splittable, and its use of resources might well need to be specified in a complex manner; that is, for each resource used by the activity the planner would specify not only the code and the amount required, but also the number of days for which the resource was required and at what point within the activity duration.

It is valuable to be able to specify that activities can be split into sections if there is no major penalty involved in so doing. Some programs contain facilities for the planner to control such splitting by specifying a minimum size section in to which the activity may be divided, a maximum elapsed interval between the end of one section and the start of the next, a minimum size for the first section and/or for the last section. In general, 'serial' resource scheduling handles activity splitting better than 'parallel' methods, which work best if every activity can be split into single time units if necessary. If this capability is important to the project, it might be as well to know which candidate programs use the parallel and which the serial method.

In the early days of resource scheduling, activity splitting was the only way in which complex working shift situations could be expressed. In cases where, for example, three 8-hour shifts per day were available to carry out the project, some activities could be worked 24 hours per day, some 16 per day, and some only eight hours per day ... in prime shift. A resource levelling program with the capability of splitting activities could be persuaded to deal with this kind of situation. A 'prime shift' resource would be defined. The availability of this resource would be very large — say, the largest number the program would accept as an availability — during the eight hours of prime shift, but would be zero at other times. Any activity which had to be operated during prime shift only would have a requirement of one unit of this resource throughout its duration, and would be marked as being 'splittable'.

This technique produced reasonable results, but was not entirely satisfactory. Activities marked as being splittable in order to work the correct shifts tended to get split for other reasons too ... the temporary lack of other resources ... and jobs would become fragmented over time for no good reason. The time analysis float of such activities would be hard to interpret, as it would include large quantities of unusable second- and third-shift time. A number of inadequacies in reporting were experienced — computer programs were capable of showing each split section of an activity separately in a report. An activity working prime shift only would tend to appear in reports as many times as there were days covered by its duration unless special action was taken to prevent this.

Multiple calendars

Multiple calendars are used by some more recent programs to overcome the problem of a project in which the workforce includes groups of people who work shifts in addition to others working a normal day. When the planner specifies the activity data, he states not only the duration, but also the calendar on which that duration is based. To illustrate and explain this point, a schedule could be prepared using three calendars as follows:

1 A calendar based on a 24 hour round-the-clock day of 3 shifts
2 A calendar using two shifts, totalling 16 hours each day
3 A calendar incorporating only one 8 hour shift each day.

In this example, an activity using people only working the single 8 hour shift would be coded as using calendar 3.

Activity float is expressed according to the calendar relevant to the activity, and so the time analysis float of such activities would be meaningful. The activity could still be made coded splittable or not, relative to its own calendar. It would not be necessary for the program to generate a printable result for each day of the activity.

Multiple calendars are of use in many different situations — not only that of shift work. Working weeks of different lengths may affect a project. Some activities may be carried out in offices where a five-day week is worked, and others on-site where a six-day week is worked; a seven-day week may be appropriate for such activities as allowing concrete to cure.

In international projects, activities may have weekends located around Saturday rather than Sunday, or around Friday rather than Sunday (though rarely both, in the present political climate). Different countries have different patterns of national holiday. Some companies shut down altogether for two or three weeks in the year. Large projects involving consortia can involve the use of thirty or forty different calendars to account for all the different combinations.

Other practical considerations can be approximated by multiple calendars. Activities will be more or less affected by weather conditions. It is common to set up several 'weather' calendars one of which might show a six-day week in the summer, five-day weeks in spring and autumn, and four-day weeks in the winter, to approximate the effect of weather conditions on a certain type of activity. In extreme cases, the calendar might show a complete gap in the winter. Activities showing planned operations on oil-rigs in the North Sea are sometimes of this type, as certain tasks cannot be scheduled for times when the wave-height is likely to be above a certain threshold.

Totally irregular 'calendars' are sometimes worthwhile. Consider a network where progress has to be reviewed by a committee before certain tasks are undertaken. This can occur in local government work, where networks are used to express the procedures that must be undertaken before a section of new road is to be constructed, for example. If the committee meets on an irregular, but known, schedule, a calendar can be constructed which consists of only the dates in that schedule. Activities requiring a decision from the committee are preceded by short activities based on the committee calendar, so that if all the other preceding necessary items have been completed just after a meeting, nevertheless the next step will be delayed until the next meeting occurs. It might even be possible to estimate the maximum number of decisions such a committee could take in one session, and express that as a resource availability — each activity requiring a decision could use up one unit of that resource! To enter further into the realms of fantasy, the resource availability could express the number of useful minutes of meeting time in each session, and the resource requirement of each activity might be the estimated time required to discuss it.

An additional example of an irregular calendar might occur in building work, where an architect has to inspect certain phases of the construction before they are covered up and become inaccessible. If the architect has a defined inspection schedule, then a job which misses one of those days will have to wait until the next before it can be continued. The architect's inspection schedule could be specified to the system as an irregular calendar in this case.

It can be dangerous to mix weekly time units with daily time units in a multi-calendar network when resource levelling is used. Depending on the procedure used by the computer program, a week on a weekly time-scale may not be a full week, but may just cover the Monday. This will not matter greatly in the case of time analysis, but if the same resource is used by activities with both weekly and daily time units, one should take care that the weekly activity really uses the resource during the whole week. It may be necessary to multiply the durations of the weekly activities by the number of days per week, and treat them on a daily calendar. The same consideration can apply to mixing activities whose durations are expressed in terms of whole days with activities whose time units are in shifts or in hours.

One objection to the use of multiple calendars in networks is that float does not always remain consistent down a chain. Planners have been accustomed to selecting all the activities with zero float (or the maximum negative float, if targets have been used) for concentrated analysis in order to reduce the network duration. With a single calendar, this will isolate the entire critical path or paths in coherent chains. With multiple calendars this is not necessarily so.

It should be noted that an activity on the critical path can quite genuinely show a float greater than zero. The simplest example occurs when one considers a mixture of activities, some of which

Planning and Scheduling

work a seven-day week, and others of which work a five-day week, say. If there is a sequence of three activities:

> A = pour concrete
> B = allow concrete to set
> C = lay railway lines

and C must follow B which must follow A, it is possible that activities A and C might use labour which works a five-day week, but B can occur on a seven-day week. If the project starts on a Monday, and the durations are: A = 6 : B = 5 : C = 6, then the project will end on the Monday of the fourth week. Activity A will start on the first Monday and finish at the end of the second Monday, and will have zero float. Activity B will start on the second Tuesday and finish at the end of the second Saturday. It will have a float of one day. Activity C will start on third Monday, and will finish at the end of the fourth Monday.

In this example, if activity B happened to take six days instead of five, this would make no difference to the project duration. If activity B had a duration of four days, this would leave the project duration the same, but activity B would have a float of two days. It would also have a free float of two days. This gives a clue to one technique which can be used to complete the chains for float analysis purposes — the selection is done not on total float, but on a figure produced by subtracting the free float from the total float. This tends to include all necessary activities in the maximum float chain, but it will associate the activity at the end of each sub-chain with the activity it enters, rather than with the sub-chain to which it belongs. The analysis may have to be done separately for sub-critical chains, if these are to be analysed at the same time as the critical chain.

It is helpful to have a key logic analysis feature when making extensive use of multiple calendars, where the float may change from activity to activity. In this feature, activities or events are picked out as key points of the network, and the computer is asked to select out all those chains which connect the events or activities in question. In the simplest case, chains connecting two points of the network which are on the critical path(s) can be selected out for examination.

It is, then, a good thing if one can define a complex activity, whose resource requirements change during its duration — either requiring different resources or different amounts of the same resources. If a complex activity is used to define a series of tasks which the planner wishes to schedule together as a coherent whole, then the amount of descriptive information that the program allows to be associated with an activity should be adequate for this purpose.

Pool resources

Pool resources differ from normal resources in that their availability is cumulative. If an amount of the resource is left unused at the end of one day, it becomes available for use on the following day. Resources available in this way are expressed as a series of lump amounts on particular dates. Pool resources are normally used either for consumable materials, like cement or bricks, or for money. For example, if there is a limited budget for a job, the available money can be made available in 'lumps' whenever the budget allows, and the activities will use up this money until none is left ... at which point any further work will have to be delayed until the next cash inflow. Similarly, bricks are used up in construction, and any activity needing bricks may have to wait until the next delivery.

Pool resources generally feature in 'parallel' rather than 'serial' resource levelling schemes. This is one of the few advantages of parallel over serial levelling. Most of the effects of a pool resource can be simulated by using a normal resource, whose availability is specified in the same way as a pool resource, with individual 'deliveries' at specific times. The activities which would normally need to use the pool resource do not mention this resource in their requirements. Instead, an extra activity with a duration of one time unit is inserted before the activity needing that resource, and the requirement is associated with the extra activity. The extra activity normally has no predecessors, so that it can occur at any time before its successor. It will then make sure that there is an allocation of the necessary money or materials before the succeeding activity begins. Sometimes activities are allowed to have negative availability, so that they can add in to the availability of a pool resource. This can be applied if deliveries of a consumable material are scheduled as activities in the network.

Delay start constant

A delay start constant is the maximum time that an activity can be delayed during the resource analysis process. Once this delay limit is reached, then the resource levels will have to be exceeded if necessary to meet the schedule. It is normally applied to activities that occur early in a project, in order to prevent them from using up all the project float during scheduling. This leaves some float for activities occurring later in the project. For example, in a project consisting of two phases, design and construction, if the design phase must be completed with very limited resources, it could use up much of the available float, causing scheduling problems in the construction phase. Delay start constants applied to the design activities will tend to limit this effect.

Imposed dates

Imposed dates have a variety of subtle differences. Most network analysis programs will contain a facility for ensuring that an activity's earliest start is not before a given fixed date. Similarly, one can usually specify that an activity's late finish must not be after a given fixed date.

A number of variations on this are possible. Simple and obvious variations that fix an activity's earliest finish as not being before a given date, or its late start as not being after a given date occur in some programs. More dangerous are features such as 'mandatory finish' dates. These occur when the project controller has determined that a particular key date in a network is going to be met. Such key events are sometimes known as: 'The sun will not rise tomorrow unless ...' events. In this case, the planner instructs the computer that the activity on which the mandatory finish is placed will happen on or before the specified date, even although the chain leading up to it contains negative float. The earliest start of the activity coming out of the mandatory finish will start at or before the mandatory finish date, even although the earliest finish of the preceding activity may be greater than the mandatory finish.

In some programs the 'Time now' date acts as an imposed start date on all uncompleted activities. One should be able to specify different time now dates for different sections of the network, or even individual activities if required. When a planner is updating his network, it will probably take more than one day to extract progress reports for all the in-progress activities. In this case, the planner might choose an 'as of' date which is the notional date at which he is updating the network. All progress reports are related to that date. The updating process involves a certain amount of mental strain on the planner who has to consider not only how much time is required to finish the in-progress activity, but also how much time will be required to finish the activity on the 'as of' date chosen (or how much was required at that date, if it happens to be in the past). It is simpler to be able to give a date to the progress information which is the date at which it was current.

Some programs allow the user to place 'expected finish' dates on activities. After they have been reported as started, such activities automatically adjust their remaining duration so as to finish at the date specified. There is a temptation to forget about such activities altogether, and to sit back and let the computer carry on blindly reducing their remaining duration. However, used with sufficient caution, this feature can help to avoid the constant updating of durations on activities involving the delivery of materials, for example.

Order and delivery activities

Order and delivery activities are mainly concerned with the ordering and delivery of materials. Such activities may be associated with fairly large capital expenditure, or they could refer to bulky items. It is prudent, therefore, not to have these activities scheduled at their earliest start for two reasons:

1 The equipment could arrive on site long before it is needed, giving rise to storage and security problems.
2 Money is spent earlier than necessary, to the detriment of project cash flow.

Some systems allow the planner to mark delivery activities with a suitable code so that they 'slip' along their free float (i.e. towards the earliest start of the activity needing the equipment) during the time analysis calculations (see Figure 20.2).

In the calculation of arrow diagrams, one should mark dummy activities with the 'order and delivery' code, so that any dummy activity will pass its free float back to the preceding activity, where it is of more practical use, and where it should appear for reporting purposes.

Planning and Scheduling

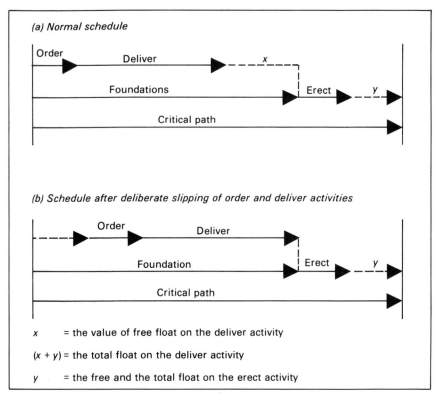

Figure 20.2 Scheduling of order and delivery activities
In the upper diagram the order and delivery activities have been scheduled at their earliest possible start dates, in the normal way. In the lower diagram, the computer has been informed by special input coding that these are order and delivery activities and it has slipped them as late as possible without affecting the float of their following activity (erect) in order that purchasing funds shall not be committed too early and that the goods or equipment is not scheduled for delivery to site until it is required

Resource aggregation

Resource aggregation is the accumulation of resource usage based on the results of time scheduling. It may be interesting to see what resources would be used if every activity were started at its earliest start (incidentally, beware of programs which claim to be capable of resource scheduling but which, in fact, can only carry out resource aggregation without being able to perform levelling).

A resource aggregation can show the amount of each resource required on each day of the project. Sometimes this will be best expressed cumulatively, particularly if the resource in question is money. The results should be available either in the form of a table, a series of printed, or plotted histograms, or a plotted curve.

It is sometimes a good idea, before carrying out the resource analysis of a project, to do a resource aggregation based on the earliest start of each activity, followed by another aggregation of resources used based on the latest starts. If it is anticipated that lack of resources will delay the project, these latest starts should be based on an estimate of the project completion date. The comparison of these two graphs will show the two extremes of probable resource usage. If they are close together, there is not much room for improvement by resource analysis.

Once the resource calculations have been done, the resulting resource schedule should lie somewhere in between the earliest and latest time aggregations. It should look much smoother than the time analysis-based results. The improvement over the earliest/latest case should show the amount of effective work the resource analysis process has carried out.

In cases where resources are effectively unlimited, and the goal is to produce a smooth utilisation of resources, then one should look at the results of a resource aggregation based on earliest and latest starts to decide where to set the initial availabilities. Most resource smoothing programs will work reasonably well if the availability of every resource is specified as being zero for the entire project, but they work better if a positive but tight availability is allocated initially. This availability can be estimated by inspection of the resource aggregation tables.

ERROR DIAGNOSIS

No matter how sophisticated the program, the output produced will be meaningless if the input data contains any significant error. Many of the program features described in this chapter are indeed sophisticated, and even more advanced techniques are discussed in Chapter 22. Among the most important features of any network analysis and resource scheduling program are its ability to detect and report input errors, in order that the planner can correct them. Of course, not all input errors can be recognised as such. If the planner inputs 100 weeks for an activity instead of 10 weeks, for example, the computer will not be able to tell him why his critical path has come out almost two years longer than expected! What the computer is able to do is analyse the network logic, to ensure that there are no unexplained discontinuities or feedback loops caused by mistakes in the input. The function of error detection is carried out just before time analysis. Until the errors have been corrected by the planner the subsequent phases of time analysis, resource scheduling and reporting cannot proceed.

Dangles

If an activity is left out of the input data by mistake, then it can give rise to an end dangle for its predecessor and a start dangle for its successor. This is explained in Figure 20.3. It is necessary for the planner to inform the computer of the intentional start and end dangles: otherwise the computer will identify these as errors. The program should be able to handle multiple starts and ends, and should believe its own analysis of the start and end points if there is any conflict between that and the planner's expectation (after giving the appropriate warning messages).

Loops

Probably the most important error detection facility in a time analysis program is the detection of logical loops in a network.

Most programs contain a facility for detecting whether a network contains logical loops. They can print out all those activities or relations involved in such loops. But, for large networks this may not be enough. Anyone who has seen a group of planning engineers faced with a network of 15 000 activities containing loops involving 5000 of those activities will realise that the more help the computer program can give in a such a situation, the better.

Figure 20.4 shows how a very simple loop can be created through an error in the input data. This is the simplest case, and the error print-out showing all activities contained in the loop gives the planner all he needs to know to put matters right by deleting the incorrect activity and replacing it with correct data.

One very necessary feature in loop detection is for the computer

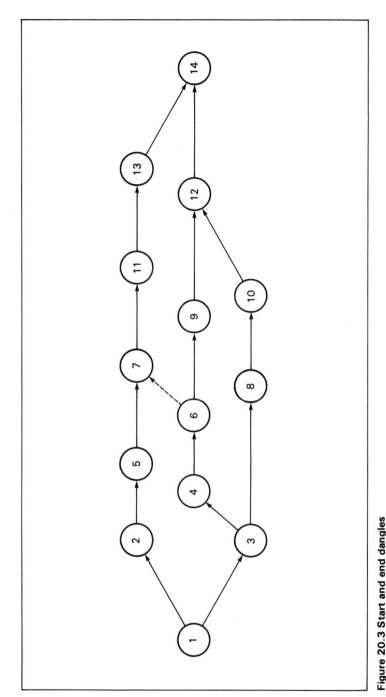

Figure 20.3 Start and end dangles
In error detection routines, critical path analysis programs should identify and report any unintentional start or end dangle. In the example above, the planner should report event 1 as a start event and event 14 as an end event. If these are not so reported, they will be printed out as logic errors. Now suppose that, by mistake, activity 8, 10 is left out of the input. The computer will identify event 8 as an end dangle and event 10 as a start dangle. Identification of these dangles by the computer tells the planner which activity is missing from the data

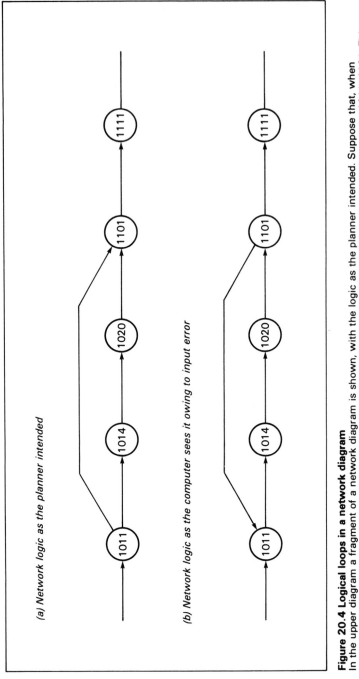

Figure 20.4 Logical loops in a network diagram
In the upper diagram a fragment of a network diagram is shown, with the logic as the planner intended. Suppose that, when preparing the input data, the planner has transposed his figures for events 1011 and 1101 when inputting activity 1011, 1101. This might be an easy mistake to make, when faced with the tiring task of inputting a large number of activities, and with numbers looking very similar. In this case, the computer would therefore be given, and would read the activity as 1101, 1011, thus effectively reversing its direction. The result is to create an endless loop, as shown in the lower diagram. The program's error detection routine should print out all the activities comprising the loop, in order to lead the planner to his mistake. Here, the activities in the loop are 1011, 1014; 1014, 1020; 1020, 1101 and the culprit reported as 1101, 1011

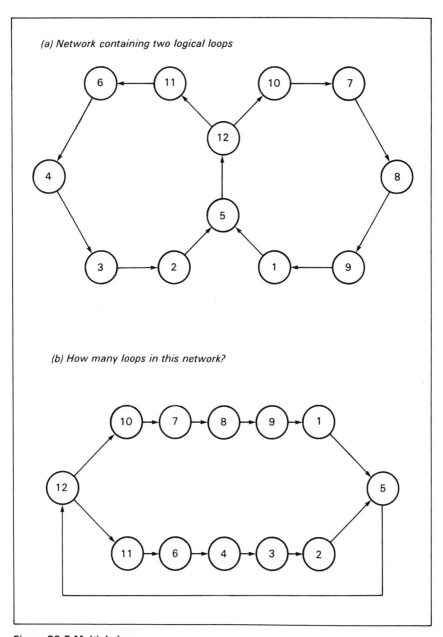

Figure 20.5 Multiple loops
Here are examples of multiple loops. In fact, the lower diagram is the same network as that in the upper diagram and both contain same two loops, no doubt caused by the planner making the mistake of calling activity 12, 5 activity 5, 12 when he prepared the input data

Planning and Scheduling

program to be capable of separating a number of loops from each other. These can be individually identified and solved by the planners. It should be able to recognise loops connected by a single directional chain, and separate those from each other.

Complex loops involving several connected cycles are more difficult to identify. For example, how many loops are there in Figure 20.5(a)? The usual answer, after a rapid inspection, is two. How many loops are there in Figure 20.5(b)? The usual quick answer is one. But a closer inspection reveals that both diagrams actually represent the same network.

Most computer programs capable of detailed loop analysis would take the view that the activities in Figure 20.5 (a) and (b) form only one loop. The more sophisticated loop analysis programs are able to suggest that the activity 5,12 is the most likely to have caused the problem, or of breaking the loop into a main chain and sub-chains of activities. See Figure 20.6.

```
            K & H   CRESTA LOOP ANALYSIS

       Analysing Loops

       Following are not a loop, but link to other loops
       1            events   5            events
       7            events   8            events
       8            events   9            events
       9            events   1            events
       10           events   7            events
       12           events   10           events
       Following are Loop Number    1
       2            events   5            events
       3            events   2            events
       4            events   3            events
       5            events   12           events
       6            events   4            events
       11           events   6            events
       12           events   11           events
```

Figure 20.6 Error detection report – loop analysis
Produced by the K and H Project Systems' CRESTA system from the network loop shown in Figure 21.5

Duplicated activities

To conclude this section on error diagnosis, having discussed the heady subjects of dangles and loops there remains one other, simple yet important error category. This concerns the problem of putting

(a) Duplicate activities created by network logic inappropriate to computer applications

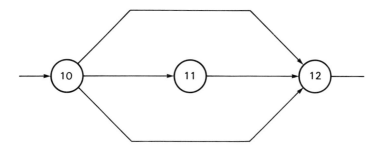

(b) Fragment of network to illustrate creation of duplicate activities through input error

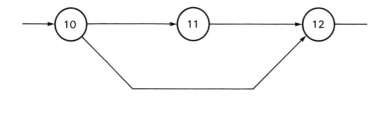

Figure 20.7 Duplicate activities
Duplicate activities can be created in several ways. In diagram (a) there are two activities which can be labelled as 10, 12. While the human brain can perceive the logical intention and calculate the network, the computer simply sees both activities as the same: it is necessary to insert a dummy in one of the activities to provide separate identification. In (b), if the planner should make an error in his input, describing activity 10, 12 wrongly as 10, 11 (it's easily done at the end of a long day) then the computer will see and report duplicate activities 10, 11

Planning and Scheduling

two or more activities into the computer file which have the same start and finish event numbers. This may be done intentionally by an inexperienced planner, or unintentionally by a person with more experience.

The intentional source of duplicated activities arises from planners who have been accustomed to mental network analysis, and who fail to realise that while the human brain can cope with two activities drawn parallel to each other in the network diagram, the computer will recognise these as twins. This point is explained in Figure 20.7(a). The inexperienced planner must learn that it is necessary to identify each activity separately, if necessary adding dummies to provide new event numbers.

Unintentionally duplicated activities occur when the planner makes a mistake in his input data, perhaps when he breaks off his input session for a cup of coffee, and repeating some of the input upon his return to the computer because he has forgotten where he left off, and failed to tick off all the activities already entered. Another cause is a simple numerical mistake in entering event numbers; this is illustrated in Figure 20.7(b).

Detection of duplicated activities is a simple matter for the program, and this can be done during the merging of file data before time analysis begins.

21

Computer Programs for Network Analysis — 2

David A. Barrett

This chapter continues the discussions of Chapter 20 with a more detailed examination of some complex ways in which the starts and finishes of activities can be related. Time analysis is taken a step further in the context of probabilistic and risk analysis. Progress reporting is included next, where procedures are described for updating networks according to progress made on a project. The chapter continues with a collection of more advanced techniques, with sections on automatic network generation and plotting, treatment of cost data, and some database applications. The concluding section is concerned with the user, and his 'interface' with the computer input and output.

COMPLEX RELATIONSHIPS FOR ACTIVITY STARTS AND FINISHES

Precedence network relationships

It is quite common that network logic has to be arranged to indicate that one activity must occur completely within the duration of another, longer, activity. In precedence diagrams it is natural to attempt to express this by giving a start-to-start relationship from the beginning of the longer activity to the beginning of the shorter one. In

Planning and Scheduling

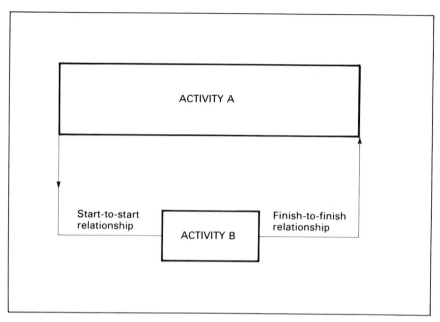

Figure 21.1 Parallel activities — precedence system
In some programs this arrangement might be interpreted as a logical loop

order to ensure that the shorter activity does not drift past the end of the longer one, it is natural to add a finish-to-finish relationship from the end of the short activity to the end of the longer one. This is illustrated in Figure 21.1. Many computer programs will consider this specification to be a logical loop. Some allow an extra type of relationship — a parallel relationship — to deal with this situation.

Other than the parallel relationship, the more common ones are:

SS	= start-to-start
FF	= finish-to-finish
N or FS	= normal, finish-to-start
SF	= start-to-finish

The SF relationship is less necessary than the others in practice, and is omitted from some computer programs.

Most computer programs will use a mathematical definition of finish-to-finish relationships which is slightly different from the intuitive view of them. An FF relationship is usually considered to

Computer Programs for Network Analysis — 2

condition the earliest start of the activity which follows it. If, for example, activity B follows activity A with an FF relationship lag of two days, then the earliest start of activity B must be at least:

[earliest start of A] + [duration of A]
+ [lag(2 days)] − [duration of B]

This is not quite the same as saying 'Activity B must finish at least two days after the finish of activity A'.

Most programs will not allow precedence relationships between activities to stretch out the durations of activities or to break them into discontinuous segments. The network shown in Figure 21.2 could have two different project durations, depending upon how the effects of its SS and FF relationships are viewed.

The intuitive approach

This approach, looking first at the SS relationships in Figure 21.2, would indicate that activity B can start on day 3, so activity C can start on day 6, and activity D can start on day 16. As the duration of activity D is 10 the project could end on day 25. Considering the FF relationships, activity B must not end before day 20, activity C must not end before day 24, activity D must not end before day 25. It would seem that the project duration is 25 days.

The computer approach

This approach to this question might run as follows. Because of the relationship A to B SS 2, the earliest start of activity B must be at least the morning of day 3. Because of the relationship A to B FF 4, the earliest start of activity B must be greater than 1 (earliest start of A) + 5 (duration of A) + 15 (FF lag) − 10 (duration of B). The answer is 11. The earliest start of activity B is 11.

Because of the relationship B to C SS 2, the earliest start of activity C must be at least day 13 (earliest start of B + lag of 2). Because of the relationship B to C FF 4, the earliest start of activity C must be greater than 11 (earliest start of B) + 10 (duration of B) + 4 (FF lag) − 8 (duration of C). This gives the earliest start of activity C as day 15.

Because of the relationship C to D SS 10, the earliest start of activity D must be at least day 25 (earliest start of C + SS lag). Because

Planning and Scheduling

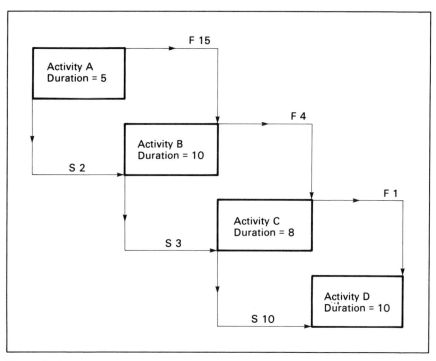

Figure 21.2 Interpretation of precedence network duration
As explained in the text, the project duration of this network might be understood as 25 days intuitively, but a computer program (using a mathematical approach) could arrive at an answer of 34 days

of the relationship C to D FF 1, the earliest start of C must be greater than 15 (the earliest start of C) + 8 (duration of C) + 1 (FF lag) – 10 (duration of D), which is 14 days. The earliest start of activity D is day 25, and the project ends on day 34.

The reason there is such a difference between the intuitive approach and the mathematical approach in this case, is that the intuitive approach would split activity B into two sections, one having an earliest start of day 3, because of the SS relationship from activity A, the other having an earliest finish of day 20 because of the FF relationship from activity A. However, the duration of activity B is only 10 days, and so will not stretch from day 3 to day 20. We can arrive at the ironical situation where, for certain activities, the longer they are, the shorter is the overall project. This effect is illustrated in Figure 21.3.

Computer Programs for Network Analysis — 2

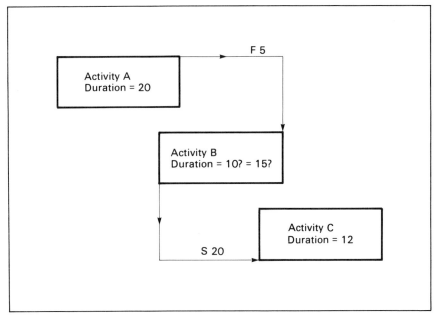

Figure 21.3 A paradox in precedence logic
When this network is subjected to time analysis by a computer, the strange result is produced that the longer the duration of activity B, the shorter the project duration

Relationships in arrow diagrams

Some relationships which can be programmed into arrow diagrams (otherwise known as IJ networks) were described in the program features listed in Chapter 20. These included slippage of order and delivery activities and tied activities.

The rules of IJ network logic imply that for two activities in sequence, the first must be 100 per cent complete before the second can start. In practice, many situations arise where this ruling does not apply to the real life project. The conventional way of expressing this in the network diagram was to break the activity into two or more sections such as 'start activity', 'continue activity' and 'finish activity'. This is illustrated in Figure 21.4. There were two main disadvantages with this approach.

1 The number of activities in the network is increased (from two to six even in this very simple example, which omits the 'continue activity' option).

Planning and Scheduling

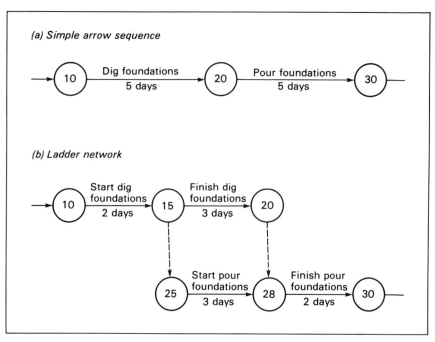

Figure 21.4 Ladder networks and transit times
The upper network, as it stands, does not reflect true life. It is not necessary for the whole length of the foundation trench to be dug before pouring can begin. It is possible to use a ladder network, such as that shown in diagram (b) to reflect planning intentions more accurately but, as explained in the text, the use of a computer program having the feature of transit times allows diagram (a) to be used without the unwelcome complications of ladder notation. The dummies in (b) have zero duration in this example, but durations are sometimes used in these circumstances

2 During resource allocation, because of possible resource availability restrictions, the completion part of each operation could be scheduled later than the start — in effect splitting a single operation into two parts scheduled at different times, even although the whole operation might not be strictly splittable.

The 'transit time' concept overcomes both of these disadvantages. A *transit time* is a number associated with any arrow, which can be negative or positive, and can refer to the beginning or to the end of an activity. Transits which refer to the starts of activities are called 'transits before' (TB). Transit times which refer to the end of activities are called 'transits after' (TA).

A positive TB is the delay between the predecessor event of an activity and the activity's start.

A positive TA is the delay between the end of an activity and its successor event.

A negative TB is the amount by which an activity can overlap its predecessor event.

A negative TA is the amount by which an activity can overlap its successor event.

In the practical example above, the overlap can be achieved by coding the activity for 'pouring foundations' with a negative TB of 3.

One of the major advantages quoted for precedence diagramming over IJ is that precedence allows for the overlap of sequential activities, by the use of SS and FF relations. An IJ system with transit times has the same capabilities, so that particular advantage disappears.

Not all IJ diagramming programs have transit time features in them. One reason for this is that it is technically difficult to combine parallel resource analysis with transit times, so that systems which use one tend not to have the other.

PROBABILISTIC NETWORKS AND RISK ANALYSIS

Right from the beginning of critical path analysis it has been recognised that the estimate of an activity duration is just that: an estimate. Attempts have been made to take into account the inaccuracies involved in estimating, both by trying to improve the estimating process and by analysing the possible consequence of bad estimates. Some early programs used the PERT technique of giving three time estimates to each activity in order to obtain a more realistic estimate of activity duration.

The planner was asked to provide an 'optimistic', a 'realistic' and a 'pessimistic' estimate. These estimates were then weighted to produce the duration estimate that was used in the calculation. This practice gradually fell into disuse. Planners found it hard enough work to produce one estimate of the duration of each task, let alone three. If these three duration estimates were also used to provide some measure of the effects of uncertainty at each stage of the project, and if these measures were comprehended and used, then the extra effort involved could become worth while.

In PERT analyses of this type, the three duration estimates for each activity were thought of as defining a continuous probability distribution for that duration. Many different possible distribution shapes were made available for the planner to choose from, specified in different ways. The best results came when there was a large body of statistical experience relevant to the estimate in question, in which case the planner did not need to be a statistician in order to choose the distribution which most closely matched his intuitive feel for the practical reality.

Once the shape of the probability of duration had been established for all the activities in the network, an analysis was carried out to determine the shape of the distribution of probable dates at each activity or event of the network. Then, the answer could be determined to such questions as:

— What is the probability of meeting a given completion date?
— What date for a given activity can we give, and be 99 per cent sure that it will be met?

By experimenting with the duration estimates of individual activities within the network, one could discover how sensitive the date distributions at the end of the network were to the durations of those individual activities.

Such networks were generally drawn at a much higher level than the critical path networks used to actually schedule the job, because of the difficulty of obtaining estimates at the lower level, and of evaluating the results. The method of calculation was a Monte-Carlo simulation technique. This method is named after the gambling casinos in Monte Carlo, and consists quite simply of carrying out a very large number of network analyses of the same network. In each calculation the dice are thrown for each activity to see what duration that activity will have (obviously this random choice is made in such a way so that it is likely to conform to the probability distribution of the duration of the activity in question). Every early start date is recorded for every calculation, and added into a distribution of early start dates for each activity of the network. After a sufficiently large number of calculations have been done, the probability distributions of early start dates can be used to draw statistical conclusions.

Because of the random method of calculation, some of the distribution shapes will tend to have strange little squiggles in them, but the results are nevertheless usable. The higher the confidence level one is examining for the dates in question, the more calculations will have to be done, in general, so that the 'tail' of the distribution (where the less likely results are recorded) becomes reasonably well formed.

This technique can take quite large amounts of computer time, and is often highly recommended by computer manufacturers.

More recent approaches to the analysis of risks in networks, and of the probabilities of achieving projects within a given time span have concentrated on direct calculation techniques as opposed to simulation. In this case, the distribution shapes remain correct within the accuracy of the computer numbers being used, and there is no possibility of a totally erroneous result due to the blind workings of untutored chance.

This approach allows a departure from the pure network model of a project for risk analysis purposes. The project is divided into a very limited number of key activities, each of which is described in detail together with all significant sources of risk associated with it. All feasible responses to each source of risk are then listed and described, and additional risks implied by those responses are analysed. From this, the interrelationship of the various possible contingencies is established.

Then, the probability of each risk is assessed, together with the probabilities of the associated consequences. The cumulative effect of successive sources of risk is then computed, giving the shape of each risk within an activity, and the contribution of each activity to the total time risk of the project.

Similar statistical analysis techniques can be applied to cost risks as to time risks, when for example a price is to be fixed in advance for a product whose component costs are not completely known.

These methods are generally much more difficult to use than pure time, resource and cost planning. Engineers with appropriate experience are in short supply, and the probabilistic analysis of the risks associated with a project can be expensive in man-hours and in effort. Nevertheless, it may be worth while for large complex projects involving significant uncertainty.

From a software performance point of view, the potential purchaser should check how long it takes to carry out the calculations for networks of the size he plans to use. The form in which probabilistic results are expressed is important, as quite subtle points are being made. The system should be able to display answers to the kinds of question that the planner is likely to ask in a form that is easy for him to understand.

PROGRESS REPORTING

When all the techniques so far discussed have been used to produce a schedule, the job of planning has only just begun. Obviously the network and its resulting schedule need to be updated with sufficient frequency to ensure that the schedule remains valid as the project proceeds and, almost invariably, is subject to changes.

Progress reporting techniques vary considerably between programs. It is quite common for a planner to wish to report progress on activities which should theoretically not have been started, according to the network logic. If one is not to plan at a very low level of detail, the network will correspond only approximately to the possible sequence of tasks in reality, particularly if an attempt is being made to catch up on the schedule. Overlaps between operations may be possible, although not planned.

Many computer programs act in a bewildered fashion when confronted by updates that are out of sequence according to the logic of the network. They remark: 'That's not logical, Captain!' and wiggle their ears. The easiest answer for a programmer is to assume that the input must be in error, and to not allow the situation at all. A network is a tool not a prison, and should not involve the planner in unnecessary work making the sequence of what has already happened look logical to the program he is using.

It makes sense to force the earliest start of any activity which has been started or completed to be 'time now' (the date relevant to the update in progress, from which the computer will recalculate the remaining schedule) even though it is preceded by items which have not yet been completed. Sometimes one may wish to ask the program to maintain the sequence, so that the earliest start of the in-progress activity drifts away from time now to allow room for the non-completed chain preceding it.

The situation as regards the calculation of the latest times of activities preceding the out-of-sequence progress is more complex than the action as regards earliest times. The answer is less intuitively obvious. One might require the following options:

(a) The backward pass is unaffected. The latest times of the activities preceding the out of sequence progress follow on logically from the out-of-sequence activities. This implies that these preceding activities will suddenly have much lower float as one reads back along the chain which includes the out-of-sequence progress; they may even develop negative float that is difficult to justify objectively and which looks bad on progress reports.

(b) The chain of logic is completely broken at the point of out-of-sequence progress. Activities followed only by in-progress or completed activities act as if they were disconnected ends. Activities followed by a mixture of in-progress and not started activities take their results from the activities which have not yet been started. This can be awkward if the following chain is in fact critical, and it is still necessary to complete some of the preceding logic before continuing with the network.

(c) The latest finish of the activity preceding the out of sequence progress is 'adjusted' so that the float of that activity is equal to or less than the float of the in-progress or complete following activity. This is somewhat artificial, but may be the best compromise. It is certainly one of the most popular calculation options chosen in the use of K and H Project Systems' PREMIS system.

Some programs allow the planner to mark particular events or activities in a special way, so that they do not follow the normal logic of network analysis. The usual convention is that an activity cannot start until all preceding activities are complete. The 'or-node' or 'short path activity' does not follow this rule. Instead, such an activity can start as soon as ANY of its predecessors is complete.

Practical uses for this kind of feature are fairly rare, but they do exist. In particular, two alternative sources of supply for a certain material for a task could exist in a network, and the one which arrived first would be used in preference to the one which arrived later.

In the network analysis of such items it is by no means clear what action should be taken by the computer program on the backward

Planning and Scheduling

pass through the network, when latest finishes are being computed. If an activity 'C' can start as soon as either activity 'B' or activity 'A' has finished, and the durations of the activities are A = 2 days, B = 4 days and C = 6 days, then, supposing the project starts on the first of January, working seven days per week, activities A and B can both start on the first of January. Activity A will finish on 2 January, and so activity C can start on 3 January. The project will then finish on 8 January, at the end of activity C. Working the late times backwards, the latest start of activity C will be the same as its earliest start — 3 January. Therefore it would seem that the latest finish of activity B would be 2 January. Its earliest finish is 4 January. It will therefore appear to have a negative float of 2 days.

COMPUTER AIDED NETWORK CONSTRUCTION

Library networks

In many projects, certain groups of activities are repeated several times throughout the network with perhaps only the duration, part of the description, and the identifying area or work-breakdown codes being different. For example, in petrochemical construction, the network logic for the design, procurement and installation of a pump is identical for the majority of pumps. Only the durations and identifications tend to change.

It is possible to generate large networks rapidly in this way. One uses a computer to generate them, needs a computer to analyse them, and may well need a computer to display the resulting network, particularly if there are extensive local changes to the library modules once called — so one cannot just use many prints of the library network drawing.

If a library of standard subnetworks has been established, it can be valuable not only as a method of creating networks rapidly for new projects, but also as a repository for a history of activity durations. If the spread of durations is recorded, together with some appropriate measure of the size of the job, if appropriate, better estimates can be produced in the future, together with some idea of the possible variation that can be encountered. If the estimate is associated with a job size, then the new estimate for a given use of the library network can be automatically made to be a function of the size factor.

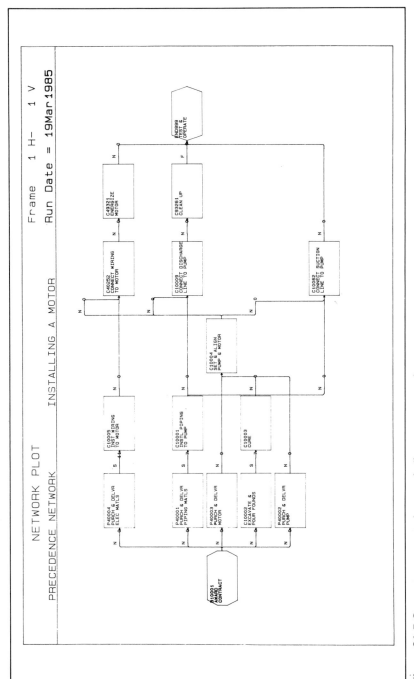

Figure 21.5 Computer generated network diagram — precedence system
Compare this with the same project network plotted in arrow notation at Figure 21.6

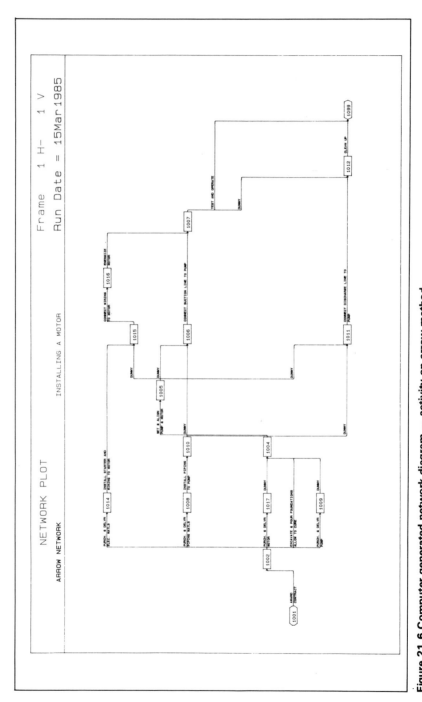

Figure 21.6 Computer generated network diagram — activity on arrow method
This shows that arrow diagrams allow more detail in a given space than their precedence counterparts — the precedence version of this network is in Figure 21.5. (Both diagrams produced by K and H Project Systems' CRESTA system)

When networks are not drawn by the planner initially, but are generated in this way, it is helpful to have automatic plotting equipment available to draw out the network once it has been created. In the absence of this, networks can be represented quite efficiently by printing out adhesive labels from the computer, each label having the information for one activity. These labels can then be stuck to a working board or drawing and the relationships to other activities drawn in by hand as required.

Graphic displays and plotters

It is not easy to program a computer to design a diagram of a network, and programs which do this vary greatly in the elegance of the network which is produced. The more clumsy the layout, and the greater number of crossed lines and linkages, the harder the network will be to follow.

More information can be drawn on a page for arrow networks than for precedence networks, where the boxes tend to get in the way of the relationship lines. See Figures 21.5 and 21.6.

A good design algorithm will react to a change in the connectivity of a network caused perhaps by adding or deleting a single activity, and will produce a new, perhaps different, layout. Planners sometimes find this frustrating because they have become familiar with a particular layout, and have learned where to find particular activities. If the computer has redesigned the layout and moved activities about, they can no longer find them in their accustomed places.

In some plotting software it is possible to define 'zones' in a network layout. These are horizontal bands which can be associated with particular activity codes. If this feature is used, then all activities of a particular area or responsibility can be confined within the same general area. This can make it easier to find activities after a re-design has been carried out.

One useful capability is that of being able to 'fix' a design and to determine manually where any new activities are to be fitted in to the drawing.

Online updating

Given computer-designed graphic representation of a network, and a terminal capable of displaying reasonably large sections of the network, it may be possible to update the project directly in network form. The planner picks out the activity he wishes to alter, zooms in for a detailed display of the information associated with the activity, and alters it in situ. New relationships and connections can be drawn in on the screen, and activities can be moved about by 'connecting' them to the screen cursor and moving them about until they are 'dropped' at the appropriate point in the display.

Not all project management software is capable of doing this.

COST FEATURES

Early attempts to integrate cost factors with the time analysis and resource analysis of critical path networks met with little success in general. When dealing with costs, it would seem logical to unify the cost reporting schemes of planners and of accountants who are working on the same project, so that costs have to be estimated only once, and reported only once, However, the working methods of planners, and their goals, differ from those of the accounting staff.

A planner will tend to break a project down into functional units. An accountant will tend to use a cost-centre breakdown. Thus, the elements against which a planner will report progress for time and resources will be different from those which an accountant will naturally use. One compromise has been to use a work-breakdown structure which can codify the lowest level of detail used by either the planner or the accountant in each individual case, or which can assign the percentage contribution to each cost centre item of each task defined by the planner. Although this adds complexity to the coding structures used by both the planner and the accountant, it does have the merit of being a 'database' approach, where each piece of information is reported and recorded in one place only.

Planners operate with rough estimates, and are pleased if they come within ten per cent of the eventual reality. Accountants strive for precision. Normally therefore, the cost estimates used by planners are recorded separately from the accountant's information in the data structure — although both can benefit from the other's information. The planner can eventually integrate more precise estimates, and then actual figures, into his reports. It is most important (and more rare than it should be) for the planner to compare his initial estimates with the actual figures eventually reported through the accounting procedures. The single most essential factor to improve the quality of estimates or forecasts in general is feedback. The estimator must be able to discover how close his estimates were, so that he can improve his future guesses. The accountant too can make use of the planner's estimates in the early stages as a cross-check to look for gross errors in his data.

The timescale of reporting is usually quite different for cost and for time. This is probably the major reason for failure to integrate costing and scheduling. The planner will know which activities are complete, and (for those that are in progress) roughly how far along they are, quite quickly. Depending on the kind of project being carried out, he might know hours, days, or a few weeks after the progress has in fact occurred. The accountant might not know for several months what the costs have been. Thus, the evaluation of in-progress work items is very difficult. Interim estimates have to be made of the value of work done, before the full accounting procedures have returned their final result. In cases where interim progress payments are important, delay in reporting work done means delay in receiving money, and possible cash-flow problems. In this sort of environment, the planner is still looking to the future. His priority is to know what work remains to be done, so that he can schedule it properly. The accountant is looking to the past. His priority is to know what work has been done, how much he can charge for it as an interim payment, how much it cost to accomplish.

The planner looking forward and the accountant looking back sometimes end up with an eyeball-to-eyeball confrontation.

It may be important for project costing that the computer program chosen is sufficiently flexible in its method of coding what activities are associated with which cost packages. In general, an activity may involve several cost items, and a cost item may involve several activities. An activity may include part of several cost elements. It must also be possible to summarise costs at different levels of the pyramid of the work-breakdown structure. There can be a limit to the number of such levels which a program will allow.

The method of evaluating activities which are in progress, or which have received partial reporting information, can be critical. It is desirable to have a wide range of methods available for this purpose.

Planning and Scheduling

It may be appropriate to compute the value of work done according to:

1. A 50 per cent rule, where half the job price is released on commencement and the rest on completion.
2. A progress rule, where the proportion of time completed on the job is applied directly to the value of work done.
3. A 100 per cent completion only rule, where the job only contributes to the value of work done when it is complete.
4. A 'started' rule, where the job is added in as soon as it has been started.
5. An 'equivalent units' rule, where some independent measure is taken and work done is evaluated according to the proportion completed (*viz*. cubic yards of concrete poured, and the like).
6. A 'level of effort' rule, based on elapsed time in the activity.
7. An 'apportioned effort' rule, where the progress of the cost element is proportional to the progress of a number of other cost elements or activities, perhaps weighted by value or work content.

And many others: the wider the range of possible methods offered by a program, the better.

For cost performance analysis it is important to determine whether or not the program being considered can be integrated with the company's cost accounting procedures. This may indeed be totally unacceptable to the accounting department, which in many cases is reluctant to accept what they term 'unfiltered' data from a planning process. Can the system easily accept files produced by the current accounting programs now, or will additional programs have to be written? Can it produce files in the form which the accounting programs will accept, or will some kind of translation have to take place? Can the program being considered replace some of the reporting functions of the current accounting system altogether?

Some programs rely upon fixed input formats. Others can accept guidance as to what information is to be provided, and in what form. It is sometimes necessary to extract data from existing computer files, to enter the project planning system. If the computer system selected can only accept data from a fixed screen panel, which is built into the system, it will not be able automatically to 'steal' data from files created by other programs. If it can accept information as a file, it is important to know whether this file must be in a given fixed form, or whether data can be captured directly from other files. If the data must be in a given fixed form, some programmer familiar with the system from which data is to be accepted will have to write a program to produce the information in the form required.

A planning system should ideally be able to accept data other than that envisaged by the suppliers of the program. Additional data can then be input to the system and associated with the activity records, and can eventually be output in reports. All kinds of data may be required to be associated with activities in the network, in which case one might need a facility for defining any kind of information, and printing it out in any way. There may be a use in particular situations for associating:

1 Material lists, quantities, prices and so on.
2 Drawing number lists, version numbers.
3 Work breakdown structure codes.
4 Purchase order numbers, delivery times.
5 Job numbers.
6 Electrical conduit routing codes.
7 Area, responsibility, department codes.

There are many other kinds of information, with activities.

If one adds to this the ability to carry out computations on any numbers stored, and place results on computer files or on output reports as listings or as tables, the result can be a system which can carry out most data processing functions. Once planning engineers have mastered such a system, they can carry out a great variety of computer processing without needing to have recourse to computer specialists. Planners using K&H Project Systems' PREMIS system, for example, have been known to establish supplementary data processing departments within their own organisations.

DATABASE APPLICATIONS

Rational database capabilities can be valuable when attaching a list of items to each activity, rather than a single value. This can be difficult to specify and manipulate, using the control instructions provided by the software supplier. If large quantities of information are associated with each activity, the network computation process is bound to become more clumsy, with gigantic lists of data rumbling around inside the machine, contributing little to the pure critical path analysis or resource levelling calculations.

The most quoted advantage of a 'database' approach to information handling is that it reduces duplication of data. This has some truth in it, but perhaps more important is its effect in simplifying the processing of lists of information.

A database structure will enable the planner to store any lists of information, or indeed any information not essential to the time analysis calculation, separately from the activities themselves. Each set of information that is associated with an activity will have a pointer to that activity. When computations involving the network are to be carried out, they do not need to refer to the associated lists in any way. When reports are to be produced for (say) materials, then relevant activity information (perhaps the activity early starts or scheduled starts) can be picked off from the activity file from the pointers on the materials file.

The nature of these pointers determines whether the database in question should be termed 'relational' or 'hierarchical'. Traditional databases were hierarchical. After the invention of the relational approach, it gradually became more popular than the older hierarchical systems. Relational systems tend to be more flexible. hierarchical systems are usually more efficient in their use of computer resources. The pointers in relational systems tend to refer to the content of the records being pointed to. The pointers in hierarchical systems refer to the physical location within the computer of the records being pointed to.

The salient differences between the systems can be visualised by comparing the processes that have to be carried out when an activity number is changed, and there is a materials file with several records for materials which are required by that activity.

In a hierarchical system, there would be no change required, other than altering the activity number itself. The pointers would still be pointing to the correct place.

In a relational system, the current activity number would have to be removed from the 'index' being used to relate materials to activities. The new activity number would have to be added to the index, and associated with the correct physical location of the altered record. All the materials records referring to the activity would have to have the activity number on them altered. Note that the relational system does involve some duplication of data — namely the data on which the matching process from one file to another takes place.

Once a hierarchical structure has been established, it is difficult to add new pathways to it. Ad-hoc enquiries on bases which have not been planned for right from the beginning cannot easily be made. On the whole, it is probably better to pay the performance penalty and use a relational system; though it is perhaps wise to use the most efficient relational system possible so as not to lose more than absolutely necessary in response speed.

INPUT, OUTPUT REPORTS AND THE USER INTERFACE

Application generators are usually, but not necessarily, associated with particular database systems. They are intended to enable personnel not trained in computer work to take advantage of the potential flexibility of modern computer systems without needing to rely upon computer experts.

Failure of communication between people is by far the greatest cause of problems in data processing. The application specialist who wants the computer to carry out some particular kind of processing has to explain what he wants to a systems analyst, who then explains it to a programmer or programmers who then 'explain' it to the computer. Application generators try to cut out the middle man, so that the application specialist talks directly to the computer system.

If a prewritten program is to be acquired for project planning, it is not ideal if the operations of the company acquiring the program have to be distorted to fit the pre-set reporting formats of that program. A program may have a sufficiently well-chosen variety of standard reports that current and future conceivable needs are covered by them. Alternatively, it may contain a 'report generator' facility whereby the planner can specify his own reports.

The best situation is probably a mixture of these two solutions, where the planner may

1 Choose a standard report.
2 Ask for simple variations in that standard report such as

different sort sequence, activity selection, or control-break field for totalling.
3   Make temporary or permanent changes to the standard report and create new standards of his own from it.
4   Build his own reports from scratch.

Where a report generator language is used, it should be designed for use by personnel not trained in computer work. Some generators have several levels of use, where the program predefines more or less of any given report, giving correspondingly greater or less ease of use and increasing flexibility with greater complexity.

A program should be capable of producing

1   Listings in almost any form, sequence, or selection, with totals and page changes as chosen by the planner.
2   Bar charts on computer printers (even if automatic plotting equipment is available, a computer-printed bar chart is produced much faster and more cheaply).
3   Tables, especially of resource usage, resources remaining, cost by time, cumulative cost curves, and so on.
4   Histograms of the above. (Again, computer-printed histograms are more efficient than plotted histograms, and should be used unless quality presentation is the overriding factor.)

The reporting system should be capable of handling lists of information, and in particular of expanding any of the codes used in the activities — resource codes, department codes, area codes, etc. — for reporting purposes. It should be possible to direct reports to other systems or back into the input phase of the planning program as well as to the printer. This is useful if one wishes to 'print' an update candidate list containing all those activities likely to show progress during the next update cycle, to use as a basis for the inputting of progress information.

Opinions vary as which method of inputting and updating information is the easiest to use. Some prefer to be able to select from a number of options displayed on a menu. Some prefer a question-and-answer method of working. Others prefer a 'command' language structure, consisting of a keyword followed by options.

It is common for a user to prefer the use of menus when he first starts to use a system. He knows where he is and what is expected of him at any time. After he has become familiar with the menu structure and options, they can become irritating, and he may begin to prefer a command-orientated system. By the same token, inexperienced users will prefer to carry out updating one activity at a time, editing a screen-full of information, with the maximim amount of on-line error checking from the computer system. More experienced users will become impatient with this, and may graduate towards the preparation of update lists, with many activities on the screen simultaneously, with minimal delay produced by the computer system.

Ideally, a computer program should have a wide variety of possible input methods, to suit users with different tastes and different amounts of experience with the system.

As an extreme case, there is one system which attempts to judge the competence of each user, who is identified by his log-on code. It adjusts the degree of 'user-friendliness' downwards as the number of user mistakes decreases. Eventually it allows short-cut methods and rapid bulk input.

There are many special updating operations which are useful in practice, but are not included in all computer programs. It is worth while to have a transaction to change activity numbers or node numbers in arrow networks. In precedence networks such an operation should automatically alter any relationships pointing to the activity whose number is being changed.

It is important to determine how long the program will take to handle networks of the size normally used by the planner, using the computer equipment which has been chosen.

Times to carry out updating, time analysis, resource analysis, and produce reports are all important. When updating activities or other data, how long will the user have to wait while the computer finds the appropriate record, and paints the appropriate screen to be filled in, if a full-screen approach is to be employed?

Older systems are mostly based on 'batch' processing. Newer systems tend to be more 'interactive'. There are advantages and disadvantages to both approaches. With a batch approach, the planner makes all the alterations he is going to make to the network, and submits them to the computer to be analysed. With an interactive approach, the computer makes each change as it is typed in, and may produce error diagnostics at any stage. The added convenience of immediate error detection has to be balanced against any additional delays between updates as the planner sits at the screen and waits for the error checks to be performed and against the larger amount of computer time used by an interactive system. If the planner is using his own dedicated micro computer, there is no advantage in operating in batch mode, providing that the micro computer is fast enough to carry out all the updating functions he requires without appreciable delay.

It is important to know how much help and assistance the producer of the program, or his local agent, will provide in the implementation process. How much will this assistance cost?

The quality of the program documentation is important. Possibly the perfect program, perfectly documented might need no support from the supplier. Especially for the perfect user. Most systems do not aspire to these heights.

Any training offered by the program supplier should be gratefully accepted. It should produce more rapid learning than that obtained by trial and error from the use of the system itself and from its associated manuals; but more important, it will give a feeling for the emphasis provided by the supplier on the different features of his system, and for the particular interpretation made of some of the claims in the publicity literature for the product.

Some software suppliers offer a telephone support service, sometimes called a 'hotline', whereby users can ask questions of experienced personnel. This is a major advantage, where it is available, and if the service is reasonably priced (sometimes it is free).

It is advisable to have a definite procedure to follow when the computer system appears to have gone wrong. Most software suppliers do not find it helpful to receive a telex or telephone call stating that 'the program does not work'. Greater detail is preferred. One good procedure is to build up a standard test network containing examples of most of the features of the program that one uses. Whenever an error appears in the results, this standard network should be run to see if it still comes to a successful conclusion, and produced the same results as before. This procedure should also be carried out whenever a new version of a programme is received from the supplier. Any changes in results from the standard network should be investigated to determine whether they are really improvements to the system.

In this way, it may be possible to give the supplier a clue as to whether the problem lies with his software or with the computer hardware being used, and to locate and correct any error with maximum dispatch. Sometimes, the problem may be caused by an intentional software 'time-bomb', and may be a tactful way of saying 'Have you paid your rental for this year?' Some suppliers arrange for their software to degrade gracefully (or, according to some of their clients, disgracefully) if payments are not made where appropriate, in order to defeat the processes of software piracy.

It is not ideal to introduce intentional errors into software, which suffers quite enough from unintentional ones. Such anti-piracy measures, although being more complex, are still fairly easy to defeat, for the most part. Those that are based on dates can be circumvented by the user lying to the computer as to what is today's date. They can be brought into action unintentionally by an operator who mistypes today's date into his machine, and thereby perhaps destroys copies of such intentionally sabotaged software.

An additional advantage can be derived from making a standard test network in the initial stages of using a program. It is important to learn how the program reacts to different situations.

Make a test network and try out typical practical operations. For any special features which look interesting, try to produce the situation in which you would use them, and see if the results indeed correspond to what one would expect from the manual.

A good way of judging the support offered for a given product is to speak to as many as possible of the existing users. Try not to talk exclusively to those clients recommended by the supplier as good contact points, nor exclusively to those who have just got out of bed with a bad hangover after celebrating the successful conclusion of their latest project. The worth of any individual opinion should be weighted by the length of time the organisation in question has been using the software.

Part VI
MANAGING PROGRESS AND PERFORMANCE

22
Managing Progress

Dennis Lock

This chapter starts with a crop of assumptions, the first of which is that progress needs managing. The importance of carrying out all project commitments on or before the promised dates should be obvious to all. A project is not successful if its late completion results in delayed start-up of a process or production plant, causing lost revenue for the owner. A project is an obvious failure if the exhibits being prepared for a trade exhibition are ready two weeks after the exhibition has closed. It is a general rule that any extension of a project beyond its agreed timescale must lead to extra expenditure or losses, simply through the cost of the money and other resources (accommodation, people, materials) which are locked into the programme. No one should, therefore, argue with the assumption that project time is itself a vital and expensive resource. Just as all other project resources have to be managed, so does time.

THE FRAMEWORK OF PROGRESS MANAGEMENT

In order to give a project some chance of being carried out according to the client's delivery wishes, the management methods and structure have to be suitable. The following assumptions are made: if any of these is not met in a particular project, progress management will be made more difficult, if not impossible.

1 **Organisation**

It is assumed that the project organisation is appropriate to the size and nature of the work, and that all members of the organisation are clear on their roles.

2 **Project definition**

Another assumption is that the project is clearly defined, so that the project manager knows exactly what has to be achieved.

3 **Supportive management**

The project manager cannot operate in a vacuum, without the support and encouragement of his superiors. It is assumed that this exists, both in the provision of facilities and in backing up any requests for action which demand intervention at senior level, either within or outside the contractor's own organisation.

4 **A reasonable client**

The client (or customer, or owner) must act responsibly by providing funds when they are required, by avoiding unnecessary requests for changes, by approving designs and authorisations for expenditure when asked without undue delays, and generally by appreciating the problems which face his contractor and acting to co-operate rather than hinder progress. A reasonable client is assumed.

5 **Competent people**

A lot of people are involved in a major project. They will be spread throughout the contractor's own company, the organisations of subcontractors and suppliers, in the firms responsible for moving materials by rail, road, sea and air, in government and other official functions, and in the client's own management. Some of these people will be competent. Others might be less so. We have to assume that the majority are capable of

6 A workable schedule

It is not enough to plan a project by simply drawing a few lines on a piece of paper, calling it a bar chart, and then attempting to use it as a working programme. Schedules have to be thought through carefully, taking into account all task interdependencies, resource constraints, and so on. A workable schedule is one which does not expect impossible things of the resources employed. Scheduling is dealt with fully elsewhere in this book, but it is assumed that the project manager to whom this chapter is addressed has the benefit of a schedule which exists in sufficient detail to highlight the dates when measurable events should take place if the programme is to be met. Given a set of targets at which control can be aimed, there is some basis for control. A good schedule is to progress management what a properly authorised budget is to cost control.

With all these assumptions, perhaps it is a wonder that any project ever gets finished on time. And, so far, we have not even thought about all the other things which can go wrong accidentally, seen in any insurance company's catalogue of policy disasters (fire, storm, tempest, civil commotion, riot, war (civil or otherwise), strikes, lockouts, objects dropped from aircraft, other natural disasters, unnatural disasters — (you know the sort of thing). What chance does any project ever have of being finished on time? The truth is that many do finish late.

Efficient progress management seeks to plan the project effectively, to foresee possible risks to the programme, to monitor work in progress and identify any current problems, to assess priorities for using scarce resources, and (above all) to take action whenever problems do arise which, if left alone, would threaten the programme.

COMMUNICATING THE WORK PROGRAMME

Consider a contracting organisation into which is received a prized order for a new project. Possibly over one hundred of this contractor's staff are going to be working on the new project for a prolonged period. All good news. But how do they know when to start and what to do?

Project authorisation

The first official document used in many companies to start up a new project is a works order. This sets out the most important dates, is accompanied by budget instructions, summarises the technical details, and notifies everyone of the cost codes and project number to be used. Much of the works order content is derived from the sales engineers who worked with the client when the project negotiations took place, so that the works order should be seen as part of a detailed project specification. If the engineer who headed up the sales team can take over as project manager, so much the better.

Apart from containing information about the project, the other important function of a works order is that it authorises work to start: in other words the start of project expenditure is approved.

Although it is a general rule that no work should ever be allowed to start without such authorisation, it can sometimes be worth taking a small risk on a big project by allowing one or two exploratory tasks to start before the issue of a formal authorisation document — indeed before a contract has been received. If this sounds dangerous and reactionary, consider that the build up of work on any project is usually slow, requiring only a few people at the front end. They would be engaged in finding out about the client's drawing and engineering standards, sorting out any remaining problems on broad design concepts, and other tasks which, although time consuming, do not require the full time use of more than one or two engineers. By taking a risk such as this, it is sometimes possible to gain up to a month on the engineering programme. It is at least worth considering.

Task lists

Whilst the works order or other project authorisation document gives instructions in broad management outline, it does not carry enough detail from which to issue work down to the level of separate jobs.

Before the days of computers, the project manager could arrange

```
DEPARTMENT - ENGINEERING DESIGN    RESOURCE SCHEDULE ALL ACTIVITIES    SINGLE TRANSFER MACHINE
```

PREC EVENT	SUCC EVENT	DURN DAYS	WORKS ORDER	..ACTIVITY DESCRIPTION..	EARLIEST START	SCHEDULED TIMES START	FINISH	LATEST FINISH	REM.G FLOAT	RESOURCES
1001	1002	12	75001	DESIGN TRANSFER LAYOUT	22FEB82	22FEB82	09MAR82	22MAR82	9	1 ENG.R
1012	1020	15	75001	DESIGN BORE HEAD LAYOUT	22FEB82	22FEB82	12MAR82	25MAR82	9	1 ENG.R
1004	1009	15	75001	DESIGN FIXTURE LAYOUT	22FEB82	03MAR82	23MAR82	23MAR82	0	1 ENG.R
1002	1003	8	75001	DESIGN TURNOVER LAYOUT	10MAR82	10MAR82	19MAR82	01APR82	9	1 ENG.R
1002	1006	1	75001	REVIEW TRANSFER DESIGN	10MAR82	10MAR82	10MAR82	26MAR82	12	
1020	1023	2	75001	REVIEW BORE HEAD LAYOUT	15MAR82	15MAR82	16MAR82	29MAR82	9	
1003	1007	1	75001	REVIEW TURNOVER DESIGN	22MAR82	22MAR82	22MAR82	02APR82	9	
1019	1025	2	75001	CHECK TOOL LAYOUT	22MAR82	22MAR82	23MAR82	20APR82	18	1 ENG.R
1009	1013	2	75001	REVIEW FIXTURE LAYOUT	15MAR82	24MAR82	25MAR82	25MAR82	0	
1010	1014	5	75001	DESIGN MACHINE LAYOUT	15MAR82	24MAR82	30MAR82	30MAR82	0	1 ENG.R
1014	1018	1	75001	REVIEW MACHINE LAYOUT	22MAR82	31MAR82	31MAR82	02APR82	2	
1015	1021	10	75001	MAKE FOUNDATIONS DRAWING	22MAR82	31MAR82	15APR82	15APR82	0	1 ENG.R
1016	1026	2	75001	PRE-ISSUE CHECK TRANSFER	01APR82	01APR82	02APR82	22APR82	12	1 ENG.R
1017	1026	2	75001	PRE-ISSUE CHECK TURNOVER	06APR82	06APR82	07APR82	22APR82	9	1 ENG.R
1025	1026	2	75001	PRE-ISSUE CHECK HEAD	06APR82	08APR82	13APR82	22APR82	7	1 ENG.R
1021	1026	5	75001	CHECK FOUNDATION DRAWING	05APR82	16APR82	22APR82	22APR82	0	1 ENG.R
1024	1026	2	75001	PRE-ISSUE CHECK ASSEMBLY	06APR82	19APR82	20APR82	22APR82	2	1 ENG.R
1022	1026	2	75001	PRE-ISSUE CHECK FIXTURE	08APR82	21APR82	22APR82	22APR82	0	1 ENG.R

Figure 22.1 Example of a work-to list produced from a computer based resource schedule

The computer has analysed the project network diagram, scheduled the activity times according to the available resources, edited the activities by departments (in this case engineering design) and printed out the results in sequence of scheduled start dates. This provides the departmental manager with a valuable checklist and a schedule from which to issue work to individual engineers according to the project programme requirements

```
            DEPARTMENT - DRAWING OFFICE      RESOURCE SCHEDULE ALL ACTIVITIES        SINGLE TRANSFER MACHINE

                                                          EARLIEST    SCHEDULED TIMES    LATEST   REM.G
PREC  SUCC  DURN  WORKS                                                                                      RESOURCES
EVENT EVENT DAYS  ORDER  ..ACTIVITY DESCRIPTION..         START       START    FINISH    FINISH   FLOAT

1006  1016   15   75001  DETAIL & CHECK TRANSFER          11MAR82     11MAR82  31MAR82   20APR82   12        3 D.MAN
1023  1025   14   75001  DET. & CHECK BORE HEAD           17MAR82     17MAR82  05APR82   20APR82    9        2 D.MAN
1007  1017   10   75001  DETAIL & CHECK TURNOVER          23MAR82     23MAR82  05APR82   20APR82    9        2 D.MAN
1013  1022   16   75001  DETAIL & CHECK FIXTURE           17MAR82     26MAR82  20APR82   20APR82    0        2 D.MAN
1018  1024   10   75001  DET.& CHECK MACHINE ASSY         23MAR82     01APR82  16APR82   20APR82    2        1 D.MAN


            DEPARTMENT - ADMIN              RESOURCE SCHEDULE ALL ACTIVITIES         SINGLE TRANSFER MACHINE

                                                          EARLIEST    SCHEDULED TIMES    LATEST   REM.G
PREC  SUCC  DURN  WORKS                                                                                      RESOURCES
EVENT EVENT DAYS  ORDER  ..ACTIVITY DESCRIPTION..         START       START    FINISH    FINISH   FLOAT

1026  1027    3   75001  PRINT & ISSUE TO PRODUCN         14APR82     23APR82  27APR82   27APR82    0
```

Figure 22.2 More examples of work-to lists

The above examples are complementary to that shown in Figure 22.1, and complete all design engineering activities for the machine design project up to the issue of drawings for production. The upper schedule would be used by the drawing office manager to issue and progress work, while the lower list shows when drawings should be issued to production control for the project schedule to be broken down into a series of tasks, each of which was sufficiently small to be handled by an individual member of staff, or by a small department. Task lists would be handed out as a means for authorising work on the tasks, and to tell the working staff exactly what had to be done.

Computerised schedules, derived from network analysis and subsequent resource scheduling, have opened up a new dimension in progress management. Such schedules can be 'personalised' for each departmental manager or specialist chief engineer by editing, so that these departmental schedules only contain activities for which each particular department is responsible. From the point of view of progress management, the individual schedules become invaluable when the activities are listed in order of their scheduled start dates. Thus, each manager has what is known in production management terms as a work-to list. The lists are also useful checklists, since (provided the schedules are complete) they help to ensure that no essential task is forgotten. Another condition for success is that the resource scheduling has been properly carried out, based on reasonable estimates and realistic levels of resource availability. Examples of these edited schedules are given in Figures 22.1 and 22.2.

Please refer to the work-to list in Figure 22.1. This is adapted (for clarity) from an actual project for the design and manufacture of a special purpose heavy boring machine. The manager of the engineering department can see all the activities needed from his department, when they should take place, and how critical each job is (from the amount of float left after the computer has scheduled the resources). Consider activity 1002, 1003 for example. The duration is eight working days, the job can start on 10 March 1982 according to the network logic (earliest start). The computer has scheduled the job, in fact, to start on the earliest date because, presumably, resources are shown to be available (i.e. not all engineers have been committed to other work on that date). The job is scheduled to finish on 19 March 1982. If, for any reason, this job ran into difficulties, it would not matter to the programme if the finish were to be delayed until 1 April 1982. All jobs in the department are seen to require the employment of one engineer, except the design review activities, which are carried out by the manager. Several jobs are seen to have zero remaining float, with their scheduled finish dates equal to their latest permissible finish dates. These jobs are critical, either as a result of the network logic analysis or as a subsequent result of the computer delaying the jobs until resources have become free to work on them.

Figure 22.2 shows the two other lists which, together, complete all the design engineering and drawing activities needed for this machine project. Note, for example, that detailing and checking the machine assembly (which follows 1014, 1018 review machine layout by engineering design) will take an estimated ten working days to finish and requires one draughtsman. The computer has delayed the start of this activity from the earliest date of 23 March 1982 (no draughtsmen free) until 1 April 1982. The job still has two days' float left.

The report for the administration department which is shown in the lower half of Figure 22.2 shows the vital dates when drawings should be issued for production (although, in the case of this simple example, only one batch of drawings is involved). It is excellent practice to arrange that schedules highlight such important events, which are worthy of vigorous progress monitoring.

Similar work-to lists can be produced for production departments. These would be unlikely to contain sufficient detail for the day to day loading of machines and shop floor facilities, but they ensure that work packages are loaded to production engineers and production control at a rate consistent with the total production capacity available. All this assumes that the computer has scheduled the total company workload together in a multiproject calculation, which was the case in the example shown in Figures 22.1 and 22.2. This was only one of several projects being undertaken, and all project networks were indeed put into the same computer resource allocation run. Detailed shop floor loading is a separate function, to be carried out by the usual production control methods.

For large scale construction projects, although design and drawing schedules could be produced in the same way the practical approach is usually somewhat different. Here, the workload is set out in the form of drawing and purchase control schedules.

Drawing schedules are prepared at the start of the project and attempt to list every drawing needed for construction. They are typically set out in sections according to different parts of the plant to be built, and the drawing numbers are determined at this stage. They can be converted into work-to lists by the computer, taking either single drawings or groups of drawings as network activities, depending upon the amount of time and work needed for each drawing. At one time target start and completion dates were written by hand on the schedules, which was a tedious and unsatisfactory exercise from the progress point of view, especially when a change in programme requirements demanded that all dates had to be rescheduled. With the computer-based network techniques, such problems become far easier to manage.

Purchasing activities

Since every respectable network diagram for a project must show purchase order activities and material lead times, it is a simple matter to sort out work-to lists for the purchasing department in the same way as for other departments, although it may not be necessary to attempt resource scheduling of buyers. For the purposes of expediting and inspection of suppliers, the expediting section of the purchase department can be given the list of order activities sorted by completion dates, so that the expediters can plan their letters, telephone calls, telexes or visits accordingly when monitoring progress. Of course, the instruction to start actual work in a supplier's organisation is contained in the purchase order and its attached specification, so there should be no ambiguity there.

In large construction contracts, the individual purchases are probably going to contain some high value orders. This is especially true for projects such as mining or petrochemical plants, where some of the purchase orders are for the supply of major items of capital equipment, or for the employment of subcontractors on site. Purchase control schedules list all the purchases which can be foreseen at the start of the project. Like the drawing schedules used to control the preparation of project drawings, the purchase schedules are used to carry scheduled target dates for the various stages leading to the issue of purchase orders. Again, this was a tedious practice, difficult to change with changing project needs. Modern practice links such schedules to the project network, and the computer can produce the schedules and, if necessary, reschedule all the dates.

Since each major purchase activity starts with the preparation of a purchase specification, the purchase schedules are intended to cover the issue of work to engineers who will have to write these specifications, then the subsequent stages of purchase enquiries (invitations to suppliers to bid), the preparation of final specifications and requisitions, and the issue of the purchase orders themselves.

On a major project, it will also be necessary to list as network activities the purchase lead times, and some principal shipping activities (at least to allow for the time required for goods to be shipped from supplier to project site).

All of this information, appropriately edited, sorted and listed by the computer, gives the progress engineers and progress chasers valuable control checklists for the purpose of monitoring progress.

Subcontracted services

Companies providing manufacturing services as subcontractors (e.g. heat treatment, plating, special gear cutting, etc.) can be instructed through the official purchase order system.

When engineers and draughtsmen are supplied for work on a project by external agencies the issue and control of work can become a little complicated, especially when these people are going to work away from the project home office in the offices of the agency companies. One way around this problem is to give each subcontractor a self-contained piece of design work that starts with engineering design and layout, and then proceeds through detailing and checking to arrive at a batch of drawings which are issued to production (or to construction, depending on the type of project) as a discrete part of the works. The main contractor arranges for the subcontractor to provide a senior design engineer to work in the main engineering offices for as long as it is necessary for him to learn the engineering standards required, and to produce the first layout drawing. This engineer then returns to his own company, and supervises the day to day work of the draughtsmen and checkers needed to finish the drawings. The completed parcel of drawings must be rechecked by a responsible engineer in the main contractor's organisation, naturally. Once this process has been carried out, it should be possible to place further work with the subcontractor without the need for the design engineer to work in-house. Then, the following procedure can be followed to ensure that the work commitments are made known and followed up.

The main contractor appoints a subcontract liaison engineer. This person should be of sufficient technical competence, and have

Managing Progress

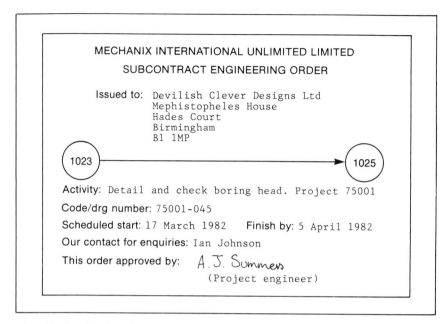

Figure 22.3 A simple subcontract engineering order
The idea of showing each subcontractor's assignment as its corresponding network activity may appear at first sight to be a gimmick, but it does highlight the fact that the job is part of a larger schedule, and that the timescale commitments are important. These little orders are printed on cards, a copy of which is kept in the subcontract liaison engineer's files from which he monitors and expedites progress

enough knowledge of the main contractor's standard engineering practices, to be able to answer queries raised from the outside offices. This liaison engineer carries out the functions of issuing work, and progressing it. It is unlikely that a purchase order will be issued for each piece of design: rather the work would be carried out at agreed hourly rates against timesheet control. The simple job sheet shown in Figure 22.3 has been used to good effect in issuing work of this type.

Note that the example given in Figure 22.3 does not indicate how much float is available, and it does not show the budget estimates or the number of draughtsmen required. The company from which this example was taken took the view that subcontractors must finish within the dates given, regardless of float and that to give details of cost estimates in advance would preclude any possible savings. (Suppose, for example, that a job was estimated to take two weeks for three men, and that the subcontractor was given this information. If in fact he managed to complete the job in less time, this company argued that the subcontractor might be tempted to submit his invoice for the full estimate.) Readers will hold different views on these points, but the principle of using small engineering subcontract orders of this type, printed on handy cards, is a useful aid to progress control. The subcontract liaison engineer retains copies of all orders issued and in progress, and uses these to follow up progress.

MONITORING AND CONTROLLING PROGRESS

This chapter began with a series of assumptions. Here is another. It must be assumed that the project organisation contains a sufficient number of individuals whose task is to ensure that progress is watched, measured and controlled. The subcontract liaison engineer discussed in the last section of this chapter is one example of such a person. The expediters in the purchasing department and the progress chasers in the factory are others. On site, quantity surveyors work with site management to ensure that work is progressing at the planned rate, measured in terms of tonnes of earth moved, the number of bricks laid, and all the many other quantities involved. Back in the home office, it is usual to appoint a project co-ordinator, responsible to the project manager for monitoring and following up the progress of many of the routine, yet vital, office tasks. The project planners may also be assigned to following up progress: in some organisations this job will be left to the co-ordinator and to the discipline managers, with the planners simply using the progress information to update their network schedules.

In addition to the obvious need to keep the programme on schedule, progress measuring has another important function. This concerns the establishment of equitable charges for work done which each contractor can invoice (subject to the contract terms). Thus the work of subcontractors has to be measured to establish how much they can bill the main contractor (or the client, depending on the payment structures agreed in the contract) and the main contractor's own work should be measured for similar reasons. Even where the contract does not allow for such progress payments, it is still necessary to know, at any stage in a project, the actual value of work done by measurement in order that expenditure trends are known by comparison with cost estimates and budgets. This subject is dealt with more extensively in the chapter on cost control.

Engineering design and project administration

It is common practice to measure engineering and drawing progress in terms of percentage completion. Thus, if a particular design job were to be estimated as taking four weeks, the progress might be reported as (say) 75 per cent complete, from which the project manager and any other interested person would conclude that one week's work remained. It is, unfortunately, true that most people tend to be optimists when making assessments of their achievements. Thus, the project manager with several years' experience under his belt should not be surprised when this particular job is presented to him not one week later, but after two weeks, and then with questions still to be answered on some finer engineering point or other.

Another problem facing the manager trying to get a project designed on time is the frequency with which engineers and draughtsmen report their work as 90 or 95 per cent complete, leaving that last tantalising 10 or 5 per cent just out of reach.

The shrewd manager will quickly learn to apply a few simple rules that should get progress back on course. The first requirement is for a set of milestones, key events, happenings (call them what-you-will) which allow no compromise in interpreting whether or not they have been achieved. These events, which should appear on the project network (and therefore have the benefit of scheduled dates) must be chosen at intervals which are not too far apart. Two or three weeks is about the limit. This reduces the risk of being deceived by optimistic promises. A good general rule when setting targets is to choose events where jobs pass from person to person, or from department to department. Thus, the handover of a drawing from draughtsman to checker, or the number of isometric piping drawings completed as a proportion of the total might be firm indications of real progress.

Design activities very often depend on information from outside sources. In the case of a large construction project, this information can include considerable correspondence from suppliers, and from the client. Engineering can be held up while the client approves (or rejects) design layout drawings, and the project co-ordinator's job should include close monitoring of all such correspondence against the target dates. Another function of the project co-ordinator is to ensure that every letter and telex, both outgoing and incoming, is answered within a reasonable time. This is important for keeping progress on the move, and for checking against the possibility that messages have gone astray — which often happens on very large international projects. Where regular correspondence and telexes exist between participating organisations (the client, contractors, site management, purchasing agent, etc.) all messages should be numbered serially so that any gap in the series is seen as a lost message.

Another check on engineering (or indeed any other) departmental progress is to compare the number of people engaged in any discipline with the resource schedule. The author remembers one occasion when he carried out such a check himself on an engineering project and discovered that instead of about 30 agency draughtsmen, only about six could be found actually working on the project under review. Yet engineering appeared to be in step with schedule. The reason was found to be that the engineering designers were declaring that their layouts were 100 per cent complete, but were not releasing them for detailing because, in fact, they were simply reluctant to let their work go. The engineers were, perhaps, a little uncertain. They wanted to give a few last minute tweaks to their designs to arrive nearer perfection. This was a case where an appeal to the engineering director soon put things right, and got the show back on the road.

Engineers must be encouraged to release information ahead of drawings when it comes to purchasing items with long delivery times. These include such things as special bearings, weldments and castings, flameproof motors, and so on. It is not good enough to await the final parts list, bill of materials or purchase schedules to get such equipment on order.

Production progress

A factory organisation is used to controlling progress, and it should be equipped with an established production control system which ensures the efficient scheduling of work. Progress chasers ensure that work is moved from each work station to the next without undue delay.

The physical movement of machined parts, subassemblies and

other production jobs between work stations is all important to progress. If a job requires (say) 10 operations from raw material to completed part, including inspections, and if it takes a day to move the part between each work station, then that part will spend two weeks of its time in the factory sitting on racks or trolleys. There are methods used to overcome such delay possibilities in factories. A project manager who has access to the production facilities employed on his work can spend profitable time walking through the factory regularly (perhaps once a day). Just ten minutes is often sufficient for the project manager to note whether any job of his is held up. A stack of steel piled in a corner for a few days might be an indication that the production management have downgraded the priority on the project work to the advantage of some other project manager who is able to shout louder. One project manager once became frustrated that his work did not move as it should through the factory, and his protests had no effect on the production manager. During one lunch hour, when the factory was deserted, this project manager collected some stalwarts from the engineering office and, together, they lifted a heavy steel workpiece from the factory floor (where it had lain neglected for a week) and laid it across the production manager's desk. Of course there was a terrible row, and the production manager felt embarrassed because he had to get his own labourers to move the offending workpiece. But he never ignored that project manager again.

It is not good practice to attempt the allocation of priorities to production work outside the normal scheduling routine. It is true that some companies operate systems with 'Priority A', 'Priority B' and 'Priority C' jobs, but in practice these are prone to problems. If the factory is heavily loaded, the chances are that all managers calling on the production resources will demand that their jobs are given 'Priority A', and the 'Priority C' jobs will never get done at all.

There are occasions, however, where special action is needed to accelerate production. One obvious situation is a job held up for shortages, caused by the failure of suppliers to deliver materials (or by the failure of the purchasing department to order them on time) or by the inadvertent scrapping of materials or components through manufacturing errors. The progress chasers will usually follow up such delays vigorously, informing the managers of the relevant production departments to ensure that prompt corrective action is taken.

Managing Progress and Performance

The cost to a project of a delay in the production of one small item can be out of all proportion to the production cost of that item. This is especially true for any specially manufactured item which lies on the project network critical path. Particularly disastrous is the case of an assembly, possibly containing complex electronic or electromechanical gadgetry, which fails catastrophically on its final test. Possibly some single component has broken down, causing other components to be lost. Situations such as this are even more serious when it transpires that the failures were caused by fundamental design errors, so that the dud components were destroyed by overloading. When such calamities arise they demand urgent action. Here is real cause for allocating top priority — covering not only the production facilities, but also going right back to the drawing board where the design errors occurred. There is a procedure which copes with such problems very well. It depends upon the issue of immediate action orders.

The usual documents seen in the factory or engineering offices are printed on ordinary white paper, so that one document looks very like another. The first thing which strikes the observer about an immediate action order is that it is anything but an ordinary piece of white paper. These top priority documents are printed on paper with brilliant diagonal stripes. They cannot fail to be seen on a desk or worktop. Another feature of such orders is that, because they are so special, they have to be authorised at general manager or managing director level. Once so authorised, there is no limit placed on the expenditure authorised to get the job done. If the factory has to keep open all night, or over Christmas, then so be it. If materials are only available in Scotland, and the factory is in Cornwall, then those materials must be obtained by the quickest route regardless of cost. The immediate action order commits all project departments, so that in any case where a design fault existed the engineering department would be expected to modify the appropriate drawings without delay. So important is the emphasis placed on these special immediate action orders that only one is allowed to be in existence at a given time. The order is hand carried from department to department by a progress chaser, and it is date and time-stamped when it arrives at and leaves each departmental manager's desk. In companies where this system operates, managers actually learn to fear immediate action orders. They are a nuisance. They command priority over all other work —

even to the extent of stopping a machine in mid-cut, removing the workpiece, and resetting the machine to take the immediate job. The logic in this approach is seen when by spending, perhaps, £2000 to finish a job which should only have cost £200 the project programme is retrieved by several weeks, equivalent (say) to a saving of £20 000 in penalties and lost reputation.

As an example of what can be achieved by an immediate action order, a special high voltage, high frequency transformer was produced for a prototype piece of military defence equipment. The transformer took six weeks to make, being mounted in special screening, and with an aluminium frame, all encapsulated in epoxy resin. The transformer had to be subjected to rigorous inspection routines at each stage. It failed on overload test. The replacement, including modified design, was produced against an immediate action order in only three days.

Construction site progress

At a production site, which may be thousands of miles removed from the project manager and the home office, it is customary to establish a management team which controls progress on the spot. But the size and organisation of that team can vary, from just two or three individuals on a small project to a semi-permanent management group for a large job. Progress measurements and actions depend very much on the contractual arrangements, so that a managing contractor would leave day to day progress to the many subcontractors employed, satisfying himself through site quantity surveyors and quality control engineers that work was being performed on schedule and to the required standards of materials and workmanship.

The contract conditions existing have a marked effect on the degree of management control that the site manager must exercise on the individual subcontractors. This point is amplified in the chapter on cost control, where the same arguments apply.

In order that site progress can be maintained according to schedule, it is obviously essential that all materials are delivered to site at the right time and in good condition. Thus the project purchasing organisation has a prime responsibility to the project site progress.

No less important than the flow of materials and equipment to site is the supply of construction information. This exists in the form of drawings, suppliers' installation instructions (for equipment), take-off lists, engineering standards, and similar specifications and erection instructions. It is usual for construction to start while engineering design is still in progress, albeit in the later stages of completion. Thus there is real danger of construction work outstripping the supply of drawings and other engineering information. The project organisation must provide a channel of communication, preferably using telex or some other electronic means, by which the site management can make known any engineering problems or deficiencies in information. The project co-ordinator in the home office would be expected to monitor the progress of the home office engineers in responding to such requests, so that no undue delays are allowed.

Drawings sent to site for use in construction are usually stamped to show that they have received all the necessary checking and approval stages. 'Released for construction' is a typical rubber stamp legend used for this purpose. It often happens on large projects that the design engineers are not able to release complete drawings for construction, although they have the drawings nearly ready. Possibly they await details of holding-down bolt positions for some item of equipment, or the exact location of a hole for pipes cannot be shown in a floor slab. In these circumstances drawings may be released for construction as incomplete, a rubber stamped legend reading 'Released for construction with holds'. Although a drawing released with holds is probably better than no drawing at all, since it allows some site calculations and planning to take place, project management in the home office must not be complacent about such issues, and all steps have to be taken to get the missing information needed to complete the drawings and allow construction to proceed unhindered.

The use of network float is another point worthy of consideration. It is too easy to allow all float to be taken up in the design phase, so that the construction site team are left with no remaining float, and therefore find themselves squeezed for time. One way out of this difficulty is to include a special activity in the network which does not represent work, but which adds an artificial delay of, perhaps, four weeks to the end of the construction programme. This has the effect of removing float from the front (engineering) end of the network, and emphasises the need to get design finished. This is not unfair to the engineers. Most project difficulties, at least most of the excusable ones, occur on site. The engineers are not likely to be affected by ice, snow, floods, running sand, strikes, fights, thefts, or any of the other myriad unforeseen problems which the site manager has in store.

MODIFICATIONS, CHANGES AND VARIATIONS

Any change to a project during progress is likely to pose a threat to progress and to cost control. It is true that some contractors on construction projects (and other projects) welcome requests from their clients to make changes, since such requests can provide an excuse for levying additional charges and for extending the programme with the client's permission and funding. Project managers, however, usually view all changes as nuisances.

Because of the risk which all changes represent, it is usual to examine the possible effects of any proposed change carefully in all respects (technical, commercial, timescale and cost implications). Since no one person can usually be found in the organisation capable of assessing all these factors, the job is assigned to a change committee, which meets as often as necessary to approve or reject proposals. This subject is also discussed in the chapters on cost control and quality assurance.

In one company the view was taken that, unless requested by the client (and therefore paid for), all changes would be classified as either 'essential' or 'desirable'. Essential changes would be those necessary to guarantee the safe and reliable operation of plant. They would probably be approved by the committee, or they would be sent back to the engineers with tacit approval but with a request to find a cheaper solution. Desirable changes, on the other hand, would always be rejected. 'If it's essential we do it, if it's not then we don't' was the official slogan.

All requests for variations must be recorded on suitable forms, serially numbered (usually by the project co-ordinator) to allow easy reference for progressing and later invoicing (when client-funded). The co-ordinator must follow up every change to ensure that it gets to the change committee, and that the committee decision is made known by circulating the approved or rejected copies of the change form. If the change has been approved, the co-ordinator must then follow up the actions listed on the change request, and he or she will make sure that drawings are properly modified and re-issued to all those who need the information.

PROGRESS MEETINGS

Progress meetings usually serve two purposes. They provide a forum in which progress difficulties and risks can be discussed, and actions are agreed. The other function of progress meetings is secondary to the main project management theme of this book, being concerned with the inevitable technical discussions that arise. It would be unrealistic to expect that a gathering of project technical and management staff would not raise technical problems when they had the opportunity provided by a progress meeting, but such discussions should be limited strictly to those technical problems which are a danger to progress. A progress meeting should be managed efficiently by the chairman, with the aid of a sensible agenda, so that it concentrates on matters related to keeping the project on schedule. Progress meetings should also be kept as short as possible, given that those attending are probably busy, short of spare time, highly paid, and needed back at their own departments for actually doing work rather than simply discussing it. It is not a bad plan to arrange that progress meetings, at least those which only contain in-house staff, are started at a fairly late hour in the working day. Then there is a real incentive to get on with the business. Of course, this argument would not apply to a project where the client had travelled thousands of miles to attend the meeting.

The frequency of progress meetings depends on the duration and complexity of the project. For a highly intensive project carried out at feverish speed over just a few weeks or months it might be deemed appropriate to hold short progress meetings every week. Monthly is a more usual interval for most projects. But progress meetings can be avoided altogether if (a very big 'if') the planning, scheduling and project management are perfect. Why hold progress meetings when everyone on the project has been told exactly what to do, when those instructions are carefully planned to be achievable, and when the follow-up by supervisors and managers ensures that any difficulty is immediately corrected? One company did, in fact, abolish regular progress meetings by the successful establishment of effective day to day control. These arguments apart, a project manager has no alternative to the calling of a progress meeting, or series of meetings, when the participants come from different departments or organisations and either cannot agree with their planned commitments, or have to meet to agree jointly actions needed to overcome genuine difficulties and get the programme back on course.

During progress meetings it is common for individuals to be asked to make estimates, or to give promises of fresh dates by which late or additional jobs can be finished. The chairman will ensure that promises with vague wordings such as 'the end of the week', or 'sometime next month' or (worst of all) 'as soon as possible' are not allowed. The chairman must insist on firm, measurable commitments. If any member of the meeting feels that the promises being made by others are unrealistic, he should (politely) say so, in order that all possible consideration is given in advance to the likely problems. All promises and commitments must be as realistic as possible. How many readers have attended progress meetings where, from one meeting to the next, the same item keeps cropping up with the only result being that a new, later, promise is given each time?

Progress meetings are a waste of time when the agreements reached are not followed up by the relevant project management personnel to ensure that promises are kept. The control document for this purpose is that containing the meeting minutes. It is most important that such documents are:

1 Concise, using short statements of actions required.
2 Annotated to show clearly those persons who are required to perform or manage the agreed actions.
3 Issued promptly, as soon after the meeting ends as possible.
4 Distributed to all those present plus any person not present but to whom action had been delegated by the meeting.

PROGRESS REPORTING

Progress reporting takes place at many levels, formally and informally, on any large project. At the simplest level reporting is person-to-person when, for example, a supervisor performs the daily rounds and asks how individual jobs are progressing. Then follows an ascending hierarchical structure of reporting, involving other departments, subcontractors, purchasing and shipping organisations, finally reaching the level of regular, comprehensive cost and progress reports to the client.

Progress reporting for network updates

As a project proceeds, those responsible for planning and scheduling have to ensure that their carefully laid plans are not rendered useless by events or activities which deviate from the network logic. It may be necessary to update the network from time to time, and re-run the computer schedules. For this purpose, the computer has to be given at least the following information:

1. A list of activities which have been completed since the first run and all previous updates.
2. A 'time now' date. The computer will use this date as a new zero time from which to start the scheduling of all remaining work. Occasionally, the time now date used might be slightly in the future. This would be done where the time taken to produce a revised schedule was significant (perhaps a week or more) in which case a small risk is taken by forecasting results, to gain the benefit of a new schedule with an issue date that looks reasonably fresh.
3. If time now is in the future, activities expected to be finished by time now must be reported as actually complete.
4. All activities which are started at time now, together with their percentage completions, or the durations remaining after time now (the actual method depending on the program used).

It will be appreciated that this kind of detailed progress information requires a good deal of effort to collect, especially where some of the activities are concerned with shipments of materials in remote places, and in the activities of those on a far away project site. Although good management practice should concentrate only on those aspects of progress which are likely to go wrong (management by exception) the computer does not understand management principles, and demands that simply everything is fed in. Thus, here is a level of progress reporting that must be set up to gather and use facts on the progress of every activity on the network.

Exception reporting

Strictly speaking, the more senior the person in the management structure of the project organisation, the less detail should be given about progress. Those managers responsible for taking action when things look like going wrong should not just be given a long list of jobs which are on course, with the few problems hidden among them. It is necessary to edit out the problems and highlight them. Then managers' time can be focussed on the problems. When a computer is used for scheduling, it is possible to edit lists so that only critical activities are shown, and there are several techniques for reducing the number of activities in reports for individual managers still further, so that each only receives information on critical activities within his or her area of responsibility.

Although material shortage lists produced by stores staff are a good example of exception reporting, the control of material movements for overseas work may demand complete reporting in great detail, at least to the purchasing staff concerned. This is one example where exception reporting may not be enough, it being essential to know for each purchase order where the materials are at any given time. There is usually some difficulty in getting information together from all the various organisations involved in supplying and shipping equipment and materials, which is unfortunate because the data is essential.

An example of exception reporting might be that the general manager receives a simple statement that the project is either on course or expected to finish at some other (early or late) date. He may be given an overall reason. The general manager would also expect a cost performance summary, in terms of total sums involved. A manager of a department engaged on the project, however, needs to be told clearly and quickly about any activity under his control which is not running to plan, together with the forecast consequences to the project if the departmental manager is not able to put more effort into getting the job finished on time. This departmental manager would also expect to receive regular statements of his department's project expenditure against the set budgets. This manager should also be

Managing Progress and Performance

given advance information about any jobs running late in other departments, where such delays are going to have a direct effect on the start of work in his department.

Progress reports to the client

If the project is large in terms of timescale and overall cost, then the client will want to know how well the project is progressing at any time, and he will need this information in the form of an official progress report (usually issued monthly).

It is usual to combine progress reports to the client with cost reports and statements showing how project funds are being used. When a large project starts, most of the activity takes place in the contractor's home office. It is obviously from that office that the first series of monthly reports to the client will be issued. When a site office is established, and work emphasis shifts from the home office to the site, most of the information contained in the report will be generated from site. However, facilities for typing, printing and binding the report to the presentation standard which the client of a large and expensive project should expect may require that the home office continues to produce and issue the monthly reports. Where the site is new, and remote from the client's own headquarters, then the home office will probably continue to be the source of all bound reports throughout the life of the project. Where, however, the site is at or close by the client's existing plant, then it often falls to the site manager to have the responsibility of taking reports to the client each month, and being prepared to explain the contents.

The main contractor of a major international project might include the following items in his regular reports to the client:

1. A written account of progress achieved to date, with special emphasis on progress achieved since the previous report.
2. Photographs showing the current state of progress at the project site.
3. Some form of quantified evidence to back up the achievements claimed. This might include a table of drawing achievement showing:
    Total drawings required for the project
    Number of drawings issued this reporting period

Managing Progress

      Total number of drawings issued to date
      Number of drawings in progress and not started
      Percentage of total engineering design and drawing finished

and for purchasing, a statement of engineering progress showing:

      Total number of purchase specifications required for the project
      Number of purchase specifications completed and issued as enquiries during the period reported
      Total number of purchase enquiries issued to date
      Number of enquiries remaining to be prepared and issued
      Percentage of engineering work completed on purchasing tasks.

These tables might be divided into rows, each row representing a major area of the plant or work package, with the total figures given at the foot of each column.

4 A statement of the position regarding purchased equipment, possibly in the form of purchase and order schedules
5 A cost report, showing in tabular and graphical form the expenditure to date on major areas of the project, and the totals. The cost report would include the latest predictions of total final project expenditure, and would also give the client up to date cash flow forecasts
6 A summary of the work planned for the next reporting period.
7 A list of any problems caused by the client in holding up the supply of information, approvals or funds. In other words, a schedule of actions which the contractor requires from the client.
8 A summary of project variations, separated into those which have been approved and those which are undergoing appraisal
9 Where projects involve complex communications, and especially where the clerical facilities at one or more project locations cannot be adequately staffed, lists of all communications sent and received during the reporting period. These would show the serial numbers of all telexes and letters sent, highlighting any gaps in the series. Strictly, such reports should be unnecessary, since any gap in any series should automatically cause action to get the missing document or message traced, but

some clients, especially in third world countries, have been known to insist on this 'belt and braces' procedure.

Project managers or their superiors should edit reports for clients carefully to ensure that the contents represent a true picture of the project progress. It is not necessary, obviously, to tell the client of every silly mistake made during design or manufacturing, provided that such mistakes are correctable within the time and cost constraints of the contract. The client must, however, never be misled or intentionally misinformed. If a problem is foreseen which poses a real threat to the timescale, to the budget, or to the technical performance of the finished project, then the client must be told. If the client is left to find out for himself, much later in the project, he will not feel that the project manager has acted to protect his interests, and should feel justified in asking how the contractor felt able to ask a fee for managing the project when, at best, there appears to have been no awareness of the problem and, at worst, the project manager has practised deception.

23
Project Quality Assurance

L. E. Stebbing

Quality has been defined as 'The totality of features and characteristics of a product or service that bear on its ability to satisfy a given need' (BS 4778: Glossary of terms used in quality assurance, including reliability and maintainability terms). In short, this means the production of an item or the performance of a service which is fit for the intended purpose.

THE CONCEPT AND PHILOSOPHY OF QUALITY ASSURANCE

No simple definition can adequately define the all embracing philosophy of quality assurance. It has been described as a management tool, but this only produces the reaction that it is something for management to use. Similarly, where a quality department exists the reaction is that responsibility for quality lies only within that department. Such reactions result in a 'them and us' situation, which should be avoided at all costs. Quality is the responsibility of everyone, and every member of the project task force should understand this. Each activity should be properly identified and defined and, where it interfaces with other activities, integration and co-operation are important.

British Standard (BS) 4778 defines quality assurance as 'All activities and functions concerned with the attainment of quality'. Note that this definition embraces all activities and functions, which means that all departments within an organisation are responsible for the quality of work produced, whether they are administrative, design, manufacture, or installation, etc.

The Norwegians, in their publication *The Continental Shelf*, use the term 'internal control', which is defined as 'All systematic actions that are necessary to ensure that the activity is planned, organised, executed and maintained according to requirements in and pursuant to laws and regulations'. Internal control covers all parts of the organisation and all phases of an activity.

This definition is somewhat similar to that contained in BS 4778 but the final sentence makes it clear. Therefore, the assurance of quality must be fundamental for all work undertaken within an organisation and must be practised by all personnel in their daily activities. Quality can be achieved only by working in a systematic (well disciplined) manner, to formalised procedures which are designed to eliminate the occurrence of deficiencies.

It is possible that quality (fitness for purpose) can be achieved within budget and schedule, but with avoidable expense incurred to achieve the fitness for purpose state. These expenses, the 'quality costs', are the cost to the contracting organisation of putting things right. Even though the customer might receive the end product according to specification, the costs of design revisions, rework, scrap, replacement materials and so on may not be considered. The application of quality assurance concepts to ensure that all activities and functions are carried out in a systematic manner (so that they are right first time) ensures that fitness for purpose is achieved in the most efficient cost effective way.

During recent years, with design, manufacture and installation processes becoming increasingly complex and with safety and environmental requirements becoming more stringent, the old inspection practices have been found to leave too many areas open to human error, notwithstanding the quality and extent of inspection coverage. Occasionally defects were not discovered until a project was at an advanced stage, often resulting in costly repair work, and sometimes involving scrapping, with the inevitable schedule delays. Sometimes defects, in spite of frequent inspection, were not detected at all and resulted in the in-service failures with which we are all too familiar.

Unfortunately, there is still the tendency to cling to these old inspection practices which only serve to identify that an item or service is acceptable or unacceptable. Instead, one should now be looking at methods which reduce the amount of inspection and non-destructive testing activities. Everyone in an organisation should be responsible for the quality of the work they produce rather than relying on the activities of others subsequently to discover any faults.

It is not surprising that customers often criticised the poor quality and delivery performance of their contractors. This has seriously affected the ability of companies to be competitive in home and overseas markets. The philosophy now is to insist on objective (or real) evidence of quality, rather than assuming the achievement of quality through inspection, or by relying solely upon the guarantees of contractors and suppliers that the required quality does exist. This real evidence of quality must be seen to exist not only in the completed item, but in all activities involved in the completion of that item (design, procurement, manufacture and installation). By controlling all these functions systematically, one can be reasonably assured that each activity is right before the next starts.

OBJECTIVE EVIDENCE OF QUALITY

The real, or objective, evidence of quality collected during the design, procurement, manufacture and (in the case of large projects) site construction and commissioning, consists of:

Procedures

The documents which detail the purpose and scope of activities and specify how they are to be properly carried out.

Documentation

Derived from recording the results of tests or activities.

Certification

Resulting from documentation, this states that an item or service conforms to requirements. Thus, procedures are necessary to cover all activities and functions throughout all phases of a project. In order to ensure that these procedures are followed, a compliance audit has to be undertaken.

Compliance audits

A compliance audit is arranged in order to determine whether or not a procedure or system necessary to ensure quality and safety is working satisfactorily. It highlights deviations and leads to corrective action aimed at preventing their recurrence. In other words, the compliance audit examines the objective evidence for quality.

ORGANISATION FOR QUALITY ASSURANCE

Implementing quality assurance audits must be a management commitment and the conduct of audits is itself a function of management. As such, the responsibilities and organisation of the quality assurance function must be defined and integrated into a quality assurance programme. In order for any audit to work effectively, the group concerned with audit implementation must have sufficient organisational freedom to oversee the development, implementation and maintenance of the quality programme. For the sake of convenience, this group is usually called the 'Quality Assurance Department', but this is unfortunate since quality assurance is a philosophy relevant to the whole organisation rather than a subject limited to the responsibility of a single department. Finding a better title for this particular department could lead to an improved understanding and appreciation of quality assurance.

To secure the required organisational freedom and independence it is necessary for the quality assurance manager to report direct to senior management, and not to any specific lower management level within engineering design, procurement, production or installation. (see the organisation charts in Figures 23.1 and 23.2).

In order to assess and report procedural non-conformances within any discipline or department, and to be able to specify and obtain positive corrective action, it is obviously necessary that all personnel in the quality assurance group are sufficiently qualified and experienced.

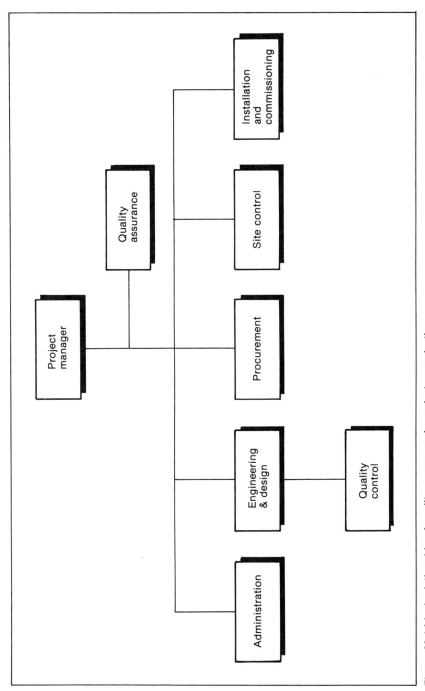

Figure 23.1 Ideal relationship of quality assurance in project organisation

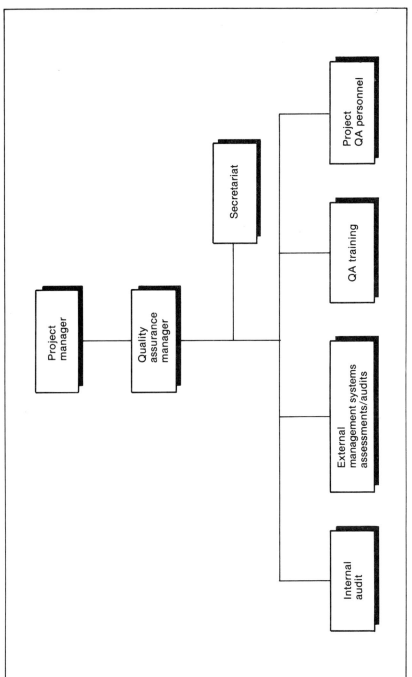

Figure 23.2 Project quality assurance department organisation

Project Quality Assurance

QUALITY ASSURANCE PROCEDURES AND SYSTEMS

To implement a quality assurance programme, and to assess and report shortcomings within the programme, the quality assurance department must have bases upon which to work. These bases are the written procedures which describe how the quality and safety requirements will be accounted for during the various phases of the project. Every procedure must detail clearly:

1 *What* is required, or What has to be controlled?
2 *Who* is responsible for ensuring that the requirement is met or the control carried out?
3 *How, when, where* (and possibly *why*) it is to be controlled.

As well as taking account of quality and safety requirements, it is also important that procedures indicate how interface problems between departments are to be avoided. Procedures dealing with or involving interfaces between departments or disciplines must have the approval of all groups who are concerned with their implementation. Each procedure should be written by the discipline or department which is principally concerned, and this must be done in consultation with the quality assurance manager to ensure that all relevant quality and safety requirements have been included, and that the finished document is auditable.

DEVELOPING THE PROJECT QUALITY PLAN

Development of the quality assurance system for any given project will depend largely on the total project work scope. In most major projects the work will involve design, procurement, manufacture and installation, in which cases procedures would be needed to control every one of these activities.

There is a large number of standards which give guidance on the development of quality assurance systems but, in the main, they all say the same things regarding the criteria for control. Some of these standards are identified in Figure 23.3.

Before a quality assurance system can be finalised, the system objectives have to be decided — what is the system intended to achieve? A design contractor, for example, would place the emphasis

U.K.	BS 5750	Quality Systems.	
		Part 1 — Specification for design, manufacture and installation.	(Guidance notes — Part 4)
		Part 2 — Specification for manufacture and installation.	(Guidance notes — Part 5)
		Part 3 — Specification for final inspection and test.	(Guidance notes — Part 6)
	BS 5882	Specification for a total quality assurance programme for nuclear power plants.	
	DEF STAN 05-21/1	Quality Control System Requirements for Industry.	
	05-24/1	Inspection Requirements for Industry.	
	05-29/1	Basic Inspection Requirements for Industry.	
NORWAY	NS 5081	Requirements for the contractor's quality assurance. Quality assurance system.	
	NS 5082	Requirements for the contractor's quality assurance. Inspection system.	
	NS 5083	Requirements for the contractor's quality assurance. Basic inspection.	
CANADA	CSA Z299.1	Quality Assurance Program Requirements.	
	CSA Z299.2	Quality Control Program Requirements.	
	CSA Z299.3	Quality Verification Program Requirements.	
	CSA Z299.4	Inspection Program Requirements.	
USA	ANSI/ASME NQA-1	Quality Assurance Program Requirements for Nuclear Facilities.	

Figure 23.3 Typical quality assurance standards

on different in-house controls than those applicable to (say) an installation site. The company's requirements should therefore be established from the start, taking into account requirements imposed by relevant regulations. The total control scope of work will be taken into account, and an outline of each function must be established and documented. These outlines will assist in formulating a quality manual and in the eventual development of the detailed procedures.

Quality manual

British Standard 4778 defines a quality manual as 'A document setting out the general quality policies, procedures and practices of an organisation. The word 'general' is important in this definition. A quality manual is usually the first indication which a prospective client gets of a company's approach to quality. The manual should set out the company's intentions. It should not, however, contain detailed procedures since these would increase the production costs of the manual and their updating would present a continuous problem. By keeping the detailed procedures separate, and made available at their point of use, they can be updated independently without affecting the outline procedures contained in the manual. Contents of a quality manual would typically include as a minimum:

1. Policy statement.
2. Authority and responsibilities.
3. Organisation.
4. Procedure outlines.
5. List of procedures.

Quality programme

A quality programme is defined in BS 4778 as 'A documented set of activities, resources and events serving to implement the quality systems of an organisation'.

It is seen (above) that the quality manual describes the intent — i.e. WHAT is to be done.

The separate, detailed procedures not only WHAT is to be done, but spell out BY WHOM, HOW, WHEN, WHERE and WHY.

Thus the quality programme comprises all of these documents, viz the quality manual together with all the supporting procedures.

Managing Progress and Performance

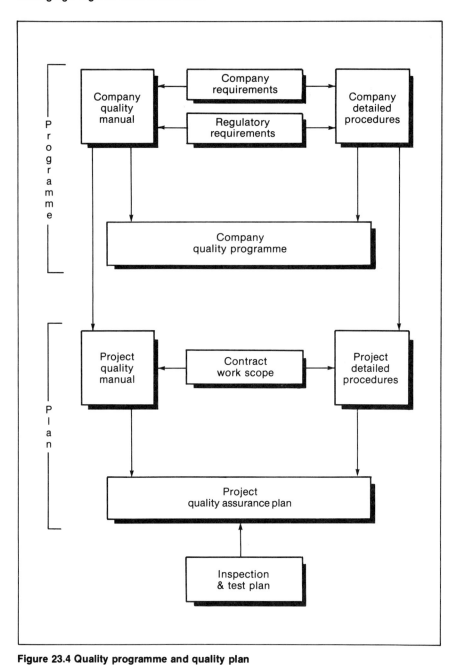

Figure 23.4 Quality programme and quality plan
This diagram illustrates the relationship between a company's quality programme and a quality plan

Quality plan

Again referring to BS 4778, a quality plan is described as 'A document derived from the quality programme (extended if necessary) setting out the specific quality practices, resources and activities relevant to a particular contract or project'.

When a company's quality programme is applied to a given project it invariably needs modification to suit the project. Such modifications can take the form of additions to or reduction of the corporate programme. For example, a project management contractor with involvement in all project activities must develop a programme covering all functions from design through to installation. If this contractor, however, were to be engaged for design only, he would need only those detailed procedures applicable to design, 'fronted' with a quality manual produced specially for that contract. The unique manual, together with its supporting procedures, comprises the set of documents called the project quality plan (see Figure 23.4).

That, in essence, is how things should be, but there are instances of confusion, with plans being called programmes and vice versa. On occasions there have even been documents entitled 'QA programme/plan'.

Project quality policy

Before leaving this subject it is worthwhile identifying who defines project quality policy. There are a number of ways in which a project management task force (PMTF) can be arranged, including (for example):

Client PMTF

This is where the client will manage the project with his own staff and resources. In this case project quality requirements will probably be established by the client and imposed upon all the main contractors who will each, in turn, develop a quality plan in accordance with their scope of work.

Integrated PMTF

This is where the client and a main contractor manage the project with staff and resources from both organisations. In other words, they pool their resources and assign the best person for each given job. Here, the project quality requirements will be established jointly by the client and contractor although, in all probability, the emphasis will be given to the client's philosophies. Again, main contractors will be expected to develop quality plans in accordance with the quality requirements applicable to the tasks within their scope of work.

Contractor PMTF

This is where a contractor is employed to manage a project. The quality requirements will be identified by the client, and the contractor will develop a project plan. Such project plans will be reviewed by and, possibly, approved by the client before implementation.

Detail design contractor with project management responsibilities

This is where a contractor is engaged to undertake the design of a given structure, and to manage the procurement, manufacture, site fabrication and installation. This design contractor will develop the project quality plan and implement it throughout all phases of the project.

Detailed procedures

As quality assurance should be a company wide philosophy, so the procedures must cover all activities and functions. Thus every department should organise itself so that the work produced is not only correct but, more importantly, correct first time. This will obviously promote efficiency, improve productivity and reduce costs. The establishment and implementation of procedures should be undertaken only by personnel familiar with the particular activities and functions and, to be effective, each procedure will define the purpose and scope of the relevant activity and specify how it is to be properly carried out. Unfortunately, the 'quality assurance department' is

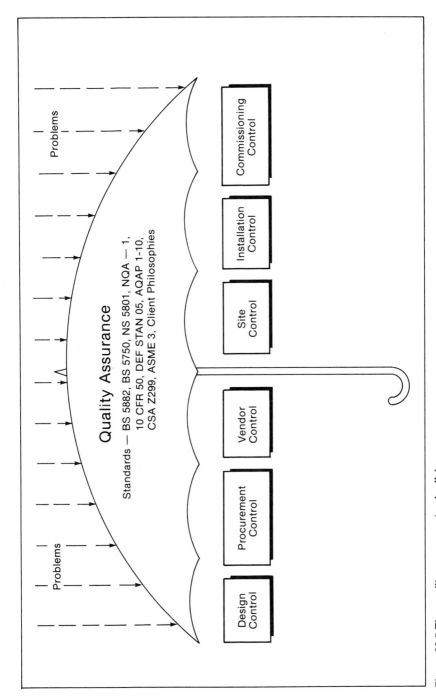

Figure 23.5 The quality assurance 'umbrella'

generally given the task of procedure writing, whereas it could be argued that the only procedures which should really be written by the QA staff are those confined to auditing, corrective action, and to auditor qualification and training.

The concept of QA could be depicted as an umbrella for protection against problems (Figure 23.5). Within the umbrella are the various QA standards which assist in establishing quality programmes (although no single one of these can itself fulfil all requirements). Each of the six elements beneath the umbrella needs procedures to cover all of its activities and functions.

What has to be determined is who is responsible for controlling and checking the quality of work for each element. In every case, this responsibility must lie with personnel familiar with that work if the checks are to be effective: yet, in order to ensure unbiased results, the checks must be carried out independently, by people not actually engaged in the relevant activities. Checking is an activity in itself and, as such, it too must be procedurally controlled.

Thus, design documentation can be properly checked for technical detail and accuracy only by design engineers; procurement activities only by personnel familiar with those activities; manufacturing work only by manufacturing personnel (in-house inspectors) and so on. Even those engaged in simple unskilled tasks (such as housekeeping) contribute indirectly to the quality of the finished item, and their activities and functions should be similarly controlled and checked.

Referring again to Figure 23.5, the quality assurance department would be located within the umbrella. It would be responsible for:

1   Verifying, by audit, that the QA philosophy is being followed throughout the organisation and that procedures and work instructions are implemented by all departments.
2   Verifying that those responsible for controlling and checking an activity have done so in a systematic manner and that objective evidence is available to confirm such.
3   Ensuring that all procedural non-conformances are resolved.
4   Ensuring that fundamental working methods are identified and that fully approved procedures are raised to cover them and that all departments are in possession of current versions.
5   Verifying that all procedures are regularly reviewed and updated as necessary.

As all these activities are under the control of the project manager, then he and he alone is totally responsible for the ultimate quality of the project on completion.

The assurance that each activity is right first time can be verified by audit and it is the responsibility of the quality assurance department to undertake these audits and report the findings back to the project manager.

Where difficulties are encountered in resolving problems the project manager will be the final authority. Hence the requirement within all quality assurance standards that a management representative, preferably independent of other functions, shall be appointed who has the necessary authority and the responsibility for ensuring that the requirements of the quality system are implemented and maintained.

The remaining sections in this chapter describe the application of quality controls to design, procurement and to an installation site.

DESIGN

It is regrettable that most expertise in quality engineering currently lies in controlling the quality of manufacture, and a great deal of time and effort is spent in assessing manufacturers' ability to control their own quality. Manufacturers can be assessed and audited regularly and indeed they often are. In fact, it is not unknown for a single manufacturer to be audited or assessed a dozen times in as many months. But what do such activities tell the customer? Only how good this manufacturer's systems and controls are. Yet, if the design is in error, this manufacturer, even though his systems and controls are more than adequate, will present the customer with hardware which is unsuitable for the service requirements.

At the risk of stating the obvious, it is therefore essential for the design to be right before placing the specification with a manufacturer. This means that not only has the design got to be right, but it has to be right first time. In order for this to be achieved it is necessary to put quality assurance controls on a formal basis, and to develop a design control plan which meets the needs of the contract scope of work. It is worth while considering how an engineering contractor can use quality assurance as a means of controlling his design.

The first problem facing an engineering contractor is that, in the main, industry has not as yet agreed the need for (let alone a uniform approach to) quality assurance. Existing quality programme standards are inadequate as far as engineering design is concerned. While BS 5882 and ANSI/ASME NQA-1 go a long way towards meeting design control requirements they would be generally unacceptable to most of the industry because of their nuclear connotations. Therefore some of the controls discussed here will not be found in any of the quality programme standards, yet they do reflect what is perhaps becoming the general custom and practice.

Design procedures and instructions

The project procedures, methods and instructions will probably comprise corporate documents, amended where necessary to suit specific contract requirements. In all cases the project procedures should be approved by the project manager, the project quality assurance manager and the relevant discipline or department manager. The client will very probably wish to see and review them also and give his agreement before they are released.

Each manager of an engineering discipline or department should be responsible for maintaining up-to-date procedure manuals for his area of management, including procedures for:

1. The checking of drawings, data, calculations, specifications, etc.
2. The control of design or construction work by the use of philosophies, procedures and standards.
3. Standard preparation methods for specifications, data sheets, drawings, work packages, etc.

Each lead discipline engineer or supervisor should ensure that all significant activities are properly conducted and documented throughout a project, verifying that:

1. All necessary data, specifications and other documents are available before the start of any activity.
2. All the required work, drawings, reports, calculations, etc., are in fact produced during each activity.
3. All the required checks, reviews, audits, etc., are carried out on completion of each activity.

4 Any deviation from the above requirements is properly documented.
5 All documents are systematically numbered or otherwise identified, filed, updated as required, and held securely in a system which ensures that they are readily available upon request to assist reviews or audits by the project team, the corporate discipline manager, quality assurance staff or the client's representative.

DESIGN CONTROLS

The most important design controls are:

1 Contract review.
2 Document preparation.
3 Discipline check.
4 Interdiscipline check.
5 Internal design review.
6 Design interface control.
7 Change control.
8 External design reviews.
9 Audits and corrective action.

These are summarised in Figure 23.6.

Contract review

This is a most important activity, but unfortunately insufficient emphasis is given to it in most QA standards. Before any work starts, it is important that all concerned are aware of their responsibilities within the design contract, and that they have the right tools with which to perform their job. A review team must therefore be pulled together comprising project management, discipline lead engineers and quality assurance representatives.

Work scope

The review team considers in detail the scope of work and establishes that this is fully understood and that the quality assurance plan identifies the true scope.

Design Control

Design Control Activity	Scope	Performed by	Action by QA
1 Contract Review	Review: Work Scope Specifications Philosophies Design Criteria CA Rules/Regs. Organisation	Project Management Discipline Engineers Quality Assurance	Verify that missing or ambiguous information has been followed up and satisfactorily closed out by the responsible person.
2 Document preparation, control & retention	Ensure correct and uniform presentation of documents. Ensure formal preparation, identification, checking, approval and distribution, including amendments. Verify retention, retrieval, storage and handover requirements.	Project Management Discipline Engineers (Client)	Audit adherence to procedure
3 Discipline Check	Verify content and accuracy of documents originating from own Discipline.	Relevant Discipline	Audit adherence to procedure.
4 Inter-Discipline Check	Assure compatibility of design between Design Disciplines. Accuracy of content.	Project Management Discipline Engineers	Audit distribution and approval. Verify as necessary that comments have been closed out by the originating engineer.

5 Internal Design Review	Review of Design activities in progress or completed.	Project Management Discipline Engineers Q.A.	Verify that comments have been closed out.
6 Design Interface Control (See also 4)	Check physical interfaces between Systems/Contractors Authorities	Project Management Discipline Engineers (Other Contractors) (Client)	Audit distribution and approval. Verify that comments have been closed out.
7 Change Control	Check Changes in design criteria.	Project Management Discipline Engineers	Monitor, changes as required, to close out and approval.
8 External Design Reviews	Detailed Design Audit — Adequacy of Design — Adherence to Contract — Account taken of studies	Independent teams of Discipline Engineers (In House or Client)	Project Management also involved. Audit to verify that any non-conformances have been closed out.
9 Corrective Action	Ensure non-conformances promptly identified and corrective action taken to prevent recurrence.	Project Management Discipline Engineers Q.A.	Co-ordinate and verify that corrective action completed and that action has been taken to prevent recurrence.

Figure 23.6 Matrix summarising the most important design controls

Specifications and standards

It has to be ensured that all applicable specifications and standards, of correct issue, are readily available at all activity locations.

Philosophies

These can cover studies, design philosophies — even QA philosophies (where these could be interpreted in different ways). Are these philosophies agreed upon and understood?

Design criteria

Are they all available and understood?

Regulatory requirements

If any regulatory authority is involved regarding safety and/or environmental requirements, then the project team should be aware of all parties involved and the exact nature of the statutory requirements in their current form.

Organisation

Who does what in the project task force? Who reports to whom, and what are each individual's terms of reference? If the organisation is defined and made generally known immediately, then there can be no misconception about reporting responsibilities. A considerable amount of time and misunderstandings can be avoided when the right person to approach concerning any given issue is known.

Document preparation

Document preparation is another important activity not given sufficient emphasis in QA standards. Documents in this context covers drawings, specifications, data sheets, and so on. These must be presented in a correct and uniform manner. On many occasions project personnel have different ideas on how documents should be formulated. Sometimes ideas developed for previous projects may

Project Quality Assurance

not be compatible with current projects, and the rules need to be overhauled. A uniform approach should be agreed, defined and made known to all before work starts. The client should be brought into these discussions, since he may have his own ideas and requirements. For example, the client may have standard drawing files based on A1 sized drawings: he will be very concerned to find that at the end of a project the design for which he has paid is presented to him as a large number of A0 sized drawings which are too large for his existing files, and which cause him the expense of purchasing new filing equipment for which he has no suitable accommodation.

Uniform document presentation helps to avoid errors and facilitates checking, allowing more use of standard checking routines. It is far easier to handle documents when, for example, the project number can always be found in the same corner. It is difficult and time consuming to check documents whose contents are distributed in different patterns or sequences.

Document identification

Identification of documents should be standardised and controlled using logical procedures. Complex numbering systems should be avoided, as these tend to confuse rather than assist in identification and retrieval of documents. The simpler the system, the easier it is to operate and control. Numbering systems should, as a minimum, contain the following:

1. Contract or project number.
2. Document type (denoting whether it is a specification, purchase requisition, design brief, data sheet, drawing, etc.).
3. Document serial number.
4. Document revision status.

The following is a typical arrangement for document identification:

```
                                          8742-S-345-1
       Project number ──────────────────────┘   │ │
       Document type  ─────────────────────────┘  │
       Serial number  ──────────────────────────── ┘
       Revision status ─────────────────────────────┘
```

Whatever the identification system to be used, the client will probably require some input and he should be consulted before the system is put to use on his project.

Document approval

Document approval procedures need to be formalised, and all those carrying the authority to give approval at each stage (including the client's representatives) need to be named. It is desirable that specimen sets of initials or signatures should be registered in project records.

Document distribution

Document distribution procedures must be established to identify who gets what. More importantly, the procedures need to be based upon the principle of who really needs what. Many people may wish to be included on the distribution list, whether they need to be there or not. Involvement by those who have no need to get involved creates confusion. A matrix chart, which lists document types along the left hand vertical column, and has the remaining columns headed with all potential recipients is a useful and concise method for denoting the standard distribution arrangements for project documents. In the matrix, each box will link a document type with a possible addressee, and the matrix will automatically cover all possible permutations. It is simply necessary to leave blank boxes where there is to be no distribution. In each case where documents need to be sent to an addressee, the number of sets to be sent is written in the relevant box. It is stressed again that this must be arranged strictly on a 'need to know' rather than a 'want to know' basis.

A formalised procedure for distribution is also essential to ensure not only that each person needing documents appears on the list, so that he or she gets them in the first place, but also to ensure that they are in the right quantities (number of sets), of the correct form (e.g. full sized drawings or microfilms), and that the initial issues are backed up by all revisions.

Project Quality Assurance

Discipline check

A discipline check is carried out to verify the content and accuracy of a document originating from a single engineering discipline. Such checks should be performed by engineers of the appropriate discipline, but the checking engineer must not be the same person who carried out the original work. The checker must be of at least the same grade of seniority as the originating engineer. In the case of a one man discipline (which often occurs on small projects) it will be necessary to appoint the checker from outside the project, either from a corporate department or from another project team.

Interdiscipline check

Interdiscipline checking assesses not only the content and accuracy of a document but assures compatibility between all the design disciplines involved. Here, the document distribution list (previously described) would be important, and it would need to list all those required to comment on a document. There are various ways of distributing documents for interdiscipline checks (see Figure 23.7).

Parallel issue

This issue, although expeditious, entails considerable copying of documents and requires strict control. The document to be reviewed is issued simultaneously to all interfacing disciplines for their review and comment. The latest date for the return of comments should be indicated, and every involved discipline should make comment, even where this means writing 'no comment'. The department responsible for document control should issue the review copies on behalf of the originating discipline, and should control and expedite progress to ensure the return of all copies within the latest completion date. Parallel issue is obviously the method best suited where a fast turn round of documents is required.

Circular issue

As its name implies, this depends upon the circulation of a single issue of the document to all interfacing disciplines on a 'round robin' basis.

Managing Progress and Performance

Documents produced by Mechanical Discipline	Architectural	Electrical	Fire & Safety	HVAC	Instrumentation	Mechanical	Process	Structural	Quality Assurance	Project Manager	
General Specifications		✓	A			O					
Unique Specifications		✓	A			O					
Philosophies		✓				O				✓	
Reports		✓	A			O				✓	
Studies		✓	A			O				✓	
Calculations	Not given an IDC										
Drawings	✓	✓	A					✓	✓		
Data Sheets	✓	✓	A					✓			
Requisitions	Not given an IDC										
Mechanical Equipment		✓	✓			O	A				
IDC Matrix Minimum Distribution O = Originator ✓ = Review A = Review as applicable											

Figure 23.7 Example of a document distribution matrix chart

Project Quality Assurance

This type of distribution is used where urgency is not the first priority. Care has to be taken in arranging the circulation list to include the disciplines required to make comment in order of priority. Here, again, the department responsible for document control, after issuing the document on behalf of the originating engineer, must expedite and control its progress around the circuit. As with parallel issues, all involved disciplines should make comment.

Flood issue, in conjunction with a review meeting

This is similar to a parallel issue but, instead of inviting comments through the distribution circuit, a meeting is called to review and co-ordinate any such comments. As for any meeting, minutes will be tabled, and these will list the comments made for the subsequent attention of the originating discipline. Minutes of meetings are objective evidence of quality and can be used by QA engineers as checklists for audit purposes.

Internal design review

At important stages throughout design activities internal design review meetings will be called to review progress. These meetings will consider all aspects of project activities to date. There may be areas of concern, perhaps even updated information from the client, or new legislation concerning safety, certification, etc. All meetings of this kind will be minuted, and actions placed on individuals.

Design interface control

Although the design interface control could be linked to the inter-discipline check, it goes far deeper. Design interface control sets out to control the interfaces between systems, contractors, and even regulatory bodies. There are many instances where projects use more than one design contractor, creating not only interfaces between disciplines within one organisation but complex interfaces between different contractors. The problems encountered in persuading all parties to liaise with one another are enormous, but not insurmountable. Providing that each of the participating organisations has a compatible design programme, the interface control can work

Managing Progress and Performance

XYZ Company	Design Modification Proposal	Project Title Project No. DMP No.
\multicolumn{3}{l}{Part 1.}

Part 1.
Activity
Originator   Discipline   Date
Source of Modification Proposal — Indicate ☐ Client ☐ XYZ Company ☐ Other
Description of Modification (sketch, description, general information e.g. Affected documents)

Part 2.
This modification proposal is rejected/accepted for further processing
Reason/affected discipline
 	
            Signed ....
            Project Manager

Part 3. .... discipline. Please estimate the effect of the above proposed modification on your discipline Documents affected

Part 4.
Summary of Modification Impact.
 	
            Signed ....
            Project Planning Engineer

Part 5.
This modification proposal is accepted/rejected. Prepare DMR Yes/No
 	
            Signed ....
            Project Manager

Documents affected:

☐ Flow Diagrams	☐ Fire Protection	☐ Certification
☐ P & I.D.	☐ Telecoms	☐ Commissioning
☐ GA/Layout	☐ Operations	☐ Maintenance
☐ Struct. DRG	☐ Studies	☐ Fabrication
☐ Piping DRG	☐ Requisition	☐ Installation
☐ Instr. DRG	☐ Specification	☐ Hook-Up
☐ Elect. DRG	☐ Interface	☐ Histograms
☐ Other DRG	☐ Weight	☐ Schedule
☐ Vendor DRG	☐	☐

Figure 23.8 An example of a change control form

Project Quality Assurance

smoothly. A strong client is needed to set the rules and to get all concerned to keep to them. If different philosophies are allowed to prevail, then interface control can be a great problem.

Change control

The control of changes is another very important activity which most QA standards treat much too lightly. It usually receives only a passing mention under the subject of 'document control'. It is generally accepted that many of the major project problems arise through the lack of change control, with changes being made to a design without reference to the original design source.

Design changes can emanate from many areas; changes in client requirements, updated information from external sources, new legislation from government bodies relating to safety, etc., and internally from departments within the contracting organisation. All must be documented, and they must be subjected to consideration and review in the same systematic manner as the original documents. In addition to aspects of quality, these reviews have to take into account the likely effect of each proposed change on the project costs and progress. Formal procedures for controlling engineering changes will ensure that the client is always consulted where this is relevant, and a suitably qualified group of people will be selected to give approval to or reject each change considered (typically known as a change committee). See Figures 23.8, 23.9 and 23.10 for examples of change control documents.

External design reviews

External design reviews can be carried out either by the contracting company, using its own corporate disciplines, or by the client. The reviews amount to a detailed design audit, verifying such items as design adequacy, adherence to contract and the account taken of studies. The timing of these reviews is usually identified in the project schedule, so they should come as a surprise to no one.

Adequacy of design

Does this accord with the scope of work? This corresponds with the first listed design control, 'contract review'.

Managing Progress and Performance

XYZ Company	Design Modification Request	Project Title
		Project No.

To:	Date:	Initiator ☐ Client ☐ Contractor
Title:		Payment ☐ Lump Sum ☐ Reimbursible ☐ Unit Rate

Contractor is hereby instructed to proceed with the work described hereunder:

Applicable Correspondence

Adjustment to Contract:
Total Estimated Manhours   Total Estimated Cost

Documents Affected

Estimated Impact on Programme

Work to Commence by:	Effect on Contract Schedule:
Planned Completion Date:	Effect on Manning

Accepted by Contractor	Approved by Client
Name:	Name:
Signature:	Signature:
Date:	Date:

Figure 23.9 Example of a change form for external issue to contractor

Project Quality Assurance

XYZ Company	Summary of Additional Manhours & Costs	Project Title
		DMR No.

Discipline \ Position	Engineering & Draughting Hours									
	Director/ Project Manager	Senior Engineer	Engineer	Interface Engineer	Weight Control Engineer	Senior Designer/ Checker	Draughts-Person	Planning Engineer	Document Controller	Quality Assurance
Architectural										
Electrical										
Fire & Safety										
Instrumentation										
Interface Control										
Loss Control										
Mechanical/HVAC										
Process/Piping										
Structural										
Quality Assurance										
Weight Control										
Estimated Totals										
Project Control										
Purchasing Expediting										
Estimated Totals										
Estimated Overall Manpower Costs										

Summary of Modification Costs	
Manpower Costs	
Communications	
Printing & Computer	
Travel & Subsistence	
Other	
Overall Total Costs	

Figure 23.10 Form suitable for summarising the estimated costs of a change

Managing Progress and Performance

Adherence to contract

Has due consideration been given to all contract clauses?

Studies

Has due consideration been given to the results of all field studies which may have been carried out by others?

Audits and corrective action

It is most unlikely that a project will be completed without some corrective action becoming necessary. This is where the QA department needs the support of senior management. Without it, they would not have the authority to carry through their job. All non-conformances identified during the checks and audits already described, whether discovered by the QA staff or by the engineers themselves, should be dealt with immediately and steps taken to preclude their recurrence. Where a non-conformance is identified, but the corrective action taken by the department responsible is considered to be insufficient to prevent repetition, then the QA engineer must be able to call upon support from management in order that the problem can be resolved effectively. The intention of design control is to ensure that the eventual design meets all client and regulatory requirements. At the end of this activity, the design will result in the commitment of expensive resources to produce the hardware. So, it is essential that the audits carried out by the QA engineer are taken seriously and their results acted upon.

CONTROL OF PROCUREMENT AND VENDORS

The activities considered to be the most significant in controlling procurement and vendors are:

1 Inspection and test plan.
2 Supplier assessment.
3 Tender package development.
4 Bid package review.
5 Pre-award meeting.

6   Contract award.
7   Post-award meeting.
8   Quality control.

The inspection and test plan

During the design activity the QA engineer should be working with the design engineers not only in an auditing capacity, but also to determine that the criticality and traceability requirements for equipment and materials have been evaluated. These factors decide respectively the importance attaching to inspection of the items and the need or otherwise to be able to trace the origin of the particular consignment in order to verify the quality from source or to trace back the supply path in the event of subsequent failure, in order that the remainder of the batch can be identified and withdrawn from production or service. In order to determine such criticality and traceability, the following have to be taken into consideration:

1   Design complexity.
2   Design maturity.
3   Service characteristics.
4   Manufacturing complexity.
5   Safety.
6   Environmental requirements.

The Canadian standard CSA Z299.1, section B2 (Evaluation and selection) can be used as a guide to establishing a criticality and traceability procedure. The results of any such determination should be compiled into an inspection and test plan.

The inspection and test plan will identify all inspection check points relevant to the criticality of the equipment. It will also identify requirements for non-destructive testing, acceptance testing, certification and documentation. It is basically a schedule of inspection points which the design engineer would expect the potential supplier to include in his own controls. It becomes a guideline that sets the minimum requirements for control and surveillance.

The inspection and test plan is not considered to be a mandatory exercise, but it is recommended if only to place the criticality of the material or equipment at the right level. Too many times materials and equipment have been subjected to unnecessary inspection, and other items have not been inspected when they should have been.

Responsibility for inspection should lie with the supplier. His own in-house programme should identify the areas of quality control.

Supplier assessment

A supplier

A supplier in this context is taken to mean an organisation which supplies materials and/or equipment, either as a manufacturer or as a vendor.

A fabricator

A fabricator is an organisation which uses materials and equipment to assemble or build a structure. For the purposes of this section, the term 'supplier' also refers to fabricators.

When choosing a supplier, particularly when the firm is unknown, it is necessary to examine critically a number of factors in order to assess his suitability. These are:

1. Engineering capability.
2. Quality.
3. Price and delivery.
4. Financial stability.

Engineering

Does the supplier have the capabilities to manufacture or supply the materials or equipment in accordance with the required specification? What is his track record, from a study of his fulfilment of recent orders of comparable size and complexity?

Quality

Does the intended supplier have an effective quality programme which operates well in practice with full management support? At this stage, with no contract made, there is nothing binding upon a potential supplier to conform to any given requirement. It is only possible to review the quality programme and to make observations on any apparent deficiency, perhaps advising the supplier that this deficiency could have an adverse effect on contract award if it not rectified.

Price and delivery

Are the prices right? Can the supplier show proven ability to deliver goods on time? Is the delivery date actually promised acceptable?

Financial stability

Are the supplier's finances in order? Nothing would be worse than to place an order, only to have the supplier go bankrupt during production (possibly after considerable advance progress payments have been committed — and lost for ever). It is often prudent to examine the supplier's published accounts, or to seek a report from an agency such as Dun and Bradstreet.

Tender package development

During the assessment period — possibly even earlier — tender packages will have been assembled. These will comprise the specifications, drawings, data sheets, delivery requirements, inspection and test plans and so on which, together, define the commitment which the supplier is being invited to undertake. Although the purchasing department should compile and issue the tender package, both the engineering and quality assurance departments should be involved. The tender package is, in effect, subjected to an interdiscipline check, as in design control. Thus the tender package receives a review for completeness and accuracy. The tender package will then be issued to approved potential suppliers.

Bid package review

When all tenders from suppliers have been received, they will be reviewed for engineering content, quality, price and delivery.

Engineering department

This department will review the tenderers' proposals for supply. There may be cases where a supplier proposes alternative methods, materials or equipment from those listed in the specification, and the engineering department will comment on this, stating whether or not the changes represent improvements or otherwise, and whether or not they are acceptable.

Purchasing department

This department will consider the price and delivery proposals. When the potential sources of supply are remote from the sites where goods are to be delivered, especially where overseas transport and international boundaries are involved, it is necessary to consider not just the ex works price quoted, but the total cost of purchase, transport, insurance, duties and taxes payable to obtain an on-site cost.

Quality assurance department

This reviews the package for compliance with the quality programme level, quality acceptance criteria, inspection and test plan and certification.

Bid summary

When a choice has to be made between a number of suppliers, it is of benefit to tabulate the main points arising from the review on a bid summary sheet. This is arranged to display the various price and delivery promises, all translated to a common set of units for easy and meaningful comparison (eg all the costs converted to pounds sterling). Tabulations are less useful for technical and quality comments, being too limited in space, but they can be used for brief comments, especially where such comments give a definitive preference or rejection. Final choice of supplier is often a complex affair, involving the company's technical and commercial departments and, usually, the client.

Pre-award meeting

Pre-award meetings with suppliers are held to review jointly the contract requirements, and to obtain the suppliers' understanding and agreement. Such meetings correspond to the contract review meetings discussed in design control.

Each pre-award meeting will verify the supplier's intended compliance with the contract, and will also take into account quality programme deficiencies observed when the supplier was assessed, prior to bid package issue. Items identified on the inspection and test plan are reviewed against the supplier's own inspection and test plan, and this comparison will confirm whether or not the purchaser will need to exercise any quality control activities himself. Any contentious issues should be resolved at this meeting, or at least very shortly afterwards. Ambiguities and unresolved problems could result in delays or additional costs later on.

Contract award

The purchase order or contract package issue, apart from being issued only to the chosen supplier, is treated in the same way as the invitation to tender documents. Again, it involves the interdiscipline check and review to verify completeness, accuracy and compliance with any agreements arising from the pre-award meeting.

Post award meeting

Among the scheduled dates proposed in the tender documents and firmed up in the issued contract should be the date by which the supplier is expected to present the purchaser with his quality plan. About 7 days after receipt of the quality plan, it should be reviewed between purchaser and supplier in a post award meeting. An audit schedule can be agreed at the same time, together with inspection hold points, certification and other documentation requirements, and the test programme. The audit schedule should include an internal audit to confirm quality plan awareness, with subsequent audits arranged to cover weak or possible non-compliant areas exposed during the original supplier assessment.

Supplier (or fabricator) quality assurance

Quality control activities should be reviewed with the supplier, who should be made responsible for the quality of the materiel and/or services which he is contracted to provide. There may be, however, additional inspections and tests required by the design engineer to prove the materiel, in which case these will be identified on the inspection and test plan. These could well be the subject of mandatory hold points, beyond which the supplier cannot proceed until cleared by the purchaser. Such inspections and tests would come under the control of the project's own quality control department, and they would also be monitored by the project quality assurance representative to verify compliance with instructions. The project quality assurance representative will also audit the supplier's activities to confirm compliance with the agreed quality plan.

Where a non-conformance is identified the quality assurance representative should issue a corrective action request (CAR) on the appropriate party.

In the case of a supplier non-conformance, a CAR will be issued on the supplier, with a follow up audit scheduled to verify 'close out' — in other words to verify that the corrective action has been taken and that action has also been taken to preclude a repetition of the non-conformance. If the action taken is not instrumental in correcting the deficiency, then another corrective action request must be issued. Should this still not produce the desired result, the project manager must be informed in order that he can lend support in resolving the problem.

In the case of purchaser quality control non-conformance, the quality control representative, together with his appropriate supervisor, should be advised of the non-conformance and corrective action agreed and followed up.

The quality assurance representative should liaise at all times with the appropriate lead engineer and with the project manager.

The remainder of this section is concerned with the quality control of materiel (*sic*.) used on site. Materiel is a word which covers all materials, supplies, stores, equipment, spares needed for contract fulfilment. Two main categories of materiel occur, and these have different implications for quality control. One category includes materiel bought by the contractor (and charged to the customer within the contract price). The other category covers materiel supplied to the contractor by the customer as free-issue items.

Customer supplied materiel (free-issued)

British Standard 5750 gives the following definition:

> Supplied materiel is materiel owned by the purchaser and furnished to the supplier for his use in meeting the requirements of the contract. Where the supplier takes delivery, he has to realise that he is accepting full responsibility for freedom from damage, identification, maintenance, storage, handling and use while the materiel is in his possession.

The site management must therefore ensure that there are satisfactory arrangements for the following:

1. Examination of the materiel upon receipt to check quantities, identities, and to detect any damage caused during transit.
2. Periodic inspection during storage to detect any sign of deterioration, to check on any out-dating risk where storage time exceeds recommended shelf life; to ensure the maintenance of storage conditions which will not cause deterioration and to check generally the condition of stored materiel.
3. Compliance with any contractual requirement for reinspection.
4. Appropriate identification and safeguarding of materiel to prevent unauthorised use or improper disposal.

Procedures should exist which define the manner in which any shortages, damage or other factors rendering the materiel unfit for use are reported to the customer.

Control of materiel purchased by site

In addition to materiel delivered to site by the customer, the site will be purchasing other items that demand local control to ensure that they conform to contract requirements. Control of such purchased items is an essential ingredient of the site quality programme.

Arrangements for choosing potential suppliers for large items of equipment or for high value items will be similar to those described for vendor control in the procurement section of this chapter. It is unlikely, however, that the quality level of any potential supplier in this area will be higher than that imposed on the main contractor.

Incoming (goods inwards) inspection

This inspection is carried out to verify that the supplier has conformed to contract quality requirements. Procedures must be established (including the provision of correct-issue drawings, specifications, purchase order copies, etc.) to ensure that the goods inwards inspectors have the means for confirming that each shipment is complete and undamaged, and that the goods are correctly identified with part numbers or purchase order number (as specified). The inspectors will also ensure that supporting documents such as test certificates, material certificates, letters of conformance, non-destructive test results, etc. are available. The procedures will deal not only with acceptance of incoming goods, but also with the actions to be taken when the goods do not conform.

Special processes

The site has now received the purchased materiel and that supplied by the customer. All has been inspected, accepted and documentation verified as correct. The next step is to translate all this into the finished product. Special processes are paramount in this operation. BS 5750 gives the following guidance on special processes:

> Special processes are processes whose effectiveness cannot normally be verified by subsequent inspection/testing of the processed materiel. Accordingly, continuous monitoring and/or adherence to strict procedures is essential to ensure the specified quality. For such processes it is essential to define the parameters and procedures to be adopted. Certain inspection and testing processes also fall into this category. For these special processes, the quality system should ensure that the process control procedures are adequate and that appropriate processing environment certifications, inspections and monitoring are provided.
>
> Among the processes that can be classified as special are certain applications of the following: concrete mixing,

welding, casting, forging, forming, plastics and wood fabrication, heat treatment and the application of protective treatments.

Among the inspection and testing processes that can be classified as special are temperature and humidity cycling, vibration, radiography, magnetic particle inspection, penetrant inspection, ultrasonic inspection, pressure testing, chemical and spectrographic analysis and salt spray tests.

Note that some everyday activities are listed among these special processes — concrete mixing, welding, heat treatment and non-destructive testing. Problems arise because such activities are not regarded as special. If they are treated as special, and the necessary control procedures developed and implemented, then many of these problems can be prevented.

The quality of a special process cannot usually be verified by subsequent inspection and testing of the processed material. It will therefore be necessary to establish full conformance by evidence obtained during the process. This is achievable by:

1. Establishing documented procedures to ensure that such special processes have been carried out under controlled conditions by qualified personnel using calibrated equipment in accordance with applicable codes, specifications, standards, regulatory requirements, etc.
2. Maintaining current records of qualified personnel, equipment, processes, etc. in accordance with the requirements of the applicable codes and standards.
3. Defining the necessary qualifications of personnel, equipment, processes, etc. not covered by existing codes or standards or when contractual clauses define stricter requirements than those already established.

Document control

The supporting documentation for all activities should be controlled, therefore a document control centre should be established. This is an important function — too many times has a project been completed without the supporting documentation being available. This leads to inevitable delays in completion and commissioning.

The methods for determining documentation/certification requirements should be established at project start up. The documentation which causes most problems is that related to testing and inspection of materiel. It is considered of great importance to identify which materiel requires certification and then to verify that such certification is made available at the right time and in the correct format. Verification can be undertaken by the project quality control personnel at the time of their inspection. When no inspection is required, then the submission of each certification should be made a contractual requirement. A well organised document control centre can be instrumental in achieving any requirements for mandatory fitness-for-purpose certification (such as a certificate to operate) in a timely manner.

It has already been defined that quality assurance is 'All activities and functions concerned with the attainment of quality'. What a quality assurance scheme will give, if well implemented and totally supported, is confidence to the project manager that all activities and functions are right first time. This confidence can be achieved only by the co-operation of all concerned. This co-operation, together with communication, must inevitably lead to capability. Quality assurance can be summed up, therefore, by four C's — communication plus co-operation leading to capability which results in confidence. The confidence that fitness for purpose has been achieved in the most efficient and cost effective manner.

Acknowledgement

This chapter includes material adapted with permission from: L. Stebbing, *Quality Assurance — The Route to Efficiency and Competitiveness*, Chichester, England: Ellis Horwood, 1986.

24
Motivating the Participants

F. L. Harrison

The bulk of this book is concerned with the techniques and systems of project management. One system without which all the other systems will not work is the 'people system', or the system of human relations. Effective project systems and a good system of human relations are both necessary for good project performance, neither being sufficient by itself. Thus, in addition to his professional skill in planning and control, a project manager must develop his skills in managing people.

ORGANISATIONAL DIFFICULTIES

The project manager has to manage an organisation which is complex, and which requires the work and contribution from many people of different professional backgrounds and trades, operating from different departments and different companies. Even in the best of circumstances the management of a project is a difficult problem. It is a very difficult task to co-ordinate, communicate, plan, organise, provide leadership and drive and generally motivate everyone towards achievement of success.

The project manager's task is made more difficult by the fact that he acts as a junior general manager, usually with ill defined authority. His lines of authority or influence are grafted on to the existing pyramid structure of his company, cutting across the normal vertical lines of command and departmental boundaries. He does not work in the usual superior-to-subordinate relationships but must motivate and control his juniors, his peers and even his superiors in other departments and companies. People in those other areas find that they are responsible in varying degrees to two managers, namely their own departmental or company managers on the one hand, and the project manager on the other.

Thus, in a typical project organisation, personnel and groups from several different functional departments, contractors and subcontractors must all work together, but their individual pay rises, promotions, performance assessments and other line matters are not the responsibility of the project manager. These people all have different loyalties and objectives. They have probably never worked together before, and may never do so again. They are bound only by the project and its organisation. The project manager must, therefore, deal with the managerial problem of developing a project organisation out of these diverse groups. This involves handling complex relationships with many other managers in these departments and companies.

The project organisation has a life which lasts only as long as the project, especially if it is set up as a task force type of organisation. The temporary nature of the project group means that its members work together only for a limited period, leaving insufficient time for interpersonal relationships to develop and stabilise as in the more usual line management. Group performance has to be effective from the very beginning of a project, since mistakes made and time lost at the start are often impossible to correct later.

The composition of a total management group on a project is usually changing continuously, with new members joining from time to time and other, older members either departing or assuming diminished roles. And, in this environment, the project manager is expected to work under pressure to get the project finished on time, within budget and time constraints. He, in his turn, has to apply pressure on all the other people engaged on his project.

THE AUTHORITY PROBLEM IN PROJECT MANAGEMENT

The principle of organisation from which project management varies most is that responsibility should always be coupled to corresponding authority. The project manager is responsible for the success or failure of his project, but is only able to exercise limited authority over the personnel employed. Yet if he is to manage effectively he must have some authority over them all.

The project manager must manage across functional lines of command in his own company, and across organisational lines of command in other companies. In a traditional bureaucratic organisation, business is conducted up and down the vertical hierarchy. The project manager on the other hand is more concerned with the flow of work in horizontal and diagonal directions than he is with flows in the vertical direction. Problems of motivation exist for the traditional manager but these problems are compounded for the project manager, because the traditional leverages of hierarchical authority are not at his disposal. However, he must act as a focal point for making project decisions. If he is to manage his projects and not be simply a co-ordinator, he must be given adequate power to accomplish these objectives, but often this power is not the formal authority of superior-subordinate relationship.

No project manager whose activities cut across functional lines and other companies can have complete authority. Authority is granted relative to many considerations. The project manager normally has written contractual relationships with other companies and these companies generally want to maintain goodwill to ensure future business. Therefore he does have a formal basis of authority which exists in contracts or purchase agreements. The personnel working for these other companies can never be fully integrated into the one project organisation, but for all practical purposes in a healthy situation they can work together as part of an effective project team.

In his own company the project manager's position is usually one of getting the job done without the line of authority or binding contractual arrangements for controlling this in-house work. Thus it is often more difficult for the project manager to exert authority over his own company's departments than it is for him with outside firms. Although a considerable amount of a project manager's authority must depend on sources of authority other than that formally given, his position will be strengthened in his own company by the publication of documentation to establish his position and stating what his legal authority and responsibilities are. This will include identifying his role in managing, organising, planning and controlling the project, and the explicit recognition of the project organisation form used.

Project managers in the matrix form of project management are thus faced with the difficult task of obtaining performance from others not under their direct control. To accomplish this they must often rely on sources of power or influence other than formal authority. The more limited the formal authority, the greater the pressure on a project manager to devise other methods for obtaining authority. Authority is difficult to define. Words such as 'authority', 'influence', 'leadership' and 'power' tend to be used interchangeably and in a rather loose association. It is therefore useful to establish an understanding of the meanings of these words.

Authority

This is usually defined as the formal, legal or rightful power to command others to act or not to act. In the traditional theory of management, authority is a right granted from a superior to a subordinate. Authority (at least formal authority) is the right of a person to be listened to and obeyed. It is delegated through job titles, organisational titles, standard operating procedures and related policy. Authority is sometimes termed 'position power'. A duly appointed superior will have power over his or her subordinates in matters concerning pay, promotion and performance reports.

Influence

Influence, on the other hand, can be assumed by an individual without legitimacy or an organisation position. This is often termed 'informal authority'. Influence can thus be based on an individual's competence and reputation, and on his or her personality.

Leadership

This is a particular form of influence. It is often associated with attempts of a superior to influence the attitudes or behaviour of subordinates, but it can also apply to someone other than a formal superior who attempts significantly to influence the behaviour of others. The distinction between influencing and leading is that the exercise of leadership will nearly always involve an attempt to influence attitudes and behaviour, whereas not all attempts at influence involve leadership.

Power

Power is a concept frequently associated with authority. It is defined as the ability to determine unilaterally the behaviour of others, regardless of the basis of that ability. The simplest way of looking at power is to regard it as the sum total of a person's authority and influence:

$$\text{Power} = \text{Formal authority} + \text{influence}$$

As power and authority tend to be interchangeable terms in practice, this equation can also be expressed for any individual as:

$$\text{Total authority} = \text{Formal authority} + \text{informal authority}$$

A manager's power or total authority is a combination of formal authority and influence such that subordinates, peers and superiors alike accept his or her judgement. Thus the individual's personal effectiveness complements the formal authority to yield the degree of authority realised in practice. This is demonstrated when two people with different amounts of personal influence occupy the same management position in succession. Though their formal authority is identical, the total power or authority which they wield can vary considerably.

The project manager accomplishes objectives through working with personnel who are, for the most part, professional people. Consequently the use of authority must be different from that expected in the simple line organisation superior-subordinate relationship. For professional people project leadership must include explaining the rationale of the effort as well as the more obvious functions of planning, organising, directing and controlling.

Unilateral decisions, dogmatic attitudes and resorting to the authority of a hierarchical position are inconsistent with the project environment. The project manager's approach must be to search for points of agreement, to examine situations critically and think reflectively and only then take decisions based on the superiority of his knowledge. This, rather than the formal position in the organisation, is the basis for the project manager's authority.

The effective authority of the project manager is thus seldom autocratic. His most effective authority may be based on his ability to build alliances with other managers involved in the project, and in resolving conflicts which may arise between them. One asset of a good project manager is that people from different departments and companies working on the project should regard him, in their own specialised way, as an asset. Technical, engineering or scientific people may think of him as a buffer between them and the irresponsible demands of others. The finance people may think of him as a businessman. Computer people might view him as someone able to understand them and be capable of communicating with operations people.

The project manager must therefore earn the respect of, and gain authority over, elements of the project which are not under his direct authority. He gets much of his work done through influence, and through authority other than that 'legally' extended to him. Voluntary co-operation is more effective than that which is forced through legal power (but, if informal authority fails to work, formal authority becomes necessary). In the project setting, the naked use of authority is one of the least effective ways of obtaining commitment and performance.

The project manager has tools which he can use to establish his authority over those involved in the project. Among the most important of these are the plan and budget. Provided these are constructed with the involvement of all those concerned, then they commit the individuals and groups involved to specific allocations of resources and performance. The project manager then has the authority to hold them to this commitment. Similarly, the use of pseudo subcontracts for organisational cost accounts and work packages also obtains commitment and establishes the project manager's authority.

The project manager is also at the centre of the information system and this in itself can be a means of obtaining influence. When combined with responsibility for control analysis and reporting, it enhances the positional power of the project manager. In addition the ability to call meetings, to chair them and to minute them gives the project manager a measure of informal and formal authority.

Finally, if the project manager is involved in the formal performance assessment of people from other functions involved in his project, he has in effect achieved some measure of formal authority over them.

Authority, organisation and managerial philosophy

The extent of the project manager's authority in his own company is the deciding factor in the form of organisation actually used. As a staff co-ordinator he has very little authority; as a divisional project manager he has complete authority over his own company personnel and, in the matrix organisation, he shares it to varying degrees with departmental heads. For descriptions and illustrations of these kinds of organisation, please refer to Chapter 2.

In the case where the project manager acts as a co-ordinator (basically a staff function but with some given line responsibilities) the project manager must pursue performance objectives with a great deal of skill and persuasiveness. He must constantly refer back to his line manager for authority. This situation is not inherently incorrect, provided that all concerned are aware of the project manager's limited authority and are willing to allow occasional delays or lack of achievement in pursuing project goals. However, when a crisis arises, speed in the implementation of instructions or corrective action is required, sometimes on the inconclusive early evidence of advance trends. The manager with some real authority has a much better chance of success because he can redirect personnel and money and make decisions with the minimum of consultation. With limited authority the project manager who is a co-ordinator must take some considerable time to consult with supervisory authority and must attempt to persuade other personnel on the basis of inconclusive information.

In the matrix organisation, the project manager is working with shared or indefinite legal authority and thus he depends a great deal on his unofficial authority. The actual working form of matrix management depends on the respect and loyalty held for the individual project manager by his colleagues. Before the matrix form of project organisation is introduced, it must be preceded by a careful analysis of the projects to be handled, the existing organisation both unofficial and official, the personalities involved and the managerial philosophies of the firm. The extent of the project manager's authority will vary with each organisation and with each project manager.

Experienced departmental managers cannot be expected to share authority with a lesser executive who is appointed as a project manager. Therefore project managers must have the respect of their fellow executives and the degree of authority together with relationship to functional departments spelled out. Where there is mutual respect and confidence in each other, the functional managers will accept a project manager's decision as a generalist and a manager, and he must accept their technical recommendations. The basis for this healthy situation is the appointment of project managers who have their fellow executives' respect and confidence and a logical division of authority based on a careful analysis of the situation.

Thus one factor which determines which is the most applicable form of project organisation for any individual company is the managerial philosophy of that company. Each individual organisation is as distinctive and unique as the people in it, and each has its own personality and character. Thus the form of project organisation which works for one firm will not necessarily work for a seemingly similar firm, as a company's organisation and philosphy of management must be compatible.

Any company's management philosophy evolves over several years and reflects the personal convictions of the senior management of the company. Therefore any changes in organisation which are not compatible with the deeply held views of the top men will fail. For example, the following points will illustrate a few aspects which affect the success or failure of any new organisational form and which cannot be changed overnight.

1. Is the prevalent managerial style historically autocratic or democratic?
2. Is the company conservative or will it try out new ideas?
3. Does it encourage delegation of decision making to lower levels of management, or persist in having every decision referred to senior management?
4. Is personal accountability emphasised, or must all important decisions be taken by a committee?

These factors generally represent deeply held beliefs and convictions of senior management and are very difficult to change. Therefore whatever type of project organisation is used, it must not only reflect the needs of any particular project but also the 'givens' of the situation. If powerful functional departments or individuals are dominant, conflict and frustration will certainly arise if a strong project organisation is attempted. A weak project organisation emphasising communication, co-ordination, planning and monitoring of progress may be the best solution for such a situation. Where a company's philosophy is participative and encourages delegation, a strong or fully mixed matrix organisation will achieve better results on project work. It can lead to effective team building and the generation of a project attitude of mind with good human relations.

THE ENGINEER AS A MANAGER

Much has been written and many studies carried out relating to the engineer's success and failure in the field of management. It is generally recognised that many engineers encounter problems when they reach the stage in their career that marks the transition from engineer to manager. They often find difficulty in overcoming the problems caused by the lack of compatibility between the purely technical role of the engineer and the non-technical requirements of the managerial role. This can lead to engineers as managers having difficulties in communicating with people, having a lack of knowledge of other disciplines because of their narrow technical interests and feeling conflict between their role as an engineer and their role as a manager.

As the majority of managers working on a project are engineers, the project manager must understand the problems facing engineers when they perform the role of managers. It is useful in this context to examine the task, role and character of an engineer in relation to the organisation and to compare the task, role and character of the manager with those of the engineer. This can give the project manager a greater understanding of the interpersonal conflicts arising from these aspects of the essentially two different professions.

The engineer

The engineer works in an environment where physical rules and laws are his tools. His designs are based on these laws and consequently a high degree of physical certainty is attached to the solution of his problems. His world is one of black and white, right or wrong, clear decisions with clear outcomes. He generally performs tasks of a technical nature, calling for precision, mathematical ability, the application of well-proven, precise theory, the mechanical approach to problem solving and the need to seek a single, lasting solution in an environment of high certainty and little change. The engineer's role thus requires an attitude of precision, a mechanistic approach to problem solving and a bias towards technical factors.

Thus the general conception of an engineer is that he is unemotional, prefers to deal with things rather than people, has narrow technical interests and chooses to specialise in physical sciences. Some of the engineer's typical personality traits are symptomatic of the problems encountered by an engineer in his transition to management. Traits such as difficulty in dealing with people, procrastination in decision making, fear of being proved wrong, resistance to change, maintenance of the self-image as an engineer and not as a manager, sensitivity to criticism, a bias towards short-term rather than long-term planning and a distinctly task-oriented behaviour.

The manager

The manager on the other hand performs the task of planning, organising, directing and controlling the resources of his firm, (principally men, money and materials) in a world of uncertainty, intangibles and constant change. These tasks call for a much broader, creative approach, and ability to diverge and search for many alternative solutions to a problem and then to choose the best solution applicable at that particular time. The manager's role in contrast to that of the engineer, thus requires an attitude of precision only in so far as its usefulness is justified for the goal to be achieved and the time available to reach that goal. It requires a non-mechanistic approach to problem solving and a bias towards efficient resource utilisation and more people orientation.

The engineer as a project manager

When an engineer moves into the general or project management area he is faced with several problems. He has to lose the greater part of his identity as an engineer and acquire an understanding of and sympathy with the needs of the total role comprising all parts and functions of the organisation. He has to have, or acquire, the skills needed for this new role. It is here that the engineer may find his problems are at their greatest, due possibly to the lack of management education and training, and the incompatibility of his personality with the requirements of his role.

Symptoms such as differences of perception and orientation of the different departments and organisations contributing to the project, time needed for the task, interpersonal orientation and environmental needs arise. The project manager must master these skills and understand these needs in order to carry out effectively the task of managing and resolving the inter-group conflicts arising.

Engineers in general thus tend to be tremendously conscientious and work oriented. Their loyalty or commitment is very often to the plant, equipment or project on which they are working rather than to the overall company. They have a great deal of pride in their work, but this can often be a disadvantage to the project manager. This pride leads to the engineer being very sensitive to criticism and having an enormous need to be right. He is more concerned with being technically correct than with time and cost objectives, or with people. Promotion to managerial position often depends on the engineer's technical ability, rather than the ability to manage people, and thus the engineering manager often takes with him this emphasis on technical perfection, pride in his work or group, and sensitivity to criticism.

When this is combined with the fact that in many organisations the level of interpersonal trust, support and co-operation is low, it means that the project manager has a very difficult task in managing the many people and organisations involved in his project.

INTERPERSONAL BEHAVIOUR IN THE PROJECT SETTING

The project manager must overcome the many problems involved in obtaining his personal and group performance from individuals and organisations in achieving the project's objectives, within the 'givens' of the managerial, organisational and technical systems they work in,

Managing Progress and Performance

that is, the sociotechnical system. Any individual's performance on his job is a function of this sociotechnical system, his or her ability and motivation. Given that many of these factors are not under the project manager's control, the main behavioural factor he can influence is the motivation of the personnel working on his project. The skills of the project manager in dealing with people can make a significant difference to performance on his project, and in this an understanding of the work of the many people who have studied the problems of human behaviour in management is well worthwhile.

Very few organisations are ideal and a person's management history can lead to attitudes, which can perhaps in the short term of a typical project life be modified, but rarely can be changed. Man is a complex being, highly variable, but capable of changing. The same manager may perform poorly in one part of the organisation, where he feels alienated, but perform satisfactorily in another part. Managerial styles may be required to be different for different individuals and different groups. No one set of assumptions is generally applicable; different people and different groups of people will show behaviour that can be accounted for satisfactorily by several different sets of assumptions about people. Thus each manager in each situation must avoid making assumptions too soon and must draw on a range of models of human behaviour to see which one suits the behaviour he observes around him at work.

The classic assumptions about human behaviour have been crystallised by McGregor in his Theory X and Theory Y, and both may be appropriate at the same time in any one project organisation. Theory X postulates that man is a rational economic being with the following characteristics:

1. The average human being has an inherent dislike of work and will avoid it if he can.
2. Because of this characteristic, most people must be coerced, controlled, directed and threatened with punishment to get them to put forth adequate effort towards the achievement of organisational objectives.
3. The average human being prefers to be directed, wishes to avoid responsibility, has relatively little ambition and wants security above all.

Theory Y, on the other hand, postulates that:

Motivating the Participants

1 The expenditure of physical and mental effort in work is as natural as play and rest.
2 External control and the threat of punishment are not the only means of bringing about effort towards organisational objectives. A man will exercise self-direction and self-control in the service of objectives to which he is committed.
3 Commitment to an objective is a function of the rewards associated with their achievement.
4 The average human being learns, under proper conditions, not only to accept but to seek responsibility.
5 The capacity to exercise a relatively high degree of imagination, ingenuity and creativity in solving organisational problems is widely, not narrowly distributed in the population.
6 Under the conditions of modern industrial life, the intellectual potentialities of the average human being are only partly utilised.

In the project setting, the project manager does not normally manage workers at shop floor level but is involved with other managers and professional people and this concept of a self-actualising man outlined in Theory Y is probably more realistic, given a healthy sociotechnical system. The problems of motivating professional people have been studied by Herzberg and others who found that accomplishment and a feeling of job growth are genuine motivators for people like accountants and engineers. He found that what they call hygiene factors such as pay, working conditions and canteens could cause dissatisfaction, but their improvement did not lead to satisfaction, merely to the elimination of dissatisfaction. They were essentially prerequisites for motivation but did not motivate by themselves, just making it possible for motivation to operate. Motivating factors are more associated with the job itself. Thus self-actualising man had a range of motives ordered in a hierarchy of importance depending on how they contributed to his survival. Given that his basic body and safety needs, and his desire for fellowship are met, his desire for autonomy in the work he does and the fulfilment of himself in his work are such that a suitably designed job will enable him to engage himself fully in it and so satisfy himself and the needs of the organisation. In the project environment where hygiene factors are generally reasonably well cared for, the personnel can be assumed primarily concerned with a search for fulfilment of their self-esteem needs. In this the characteristics of an engineer may be both a disadvantage and an advantage to the project manager.

The project manager can in this environment benefit from the use of participative methods of management. In fact in the matrix set-up he is always forced to use participative methods to varying extents with other functional managers and other company's managers. Participation means a willingness of the project manager to consult with his fellow managers and other personnel working on the project, to acquaint them with the project's problems and to involve them in the decision making. The participative project manager does not abdicate his organisational responsibilities. He is still responsible for his project, but he has learned to delegate and share operating responsibility with those who actually perform the work. Participation increases this opportunity for those working on the project to develop increased ability, satisfaction and thus motivation for the project. It can lead to the removal of conditions which set the personnel and groups apart.

However, each individual and group involved in a project may differ widely in their human relation problems, and in how much they may be trusted to achieve sub-goals on their own, or how much they require to be closely monitored. The project manager has to analyse quickly the individuals and groups working upon his project, and ascertain specifically what are the best methods of dealing with them and what motivating factors are most important to them.

He must be a good human observer and be looking for signs and symptoms of what makes them tick right through the life of the project. The abilities and motivations of the people in the various sub-organisations are so variable, that he must have the sensitivity and diagnostic ability to be able to appreciate any differences quickly.

It may be necessary to be detailed and autocratic with one individual, delegate with mild control with another group or individual and be fully participative with others. Each management style or strategy will be the correct one for each individual or group. The project manager should become skilful in several different kinds of managerial styles, each consistent with the particular situation. The authoritarian style is more consistent with many traditional organisational forms, whereas participative management can work well in a matrix organisation. To do this the project manager must be

Motivating the Participants

aware of his actual managerial style and consciously switch styles when required.

The temporary nature of the project group means that its members work together for a limited period without time for interpersonal relationships to develop into a static state, as in normal line management. Group performance is also necessary from the very beginning of a project, as mistakes made and time lost at the start can never be recovered. In addition, the composition of the group is constantly changing with new members joining it and the role of some older members diminishing in importance.

The manager must be able to size up people quickly and be aware of the electricity in the air depicting tension between groups. It is a fact that in the temporary nature of the project setting, attitudes and relationships are 'set' very quickly. The position is made more complex as project managers must work under pressure to achieve cost and time objectives, and their function includes keeping the pressure on the personnel involved in the project. They have to gain a feel for how much pressure can be usefully applied. Most personnel work better under a certain amount of pressure, and indeed accept and welcome it in the project setting in order to achieve reasonable objectives. This comes from accepting the new challenge and taking risks and increasing their abilities, but too much pressure leads to resistance, conflict and unproductive tension.

Therefore, the project manager must be sensitive to the reactions of people and endeavour to act supportively instead of threateningly. He must be perceptive to the reaction of people to him, and the interactions between people. This involves such factors as being aware of body language, and of the factors that indicate threatening behaviour or supportive behaviour. For example, the first word chosen, tones of voice, points omitted, can tend to increase defensive reaction, restrict communication and impair the person's commitment and motivation to the project. Supportive behaviour from the project manager or other people can tend to reduce defensive behaviour and lead to greater project commitment.

The project manager does have one important factor going for him in obtaining good personal performance. Project work by its very nature can be very stimulating, satisfying and give to those involved a real sense of achievement. Many professional and supervisory people feel alienated by the nature of their work and their failure to see how it fits in the overall company picture. The many layers of management in a large organisation leave those at the lower levels feeling a sense of powerlessness and remoteness from decision making, and it is difficult for them to equate their own personal needs with that of the organisation. This leads to a loss of involvement and commitment to their work and the objective of the groups to which they belong.

Project work with its definite visible goals can lead to a high level of personal commitment and satisfaction. Everyone on a project can become associated with its success or failure. For example, the objectives of a project group may be to design and build the physical plant required by the company to fulfil certain market demands. With this objective in mind, the personnel involved can readily visualise and adopt the company's objectives for their own. Projects can be extremely frustrating for a project manager caught in a power complex with little authority, but more often, people in all kinds of occupations involved in a project comment on the pleasure they had working on it. They can see how their contribution fits in to the overall picture, and if they work a little harder, they can see what effect it has on the progress of a job. This kind of feedback leads to a greater interest and motivation in the job. It leads to the development of the project attitude of mind, in which people's interests are subordinated to the overall project and they associate themselves with the project.

In addition the concept of cost accounts and work packages as pseudo subcontracts may be partially threatening in a control sense, but in fact give people clear objectives and clearly delegated responsibility. This gives them personal targets and essentially is equivalent to the methods used in management by objectives, and can lead to a greater commitment to the overall project and their part of it, which is clearly defined.

The project manager must thus make use of this unique motivational opportunity to obtain personal, group and global organisation performance. He must deal with people, with the assumption that most individuals have drives towards personal growth and development, and these are most likely to be actualised in an environment which is both supportive and challenging. Most people desire to make and are capable of making, a much higher level of contribution to the attainment of organisation goals than most organisational environments will permit. However, the project manager is working with many different people from many different organisations, and therefore with the 'givens' of any situation he may have to treat different individuals and different groups in entirely different ways to achieve the best performance for his project.

GROUPS IN THE PROJECT SETTING

The great majority of human beings have a natural desire to seek the companionship of other human beings in informal or social groups. They seek this for basic personal and psychological reasons such as satisfying human needs for friendship, for association with others, for a sense of increased security and as a home base. Thus most people wish to be accepted and to interact co-operatively with at least one small reference group, and usually with more than one group. One of the most psychologically relevant reference groups for most people is the work group which includes peers, superiors and subordinates.

These groups can make a considerable contribution to achieving an organisation's objectives in that they can give a member of a group a feeling of security and of belonging, can maximise the contribution of each individual involved, lead to a greater participation in decision making and problem solving, and result in a greater commitment of the individual to the group's and hopefully the organisation's objectives. On the other hand, if the group is unhealthy, it can lead to internal bickering within groups, the group's objectives not being the organisation's objectives and to serious conflict between groups, all of which are detrimental to achieving the organisation's and the project's objectives. The project manager must therefore be aware of the characteristics of groups and of intergroup behaviour and of the factors which can lead to the evolution of effective groups.

Principal factors contributing to the formation of a group are:

1 They are engaged together in a task or operation.
2 They come into day-to-day contact with each other.
3 They are interdependent.
4 They have the same backgrounds, skills and sense of values.
5 Leadership and management.

Several different types of group have been classified and all exist in the project setting, namely:

1 Vertical groups
2 Horizontal groups
3 Mixed groups.

A vertical work group consists of people from different levels in the same company, department or function. Formal, permanent, vertical work groups form part of the organisation of most companies, and provide a home base for the majority of people involved in a project. They are normally created to carry out or perform one specific function and are made up of people with the same background, skills and values, and can be considered as a uniform group.

A horizontal group in a project is a group of managers or technologists at the same hierarchical level or status, often, but not necessarily so, in the same profession. For example, the project managers of the owner, the principal contractor and main subcontractors may form a group by themselves, or may form a group with the heads of the various functional groups contributing to a project, all more or less at the same hierarchical level.

The mixed group is one which includes people from different levels from different companies or departments involved in the project.

Groups are very necessary in the project setting because a project is never a one-man or one-manager task. The complexity of a project, the contributions required from the many different specialised skills which no one man can have, the amount of work involved, the large number of activities that require to be managed, organised, planned and controlled, the mass of information necessary and normally the number of companies involved, all necessitate the involvement of a number of managers and specialised technologists from different functions. Thus in a large project there is not one group but many formal and informal groups. Likert in his book *New Patterns of Management* states that organisations can be considered as systems of interlocking groups. The typical project organisation is thus not just a set of relationships between individuals, but between sets of interlocking and interdependent groups. These interlocking groups are connected by individuals who occupy key positions of dual membership of groups and serve as links between these groups. In the typical project organisation there are many groups of all three types: each individual department or section will tend to form a vertical group, the people in each company working on the project will tend to form a mixed group, and ideally, all the people working on the project will form another mixed group. These groups may lead to greater effectiveness, but they can also lead to a consolidation of a 'we/they' attitude.

The vertical group, consisting of people from different levels in the same company or department, is probably the group that forms most naturally in the project setting, but it may be the least desirable from the project manager's point of view. It can be a healthy group, with greater cohesion and team spirit, and can lead to greater effectiveness within the company or department on internal matters. The great danger is that a 'we/they' attitude can be established between this group and other functions, departments and companies working on the project. That can lead to complex intergroup resentment and conflict, and as all groups in a project must work together, this in turn leads to a less effective overall project group.

The senior members of the departments, functions and companies in the project are usually involved on a day-to-day basis and form a horizontal group which can link the overall organisation of the project together. They occupy key roles in the project organisation and serve as channels of communication, influence and policy integration from one group to another. The personnel in the various groups may not all be aware of each other, but if the horizontal linking group is effective this will set the whole tone of the organisation and tend to lead to the other groups becoming effective teams. It is possible for a project group involving several sub-organisations with different management philosophies to work effectively together provided that the linking members of this horizontal subgroup form an effective team. They can be bound together by mutual respect and an over-riding commitment to the project.

Horizontal groups may tend to form in each function, for example, the construction staff of the contractor will come into contact on a day-to-day basis with the client company construction staff. This may lead to conflict if each forms a separate group with the 'we/they' attitude, but if they can combine to form one group, this will lead to greater overall effectiveness. This does not mean that there will not be conflict, but can mean that conflict can be resolved by the logic of the situation. It involves mutual respect of both ability and commitment to their common objectives. Among the factors affecting the chance of achieving this type of group is the simple one of physical contact. Take the construction group, if each has a separate site office the tendency is to form separate groups. If they share the same building, have day-to-day contact, have lunch and coffee together, there is a much greater likelihood of their forming one effective group.

The principal group the project manager must endeavour to establish is a mixed group, which includes people from different levels and different functions of the departments and companies involved in the project. This kind of group leads to greater cohesion of the total project group and a commitment to the total project objectives. However, this is probably the most difficult group to create as the project group is a temporary formal group created to carry out a specific project, and when the project is finished, the group is broken up. The group may exist for several years, but the fact that it is temporary has an influence on each member. They may feel the group may be broken up at any time, and are more or less looking over their shoulders all the time to their parent company or department.

The members of this former project group carry out the formal tasks necessary for the completion of the project and this can be regarded as the basic function of the group. If this is the only function of the project group then it will not develop into an effective team. Hand in hand with the formal functions must go the informal functions of satisfying the behavioural, personal or psychological needs of the group members. The objective of the project manager is to get the aims of the informal groups and formal groups in the project committed to the same objectives. If he fails on this, the informal groups may be hostile or apathetic to the formal project goals and waste time and energy on intergroup conflict. If he succeeds, the project is on the road to success if it is humanly possible.

There is a great difference between a number of individuals working together and an effective group or managerial team. One needs only to note some of the observable signs of an effective team namely, team spirit, enthusiasm for the project; the members are supportive of one another and use the term 'we' instead of 'I'; they manifest towards one another, if not friendliness, at least respect for other members' competence and points of view; they show staying qualities when things get rough and a resistance to frustration; there is a minimum of bickering and members do things because they want to, rather than because they have to. An ineffective group will have apathy, jealousy, bickering, disjointed effort and pessimism about the project. Instead of saying 'we will have a go and make it', members will point out all the difficulties involved and will be negative about achievement.

If the co-operative relationships and interdependence of teamwork can be achieved, the interest and enthusiasm of all concerned, regardless of their organisational responsibilities will be committed to the project. The great advantage of an effective group in project organisation is that greater emphasis is given to the total organisational effectiveness than to that of the departmental or individual companies contributing to the project. Objectives between companies will differ, but all will have a commitment to the success of the project.

TEAM DEVELOPMENT

Effective groups or teams do not just coalesce as soon as people are brought together. Groups are dynamic entities which are not static and unchanging. Studies of groups have shown four stages in the process of formation of an effective group. Effective in this instance means working towards project objectives, without interpersonal or intergroup conflict, and with satisfied and involved members. These stages are:

1. The development of mutual acceptance and trust leading to a diminishing of defensive behaviour
2. Open communication
3. Co-operation and sustained productivity
4. Resolving of problems and control by mutual agreement.

Thus an effective group takes time to develop and at any stage in process can go in reverse. That is, an effective team can be destroyed by many factors; unsupportive management philosophy of any contributing company, a rogue key member, or failure of the project. Once a team has reached full effectiveness, however, it is reasonably resilient to minor factors affecting it. Such a team is a good training group for new staff and has also been used to endeavour to correct the behavioural practices of problem members of staff, provided that they are not key linking members.

Thus for a project to be successful, the project manager must provide the leadership necessary to develop a managerial team and the organisational environment must be favourable to his work. Where a company's philosophy is participative, a strong or fully mixed matrix organisation will achieve good results. It can lead to effective team building and generation of a 'project attitude' with wide behavioural consequences. This project attitude is a way of thinking that penetrates throughout the organisation and unifies all activities towards accomplishment of the project's common goals. It will become no longer enough to say 'that our department's effort was satisfactory but that the project was held up because of someone else'. No single organisation effort is satisfactory in a project unless the project is a success, and every effort should be made to assist other organisations to carry out their tasks successfully. It involves taking off departmental 'blinkers' and co-operating by helping one another to complete the project successfully in terms of all its objectives.

In order to build up an effective team and generate this project attitude, the company's managerial philosophy must permit the project manager to use participative management with its emphasis on creativity, open communication and participation. The project manager has also thus to be more aware of human relations and personal sensitivity than the normal functional manager.

The leadership capabilities of the project manager are essential to the growth of an effective group, that is, the personal qualifications, skill role and strategy of the project manager. The development of mutual acceptance, trust, co-operation and open communication can be helped or hindered by the project manager, but cannot be brought about by him alone. Nevertheless an essential factor leading to an effective group is the perceptiveness and the ability of the project manager to recognise and resolve group problems. The sort of signs the group manager must be on the lookout for are, for example, members of a group at a project meeting who fail to pay attention to each other and show lack of respect, members preoccupied with their own personal objectives, the existence of threatening attitudes, etc.

For a group to optimise its effectiveness, the project manager cannot perform all of the leadership functions in all circumstances at all times, and all group members must assist each other with effective leadership and member behaviour. Thus the behaviour of the group is not only influenced by the project manager's leadership qualities, but by attitude, knowledge, skills and capabilities of the individual members and the characteristics of the companies and departments involved in the project.

Thus the project manager must deal with the managerial problems of developing a project team out of these different groups working on a project. In this he is helped by the fact that the main advantage of project-type work is that there are clearly definable goals of schedules, cost and performance, which are ideal for managerial team building. If the co-operative relationships and interdependence of teamwork can be achieved then the intrinsic rewards associated with a successful project can generate the interest and enthusiasm of all concerned, regardless of their organisational responsibilities. In achieving a project attitude of mind the project manager has one distinct advantage in that the project is a discrete entity in itself. Thus the group has one primary task, which is the completion of a clearly defined project, within a specified time span, to a technical specification and within a budgeted cost. People working on the project are associated with something concrete, not something intangible. A successfully completed project is obvious to everyone and people even remotely connected with it can draw satisfaction from this. The project manager has to use these advantages to establish effective team work and all that arises from it.

The project also has the advantage that all contributors to it must work together in establishing plans and budget and in carrying out the work. The project manager cannot arbitrarily set time limits and budgets; he must negotiate what is reasonable with the various functional managers and companies involved, making trade-offs between time and money in the light of the overall situation which only he knows, but which he must communicate. There is also the opportunity for intrinsic rewards which are so important to professional people and which exist in the clear and unclouded achievement of the project. The complaint of members of functional groups is often that they never see the overall picture but only their small task. It is possible in project work to communicate the whole picture and for the individual members to share in the success or perhaps the failure of the project. Extrinsic salary increases and promotions can then be fairly based on project contribution and achievement with the assessment of personnel normally being carried out both by the functional department head and the project manager. Co-operative relationships and interdependence thus must exist between all those working on a project or the organisation would grind to a halt. This in itself can lead to effective teamwork.

Finally, the more successful the management of a project is, the more obvious is the attitude of mind of those involved. They have a very real confidence in themselves and in each other. This creates an atmosphere of mutual respect and collaboration, which is essential when a large group of people must work together towards a common objective.

Thus, though the project manager is faced with the problem of welding together people from various backgrounds and organisations into one, effective mixed project team, he does have certain advantages which can help him overcome the disadvantages of the matrix organisation. It is up to him to make use of these to achieve the project's objectives. Unfortunately because of the existence of different objectives and the fact that many groups are involved in a typical project, he must also have great skill in overcoming or preventing intergroup conflict.

INTERGROUP CONFLICT IN THE PROJECT SETTING

It is an unfortunate fact that in many medium to large firms, even with the normal functional and hierarchical organisation, there tends to be intergroup conflict or hostility. It is almost impossible to have a project without differences between people; differences of opinion, values, objectives, etc. These differences can lead to discussion, argument, competition and conflict. Discussion and argument are constructive, whereas competition can be both constructive and destructive, but conflict is always destructive. It would be foolish to imagine that groups can work together on a project without disagreement and some conflict. Disagreement between people is almost inevitable in the project setting, and indeed, to a certain extent, it would be undesirable if this were not so. There is bound to be some disagreement in a healthy organisation, and it is often essential for efficiency and effective decision making.

Motivating the Participants

One of the most important functions of the project manager is thus the solution of conflicts occurring among groups involved in his project. If he is to maintain an effective mixed team comprising all the groups working on his project, he must constructively prevent and overcome this destructive intergroup conflict. If he does not, the project performance will almost certainly be seriously affected.

Conflict in a project can arise between

1. Individuals in the same group.
2. Individuals in different groups and companies.
3. Groups in the same company.
4. Groups in different companies.
5. Between companies, that is, between sets of groups.

In particular there is the great likelihood of conflict between

1. Project and functional groups.
2. Engineering and operations groups.
3. Owner and contractor groups.

Consequences of conflict

Where there is hostility or conflict between key linking members of groups, or between groups, it breaks up, or makes impossible to form a healthy effective team out of all those working on a project. It leads to a lack of respect and trust between groups, a lack of harmony and co-operation, and a breakdown in communication, with information being distorted, censored or held back. Each group will tend to reject ideas, opinions and suggestions arising from the other groups, and feelings or emotion will run high with a greater chance of mistakes being made by people under stress with clouded judgement. Groups will tend to have unspoken objectives, different from those of the project, such as to 'get' the other group, block anything they propose, achieve dominance over them and show them in a poor light to senior management. Project objectives will be subordinated to the group goals which concentrate on achieving the dominance or victory over other groups. This accelerates the breakdown in communications between groups, and creates unfavourable attitudes and images of other groups.

There will be a polarisation into a 'we/they' attitude, instead of 'all for one and one for all'. Decision making and problem solving will be slow and difficult, differences will not be worked through in an open manner and you will have win/lose situations leading to more conflict and hostility, lowest common denominator compromises, or submission of disputes to higher levels of management for arbitration. In general conflict is detrimental to overall project performance and will make it almost impossible for a project attitude to develop.

On the other hand, conflict between groups can actually enhance the cohesion and team spirit of the individual group. Competition does stimulate individuals and groups to greater performance in a similar way that it stimulates an athlete to give of his best. Group loyalty will increase, differences will be buried within the group and there will be a greater commitment to the group objective, but not necessarily to the project objectives. They will tend to close ranks against a common enemy, that is the other groups. Within these groups there is thus a more purposeful atmosphere, and probably more autocratic leadership patterns, more structuring and organisation, more in-group loyalty and conformity for a solid front to the 'enemy'. The group within itself tends to be more effective in achieving its own objectives where co-ordination and interaction with other groups is not required. Though this may be advantageous for the individual group, it will prevent the formation of horizontal and mixed groups and lead to poorer overall project performance.

Reasons for conflict

It is probable that whenever individuals are involved together in any undertaking or operation that, given the variations that exist in human nature, there will always be differences and thus a potential for conflict. One of the basic reasons for this in a company is that there is a division of labour (functionalisation) and this inherently creates groups with different sets of values and objectives. In almost every medium sized and large company there tends to be to a greater or lesser extent, antipathy or conflict between line and staff, and between different functions, for example, marketing and production, operations and engineering.

Each group will have a different set of values and given the same information, even with goodwill between groups, they will often come up with different points of view, or decisions based on these values. For example, the design engineering groups will want to design the project to the highest technical standards, whereas the project group will want to compromise between time, cost and technical standards. This will influence their points of view on many decisions and problems and will inevitably lead to disagreement with a potential for conflict. It will also lead to differences between objectives between groups in the same company. For example, the operations people will want a production plant which is easy to operate, has many installed spare pieces of equipment, capacity for expansion and possibly some items which would be classified as luxuries by the project staff. The project group will want to balance time to completion and overall cost against performance standards, and thus they will have different points of view, values and objectives, and inevitably there will be differences and thus a potential for conflict. Requests for changes to design, as discussed previously, are also a source of conflict between the design, project, construction, manufacturing and operations groups within a company.

There will also tend to be competition between these divisions of labour, that is, groups, in the same company for dominance within the company, (for example, production is the prime department and 'what they say goes') and for resources of men, money and promotion. There is also the problem of priorities and competition between projects for scarce resources. Certain groups involved in a project may be handling several projects at the same time, and their managers may have to allocate their resources to the various projects in a way that the project managers of the individual projects may not like. This leads to differences, and hence conflict between the project manager and the managers of these functional groups, and also between project managers in the company for these scarce resources.

This difference in values and objectives will also extend to the owner and contractor company groups working on a project. The contractor is in business to make a profit and he can only do this at the expense of the owner, or so the owner thinks. The owner wants to minimise the cost of the contract, which he can partially do at the expense of a contractor, or so the contractor thinks. The extreme expression of this is in the cost plus contract. In the worst situation the contractor, or so the owner's staff consciously or subconsciously believes, wants to maximise the cost of the project, at the expense of the owner, to maximise his profit. Thus the owner's staff will tend to supervise the contractor closely, question his decisions and performance, and from the contractor's point of view, interfere far too much. In a fixed price contract, the extra cost of changes will be a source of friction as discussed previously.

The problems arising from the division of labour in the normal firm are increased when the matrix organisation is used. There tend to be many groups involved in the typical project and there is thus the potential for conflict at each group interface. The project management group needs to be involved in the planning and control of the work of all groups in the project and this can be resented. Where responsibility and authority are unclear, there is always the potential for conflict, and functional managers and contractors' managers will always tend to believe that the project manager is impinging on their territory or authority, but he must do to do his job effectively. The dual subordination of a functional group member to the project manager and functional manager can lead him to feel insecure in his position, and the functional manager may also resent the project manager's interference or, as he believes, reduction of his authority. With a contractor, contractual relationships may be unclear and this will always tend to cause conflict.

In a project, people are always working under pressure, and the project manager must always be a hustler, and thus will be applying more pressure to people to meet time and cost objectives, and this in itself can lead to conflict. When added to the role and territory uncertainties, it will enhance the personal stress that people are working under, emotions will be raised, tempers will be short and conflict can easily arise.

When groups or companies have different managerial philosophies, there will inevitably be differences. There will also be personality clashes in any organisation. There also tend to be problems with defensive behaviour by managers whereby they are reluctant to implement change, act on their own, delegate, take risks and make decisions. This can arise when a manager is promoted beyond his abilities, where a technologist has been promoted to a managerial position and either has not adjusted to the managerial requirements, or is now out of touch with the technology he came from and he feels insecure. There is also occasionally a rogue manager involved who is determined to succeed at the expense of everyone else. He may be autocratic, ruthless and willing to stab other managers in the back to get on. Not only does this in itself cause conflict, but the other managers involved will probably react to defend themselves, and teamwork will be lost.

There are also problems which by themselves in a healthy team would not create conflict, but when coupled with one or more of the other problems described will cause conflict. These include differences in technical opinion, differences in time, cost and technical standards and strong personal commitment to one line of action.

The methods used to resolve conflict can often in themselves cause resentment and thus lead to further conflict. In resolving differences there are several strategies a manager or group can follow. For example:

1 Forcing through their point of view by the use of formal or informal authority. The naked use of over-riding power may gain the point in question, but it will probably ensure a lack of commitment to carry it out and increased feelings of resentment and hostility.
2 Submission of the differences to a high authority, which will lead to the same result for the loser.
3 Withdrawal from the confrontation and sulk, with the same result.
4 Compromise at a low level of agreement with the probable result that both groups will lose and feel resentment.
5 Work through the differences in a frank and honest way with mutual trust and respect. This is essentially the ideal response from an effective team and the principal way of diminishing hostility and conflict, but unless one has trust and respect it is difficult to implement; which comes first the chicken or the egg?

Finally, one of the principal reasons for conflict is a history of previous hostility and conflict. At any one point in time there may be ill feeling between groups in a company which has built up over the years and which is very difficult to resolve within the temporary lifespan of a project. This may be the project manager's own company or it may be one company in the global organisation. There is generally a new global organisation for every project, and any one of the companies involved may have this situation, which if not resolved for the individual project, can spread through the total organisation like a disease.

The resolution of conflict

One of the project manager's principal tasks is that of an integrator and as such, the management, prevention and resolution of conflict is his responsibility. It is often impossible to eliminate differences, disagreements and competition, and it is questionable if it is advisable to do so. An organisation without visible signs of these natural human traits is normally mediocre, overly conformist and a dull place to work in. These factors contribute to better performance, problem solving, innovation, decision making and commitment to objectives, provided they are constructive. If they are about how best to carry out the project, then they are beneficial to the project. It is when they degenerate, and the project is not so important as scoring over the opposition, that conflict is harmful to achieving the project objectives.

A method of resolving differences, without creating conflict, is not to deny that they exist, but to accept that they occur naturally and to endeavour to resolve them by the logic of the situation. This is not just appealing to the groups to be objective, but also to take into account the more non-tangible contributors to conflict. If there can be frank and open discussion, that is, levelling, and a mutual analysis of the problem and the solution with respect for the other's point of view, then differences can be worked through and resolved without adverse conflict. This can lead to a greater understanding and commitment to the outcome, and if successful contributes to the growth of an effective team. Unfortunately the working through of differences in this manner is one of the attributes of an effective team, and without having the makings of an effective team it is difficult to achieve; a chicken and egg problem again. Thus the problem the project manager is faced with is how to create the conditions, and how to provide the leadership and management that will increase the chances of an effective team evolving and prevent or reduce the likelihood of adverse conflict arising.

The various steps he can take can be classified into three sets, namely:

1 Formal organisational steps.
2 Informal organisational steps.
3 Managerial or personal behaviour steps.

Motivating the Participants

The biggest advantage the project manager has is, as before, that there exists what the behavioural scientists call a superordinate objective, that is, the project itself. It has been shown that the biggest factor leading to a reduction of conflict is for all the groups to have a common objective to which they are committed and that requires them to interact with each other. Thus if the project attitude can be established, the project manager is half way or more to defusing adverse conflict. In addition, project work is normally challenging work, and when individuals are involved in challenging work there is less likelihood of conflict.

To encourage the establishment of this superordinate objective, all the organisations involved must emphasise that the criterion of individual and group performance is the total project organisation's effectiveness, and not that of the individual or single group. This involves such factors as performance assessments and salary increases and promotions being based on overall project performance, and thus the project manager having a say in these factors. It also involves the companies concerned recognising that the global project organisation is an entity which exists, and giving it due recognition.

To ensure that commitment to the project is built up and maintained the project manager must have a formal and informal information system that keeps everyone involved informed of progress and permits open communication. The project objectives, progress, problems and success must be communicated to everyone involved. There must also be as clear a definition as is possible of the responsibilities of those involved. The use of the work breakdown structure, cost accounts, work packages and matrix of organisation charts enables individuals right down the line to know what these responsibilities are, who they must interact with and the role of the project manager.

Not only must formal organisational factors be used to encourage the formation of an effective mixed project group, but so should informal factors. This implies encouraging the formation of informal group and social interaction between groups, for example, involvement in sports, having dinners together, dances, cocktail parties and having coffee and lunch in the same group. Physical factors should be used to stimulate project groups; for example, a common office for those involved, partitioned areas instead of a large 'bull-pen', visits to each other's companies. It is not generally possible to form an effective team with people you don't know fairly well, and thus both the owner and contractor should encourage prolonged visits of key personnel to each other's offices. Once people have had face to face contact and know each other, physical proximity is not essential in the long term. Without this, communication will be limited to formal channels, and without informal information channels, effective communication between groups will be greatly handicapped.

In dealing with the people and groups involved in his project, the project manager must be aware of the likelihood and hazards of conflict, and use tact in his dealings. Though he must of necessity use pressure, he must be aware that if pushed too hard into a corner, an individual can only resist, and the harder the project manager pushes, the harder the individual will push back. Therefore he must show respect for and listen to opposing points of view, and on occasions he may have to compromise and back down on a point, in a conscious effort to manage conflict. He cannot afford to become too emotionally involved and he must at all times keep calm. One of the basic lessons of management is that if you cannot manage your own emotions in the workplace, you cannot manage other people.

The project manager must be aware of the problems involved in the other functions involved in the project, and this often involves rotation of personnel among the basic functions. The project manager who has worked for both an owner and a contractor company will be in a better position to appreciate the other 'side's' problems and position. Finally, the project manager must be aware that in a matrix organisation he is impinging on other managers' roles, authority and territory, and he must do so with caution, respect and tact. Given all that, he must still attempt to minimise time and cost on his project and he is not in a popularity contest. At times he must throw caution to the winds and go 'bull headed' for what he believes to be necessary, but he must also be aware of the consequences and the alternatives. An effective team will respond to a greater challenge with more commitment to succeed, and he may be able to achieve his objectives without creating conflict.

25
Integrated Systems for Planning and Control

Ray Palmer

A typical project includes a number of areas and disciplines which often operate as separate, autonomous units. Major benefits can be reaped from bringing them together. This approach is termed 'integration'. Integration is the key to effective project management and yet until recently the whole concept of integrated systems had been almost impossible to apply in practice. Several key developments during the past five to ten years have created a situation where not only are integrated systems possible, they are now viewed as an essential element of successful project management. A major factor in making integrated systems available to the project team has been the revolution in computer technology. Not only have computers become faster, smaller and more easily available, but there have been fundamental changes in the nature of computer programs. Just ten years ago, using a computer required expert assistance. Nowadays, comprehensive project control systems are available that can be operated directly by the project team itself. Areas such as planning, resource scheduling, costing, design management, procurement, commissioning, in fact every aspect of project control can now be effectively managed by the project team.

THE PROJECT MANAGEMENT PROCESS

In its broadest sense, project management can be considered as a combination of the tasks of planning, co-ordinating and controlling resources such as men, machines, materials and money in order to meet the objectives of a project.

The time-tested approach begins with the formal process of planning the work and then deciding when each part of the work will take place, what resources it will require, what it will cost, and so on. In short, creating a yardstick against which the steps required to achieve the objectives can be measured. But, the problem with plans is that they cannot always be adhered to. Bad weather, low productivity, design changes, and a thousand and one other factors continually undermine the validity of the original plan. In an attempt to minimise the effect of these changes, an almost continual re-planning of the project is required to incorporate new information affecting the project.

This process of constantly re-planning ranges from day-to-day changes in the sequence of work, the allocation of equipment, materials, and manpower to meet local conditions, to formal reviews where the whole plan is revised. This process is often described as the control cycle, although this tends to suggest a far more formalised and considered process than the complex mixture of formal and informal changes that actually occurs in practice.

Decision making

The fundamental element in controlling a project is decision making. To make reasonable and rational decisions a number of conditions must be met. Information relevant to the problem in hand must first be isolated. Often this is the most difficult part of the process and, in practice, the majority of decisions are made in the knowledge that much relevant information is submerged in the mass of project related data, and is not available on demand. When as much relevant information as possible has been gathered, the process of deciding the most appropriate course of action can begin. In most cases there will be several options and the usual process is to evaluate each one in turn and then choose the most appropriate. This is in fact the approach we intuitively use in the solving of all kinds of day-to-day problems. We automatically build a mental 'model' of the situation and test various alternatives against it, forecast the outcome for each possible combination of circumstances, and then choose the most appropriate. A simple everyday illustration of this is in choosing a holiday. It is usual to examine the alternatives in terms of cost, convenience, likely enjoyment, and so on, and then to choose the option that most closely meets the objectives. The 'model' in this case is the mental image of how all these factors combine to make a good holiday.

The project model

A project is of course a much more complex undertaking than choosing a holiday. It may well require thousands of material items, drawings, and individual tasks, combined with many different types of resources and complicated cost/time relationships. A mental model is not adequate to evaluate the astronomic number of possible ways of carrying out the job. Indeed, to encompass every eventuality, the project model would need to incorporate all the factors that could possibly have an impact upon the project management process.

To be of practical use it also has to cope with the many subobjectives that are the realities of project work, such as the need to minimise overtime, increase productivity, reduce plant movement, and so on. In real life each and every aspect of a project is interrelated and interdependent. A delayed material delivery, for example, may well require a section of a project to be rescheduled. This in turn changes the required delivery dates for other materials, which can in turn affect the procurement process and ultimately, priorities in the design office. In an extreme case, the overall timing of much of the rest of the work can be affected, along with the associated cash flow, borrowing requirements, and profit margin.

With an *integrated* system the project information is interrelated and interdependent in *exactly* the same way as in real life. This can have a dramatic impact on the effectiveness of the project team. In decision making, for example, several options can be run through and tested to see the effect on each aspect of the project and examine the cost effectiveness of alternative approaches in detail before any action is taken.

The decision reached may on the basis of a clear-cut cost benefit or a complex trade-off between a number of conflicting factors. Without an integrated system, the decision can only be based on limited information, rudimentary costings, and virtually no evaluation of alternatives. With an integrated system the project team can be confident in the knowledge that they are making well informed, rational and cost justified decisions across all relevant aspects of their project.

An integrated system is essential for effective decision making. It also provides a project or even company-wide communication medium: this is (or should be) consistent in each area of application. The day-to-day work of collecting time-sheet data, or details of material deliveries is all part of the project and as such is an essential element of the integrated system. The ability to incorporate such detailed information means that the process of managing the project is based on real information that is directly available to the project team. This information should be available not just in its detailed form, but 'rolled-up' and summarised in the appropriate form for the task at hand.

The scope and complexity of integrated systems varies considerably. At one extreme, companies limit themselves to integrating cost and schedule data and at the other, there are systems that incorporate almost every aspect of a company's work. Integration can be applied to individual projects or to a number of projects running concurrently and can include central, head office work such as buying and accounts. Integration can also be viewed as extending throughout the life of a project. Information generated at the design stage is subsequently used for construction, commissioning and eventually for maintaining the resulting product.

THE REQUIREMENTS FOR INTEGRATION

Until recent years, computer assistance was not directly available to the project team. A number of computerised project management tools existed such as 'critical path analysis' and 'cost control', but these were stand-alone applications, each designed to meet *one* need in *isolation*. Integration of these techniques varied from being 'impossible' to 'possible with difficulty'. Often too, it was difficult to enhance individual applications. For example, adding an extra cost code or producing a non-standard report, could involve weeks of a computer programmer's time. Now, with computers becoming more easily available, more powerful and with dramatic software advances, a fully integrated system addressing every aspect of project

Integrated Systems for Planning and Control

management can be achieved. Although a fully integrated project control system was theoretically possible by manual methods, advances in computing now make it a reality.

Merely having a computer and a range of application packages is not however enough in itself. A successful integrated system requires a number of essential additional features. There are a number of systems which meet these requirements to a greater or lesser extent. The author's experience is of one of these systems, ARTEMIS (by Metier Management Systems), from which the following examples are drawn.

Man-machine interface

The concept of integrated systems would have remained an academic exercise had it not been for developments in the so called 'man-machine interface' — broadly the way in which we understand and communicate with computers. In this respect, it is vital that the system has the support, involvement, and commitment of the project team. *Any* obstacle presented by the system will adversely affect this situation. Metier's early research, now confirmed by their clients, is that acceptance and use of a computer system is related to several key factors:

1 The system must be based on a simple concept, and must be easy to understand and to use. This is especially necessary if staff other than computing personnel are to use it.
2 The language used to communicate with the computer system should be simple, and as much like everyday language as possible. Once again, this is necessary if the system is to be available for use by project staff rather than by computing experts.
3 It should be possible to produce and to amend reports rapidly and easily, so that project managers can react to the changing requirements for information.
4 The system should enable information from all project areas to be brought together as and when required by the changing needs of the project environment.
5 There must be a rapid method for implementing project control applications, and for their subsequent modification or enhancement to meet changing requirements.

Each of these 'man-machine' factors is essential for successful integration. The absence of any one factor will inhibit the successful adoption and use of the system. The examples given later are based upon this understanding and it is worth looking at the practical implications in more detail.

A simple concept

In practice it has been found that the simple analogy of a filing system is an ideal method for understanding the fundamental principles of database systems. Surprisingly, the analogy holds up well in a project environment, only being replaced by more sophisticated concepts for complex and extensive systems.

If the storage of information about (say) drawings is considered using purely manual methods, one would maintain a record of all relevant information on cards — one for each drawing — which would be kept in a filing cabinet drawer or drawers. Each card might list:

1. Drawing number.
2. Drawing description or title.
3. Date drawn.
4. Date first issued.
5. Subsequent revision numbers and issue dates.
6. Etc.

For a complete project records system there would probably be a considerable number of other filing cabinet drawers, containing information on subjects such as materials, costs and the project schedule.

With an integrated computer system, the storage of information can be viewed in exactly the same way. This is illustrated in Figure 25.1, in which:

1. There is a 'card' for each drawing (called a 'record').
2. Each individual item of information on the record is called a 'field'.
3. The 'filing drawer or drawers' containing each set of records is called a 'dataset'.
4. The complete collection of all the 'filing cabinets' is called the 'database'.

Integrated Systems for Planning and Control

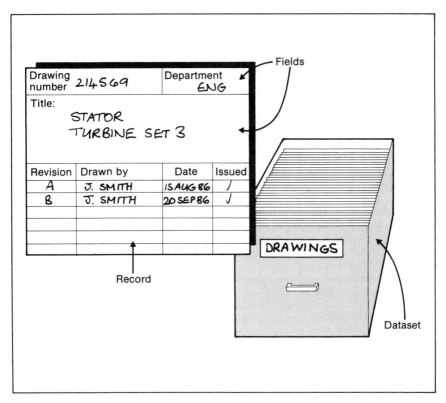

Figure 25.1 Dataset principles

With a manual system there is more or less total freedom to decide what information should be kept for each drawing and the number of cards in the file. The number of different sets of information is limited only by the amount of space available in which to store them. The ARTEMIS system enables the user to design his own record cards, and create a virtually unlimited number of 'datasets' in which to store his information. The above example uses drawings but of course each element of the project, materials, manpower, money, and so on, can be held in datasets in exactly the same way.

Thus, as a basic concept, ARTEMIS mirrors manual methods and enables users to develop systems that reflect the 'natural' organisation of information.

An extension of this analogy is to think of the computer system as a 'super-clerk', with unlimited ability to store, recall and combine information and present it as printed or graphical reports — all in response to the 'conversation-like' commands of the user.

Communicating with the system

A number of approaches are possible in communicating with the system. Advances in computing now enable the user to carry on an 'interactive conversation' with the system, but this has only been available to project teams since the mid-1970s.

Historically, using 'batch' processing computers, it was necessary to prepare a list of instructions on punch cards and then feed them to the computer. These cards would typically tell the machine which programs were needed, which data to use and which reports to produce. Preparing the data, having the cards punched and then submitting the job to the computer centre could often take anything from several hours to several days. The frustration of then discovering that a vital instruction had been omitted, causing the 'run' to fail, caused many project people to look for alternatives that could produce more immediate results.

The breakthrough came with 'interactive' computing, where the user carries on a conversation with the computer. The nature of this 'conversation' can vary from the computer acting on a spoken instruction, (an approach still being developed), to the now familiar arcade game method of using a joy-stick. Somewhere between these two extremes are the more usual 'menu' and 'command' driven systems, both of which are appropriate to the project environment.

The so-called 'menu' approach is where the system offers a list of options on the VDU screen. The user indicates his choice, usually by typing the appropriate number or letter. In the following example, the system is giving the user a choice of three report types. By entering the number '2' after the command 'GIVE NUMBER' the user has requested the 'COST THIS MONTH' report, which the computer proceeds to print.

```
         WHICH REPORT DO YOU WANT?
         1    CRITICAL ACTIVITIES
         2    COST THIS MONTH
         3    RESOURCE FORECAST
         GIVE NUMBER 2
         REPORT BEING PRINTED
```

This can be useful where the overall extent of the system is limited. Problems occur when there are many options available or a non-standard report is required. For a limited application, used infrequently, the menu approach can be the ideal means of conversing with the computer.

The alternative approach of using a command language enables the user to converse in English-like phrases. Typical ARTEMIS commands include:

> PRINT REPORT FRED
> which produces a printed report that the user has previously specified, in this case report Fred.
>
> DISPLAY IF RESOURCE IS FITTER
> which displays on the terminal screen all the activities involving fitters.
>
> DISPLAY TITLE IF START AFTER 1-JUNE-87
> an enquiry asking for the title of, in this case, drawings where the production starts after a particular date.

The advantage of the command language approach is that the user can specify exactly what is required without having to pass through several menus. The ideal arrangement is perhaps a combination of both approaches: a menu system for simple repetitive tasks and a command language for those aspects of the system that require fast response to a variety of changing circumstances.

In an integrated system the approach should be consistent across all the applications, all the system facilities such as producing printed reports, plotting graphic reports, carrying out calculations, and even in communicating to other systems. This brings benefits in that the users can use any part of the system without the need for additional training — the method of operation and the commands required are all predictable and consequently reassuring to the user.

Producing reports

Reports are the primary means of communicating information. A general rule for designing reports is that they should contain *just* the information for the task in hand. In the fast moving projects world, it is also essential that the reports can be easily and quickly modified to keep pace with changing requirements.

```
METIER      DRAWING  LISTING              ARTEMIS
Client   : METIER MANAGEMENT SYSTEMS      Project Start   :  1-JAN-85
Location : METIER HOUSE, LONDON           Timenow         :  1-JAN-85
Project Name: ARTEMIS                     Project Complete: 24-JUL-86
```

DRAWING NUMBER	DRAWING DESCRIPTION	ACTIVITY CODE	DATE REQUIRED	FORCAST ISSUE	DRAWN BY	DATE DRAWN	DATE SUBMITTED	DATE APPROVED	DATE ISSUED
E261	PIPING & INSTRUMENTS E06	9798	5-JAN-85						
E262	E06 PIPEWORK LAYOUT	9798	5-JAN-85						
E271	PIPING & INSTRUMENTS E04	6162	6-JAN-85	6-JAN-85	TRJ	20-DEC-84	22-DEC-84	1-JAN-85	6-JAN-85
E302	M.ENG. COOLING PIPEWORK	E4E7	30-JAN-85	30-JAN-85	HYJ	8-JAN-85	10-JAN-85	20-JAN-85	

Figure 25.2 Selective drawings report

Integrated Systems for Planning and Control

An effective project system will include a comprehensive and flexible 'report generator'. This will be used by the project team members themselves and should take into account the need for simple and direct operation. Using the ARTEMIS system, for example, existing reports can be comprehensively modified within a few minutes using simple commands. Take a situation where, because of problems on-site, a specific report is required which identifies all the pipe-work related drawings. Supposing the 'standard' report, report DRAW, is the drawings register, containing information on 1000 drawings, the pipework drawings can be quickly isolated as follows:

> PRINT REPORT DRAW
> SELECT IF TITLE CONTAINS 'PIPE'

The standard report DRAW is now printed but with only the piping drawings. (See Figure 25.2.)

In practice, there are several other commands that could be used:

ORDER — to put the items on the report in a particular sequence, perhaps by date or drawing number, as required.

DIVIDE — to divide the report, page by page, into a particular grouping, perhaps by department or by approval status and so on.

BAR — to add a printed bar-chart to each page, illustrating the dates in the drawing production cycle.

HISTOGRAM — to add a printed histogram to each page. This could show the drawing production rate or the number of draughtsmen required at particular times.

Indeed, all the fields of information in the drawings dataset can be included or excluded as required.

Integrating information

The situation could of course be more complex and require us to discover when each of these pipework drawings is required on-site for assembly. This requires the integration of information held in two

Managing Progress and Performance

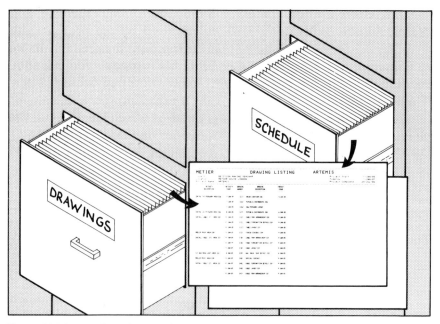

Figure 25.3 Integration of Information

separate datasets. The drawing information is, as we know, in the drawings dataset, but the pipework installation dates are held in the overall construction schedule. In order to integrate these separate sets of information we need an additional ARTEMIS command:

> PRINT REPORT DRAW
> USE SCHEDULE
> SELECT IF TITLE CONTAINS 'PIPE'

The second line (the USE line) joins the two datasets together and links the drawings to their corresponding site activities. All that remains is to specify which fields of information the user would like to see in the combined report. These steps are illustrated in Figures 25.3 and 25.4.

Rapid implementation and modification

The approach of using an all encompassing command language coupled with the ability to create new datasets as required are the

METIER			DRAWING LISTING	ARTEMIS	
Client	: DECISION MAKING SEMINAR			Project Start :	1-JAN-85
Location	: METIER HOUSE, LONDON			Timenow :	1-JAN-85
Project Name:	ARTEMIS			Project Complete:	24-JUL-86
ACTIVITY DESCRIPTION	ACTIVITY START	DRAWING NUMBER	DRAWING DESCRIPTION	FORCAST ISSUE	
INSTAL SYS PIPEWORK AREA E06	7-JAN-85	E231	VALVE LOCATION E06	5-JAN-85	
	7-JAN-85	E261	PIPING & INSTRUMENTS E06		
	7-JAN-85	E262	E06 PIPEWORK LAYOUT		
INSTAL SYS PIPEWORK AREA E04	8-JAN-85	E271	PIPING & INSTRUMENTS E04	6-JAN-85	
INSTALL CABLES ETC. AREA E01	11-JAN-85	E321	CABLE TRAY ARRANGEMENT E01	9-JAN-85	
	11-JAN-85	E322	CABLE TERMINATTION DETAILS E01	9-JAN-85	
	11-JAN-85	E323	CABLE LAYOUT E01	9-JAN-85	
PRELIM PAINT AREA E04	11-JAN-85	E331	FINISH SCHEDULE E04	9-JAN-85	
INSTALL CABLES ETC. AREA E01	11-JAN-85	E381	CABLE TRAY ARRANGEMENT E01	9-JAN-85	
	11-JAN-85	E382	CABLE TERMINATTION DETAILS E01	9-JAN-85	
	11-JAN-85	E383	CABLE LAYOUT E01	9-JAN-85	
FIT AUX MACH SEATS AREA E02	4-JAN-85	E391	AUX. MACH. SEAT DETAILS E02	4-JAN-85	
PRELIM PAINT AREA E04	11-JAN-85	E401	SPECIAL FINISHES	9-JAN-85	
INSTALL CABLES ETC. AREA E01	11-JAN-85	E402	CABLE TERMINATTION DETAILS E01	9-JAN-85	
	11-JAN-85	E403	CABLE LAYOUT E01	9-JAN-85	
	11-JAN-85	E431	CABLE TRAY ARRANGEMENT E01	9-JAN-85	
From the project schedule		From the drawings dataset			

Figure 25.4 Combined report from integrated information

basic building blocks for producing or extending project systems. The approach, broadly termed 'fourth generation', is many times faster than using more traditional, 'third generation' languages such as COBOL and FORTRAN. With a system such as ARTEMIS, the approach is further enhanced by the use of in-built project management facilities such as network analysis, scheduling, and cost calculations. In practice a fully integrated cost/scheduling system can be created from scratch in a matter of weeks. In fact, by using pre-built applications, even this time can be reduced.

This pre-built applications approach can be very effective. With sufficient experience the supplier can design-in 80 per cent of the users' needs in (say) an application such as cost control. When the system is installed either the supplier or the project team can quickly finalise the application, modifying it to meet the exact needs of the project. In the case of cost control this could include adding company cost codes, modifying report formats and adjusting calculation routines to match the existing company practices. In the case of an

ARTEMIS application not only can the project team carry out the final 'tailoring' but the experience of doing this means they are ideally placed to modify the system should it become necessary.

INTEGRATING THE REQUIREMENTS OF PROJECT STAFF

To be effective, information must reach all those who need it in a form which they can easily interpret. Failure to meet this fundamental requirement nullifies the purpose of the whole system. In the past, systems were viewed as tools for processing information. The question of tailoring the output to meet the users' needs was rarely considered. A common experience was that of receiving a stack of computer printout, without being able to discover why it had been produced.

In an integrated system the storage of data is designed around each user's view of the system. This means that the information he receives reflects this structure and, as it were, speaks to him in his own language, using *his* perception of the project.

Take, for example, a materials expediter in a typical project environment. His primary concerns are the materials required, the dates when they are required and the manufacturing location for each item. The expediter's view of the world could be considered to be that shown in Figure 25.5.

In dataset terms, therefore, it is possible to visualise the information being pulled together to generate the appropriate reports. Typical reports for the expediter could include:

1 Materials required on site in the next four weeks.
2 Late materials only, grouped by vendor or manufacturer.
3 All materials expected ex-works this week.

A typical report is shown in Figure 25.6.

The advantage to the expediter is obvious. The information he receives is tailored for his specific needs and, what is more, is drawn from the up to date situation in all the appropriate parts of the project. And, because the system can pin-point problem areas, each report contains only the items requiring action. Typical ARTEMIS selection commands could include:

Integrated Systems for Planning and Control

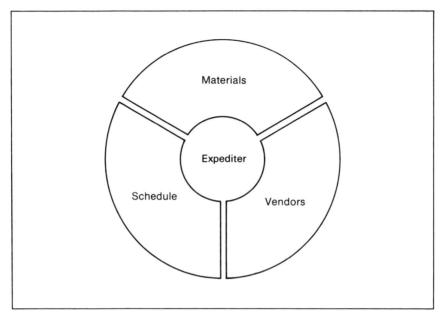

Figure 25.5 A user's view
The expediter sees only particular aspects of the database content as having relevance to him, and it is necessary to arrange that the reports can select the appropriate data and combine it for his application

SELECT IF DELIVERY AFTER 20-JUN-87

SELECT IF DELIVERY AFTER 15-SEP-87 AND SUPPLIER IS SMITHS AND DELAY > 10, (The > 10 is a shorthand way of indicating 'greater-than 10 weeks')

Graphical reports

A picture is worth a thousand words. The ability to use graphics to communicate project information is invaluable. In some circumstances, examining a chart for a few seconds can give a complete understanding of what could otherwise be thousands of pieces of data. Take for example the traditional activity lists produced from a simple, project planning system. Written out as a list of activity descriptions, start dates, finish dates, floats, and so on, it becomes difficult to interpret. As a diagram, though, the sequence of work is obvious, the relative timing of the work can be seen at a glance, and

```
METIER            PURCHASE ORDER SCHEDULE                    ARTEMIS
Client   : METIER MANAGEMENT SYSTEMS           Project Start    :  1-JAN-85
Location : METIER HOUSE,LONDON                 Timenow          :  1-JAN-85
Project Name: ARTEMIS                          Project Complete : 24-JUL-86
```

MATERIAL CODE	MATERIAL DESCRIPTION	JOB NUMBER	VENDOR CODE	REQ'N NUMBER	REQ'N LINE ITEM	LEAD TIME (DAYS)	REQUIRED DELIVERY DATE	EXPECTED DELIVERY DATE	REQUIRED PURCHASE DATE	PURCHASE ORDER DATE
MT101	50CM BOLTS	EN1869	19054	101	1	20	4-JAN-85	11-JAN-86	8-DEC-85	16-DEC-85
MT104	2CM * 12CM OAK	EN1869	09189	104	2	58	4-JAN-85	28-DEC-85	31-OCT-85	25-OCT-85
MT121	LIGHTBULBS	EN1869	25006	161	2	78	4-JAN-85	28-DEC-85	11-OCT-85	5-OCT-85
MT124	COPPER WIRING	EN1889	25006	104	1	30	4-JAN-85	11-JAN-86	28-NOV-85	6-DEC-85
MT151	ELECTRICAL WIRING	EN1889	25006	151	2	98	4-JAN-85	28-DEC-85	21-SEP-85	15-SEP-85
MT152	ELECTRICAL JOINERS	EN1889	25006	152	1	101	4-JAN-85	11-JAN-86	18-SEP-85	26-SEP-85
MT153	CROCODILE CLIPS	EN1889	25006	153	1	47	4-JAN-85	11-JAN-86	11-NOV-85	19-NOV-85
MT101	50CM BOLTS	EN1854	19054	101	2	20	5-JAN-85	29-DEC-85	9-DEC-85	3-DEC-85
MT104	2CM*12CM OAK	EN1854	09189	104	4	58	5-JAN-85	4-JAN-86	4-NOV-85	1-NOV-85
MT121	LIGHTBULBS	EN1854	25006	161	3	78	5-JAN-85	5-JAN-86	12-OCT-85	13-OCT-85
MT124	COPPER WIRING	EN1894	25006	104	3	30	5-JAN-85	5-JAN-86	29-NOV-85	30-NOV-85
MT151	ELECTRICAL WIRING	EN1894	25006	151	3	98	5-JAN-85	5-JAN-86	22-SEP-85	23-SEP-85
MT152	ELECTRICAL JOINERS	EN1894	25006	152	2	101	5-JAN-85	29-DEC-85	19-SEP-85	13-SEP-85
MT153	CROCODILE CLIPS	EN1894	25006	153	2	47	5-JAN-85	29-DEC-85	12-NOV-85	6-NOV-85
MT163	5CM PIPING	EN1934	02458	161	5	21	5-JAN-85	22-DEC-85	8-DEC-85	27-NOV-85
MT165	STEEL PIPES	EN1934	01110	165	1	15	5-JAN-85	12-JAN-86	14-DEC-85	22-DEC-85
MT169	2CM PIPING	EN1934	02458	999	23	60	5-JAN-85	22-DEC-85	30-OCT-85	19-OCT-85
MT101	50CM BOLTS	FR1874	19054	101	5	20	6-JAN-85	3-JAN-85	10-DEC-85	29-NOV-85
MT104	2CM*12CM OAK	FR1874	09189	104	5	58	6-JAN-85	3-JAN-95	2-NOV-85	22-OCT-85
MT121	LIGHTBULBS	FR1874	25006	161	4	78	6-JAN-85	5-JAN-86	13-OCT-85	13-OCT-85
MT165	STEEL PIPES	FR1939	01110	165	2	15	6-JAN-85	30-DEC-85	15-NOV-85	9-DEC-85
MT164	SAFETY PLUGS	EN1884	25006	164	1	50	11-JAN-85	18-JAN-86	15-NOV-85	23-NOV-85
MT121	LIGHTBULBS	FR1909	25006	161	8	78	15-MAR-85	3-MAR-86	21-DEC-85	10-DEC-85
MT151	ELECTRICAL WIRING	FR1909	25006	151	2	98	15-MAR-85	8-MAR-86	1-DEC-85	25-NOV-85

Figure 25.6 Typical expediter's report
This combines information from the materials, schedule and vendors' datasets

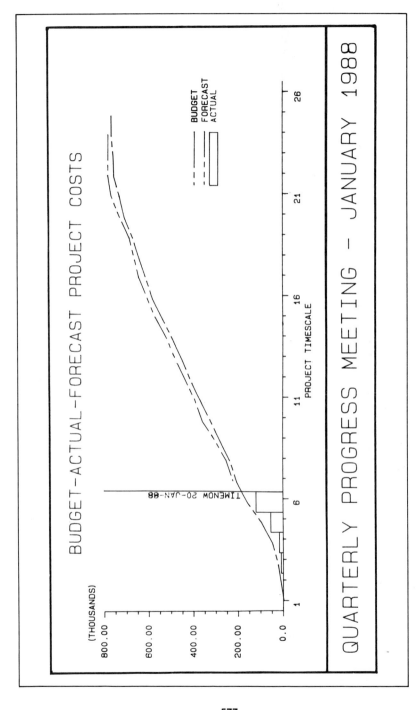

Figure 25.7 A cost forecast in graphical form

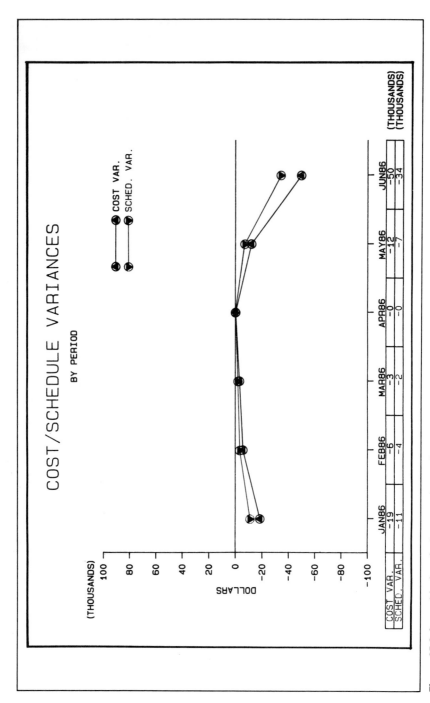

Figure 25.8 A graphical project summary report

Integrated Systems for Planning and Control

colour can be used to highlight critical work and show progress. As a means of communication it is excellent.

In an integrated system, however, the opportunities for using graphics are enormously increased. Almost every area of the system can benefit from the increased clarity that using project graphics brings.

Take for example cost forecasting, this is effectively the complex combination of cost and schedule information. As a chart, the position can be summarised on one piece of paper, as illustrated in Figure 25.7.

Quite sophisticated concepts can be used in conjunction with graphical output. In Figure 25.8 a report is shown which combines the results from progress monitoring, the schedule, and costs to give the overall status of a project in summary form.

Vertical integration

Another feature of a fully integrated system is what could be termed 'vertical integration'. Many of the available project planning systems fall down at this crucial stage. Stated simply: Without the ability to *implement* the carefully considered decision of the project team, the whole system is reduced to a conceptual exercise. An effective system must convert plans to actions *and* provide an effective means of monitoring and controlling progress. In fact this whole process can be viewed as a hierarchy of project control, as illustrated in Figure 25.9.

Referring to Figure 25.9, a number of stand-alone computer systems are capable of dealing with the top part of the triangle, the decision making and modelling part of the process. Many systems are available for the varieties of tasks which compose the lower levels of control.

Again, without a complete, integrated system, each level in the hierarchy is effectively isolated from the other. Summarised information cannot be automatically generated and so the manager finds himself without a solid basis for his decisions. He could of course demand that the information of a particular type be collected and summarised as required, but the variety and quantity of information needed would soon render this approach impractical. What is required is an automated means of producing the necessary summaries on a routine or an *ad hoc* basis.

Managing Progress and Performance

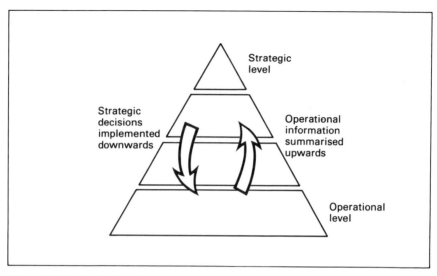

Figure 25.9 Vertical integration

These gaps in the information hierarchy also mean that management decisions cannot be directly implemented at the working level. Complex instructions, for example requiring the quality assurance testing of particular types of components for a specific area of a large project by a team of QA staff, could require considerable manual effort in simply identifying the appropriate components. An integrated system can identify the components, the suppliers, the appropriate QA persons, and reference the documentation, delivery dates, and relevant specifications! Not just that, but it can also produce the information in the form of reports: an inspection schedule, a delivery schedule highlighting potential delays, a purchase order summary showing each supplier's details and delivery commitments, and so on.

In other words a fully integrated system operates at all levels in the project hierarchy and facilitates effective communications both up and down.

INTEGRATING THE COMPUTER HARDWARE

Concerned with the cost of a new system, many new computer users limit their risk by buying the cheapest possible option to address their most pressing need. This will often be a micro-based system. This is relatively successful so they buy another to handle a second application. Eventually there are several micros dotted around the project. Having now spent the equivalent of the cost of a full function project management system, it seems an obvious step to bring all these micros into one integrated system. This is where the problems start. The individual micros were not designed to communicate with each other. Even if they could, the applications are written by different software vendors in different languages. At this stage everyone falls back on manual methods to try to integrate the separate components. Reports are prepared by each independent discipline and passed up the project hierarchy, leaving the all-essential integration to be carried out in the minds of the middle and senior managers. Horizontal integration between disciplines also suffers. Cost/schedule integration for example is almost meaningless when the 'cost' and 'schedule' programs are written in different languages on different machines.

It's not just the reporting aspects of the system that fall down; all the advantages of the 'project model' are lost. The crucial function of decision making is impaired. Testing alternative courses of action by asking 'What if ...?' just cannot operate when the individual components of the project do not form part of a 'well oiled' project system.

Reluctantly, the project team is then forced into the conclusion that the only way to achieve real integration is to scrap the existing collection of micros and start again. Sadly, they are probably right.

How then is the project team to avoid this trap? Well, there are a couple of alternatives.

Mini-based systems

The second approach requires some degree of forward thinking. A similar result to the multiple micro approach can be achieved by installing a *mini* computer with multiple terminals. This has the advantage that all the users are using the same database and consequently integration between applications and up and down the project hierarchy is immediately available. (Given care in choosing appropriate software, of course).

The cost of a mini system with perhaps half a dozen terminals may

Managing Progress and Performance

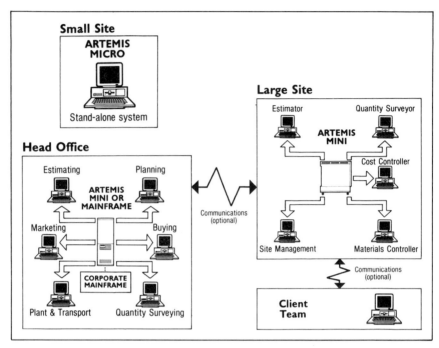

Figure 25.10 Typical configuration of computer hardware for a company using the ARTEMIS system for project management at head office and at remote sites

well be comparable to the equivalent number of independent micros. The big advantages of course are the direct integration of the system and the potential for sharing facilities such as a graphics plotter and a high speed printer.

Micro, mini and mainframe

An all-encompassing project system will operate on micros, minis and of course mainframe computers. A sophisticated system, particularly a company wide, multi-project system, may well use all three. Please see Figure 25.10.

The final choice of a computer system

For a company new to computers and with a very limited budget, an integrated system can be built up starting from a single micro. For a company with a clear idea of how their integrated system should look,

Integrated Systems for Planning and Control

then the mini or mainframe approach is the most effective. This may well involve micros as terminals into the main system, and these can also provide some element of 'local processing'. (For example, an IBM PC can operate either as a complete stand alone ARTEMIS system, or double-up as a terminal to a larger computer also running ARTEMIS).

The choice will be to a large extent dependent on the size, number and complexity of the projects and, of course, the number of applications required. There is no simple answer to this and there is no substitute for working through the available configurations with a knowledgeable supplier, who will be able to advise on the most appropriate hardware and software combinations. A few general guidelines, however, may be useful:

1. Buy one piece of software that has the potential to meet *all* anticipated application needs (e.g. cost, planning, materials, plant, maintenance).
2. Buy software that can be genuinely integrated horizontally, to other applications.
3. Buy software that can be integrated vertically, to the *same* software running on mini or mainframe computers.
4. Make sure the appropriate computer for the software is readily available, well supported, and comes from a reputable manufacturer.

To start with, particularly when buying a system for just one application, this may seem to be somewhat over-cautious. Not really. Bear in mind that the reason why this first system is being bought is to improve business performance. If it does just that, then repeating the exercise for other disciplines will be viewed as essential.

26
An Integrated Project Management System in Action

Ray Palmer

An effective way of seeing the impact that an integrated system can make is to examine the way in which it can be applied to a real-life project. This chapter, as in Chapter 25, is based on experience gained by project managers using the ARTEMIS system.

THE PROJECT INFORMATION STRUCTURE

Figure 26.1 is a diagrammatic representation of a complete project system. Each of the individual boxes in the chart represents a dataset that will, in practice, contain many thousands of information items.

The network dataset

The network dataset is the project plan. Typically, each project will contain from several hundred to several thousand activities. The network is constructed from library sub-sets which are derived from previous projects and are structured to reflect the physical construction and the resources required. Deadlines are highlighted using key events or milestones. Phases of work are identified using 'hammocks' (basically descriptive activities which span groups of more detailed activities).

An Integrated Project Management System in Action

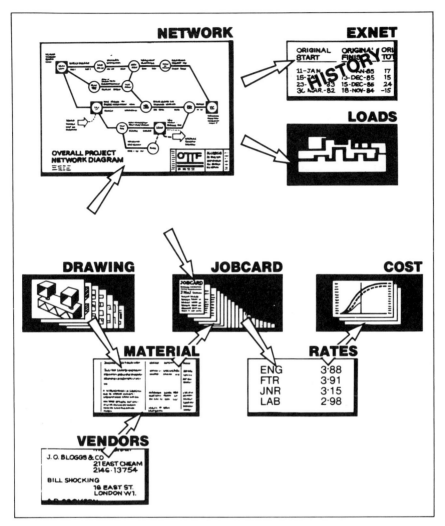

Figure 26.1 A typical project information structure

The drawings dataset

The drawings dataset is effectively a drawings register. It contains details of every drawing including its number, its description, its status (submitted for approval, approved, issued) and the dates for each of these events. It will also have revision details, the draughtsman's name, his department, the date of revision and perhaps notes on the nature of the revision.

The materials dataset

Details of each material requisition are contained in the materials dataset. This also includes purchase order details and, in practice, will often carry progress information showing the status of deliveries against each item on order.

The vendor dataset

This provides a record for each supplier, his name, address, telephone and telex numbers, the name of the usual person to contact, and the principal line of business. Often, details of past performance will be included for use in vendor rating and the initial choice of vendor.

The job cards dataset

Job card records carry details of each job to be performed on the project. Typically the cards will contain a job description, the budget or target manhours, and the planned start and finish dates. Often they are printed out as task lists for departments or trades. A full job card system will include facilities for progress control and, effectively, provides the mechanism for allocating work, collecting progress information and (via the relational database) updating the rest of the project systems.

The rates dataset

Each type of resource can be held in the rates dataset with its appropriate cost rates. Usually this will include a standard rate, the appropriate overtime rates and bonus details. The information is of course held only once in the system as any change in the rates can be communicated directly to other parts of the system, as required.

The cost dataset

This dataset contains details of each project cost account. This is usually based on a defined piece of work with an identified manager, and reflects the physical structure of the project. The basic information is generated when bidding for the work and is shown as a budget amount for each account. A large project could contain several hundred records, usually structured so that the costs can be 'rolled up' to show the position on each section of the project, and the overall position. As the work progresses actual costs are collected against each account along with an assessment of the value of the work completed to date. This enables the cost performance to be accurately monitored, and variances quickly pinpointed. It is usual to include a forecast of the cost of future work taking into account 'change orders', or variations, which can also form part of the system.

The resources dataset

All the resource types used on the project are detailed in this dataset. The information includes the times when they are needed, the quantities involved, and details of periods when they are expected to be scarce or unavailable. This dataset is closely related to the network dataset and reflects the total resource requirements of the current project plan.

The history dataset

Usually, the history dataset will contain 'snapshots' of the project taken at different times. For example, it is usual to store the details of the project as originally defined and contracted, plus subsequent updates whenever a significant change has occurred to the scope of work. These snapshots can be called up as required, and incorporated in reports to show progress compared with the original plan, slippage and so on. In fact, it is an easy matter to set up a history dataset for any aspect of the project, plans and costs being favourite subjects.

HOW THE SYSTEM OPERATES IN PRACTICE

Broadly, the system operates in the following manner.

The drawing office produces information from which the materials and equipment requirements can be calculated. This is passed to the buyer in the form of requisitions which he categorises and pulls together into orders against particular suppliers. The supplier then manufactures or procures the materials and eventually delivers to site. Once on site, the material is checked off against the orders, and allocated to a store prior to consumption.

Meanwhile the planners decide the overall approach to the work and this is converted into job cards, against which work the materials are subsequently consumed.

The cost system is set up once the scope of the project is known and this is then used to track all expenditures on every aspect of the work.

Against this backcloth we can now see how an integrated system can provide not only high level control of the project, but can provide a complete and comprehensive method for turning plans into actions and then co-ordinating the work of all the project participants.

DESIGN MANAGEMENT

Now consider some of the situations in design management where the integration of information is important. Reports are produced directly from the drawings dataset to provide a variety of information. Reports can range from a comprehensive drawings register for example, to more specific reports identifying all drawings which are not yet approved, due for issue in the next four weeks, or perhaps listing drawings for a specific area of the project. In practice though the on-site priorities can change from day-to-day. At the same time, the ability of the drawing office to produce specific drawings by a particular date can be drastically modified by conflicting priorities and the availability of staff. In other words, the drawing office should be modifying its targets in line with progress on-site but in reality is often working to priorities which were set before the start of the project. What is needed is the ability to continually draw together the *current* project plan with the *current* drawing office workload.

Using the ability to link datasets we can quickly draw information from the required areas of the system. Figures 25.3 and 25.4, in the previous chapter, illustrate this process and the resulting report compares the on-site requirements with the drawing office's anticipated issue dates. The difference between these two dates is effectively the 'float' on the production of each drawing. This may well be sufficient information to enable the design manager to plan his workload. If, however, he requires a somewhat more sophisticated approach, then the 'on-site required' dates can form the 'target completion' dates, against which he can then reschedule his workload.

With an integrated system, the user can choose the degree of sophistication to suit his requirements. A full scheduling system, itemising each drawing through each stage of production, could be called for. Or, this could be simplified by handling drawings in 'packages' for scheduling purposes, on the basis that only a complete package is of use to the on-site team.

In the earlier stages of a project where there is more latitude for solving problems, then rescheduling the drawing office to meet on site changes is a feasible approach. At the other extreme, usually later in the project when other options such as buying in additional designers and so on have been exhausted, it becomes necessary to integrate fully the design and construction process and schedule it *en masse*. This can result in design delays causing on-site work to be rescheduled, perhaps causing overall delays to the project.

A straightforward way of testing the seriousness of the situation would be to link the drawings dataset to the plan and transfer the anticipated drawing issue dates to the activities for which they are required and then reschedule using the new dates. The late drawings, we may find, only affect a small number of activities and (with luck) only activities with substantial amounts of float. If, however, this reveals unacceptable delays to the work, then we are immediately able to identify the drawings in question and take steps towards resolving the situation.

On a small project of course, it may well be possible to keep track of on-site priorities and drawing office schedules without a computer based system. On larger projects (perhaps with design and manufacture being carried out in several countries and shipments being required to a central project site) an effective system becomes an essential requirement for remaining in control of the project.

MATERIALS MANAGEMENT

Project materials fall into two main types. There are discrete components such as pumps, valves, motors and so on, and consumables such as cement and nuts and bolts. The first category in some industries will be non-interchangeable, specific components and as such will carry unique 'tag' numbers. Under these circumstances very close control is required and the facility to tailor the control system to the requirements of each different project is paramount. Consumables on the other hand are usually treated as bulk items with the emphasis being on the forecast rate of consumption and related storage requirements. In both cases of course, the need to plan the manufacture and delivery and then to track the stages through which each material passes is important.

Components however must be treated as an integrated part of the whole project system for effective planning and close control. Take for example a situation where a number of material delivery dates are slipping. The seriousness of this can be judged by linking the material dataset to the schedule and checking the latest acceptable delivery dates against the required on-site dates. In practice a report selecting only late items would be produced, probably sorted so that the largest delay is shown first, with the responsible engineers flagged for appropriate action.

Conversely, the material dataset could be linked to the schedule *and* to the supplier datasets, and reports produced which not only flag the late items, but identify each late material by purchase order number, forecast delay, and so on. This has the advantage that the report can be sorted so that the expediter is given, *on the same report*, the supplier's name, the purchase orders placed that are now late, the name of the contact man within the company, his telephone number, his telex number — in fact all the information required to pinpoint and expedite the late items. This is useful for a small project, essential for a large project, and very difficult to achieve without an integrated system. Figure 26.2 shows such a report.

Other materials-related information that could be produced may include forecasts of material to be delivered during the next four weeks (for planning storage, etc.), required delivery dates for specific items based on the current site priorities (as a guide for the buyer in placing orders), and even inspection schedules arranged to focus the quality assurance team on the current critical items.

PLANNING AND SCHEDULING

The ability to operate as part of an integrated system has transformed

```
METIER        LATE  MATERIALS  BY  VENDOR                   ARTEMIS
Client    : METIER MANAGEMENT SYSTEMS         Project Start   :  1-JAN-85
Location  : METIER HOUSE, LONDON              Timenow         :  1-JAN-85
Project Name: ARTEMIS                         Project Complete: 24-JUL-86

VENDORS CODE  :  099654        NAME : R. J. WILKINTHORPE

KEY CONTACT : JOHN MARSHALL

ADDRESS : HIGH STREET, WATFORD

LINE OF BUSINESS :

TELEPHONE : 0923-6544          TELEX :    09883

     MATERIALS SUPPLIED
     ==================

     PURCHASE ORDER -     09123
     --------------

     MATERIAL            MATERIAL              REQUIRED
       CODE             DESCRIPTION             UNITS      REQUIRED   EXPECTED
     --------          -------------           --------    --------   --------
      MT109         WATER PUMP VALVE              5S       15-JUN-85   1-MAY-85
      MT162         COCK STOP                    25S       15-JUN-85
      MT163         5CM PIPING                METRES        5-JAN-85  14-FEB-85  Late
      MT169         2CM PIPING                METRES        5-JAN-85  14-FEB-85  Late
      MT205         BALLAST PUMP MANUAL        QUIRE       25-APR-86   1-MAY-85  Late
      MT401         PUMP SYSTEM                QUIRE       25-APR-86   1-MAY-85  Late
      MT404         WATER PUMP MANUAL          QUIRE       15-JUN-85   1-MAY-85
      MT405         WATER PUMP                 UNITS       15-JUN-85   1-MAY-85
      MT549         PRECISION PUMP               10S
```

Figure 26.2 Integrated system report for use by an expediter

the work of the project planner. Large, cumbersome networks have been replaced with smaller networks designed to facilitate decision making. The detailed tasks which bogged down earlier systems are now held in the appropriate datasets and called into use only when required. The whole approach to networking is now much more that of fast-moving decision making, using the network plan to help choose the most cost-effective alternative.

Much more than before, the planner is seen as the central figure co-ordinating the effort of the whole project. The ability to integrate material deliveries, design team activities, plant movements, documentation, task lists, costs and other related items directly with the plan, enormously increases the confidence of the project team.

Network analysis and integration

In their simpler forms network analysis techniques are currently available on a large number of computer systems and, indeed, have been available since the mid 1960s. The systems vary, of course, in their ease of use but they nevertheless operate using the same principles. In the days when the only computerised project application available was network analysis, a great deal of effort was expended in 'cheating' the systems to make them behave as though they were capable of rudimentary integration, usually in conjunction with costs. This involved adding cost information to activities and then trying to produce summary reports using the resource processing facilities. By and large these efforts were not particularly effective, especially as the resulting system became totally inflexible and often unwieldy.

With an appropriate integrated system, an almost unlimited amount of extra information can be added to each activity directly or (probably more conveniently) the additional information can be held elsewhere in the system and linked to the network as and when required. So, for example, the cost information can be managed by the cost department and linked to the current plan to produce cash flow forecasts. A benefit of this arrangement is that it doesn't require special cost estimates to be made for each activity on the network (a disadvantage of the old cost-on-activity approach).

Integration has also enabled the planning team to structure their networks in more sophisticated ways. One approach is to use

```
METIER   KEY EVENT PROGRESS REPORT   ARTEMIS
Client   : METIER MANAGEMENT SYSTEMS        Project Start   :  1-JAN-85
Location : METIER HOUSE,LONDON              Timenow         :  1-JAN-85
Project Name: ARTEMIS                       Project Complete: 24-JUL-86


                                EARLY    ACTUAL   TARGET    TOTAL
EVENT   DESCRIPTION              FINISH   FINISH   COMPLETE  FLOAT    STATUS
-----   -----------              ------   ------   --------  -----    ------

STA     PROJECT STARTED          31-DEC-84                      0    *CRITICAL*

E1      READY TO INSTALL HEAVY LIFTS  27-MAY-85                200

T2      READY TO COMMISSION BOILERS   24-JUN-85                258

44      READY TO TEST WATER BALLAST   14-OCT-85                  7
        SYSTEM
T1      READY TO TEST INSTRUMENTATION 22-APR-86                 66

FIN     PROJECT FINISHED         24-JUL-86          24-JUL-86    0    *CRITICAL*
```

Figure 26.3 A milestone report

'hierarchical networks', where the top level network (management network) contains perhaps fifty to one hundred activities and this is driven by a second level of network with perhaps several thousand activities. The usual arrangement is for a group of second level activities to correspond to one top level activity. Progress information on the second level is then 'rolled-up' and summarised to the management level network. This ability to summarise data for consumption by higher levels of management is a key benefit of an integrated system. Large projects may have many levels which correspond with, and provide information to, appropriate levels within the company structure. The following paragraphs deal with reports which are typically used for these levels.

Key event, or milestone reports

(See Figure 26.3.) These reports highlight significant events (such as the beginning and end of a project), significant dates throughout the project (such as the beginnings and ends of phases) and achievements (such as 'building watertight'; 'dc control systems functional' etc.). This type of report is most useful for reporting to senior managers.

Summary bar chart

These charts show overall sections of the work in a graphical form. In this case it is produced using 'hammock' or summary activities which span large sections of work. This is useful for reporting at high level, but includes sufficient detail to be useful as a working document for senior project staff, team leaders, area engineers, and so on. An example is given in Figure 26.4. In this illustration comparison is possible between the 'before' and 'after' project dates following resource scheduling. This illustrates its use in quickly highlighting the overall effects of change on the project. Variances in a particular area can be quickly identified and more detailed reports produced to examine further the causes.

Detailed activity report

This is a typical report for what could be termed the 'working level' of the hierarchy. The report gives details of individual activities, their

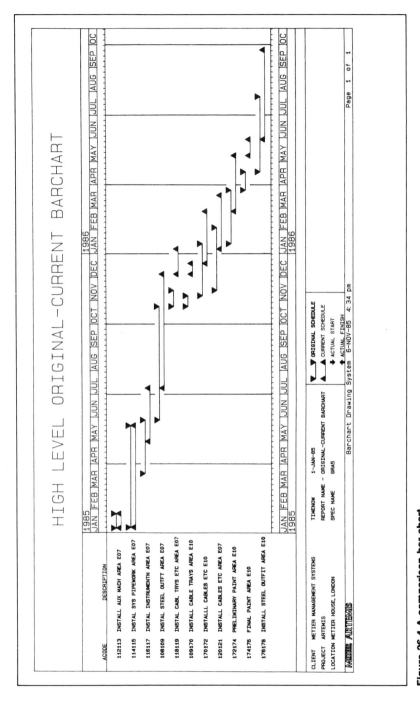

Figure 26.4 A comparison bar chart
This computer-produced report compares original and current schedule information

```
METIER
Client    : METIER MANAGEMENT SYSTEMS                                           ARTEMIS
Location  : METIER HOUSE, LONDON                                      Project Start    : 1-JAN-85
Project Name: ARTEMIS                                                 Timenow          : 1-JAN-85
                                                                      Project Complete : 24-JUL-86

                              ACTIVITY LISTING
```

PREC EVENT	SUCC EVENT	DESCRIPTION	DUR	EARLY START	EARLY FINISH	TOTAL FLOAT	TRADE	NO MEN
128	P10	PREPARE SEATS AREA E08	2	4-JAN-85	7-JAN-85	217	LABOURERS	1
110	111	FIT AUX MACH SEATS AREA E07	15	4-JAN-85	24-JAN-85	5	LABOURERS	2
11	12	INSTALL CABL TRAYS AREA E01	15	4-JAN-85	24-JAN-85	66	ELECTRICIANS	2
136	137	INSTAL CABL TRYS ETC AREA E08	15	4-JAN-85	24-JAN-85	144	ELECTRICIANS	2
140	141	PRELIM PAINT AREA E08	40	4-JAN-85	28-FEB-85	326	PAINTERS	2
19	20	INSTALL STEEL OUTFIT AREA E02	80	4-JAN-85	25-APR-85	7	LABOURERS	2
112	113	INSTALL AUX MACH AREA E07	15	7-JAN-85	25-JAN-85	5	FITTERS	2
114	117	INSTALL SYS PIPEWORK AREA E07	95	8-JAN-85	20-MAY-85	5	PLUMBERS	3
138	139	INSTALL CABL ETC AREA E08	15	11-JAN-85	31-JAN-85	144	ELECTRICIANS	2
13	14	INSTALL CABLES ETC. AREA E01	40	11-JAN-85	7-MAR-85	66	ELECTRICIANS	2
132	133	INSTALL SYS PIPEWORK AREA E08	80	4-FEB-85	24-MAY-85	200	FITTERS	1
14	1	PRELIM PAINT AREA E01	60	8-MAR-85	30-MAY-85	66	PAINTERS	1
116	117	INSTAL INSTRUMENTN AREA E07	50	19-MAR-85	27-MAY-85	0	ELECTRICIANS FITTERS	3
134	135	INSTALL INSTRUMENTN AREA E08	35	15-APR-85	31-MAY-85	275	ELECTRICIANS FITTERS	4
100	107	PRELIM PAINT AREA E06	75	13-MAY-85	10-SEP-85	206	PAINTERS	2
133	127	INSTALL STEEL OUTFT AREA E08	80	27-MAY-85	1-OCT-85	200	LABOURERS	2
117	109	INSTALL STEEL OUTFIT AREA E07	95	28-MAY-85	23-OCT-85	0	LABOURERS FITTERS	4
1	2	INSTALL STEEL OUTFIT AREA E01	85	31-MAY-85	14-OCT-85	66	LABOURERS	2
107	160	FINAL PAINT AREA E06	10	11-SEP-85	24-SEP-85	206	PAINTERS	2
109	170	INSTALL CABLE TRAYS AREA E10	10	24-OCT-85	6-NOV-85	0	LABOURERS	3
109	119	INSTALL CABL TRYS ETC AREA E07	15	24-OCT-85	13-NOV-85	120	ELECTRICIANS	2
170	172	INSTALL CABLES ETC E10	40	7-NOV-85	13-JAN-86	0	ELECTRICIANS	3
119	121	INSTALL CABLES ETC AREA E07	50	14-NOV-85	3-FEB-86	120	ELECTRICIANS	4
172	174	PRELIMINARY PAINT AREA E10	50	14-JAN-86	24-MAR-86	0	PAINTERS	2
174	176	FINAL PAINT AREA E10	15	25-MAR-86	17-APR-86	0	PAINTERS	3
176	178	INSTAL STEEL OUTFIT AREA E10	70	18-APR-86	24-JUL-86	0	LABOURERS FITTERS	3

Figure 26.5 A detailed activity report

An Integrated Project Management System in Action

start and finish dates, float, resources and so on, and as such is probably too detailed to be used successfully by workmen themselves. A simplified version with only the activity description, start and finish dates, and (perhaps) float, would be more easily assimilated. (See Figure 26.5).

Integrated checks and tests

A feature of the ARTEMIS system is the ability to generate new reports as required. For the planner starting a project from scratch, the process of setting up the network, checking the logic, allocating resources, and so on, can be quite time consuming. Producing special reports as required can considerably reduce this time. Conventional reports such as critical activity listings can be produced in minutes. However, the real power of an integrated system is demonstrated when the resources on the network can be linked to the original estimate to verify the manhours, or perhaps linked to the cost information to confirm the cash flow forecasts. In short, the planner using an integrated system substantially increases his ability to cross-check information and dramatically reduces the time taken for the system to go 'live'.

ALLOCATING WORK AND MEASURING PROGRESS

In simplistic project systems the 'grass-roots' level is often overlooked. Management may well use a system for overall planning, yet for day-to-day planning they are forced to fall back on entirely manual methods. With an integrated system, however, the control of detailed work forms a cornerstone of the project management process.

Allocating work

In many industries, the users of integrated systems have adopted the traditional job card, or task list, and have made it an essential part of their project control process. The job card now though, rather than being pre-prepared and issued manually, is produced by the system on demand. It incorporates all the appropriate information for the job in

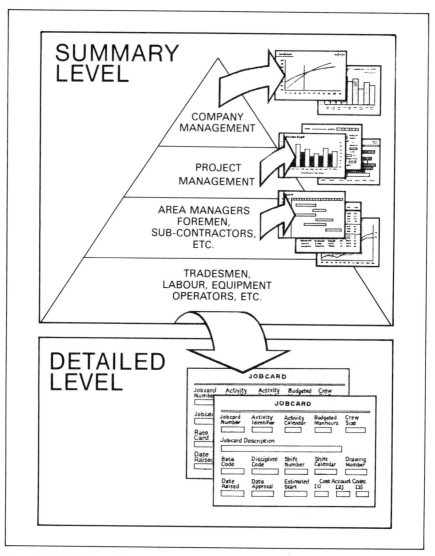

Figure 26.6 The hierarchy of project control levels

hand. Not only that, but because the information is held in the system, it provides an ideal basis against which progress can be measured. Typically, the job card level is directly below network planning in the project hierarchy. The hierarchy of control is illustrated in Figure 26.6.

An Integrated Project Management System in Action

Each network activity may contain several hundred job cards and could involve several types of resources (fitters, welders, electricians, and so on). In effect, therefore, job cards are the most detailed level of project planning.

Before issue, the latest activity dates are transferred from the network to the job cards required in (say) the coming week. Using the filing cabinet analogy, the process can be represented as shown in Figure 26.7.

In practice, the system can also hold details of any special equipment needed to carry out the work, the relevant drawings and the materials required (together with their stores locations). The job cards can then be issued as part of a complete pack of information, giving the workman all the information needed for the work in hand.

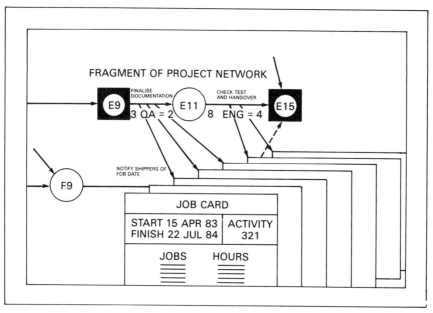

Figure 26.7 Updating job cards

Measuring progress

There are many approaches to measuring progress. They range from simple assessments based on the quantities of time or resources consumed, to more sophisticated calculations involving the value of work completed, forecasts of work outstanding, anticipated

Managing Progress and Performance

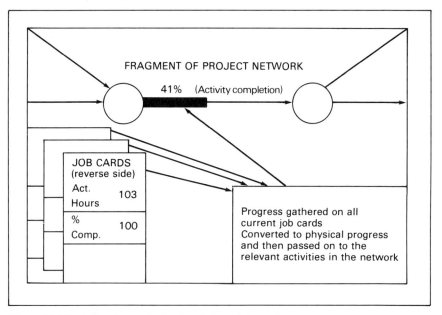

Figure 26.8 Updating the project network from job cards

completion dates and so on. The level at which the progress is measured is also important. At a sufficiently detailed level it is only necessary to know that work is either not started or completed.

The method of operation used here is to collect the progress of each 'live' job card as a 'percentage complete' figure. This is done using a 'turnround' report, a report produced from the system listing all the 'issued' but 'incomplete' job cards, with a blank column for each trade foreman to give his estimate of the 'percentage complete'.

Once the progress information has been collected, each appropriate job card record is updated to reflect the current situation. Because we are using an integrated system, we can now summarise the progress from the job cards to the relevant activities on the network (Figure 26.8).

In practice this process involves several thousand 'live' job cards and perhaps several hundred associated activities. Although the physical process of collecting the data can take several hours, the steps of updating the system and then being able to see the results in terms of progress on the overall project plan, is completed with little additional work.

Again, because of the ability to link information together, the progress position on the individual job cards is quickly turned into progress on the project network. This then enables the whole project to be re-examined in terms of overall cash flow, material delivery requirements, resources, information and completion dates. Problems can be quickly isolated and decisions made as to the appropriate course of action.

COST MANAGEMENT

It is probably true to say that every action taken on a project has a cost implication. Often though the *true* cost of an action is often just not visible to the project team. Take for example the situation where an area of a project is falling behind schedule. To speed it up the decision is made to bring in a larger piece of plant. The only cost analysis that is carried out is whether the additional cost of the machine is likely to offset the cost of finishing the project behind time. On a large project, decisions of this type are taken continually.

With an integrated system a much more comprehensive view can be taken: the extent to which the accelerated work will re-schedule activities further down the line, how this will affect their resource usage, how these resource changes will cause otherwise unrelated activities to be rescheduled, the effect this will have on material and equipment deliveries, the effect on the design office and (perhaps most importantly) how all these various changes affect the cost of the project.

In the first instance the changes to all these items may influence the overall cost. But the sum total of all the rescheduling may well affect the project cash flow. For an individual project this could mean that the amount of money 'locked-up' is increased or that the agreed borrowing limit is exceeded. For a company with several projects in hand the aggregate result of these individual changes could even prevent the financing of an additional project. With the integrated approach, the 'dynamics' of a proposed action can be thoroughly examined before any decision is made and the overall implications assessed against the overall objectives.

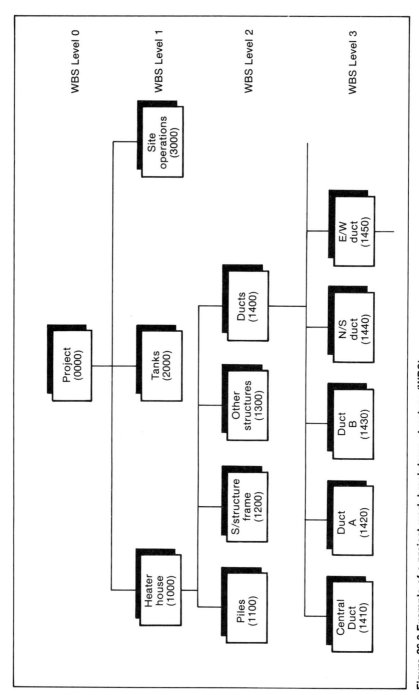

Figure 26.9 Example of a project work breakdown structure (WBS)
This example might be found in part of a civil construction project work breakdown

COST FORECASTING

Traditionally, cost forecasting has been a somewhat laborious and inexact process. Two factors have contributed to this: the cost estimate or cost accounts do not necessarily reflect the components of a project in a way that can be directly related to the construction process; and the network is usually drawn without reference to the cost structure. So, to produce a cash flow forecast, the project team have to work through the programme to pick out dates where recognisable expenditures occur and then tie these back to the appropriate costs, a time consuming task.

Over recent years the whole approach to this problem has gradually changed. Due to developments in the defence industries, particularly in the United States, there is increasing emphasis on the ability to operate integrated cost/schedule systems.

A basic requirement of the approach is that the project should be viewed as a number of packages with defined scope, responsibility and costs. A common method of arriving at this arrangement is by employing a work breakdown structure which divides the project into a hierarchy of work. Work breakdown structures are described elsewhere in this book, particularly in Chapter 10. An illustration of the concept is also given in Figure 26.9.

Once such a work breakdown exists, each item can be treated as a package of work, with the account codes being structured or 'nested' so that the total costs can be 'rolled up' to ascertain the overall position whenever required.

In the ARTEMIS system, each account is usually treated as an individual record within a cost dataset. The fields of information usually include:

1. The account code or cost code.
2. The description.
3. The person responsible.
4. The budget.
5. Actual costs to date.
6. Forecast remaining cost.
7. Percentage completed.
8. Forecast final cost.
9. The value of work completed.
10. Several variances.

Managing Progress and Performance

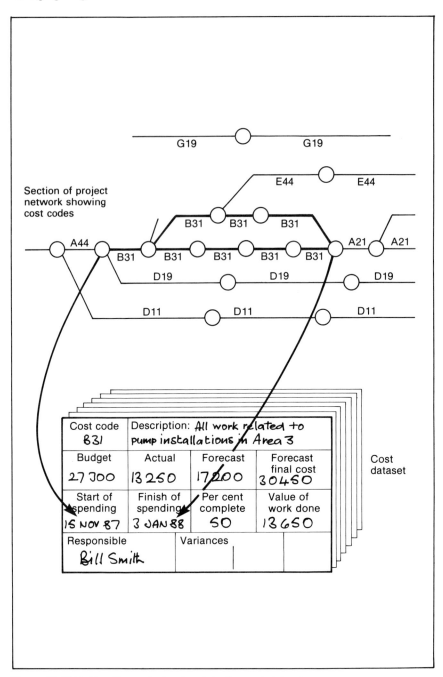

Figure 26.10 Linking the project network to the cost dataset

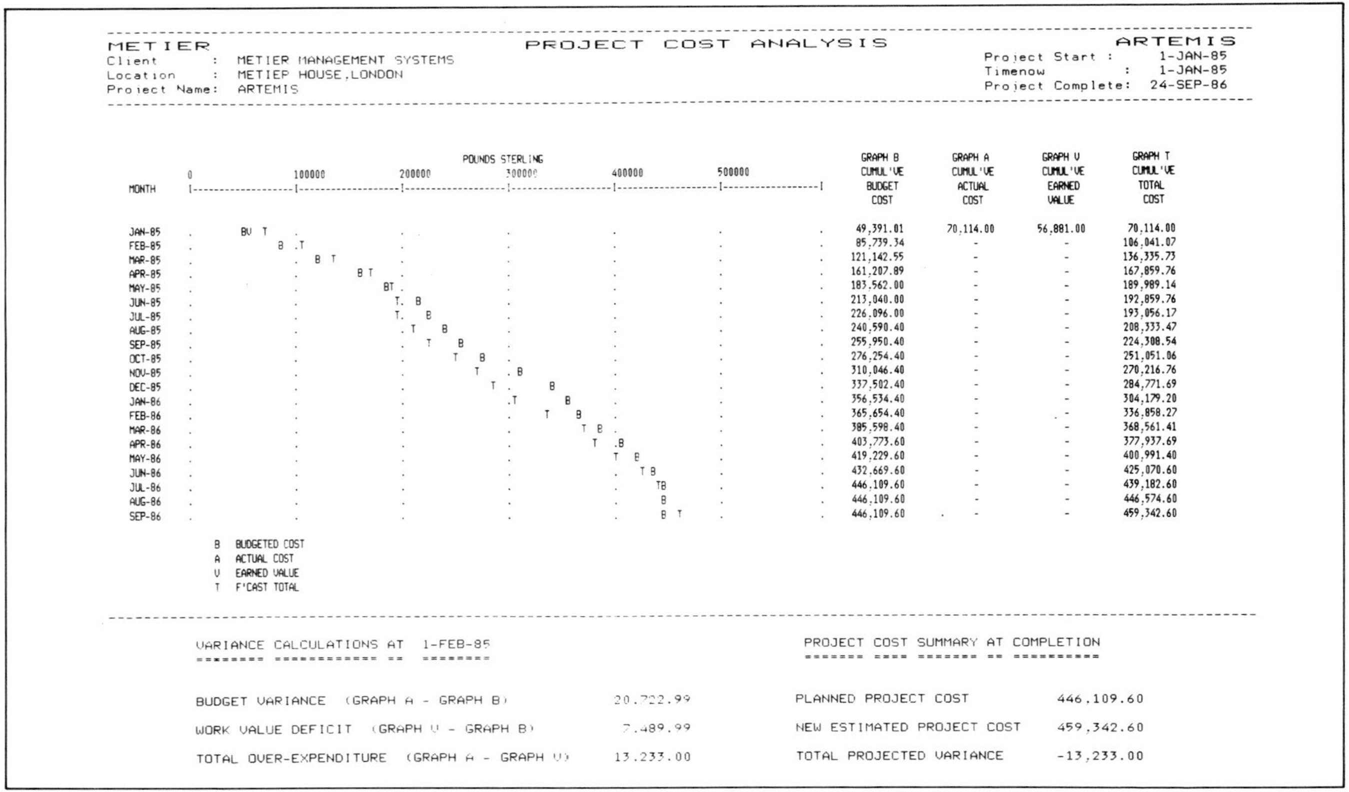

METIER — PROJECT COST ANALYSIS — ARTEMIS

Client : METIER MANAGEMENT SYSTEMS
Location : METIER HOUSE, LONDON
Project Name: ARTEMIS

Project Start : 1-JAN-85
Timenow : 1-JAN-85
Project Complete: 24-SEP-86

MONTH	GRAPH B CUMUL'VE BUDGET COST	GRAPH A CUMUL'VE ACTUAL COST	GRAPH V CUMUL'VE EARNED VALUE	GRAPH T CUMUL'VE TOTAL COST
JAN-85	49,391.01	70,114.00	56,881.00	70,114.00
FEB-85	85,739.34	-	-	106,041.07
MAR-85	121,142.55	-	-	136,335.73
APR-85	161,207.89	-	-	167,859.76
MAY-85	183,562.00	-	-	189,989.14
JUN-85	213,040.00	-	-	192,859.76
JUL-85	226,096.00	-	-	193,056.17
AUG-85	240,590.40	-	-	208,333.47
SEP-85	255,950.40	-	-	224,308.54
OCT-85	276,254.40	-	-	251,051.06
NOV-85	310,046.40	-	-	270,216.76
DEC-85	337,502.40	-	-	284,771.69
JAN-86	356,534.40	-	-	304,179.20
FEB-86	365,654.40	-	-	336,858.27
MAR-86	385,598.40	-	-	368,561.41
APR-86	403,773.60	-	-	377,937.69
MAY-86	419,229.60	-	-	400,991.40
JUN-86	432,669.60	-	-	425,070.60
JUL-86	446,109.60	-	-	439,182.60
AUG-86	446,109.60	-	-	446,574.60
SEP-86	446,109.60	-	-	459,342.60

B BUDGETED COST
A ACTUAL COST
V EARNED VALUE
T F'CAST TOTAL

VARIANCE CALCULATIONS AT 1-FEB-85

BUDGET VARIANCE	(GRAPH A - GRAPH B)	20,722.99
WORK VALUE DEFICIT	(GRAPH V - GRAPH B)	7,489.99
TOTAL OVER-EXPENDITURE	(GRAPH A - GRAPH V)	13,233.00

PROJECT COST SUMMARY AT COMPLETION

PLANNED PROJECT COST	446,109.60
NEW ESTIMATED PROJECT COST	459,342.60
TOTAL PROJECTED VARIANCE	-13,233.00

Figure 26.11 A time/cost curve
This example was produced automatically by a computer using the ARTEMIS system

Managing Progress and Performance

The last four of these items are calculated by the system.

Additionally, the individual network records can be coded, to show the account to which each belongs. Any one account could well have several dozen related network activities. For the cost forecasting exercise it is necessary to bring the cost dataset and the current schedule together. This can be considered diagrammatically as shown in Figure 26.10.

Using ARTEMIS, the two datasets can be linked and the earliest and latest expenditure dates for each found. Practically, this could require combining several thousand activities with a similar number of account records. The result of this is that we now have the appropriate dates for each account which is sufficient information to generate the appropriate cost curves (see Figure 26.11).

Again, in practice, the cost record is often more complex. There are often several versions of the 'budget' for example and there is usually a requirement to identify 'commitments' separately. Some users of ARTEMIS also split the figures into manpower, plant, materials and overheads. Additional fields can be added to the records, as required, to accommodate these needs.

The example above assumes a linear distribution of costs. Some users define 'spend profiles' for various cost types which means they can produce much more accurate expenditure forecasts. Another approach to this is just to use smaller cost code items, which in turn enables the real expenditures to be allocated to shorter and more specific periods of time. Using a sophisticated project system the possible number of approaches is quite extensive.

The improvement that integration brings transforms the whole process, from one of accounting for historic costs to that of dynamically modelling the whole process.

Figure 26.12 illustrates a perhaps surprising result from the integration of project cost and schedule information, with penalties for late completion. The 'minimum cost' finish date is shown as two weeks after the contractual completion date! Again, a calculation that is possible by manual methods. In an integrated system, however, it is just one of the many ways of analysing information and presenting the results for management action. The manual approach could take days of investigation and calculation. With an appropriate integrated system the analysis, and the production of the graphical

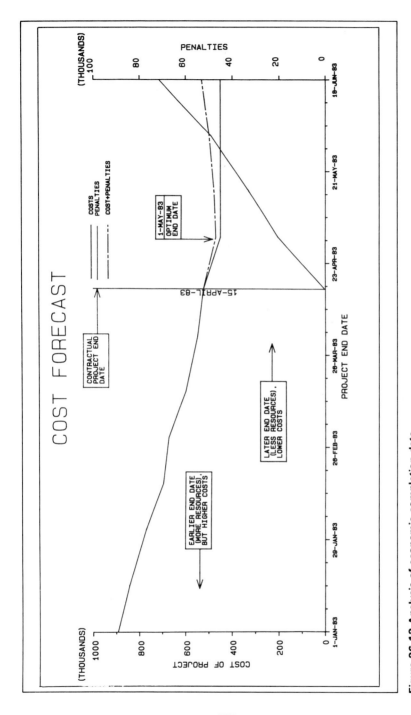

Figure 26.12 Analysis of economic completion date
The computer has taken all relevant facts to produce this calculation of the minimum-cost project completion date

output could be completed in minutes, and could even form part of a regular monthly analysis of the project status.

CONCLUSION

During the relatively short time in which integrated systems have been available, the whole approach to project management has been transformed. Disciplines that were once viewed as 'stand-alone' and even secondary (planning for example) have jumped to the forefront with the extra leverage brought to bear by integration. Clients are now aware of the benefits, and are starting to insist that their contractors manage projects using integrated systems. In consequence, contractors who still use older methods find that they are in danger of losing their competitive edge.

The breadth of the project system is also expanding. In this chapter the more 'traditional' areas of planning, materials, costs and the control of work have been discussed, but the leading project management systems now have far wider horizons. ARTEMIS, for example, is used for dozens of applications which in the mid-1970s would not have been considered as part of a project management system. Estimating, plant management, maintenance, accounting, personnel administration, claims management and many other functions now form part of successful integrated systems.

After years of being constrained by manual methods, information technology (in the form of improved computer hardware and software) has provided responsive systems which are appropriate to the needs of project managers and their teams. This field of interactive systems is barely ten years old, yet other areas of integration are already being considered. An obvious direction for development is to combine computer aided design with the management system of the associated project. Increased integration of company administration systems is also likely, with management accounting (particularly in a project orientated company) a potential area for inclusion.

Fully integrated, interactive project management systems have always been possible, but they have been limited in scope and flexibility by the cumbersome nature of the manual methods that were required. Dramatic advances in the power and availability of computer facilities have now changed the emphasis completely, so that even small projects are able to gain practical benefit from truly integrated systems.

Index

Accommodation costs 101–2
Account codes 196, 199–200
Accountability principle 54–5
Accounting, checklist 64
Accounts receivable 260
Activities 359
  relationships between 359–66
Advice notes 308
Aid and Trade Provisions (ATP) 179
Air charter 336
Air Charter Agreement 335
Airfreight 328, 334
Alarm systems 301
ANSI/ASME NQA-1 504
Arbitration 89, 129–30
Arrow diagrams 366, 382, 387–8, 415–16, 439–41, 448, 449
ARTEMIS system 565, 567, 569, 571, 573, 574, 582–4, 597, 603, 605, 606
Asian Development Bank 178
Audit function 51–2
Authorisation document 466
Authorisations for expenditure (AFEs) 215, 216, 219
Authorised Inspection Agency 286, 287
Authority 532
  and power 533
  problems in project management 530–7

Ball park estimates 191–2
Bank charges 244
Banking services 169, 172, 174–5, 180, 183, 185, 253
Bar charts 345–53
  adding information 349–51
  advantages of network analysis over 380–1

  for project control 347–9
  greatest advantage of 351
  linked 379
  main drawback of 351
  summary 594
  uses and limitations of 351–3
Bargaining counter 251
Bid analysis form 274
Bid package review 521–2
  by engineering department 522
  by purchasing department 522
  by quality assurance department 522
Bid summary 522
Bilateral aid 178–9
Bill of approximate quantities 96
Bill of lading 331
Bills of material 310
Blue Book 327
Bonded store 303
Bonds 180
Bonuses 126
Bought-out items 94
British Standards Institution 386
BS5750 525, 526
BS5882 504
Budget contingency 207
Buffers 353
Building contracts, terms of payment 109
Burst activity 362
  and merge combined 362
Butler Machine Tool Co. Ltd v Ex-Cell-O Corporation 1979: 74
Buying *see* Purchasing

Calendar features 419–23
Capital expenditure 243
Capital lock-up 112
Capital markets 177–8

611

Index

Case markings 329
Cash control 238–61
Cash crisis 247
Cash flow 110, 230–1
  example 231
  late payments 254
  safeguarding and speeding up 247–53
Cash flow forecast 231, 241–2, 244–7, 597
Cash flow management 239
Cash flow schedule 245, 252
Cash flow statement 207–9
Cash inflow 240, 241
Cash inflow statement 209
Cash outflow forecast 208
Cash purchases 242
Cash receipts 239, 248
Centro-Provincial Estates v Merchants Investors Assurance Company 1983: 73
Certification
  delays in 112–13
  in quality assurance 491–2
  of equipment 309
  of materials 289–90, 528
  of work done 114, 249
  validity of 286
Changes, financial 226
CIF (cost of goods, insurance and freight) terms 336, 338
Civil engineering contracts 113
  terms of payment 109
Civil engineering projects
  insurance 139–46
  organisation problems 5, 40
  work breakdown structure 198
Claims settlement 71
Client
  PMTF 499
  progress reporting to 486–8
  see also Owner
Client responsibility 464
Climatic factors 94
COBOL 573
Collection of accounts 254–60
Collection programmes 258
Commissioning, checklist 65
Committed costs 229
Common parts *see under* Stock control

Commonwealth Development Corporation (CDC) 179
Communications 29, 332–4
  facilities for 57
  importance of 49
Compatibility aspects 201
Competence assumptions 464
Competition 3
Completion risk 183–4
Completion time
  delaying 126
  speeding up 125
Compliance audits 492
Computer aided design 608
Computer aided engineering 163
Computer aided techniques 203
  cost control 234–6
  timesheet systems 235–6
Computer applications 205, 269
  parallel scheduling 402
  resource scheduling 394, 395, 397, 402, 467
  stock control 294, 297, 299
  see also Databases; Integrated systems
Computer based systems 203, 212–13
Computer hardware 406–10
  centrally decided policies 410
  disk speed 407–8
  factors affecting costs 406–7
  integration 580–3
  maintenance 410
  plotters 410
  printers 408
  visual display units (VDUs) 408–10
Computer languages 573
Computer programs for network analysis 405–59
  activity-on-arrow versus precedence networks 415–16
  activity starts and finishes 435-41
  anti-piracy measures 459
  automatic resource levelling 416–27
  availability 405–6, 411
  batch processing 457
  calendar features 419–23
  capacity limitations 414
  central versus local 407, 411
  complex resources 417
  cost features 450–3

612

Index

cost performance analysis 452
dangles 428
database applications 453–5
delay start constant 423–4
delivery activities 425
documentation 458
duplicated activities 432–4
error detection 458
error diagnosis 427–34
fractional resource amounts 417
general factors concerning 410–14
graphic displays 449
implementation support 458
imposed dates 424–5
input methods 457
interactive systems 457
library networks 446–9
loops 428–32, 436
maximum network size 411
memory size 407
online updating 449–50
order activities 425
parallel relationships 436
plotters 449
pool resources 423
probabilistic networks 441–4
progress reporting 444–6
report generator facility 455–9
resource aggregation 426–7
risk analysis 441–4
software price factors 415
splittable activities 417–19
standard test network 458–9
subnetting or interfacing 413–14
training 458
updating activities 457
user interface 458–9
Computer software selection 415, 583
Condition money 126
Confirming 180
Conflict
  consequences of 553–4
  intergroup 552–60
  occurrence of 553
  reasons for 554–7
  resolution of 558–60
Consideration 70
Construction information 480
Construction projects
  insurance 139–46
  organisation problems 5, 40
  organisations involved in 17, 18
  overseas labour 103
  purchasing 471
  specialist consultants 36
  work breakdown structure 198, 470
Constructional plant 94
Constructional plant costs 105–6
Consultant, role of 42–3
Contact personnel 256
Containers 326–7
Contingency concepts 206–7
Contingency forecast 229
Contingency plans 219–20, 334–6
Contract 59–60
  adherence to 518
  lump sum 93–5, 223, 284
  with customer or client 248
Contract administration 67, 119–30
Contract award 523
Contract committee authority 215–16
Contract conditions 223
Contract formation 69–76
  acceptance 72–5
  consideration 70
  intention to be legally bound 69–70
  letters of intent 75–6
  offer 72
  options 71
  settlement of claims 71
  standing offers 70
Contract law 69–92
  proper law of the contract 89
Contract price 76–7
  use of term 117
Contract Price Adjustment 110, 116
Contract price methods 93–118
Contract review 505
Contract strategy 200
  in relation to project control 217
Contract suspension 127
Contract terms 76–87
  damages 80–2
  delivery 78
  exclusion clauses 84–7
  guarantees 84–7
  passing of property 77–8
  passing of risk 78
  payment 83–4
  performance issues 82

613

Index

quality issues 82
time for completion 79–80
Contract type and cost control 218
Contract variations *see* Variations
Contractor
  appointment of 47–9
  co-ordination within 62
  organisation of 52–4
  role of 44–6
  selection criteria 48
Contractors' All Risks (CAR)
    insurance 139–46
Contractual arrangements 479
Contractual safeguards 114
Control budget 217–20
  like for like comparisons 224
Convention on the Recognition and
    Enforcement of Foreign Arbitral
    Awards 90
Corporation tax 244
Corrective action 518
Cost analysis 275–7
Cost breakdowns 277
Cost coding system 50
Cost control 8–9, 214–37
  accruals and provisions 221
  and contract type 218
  and planning functions 225
  and planning interface 195–6
  authorisations for expenditure
    (AFEs) 215, 216, 219
  authority to sanction funds 215
  checklist 63
  collecting project costs 229–30
  committed costs 220
  computer aided techniques 234
  definition of 220–2
  estimate to complete 222
  estimated final costs 222, 223, 224
  individual authority levels 216
  outstanding commitments 221–2
  overall 214–17
  sunk costs 221
Cost control engineer 46
Cost data bank 194–5
Cost data collection 194–5
Cost data elements 195
Cost dataset 586–7, 603, 606
Cost details, recording 236–7
Cost elements 7

Cost engineering function 51
Cost escalation 116–17, 236–7
Cost estimating 76, 188–213
  accuracy rating 193
  acquisition costs 189
  associated costs 189
  ball park estimates 191–2
  capital costs 189, 210
  capital equipment 210
  computer based systems 212–13
  contingency concepts 206–7
  currency exchange rates 205–6
  definitive 193–4
  detailed methods 203
  end of life costs 190
  escalation provisions 195, 204
  factoring methods 202–3
  feasibility 192–3
  instructions for 201–2
  manual systems 211–12
  methods of 201–3
  money of the day provisions 204–6
  nature of 188–90
  operating costs 190
  pre-development 192
  replacement costs 190
  work breakdown structure 196–201
  working capital 190
Cost factors in contract variation
    120–1
Cost forecasting 577
  integrated systems 603–608
Cost management, integrated systems
    601
Cost-plus jobs 97–106
Cost records 165, 234
  historical 236
Cost reimbursement 97–106
Cost reports 9, 234, 486
Cover ratio 184–5
Credit control 238–61
Credit risks 252, 253, 255
Credit terms 251–2
Critical activities 372–4
Critical events 372, 377
Critical path diagram 373
  modified 379
Critical path methods 357–91
Critical path networks
  cost factors 450–3

Index

limitations of 392
Critical task identification 8
CSA Z299.1 519
Currency exchange rates 205–6
Currency options 174, 175
Customs formalities 331

Damage in transit 291–2, 305, 338–9
Damage risk 141–3, 332
Damages 80–2, 85
Dangles 388, 428
Data collection 390–1
Databases
  applications 453–5
  fundamental principles of 566–8
  relational or hierarchical 454–5
  stock control 297
  subcontractors and suppliers 269
Datasets 584–7, 590, 603, 606
  principles of 566, 567
Debt collection 255
Debt collection letters 258–60
Decènnale liability insurance 139–40
Decision making 562–4
Definition of events 114–15
Delay start constant 423–4
Delays 95, 112–13, 120, 394–5
  costs 478
  insurance 149
Delivery promises 158–9
Delivery provisions 78
Demurrage charges 336
Dependent activities 361, 362, 363
Design
  adequacy of 515
  checklist 157
  computer aided 608
  external reviews 515–18
  internal review meetings 513
  quality control 503–8
    summary of 505
Design activities 475
Design approval 286–7
Design changes *see* Changes
Design cost 99–100
Design criteria 508
Design documentation 502
Design group 53
Design interface control 513–15

Design management, integrated systems 588–9
Design overheads 99
Design philosophies 508
Design procedures and instructions 504–5
Design work 94
Despatch notes 308, 314
Detailed activity report 594–7
Determination of amount due 116
Developed countries, finance 170
Developing countries, finance 171
Development projects 4
Discipline 120
Discipline check 511
Discounts 296
  for prompt settlement 240
Discovery of the documents 130
Disputes 129–30, 250
Document approval 510
Document control centre 527–8
Document distribution
  circular issue 511–13
  flood issue 513
  parallel issue 511
  procedures for 510
Document distribution matrix chart 512
Document identification 509–10
Document numbering system 160
Document preparation 508–9
Document procedures and instructions 505
Documents 312, 314, 466
  change control 515
  checklist 63–4
  design 502
  immediate action order 478–9
  management and supervision 162
  planning 325
  shipping 330–1
  site stores 315
  stores 306–11
Drawings 308
  changes to 163
  checklist 63
  dataset 585
  management and supervision 162
  progress 475
  release of 480
  schedules 470

Index

see also Document(s)
Dummy activities 363–6
Dun and Bradstreet 521
Duplicated activities 432–4
Duration estimates 367–8

Earned value concepts 227–9
Economic completion date 607
Education costs 102
80/20 law 295
Elapsed time 370
Electrical equipment storage 317
Enforcement 90
Engineer as manager 537–9
Engineering checklist 62
Engineering progress 475, 476
Engineering standards 10
Environment factor 155
Equipment costs 8
Equipment procurement 275–7
Equipment requirements 587
Equipment storage and maintenance 317
Erection labour 103
Erection labour costs 101
Escalation 116–17, 236–7
Estimates see Cost estimating
Eurocurrency market 174–5
Event symbol 370
Event times 370–2
Events 359
Exception reporting 485–6
Expediting 278–92
    definition 281
    function of 282
    integrated systems 591
    organisation 278–81
    report 287–9
    see also Progressing
Expended costs 229–30
Expenditure in relation to payments received 111
Expenditure curves 111, 113
Export credits 175–7

Fabricators
    assessment of 520
    quality assurance 524
Factoring methods 202–3
Fairness concept 201

Feasibility cost estimates 192–3
Feasibility study 320–2
FIDIC Conditions of Contract for Electrical and Mechanical Works 79–80
Field studies 518
Final demand 260
Finance 169–87
    amount of project loan 186
    bonds and guarantees 180
    checklist 64
    choice of currency 174, 175
    developed countries 170
    developing countries 171
    evaluation of proposals 174
    funding methods 174–81
    interest rates 176
    interest-rate premium 186
    limited recourse 172, 181
    methods of arranging 169, 173, 200
    natural resources development 171–2
    negotiation with potential lenders 173
    project situations 170–2
    see also Cost estimating
Finance department 46, 50
Financial adviser's role 172–4
Financial control 50
Financial loss control 132
Financial management 5, 239
Financial structure 173
Fire risk 314
Fitness for purpose 83
Float
    calculation of 375–7
    concept of 376
    importance of 375
    types of 374–5
fob (free on board) 324, 330
Forecast contingency 207
Forfaiting 180
FORTRAN 573
Fraudulent misrepresentation 88
free on board (fob) 324, 330
Freight forwarder 323–33, 338, 340
Frustration in contract law 89
Functional foremanship theory 27
Funding methods 174–81

616

Index

Geneva Convention 90
Geographical factors 94
Global project organisation 15
Goods inwards inspection 289–92, 526
Goods inwards receipt notes 309–10
Graphics 575–9
Group formation 545–9
  horizontal group 546, 547
  intergroup resentment and conflict 547
  mixed group 546, 547, 548
  vertical work group 546, 547
  see also Project team
Group performance 530
Guarantees 84–7, 180, 252–3

Hazardous materials 327–8
Heavy lift programme 59
High prices 277
History dataset 587
House of Lords in Reardon Smith v Hansen Tangen 1976: 82
Human behaviour 540–1
Human relations 529–60
Human resource 3
Hygiene factors 541

IJ networks 439
Immediate action order 478–9
Import procedures, checklist 64
Imposed dates 377, 424–5
Income tax 102–3, 244
Independent activities 359
Industrial disputes 334
Industrial relations 60, 201
Influence 532
Information collection 390–1
Information integration 571–2
Information requirements 56, 165, 475, 476, 480
Information retrieval 236
Information structure 584–7
Information system 534
Information technology 608
Innocent misrepresentation 88
Inspection 278–92, 305, 490–1, 519–20
  frequency of visits 286
  goods inwards 289–92, 526
  organisation 278–81

report 287–9
  role of 284–9
Inspection drawings 308
Instruction to proceed 274
Instruments, storage 317
Insurance 131–50
  all risks 141, 147–8
    warehouse to warehouse 337
  arranging 140–1, 145
  basic principles 149
  benefits of 136
  civil engineering projects 139–46
  construction projects 139–46
  Contractors' All Risks (CAR) 139–46
  contractual responsibilities 134–6
  decènnale liability 139–40
  delays in completing projects 149
  JCT contract 145
  legislation 133
  liability 143–5
  limit of indemnity 145
  limits to cover provided 137–8
  manufacturing projects 146–9
  non-availability 131
  of goods 336–9
  overseas contracts 139–40
  policy conditions 146
  project needs 138–9
  property damage 141–3
  special projects 149
  transit risks 147
  versus risk retention 133–4
  see also Risk management
Insurance claims, cargo 338–9
Insurance policy, cargo 338
Integrated systems
  allocating work 597–9
  characteristics of 563–4
  checks and tests 597
  communicating with 568–9
  computer hardware 580–3
  computer software selection 583
  computer system 582–3
  cost forecasting 603–8
  cost management 601
  design management 588–9
  expediting 591
  future development 608
  graphical reports 575–9

Index

horizontal integration 581
implementation and modification 572–4
information held in separate datasets 571–2
job cards 597–9
key factors 565
man-machine interface 565–6
mini-based systems 581–2
multi-project systems 582
network analysis 592–7
planning and control 561–83, 590–7
practical operation of 587–8
progress measurement 599–601
project control 597–9
project management 584–609
report generation 569–71, 597
requirements of 564
requirements of project staff 574–80
resource allocation 597–9
scheduling 590–7
scope and complexity of 564
simple concept of 566
user's view 575
vertical integration 579–80
Interdiscipline check 511
Interest charges 239
Interest on late payments 249, 250
Internal control 490
International bond markets 177
International Chamber of Commerce (Paris) 89
International projects
procurement policy 200
special factors to be considered 32, 36–7
INTERNET 411
Interpersonal behaviour 539–45
Invoices 229–30, 474

JCT contract, insurance 145
Job cards 588
  dataset 586
  integrated systems 597–9
  live 600
  updating project network from 600
Job list 387
Joint ventures 5, 32–5, 105, 200
Junior Books v The Veitchi Co. Ltd 91
Jurisdiction 90

Jurisdictional approval 286–7
Jurisdictional requirements 286

Key events 159, 165, 475
  reports 594
Key logic analysis 422
Kit marshalling (or kitting) 301, 306
Kreditanstalt für Wiederaufbau (KfW) 178

Labour charges for site work 125–6
Labour costs 8, 244
  overseas contracts 129
Labour productivity 94
Labour quantities and skills 94
Ladder networks 440
Late deliveries 303
Late payments 254–5
Lawyers, role of 248, 249
Leadership 532–3, 550
Leasing 179
Legal action 257
Legal liabilities 137
Letter of acceptance 274
Letter of credit 253
Letter of intent 75–6, 274
Letters, debt collection 258–60
Liability insurance 137, 143–5
LIBOR (London Interbank Offered Rate) 175
Library networks 446–9
Library sub-sets 584–7
Life annuity and pensions insurances 137
Lifting equipment and personnel 59
Limited recourse finance 172, 181
Line of balance charts 353–6
Line organisation 24
Linear Responsibility Chart 29, 30
Local amenities 95
Local labour costs 104–5
Logic diagram 47
Loops 388, 428–32, 436
Low prices 276
Lump sum contract conditions 93–5, 223, 284

Maintenance 283
Maintenance instructions 309
Man-machine interface, integrated systems 565–6

Index

Management by exception 55–7
Management committee 32
Management contracting 106–8
　agent or principal 106
　back-to-back agreements 107
　responsibility for results 106
　route for payments 108
Management information 55
Management overheads 105–6
Management philosophy 536
Management projects 5–6
Management team 5
Manhours estimate 211
Manufacturers, quality control 503
Manufacturing industry, product manager 28
Manufacturing products
　stores management 293, 299
　work breakdown structure 197
Manufacturing projects
　insurance 146–9
　organisation of 4–5, 11
　outside specialists 36
MAR policy 338
Married contracts 102
Materials
　conforming 290
　main types of 589–90
　non-conformances 290–1
Materials availability 95
Materials costs 8, 100
Materials datasets 586, 590
Materials handling function 299
Materials management, integrated systems 589–90
Materials organisation chart 300
Materials procurement 275–7
　see also Expediting; Inspection; Procurement
Materials quantities and specifications 94
Materials release note (MRN) 290
Materials requirements 587
Materials shortages 303
Materiel
　customer supplied 525
　purchased by site 525
　quality control 524
　testing and inspection 528

Matrix organisation 25–8, 52, 56, 532, 535, 552, 560
　advantages 28–9
　disadvantages 29
　fixed matrix 27
　operation of 30
　shifting matrix 27
　versus pure project 31
Measured work contract conditions 223
Mechanical equipment storage 317
Merchantable quality 82–3
Merge activity 362
Microcomputers 212, 230
　see also Computer
Microfilm aperture cards 163
Minimum cost finish date 606
Mining projects 5
Misrepresentation Act 1967, 2.2(1): 88
Misrepresentation in contract law 88
Mistake in contract law 87–8
Modifications 161–3, 481–2
Money-of-the-day provisions 219
Monitoring 8, 380, 472, 474–81
Monte-Carlo simulation technique 442
Motivation 529–60
　prerequisites for 541
Multi-lateral aid 178
Multiple calendars 419–23
Multiple command system 25
Multi-project collections 257–8
Multi-project scheduling 403–4
Multi-project systems 582

National Health Insurance 126, 244
Natural sources, development projects 171–2
Negligence 85, 91–2
Negligent misrepresentation 88
Network analysis
　advantages over bar chart 380–1
　as aid to project management 380–2
　computer programs for see Computer programs for network analysis
　computing stages 412
　integrated systems 592–7
　subnetwork calculations 412
Network construction, computer aided 446–50
Network dataset 584–7

619

Index

Network diagrams 157, 158, 357–91, 471, 584
 activity-on-node 382–5, 385
 dangles 388, 428
 hierarchies 388
 logical inconsistencies 388
 loops 388, 428–32, 436
 practical guidelines 386
 starting point 386
Network float 480
Network logic methods for resource constraints 393–4
Network planning
 detail and complexity 366–7
 difficult estimates 368–70
 phases of 358
Network techniques
 disadvantages of 381–2
 notation 358
New York Convention 90
Non-conformance report (NCR) 290–1
North Sea financing 184

Obsolescence 120
Offloading facilities 314–15
Offshore project organisation 36
Offshore Supplies Office (OSO) 269–71
Operating instructions 283, 309
Organisation, definition 15–16
Organisation chart 53
Organisation for Economic Cooperation and Development (OECD) 176
Over-run ceiling 98
Overseas companies 89
Overseas contracts 101, 105, 112
 insurance 139–40
 variations 128–9
Overseas Development Administration (ODA) 179
Overseas Economic Cooperation Fund (OECF) 178
Overtime working 94, 126
Owner 40
 co-ordination with 61
 organisation of 50
 role of 46
 see also Client

Packing 320–41
Packing criteria 327
Packing standards 326–8
Palm-tree justice 129
Parallel relationships 436
Pareto analysis 295
Participation 542
Parts lists 310
Passing of property 77–8
Passing of risk 78
Payment due dates 249
Payment forecasting 242–4
Payment stipulations 248–9
Payment structures 93–118
Payment terms 108–18
Payment verification 284
Pecuniary insurances 137
Penalty payments 7, 479
Percentage completion 475, 600
Performance issues 82
Performance requirements 9–10
Personal accident, sickness and medical expenses insurances 137
PERT (Program Evaluation and Review Technique) 368, 369, 441, 442
Petrochemical projects 5
Photo Production v Securicor Ltd 85
Physical loss control 132
Pilferage 332
Piping storage 317
Planning 21, 358
 and cost control 195–6, 225
 charts 345–56
 integrated systems 561–83, 590–7
 shipping 322–5
Plant and equipment, replacement costs 190
Plotters 410, 449
PMI 411
Political problems 251
Pool resources 423
Post-award meeting with suppliers 523
Power 533–5
 and authority 533
Preallocation 303
Pre-award meetings with suppliers 523
Precedence diagrams 385–6, 435–8, 447

Index

Precedence networks 415–16, 435–8, 449
Precedence relationships 385–6
Price analysis 275–7
Price differences 276–7
Price negotiations, timing of 123–4
Printers 408
Privity of contract 90–1
Probabilistic networks 441–4
Procurement checklist 62
Procurement control 518
Procurement costs 100
Product manager, manufacturing industry 28
Product verification plans 284–5
Production acceleration 477
Production management 477
Production priorities 477
Production progress 476–9
Productivity assessment 96
Profit 105–6, 276
Programme control 282
Progress control 474–81
Progress management 463–88
   aims of 465
   framework of 463–5
Progress measurement, integrated systems 599–601
Progress meetings 482–3
Progress monitoring 472, 474–81
Progress payments 474
Progress record 380
Progress reporting 444–6, 483–8
   exception reporting 485–6
   for network updates 484–5
   to client 486–8
Progressing 281–4
   definition 281
Project abandonment 186
Project administrative procedures 5
Project attitude 550
Project authorisation 466
Project changes 225–7, 481–2
   apparent scope changes 227
   contractual 226
   control documents 515
   defined scope changes 226
   programme 226
   specification 161–3
   technical 225

Project characteristics 3–6
Project co-ordination procedure document checklist 61–5
Project co-ordinator 21, 22, 475–6
Project control 50–1, 358, 379–80
   bar charts for 347–9
   checklists 472
   contract strategy in relation to 217
   integrated systems 561–83, 597–9
Project costs *see* Cost(s)
Project definition 151–65, 201, 464
   as built 163–5
   checklist 152–3
   commercial 158
   financial 158
   functional 154–8
   stages of 163–5
Project development 41
   phases of 44
Project diary 165
Project engineer 53
Project expenditure 221
Project finance *see* Finance
Project ground rules 155
Project introduction 62
Project liaison 56–7
Project management 200
   applications 6
   authority problems in 530–7
   definition of 3
   emergence of 10
   integrated system 584–609
   nature and purpose of 3–14, 543–4
   objectives of 6–10
   process of 561–4
   role of 357
   stages of 12–14
   techniques 14
Project management task force (PMTF) 499–500
Project manager
   accountability 54
   appointment of 40
   approach of 533
   as human observer 542
   as mini-general manager 30
   as self-actualising man 541
   authority problem 530–7
   chief 27, 30
   choices open to 41

Index

classes of responsibility 21
client reports 488
contract negotiations 248, 251
customer relationship 20
definition 17
engineer as 538–9
leadership capabilities of 550–1
motivation problems 529–60
motivational opportunity 544–5
participative 542
problems of 539
quality assurance 503
relationships with customer, specialist consultants and subcontractors 34, 35
relationships with fellow executives 536
relationships within own organisation 21–4
role of 10–14, 17–28, 535, 550
skills of 540, 542–3, 552, 560
supportive management 464
tools available to 534
use of term 6
Project model 563–4
Project monitoring 8, 380, 472, 474–81
Project network and cost dataset 604
Project organisation 15–39, 40–65, 464
 aims of 38
 as means to an end 38
 definition 15–16
 matrix form of *see* Matrix organisation
 oldest form of 25
 parties involved 41–3
 pure 31
  advantages 30
  versus matrix 31
 with more complex arrangements 31–8
Project planning *see* Planning
Project purchasing manager *see* Purchasing manager
Project reporting 199
Project schedules 159
Project specification *see* Specifications
Project sponsors 172, 173
Project strategy 196
Project summary report 578

Project supervisor 21
Project team 45, 46, 200, 549–52
 matrix organisation 27, 52
 organisation of 23, 24
Project timing 358, 367
Project variations *see* Variations
Promoter 40
Property damage, insurance 141–3
Property insurances 136
Public utility services 244
Purchase lead times 472
Purchase orders 308
Purchase schedules 471
Purchase specification 471
Purchasing 265–77, 471–2
 aims and objectives 265
 definition 265
 main sub-divisions 265
 special characteristics of 266–7
 staffing 266, 275
 see also Subcontracting
Purchasing cycle 271–5
Purchasing manager 266–7
 job description 267–8

Quality
 definition of 489
 objective evidence of 491–2
Quality assurance 10, 489–528
 concept and philosophy of 489–91
 corrective action 518
 definition 489
 detailed procedures 500–3
 development of system 495–7
 fabricators 524
 organisation for 492
 procedures and systems 495
 special processes 526–7
 suppliers 524
 umbrella concept 502
 understanding and appreciation of 492
Quality assurance department 492, 494, 495, 500
Quality assurance standards 496
Quality control 60, 278, 285
 design 503–8
  summary of 505
 manufacturers 503
 materiel 524

622

Index

Quality costs 490
Quality issues 82
Quality manual 497
Quality plan 499
Quality policy 499
Quality programme 495, 497, 498
Quantity surveyors 52
Quotations 76, 274, 275, 276, 277

Rates dataset 586
Receipt of goods 314–15
Recorded delivery 260
Records systems 566
Recovery of payments made 118
Regulatory requirements 508
Reimbursable work 224
Reject notes 310
Rejections 283
Release notes 309
Repayment profile 185–6
Report generator facility 455–9
Request for quotation 274
Residual scheduling 404
Resource aggregation 394, 426–7
Resource allocation 358, 389
  integrated systems 597–9
Resource constraints,
  detection of 394
  network logic methods for 393–4
Resource levelling 402, 416–27
Resource limits 395, 403
Resource overloads, and criticality 395
Resource scheduling 392–404
  alternative resources 402–3
  automatic 395–403
  backwards from end of project 397–400
  computer applications 394, 395, 397, 402, 467
  expansion factor 403
  goals of 395–403
  manual 394
  multi-project 403
  parallel scheduling 400–1
  serial scheduling 401–2
  simple example of 398
  summary resources 403
Resource utilisation 404
Resources dataset 587
Retention money 114, 118, 252–3

Returned to stores notes 311
Revenue curves 111, 113
Reviewing cash flow forecasts 245–7
Reviews of plan and programme 390
Risk analysis 441–4
Risk financing 133
Risk handling 131
Risk management 132–4
Risk retention 133
  versus insurance 133–4
Risk sharing 182
Risk transfer 132–4
Risks 78, 201
  economic 182
  insurable 138–9
  non-insurable 131
  political 182
  technical 182
  transit 147
  see also Insurance

Salaries 244
Sale of Goods Act 77–9, 82–4
Schedule of rates 96
Schedule workability 465
Scheduling, integrated systems 590–7
Scientific research projects 6
Security alarms 303
Security systems 301–4
Self-actualising man 541
Sequences 360
Settlement of claims 71
Settlement of disputes 129–30
Shipping 320–41, 472
  alternatives 334
  documents 314
  insurance 336–9
  planning 322–5
Shore superintendent 333
Shortage lists 306, 310
Site administration 57–60
Site arrangements, checklist 64
Site cost control 59
Site management 479–81
Site materials, stock control 315–17
Site materials controller 318–19
Site office 486
Site organisation 94
  overseas contracts 128
Site planning 57–8

623

Index

Site progress 479–81
Site stores
    documentation 315
    management 312
Site subcontracts 59–60
Site supervision
    costs 101
    overseas costs 101
Site work, labour charges for 125–6
Slack, use of term 374
Slowing down methods and costs 126–7
Sociotechnical system 540, 541
Solicitors 256, 257
Spares, checklist 65
Spares list 283, 309
Special processes, quality assurance 526–7
Special projects, insurance 149
Specialist consultants 35–6
Specifications 55, 151–81, 266
    changes in 120
    document numbering 160–1
    inadequate 119
    modifications, variations and changes 161–3
    publishing first issue 159–60
    purchase 471
    see also Document(s)
Staff organisation 24
Status reports 282–3, 316
Statutory requirements 172
Stock control 293–9
    ABC system 295
    common parts scheduling 297
    computer applications 297, 299
    database 297
    identification of common parts 295–7
    manufacturing 294–5
    quantifying common parts requirements 297
    site materials 315–17
    two bin method 298
Stock levels 294
Stock practices 294
Stock re-ordering system 295
Stock records 299, 303, 311
Stock shortages 305–6
Stock value 295

Stocklists 310–11
Stockouts 294
Storage facilities 312–14
Storage space 335
Stores documentation 306–11
Stores location system 302
Stores management 299–317
    automation 301
    bin numbers 299–300
    bonded store 303
    damage and deterioration 304
    location and retrieval 299–301
    pre-allocation 303
    site 312–17
Stores requisitions 301, 311
Stores security 301–4
Stores space allocation 304
Subcontract engineering order 473
Subcontract liaison engineer 472, 474
Subcontracting 269–71
    procedure for 272
Subcontractors 59–60, 96, 110, 472–4
    organisation 35
    payment route 108
Subsistence allowance 126
Suppliers 110, 276–7
    assessment of 520–1
        engineering aspects 520
        financial stability 521
        price and delivery aspects 521
        quality aspect 520
    databases 269
    datasets 586, 590
    payment route 108
    post-award meetings with 523
    pre-award meetings with 523
    quality assurance 524
Supportive management 464
Systems development 6

Target cost 98
Target dates 98, 475–6
Task force organisation 508
Task lists 466–71, 597
Taxation 102–3
Telecommunications 325, 333
Tender packages 521
Tendering 96
    insufficient detail 119

624

Index

Terms of payment 108–18, 250–1
  policy considerations 108–14
Test plan 519–20
Thinking time 119
Third national labour 103–5
Time analysis 389
Time-based network 390
Time/cost curve 605
Time estimates 389
Time for completion 79–80
Time limits 395–403
  for payment 117–18
Time schedules 392
Time taken to complete 238
Time-scaled diagram 379
Timescale 158–9, 367
Timescale objectives 9
Timescale planning and control 7–8
Timesheet systems, computer aided techniques 235–6
Tolerances permitted 94
Transit damage 291–2, 305, 338–9
Transit damage report (TDR) 291
Transit risks, insurance 147
Transit time concept 440–1
Transportation arrangements 329–32
Transportation insurances 136
Travelling requisitions 311

Unfair Contract Terms Act 85, 86
Unforeseeable circumstances 120

Value added tax (VAT) 241–4
Value analysis 10
Value engineering 10
Valves, storage 317
Variations 116, 161–3, 226, 227, 481–2
  balancing cost factors 120–1
  causes of 119–28
  handling 123
  overseas contracts 128–9
  pricing 122, 123
  real costs involved 123
  summary form 228
Vendors
  control of 518
  datasets 586
Visual display units (VDUs) 408–10
Vitiating factors 87–9

Wages 244
Warehousing 312–14
Work breakdown structure 30, 196–201, 603
Work in progress 7
Work packages 30, 196, 199
Work scope, review team 505
Work-to list *see* Task lists
Works order 466
Workshop facilities 95
World Bank 178